Principles and Practices of Construction Law

Nancy J. White, J.D.
Central Michigan University

Prentice Hall

Upper Saddle River, New Jersey
Columbus, Ohio

Library of Congress Cataloging-in-Publication Data

White, Nancy J.
    Principles and practices of construction law/Nancy J. White.
        p. cm.
    Includes bibliographical references and index.
    ISBN 0-13-032576-7
        1. Construction contracts—United States. I. Title

KF902.Z9 W47 2002
343.73'078624–dc21

2001036484

Editor in Chief: Stephen Helba
Executive Editor: Ed Francis
Production Editor: Christine M. Buckendahl
Production Coordination: Lisa Garboski, bookworks
Design Coordinator: Robin G. Chukes
Cover Designer: Thomas Borah
Cover photo: FPG
Production Manager: Matt Ottenweller
Marketing Manager: Jamie Van Voorhis

This book was set in Times Roman by The Clarinda Company and was printed and bound by
R. R. Donnelley & Sons Company. The cover was printed by Phoenix Color Corp.

Pearson Education Ltd., *London*
Pearson Education Australia Pty. Limited, *Sydney*
Pearson Education Singapore Pte. Ltd.
Pearson Education North Asia Ltd., *Hong Kong*
Pearson Education Canada, Ltd., *Toronto*
Pearson Educación de Mexico, S. A. de C. V.
Pearson Education—Japan, *Tokyo*
Pearson Education Malaysia Pte. Ltd.
Pearson Education, *Upper Saddle River, New Jersey*

10 9 8 7 6 5 4 3 2 1
ISBN: 0-13-032576-7

Preface

Principles and Practices of Construction Law presents the most common areas of law encountered in the construction industry in an easy-to-read format geared to college students, particularly undergraduate students. The legal concepts are simplified and presented in such a way that students can understand the legal points involved without getting so involved in the minute details of the law that they lose interest or become overwhelmed. Although such minute details are important in the actual practice of law or in any specific case, these details have a tendency to be the trees that hide the forest for people who need only a basic understanding of the important legal principles applicable to their profession.

Focuses of the Text

The Law

Chapter 1 is designed to give students an understanding of how the legal system in the United States operates. This chapter also gives students the basics that all business people should understand in order to operate effectively in the U.S. market.

Although this text does not begin to discuss specifics of the law until Chapter 6, the primary focus of this text is on the areas of law that students will encounter in the construction industry. Several chapters are devoted to contracts and contract-related issues such as differing site conditions and scope issues. In addition, chapters are devoted to torts, joint liability, and bankruptcy.

This text differs from others in that it also contains chapters on tort law and joint liability.

Critical Thinking and Reasoning

In addition to teaching students about a few laws, this text can be used to teach students how to apply these laws to real situations and to solve problems they encounter. Chapters are designed to increase the ability of students to solve problems using the law. Students are taught to think logically and to prepare valid arguments in support of some position. Chapter 4, Preparing Legal Arguments and Briefing Cases, is probably best left as a graduate student topic. It is not likely that undergraduate students will spend much, if any, time reading actual court cases, and since reading and understanding them is difficult, there is not usually sufficient time in the undergraduate curriculum to devote to this skill. Graduate students may find this topic challenging, however.

In addition, each chapter contains some THINK exercises. These are designed to encourage more active learning by students.

Problems

Each of the chapters discussing a specific area of the law (Chapters 6–17) contains problems for students to solve. Many undergraduate students find solving such problems extremely difficult, so this task has been made simpler by supplying hints that will help undergraduates solve the problems without being overwhelmed.

Frequently Asked Questions

The text ends with a chapter designed to acquaint students with some of the recent trends and the most common legal issues in the construction industry. Much of the material is a summary of material covered in the text and is a good review.

Cases

Several actual cases have been included in appendices to some of the chapters. Generally, these are best used in a graduate class where the students have a greater ability to read and understand complex writings. Cases are, after all, written by legal professionals for other legal professionals—they are not written for students.

Acknowledgments

I would like to thank the following reviewers for their helpful comments and suggestions: Frederick E. Gould, Roger Williams University; Mark Pruitt, Oklahoma State University; and John A. Wiggins, New Jersey Institute of Technology.

Nancy J. White

Contents

CHAPTER 5 LAW, ETHICS, AND MORALITY   110

CHAPTER 6 RELATIONSHIPS AMONG THE PARTIES ON THE PROJECT   132

CHAPTER 16 JOINT LIABILITY AND INDEMNITY   363

CHAPTER 17 BANKRUPTCY   385

CHAPTER 18 DISPUTE RESOLUTION   395

CHAPTER 19 FREQUENTLY ASKED QUESTIONS   410

1

Introduction to the Legal System and the Maxims of Law

The legal system in the United States is a very complex one. This text is designed to give you a basic understanding of the legal system and how it works. In addition, it will familiarize you with the types of legal problems most likely to arise in the construction industry and with the tools necessary to solve those problems.

The word *law* in the legal sense does not carry the same meaning as in a math or science sense. The word *law* in math or science means a statement that has been rigorously tested and is considered to be true; however, scientific and mathematical laws are subject to change, or modification if new information proves them to be inadequate. Nothing is considered "true." In the legal sense the term **black letter law** comes close to the mathematical or scientific definition. Black letter law is law that has been rigorously tested and is not *likely* to change. **Law** in the legal sense means rules set up by various government agencies to help regulate how people and other entities act and interact. Most laws are subject to change and interpretation.

Legal and Equitable Maxims

The **maxims of law** constitute the basic attitudes of U.S. courts toward legal disputes. The maxims are the underlying principles, often unstated, on which case law is based. Sometimes these maxims are referred as **public policy.** In some states the maxims have been adopted by statute. The California Civil Code states: "The maxims of jurisprudence here-

1-1. THINK

Name one scientific law and one legal law that you know.

inafter set forth are intended not to qualify any of the foregoing provisions of this Code, but to aid in their just application."[1] See also the North Dakota Cent. Code, § which contains a list of thirty-four maxims.[2]

Maxims of Law

1. Mistakes should be fixed, not taken advantage of.
2. For every wrong there is a remedy. No one should suffer by the act of another.
3. Liability follows responsibility.
4. Parties must come to court with clean hands. This maxim is known as the *clean hands doctrine*. A party who has treated the other party unfairly or dishonestly will not get a favorable ruling from the court.
5. The law does not require impossibilities. (This is a very important maxim applicable to the construction industry. See the section on objective impossibility.)
6. The law abhors waste.
7. Substance, not form, is important. (In other words, fairness and justice are important, not technicalities).
8. The one who takes the benefit should bear the burden.
9. When the reason for a rule ceases, so should the rule itself.
10. Where the reason is the same, the rule should be the same. (Courts use this by analogizing a case to a prior case).
11. The law does not require useless or idle acts.

1-2. THINK

If the first Maxim of Law were the following, instead of what is listed, how would the legal system in the United States be different?
The law allows remedies for acts that are contrary to law.

---

[1]California Civil Code § 3509 (1999).
[2]North Dakota Cent. Code § 31-11-05 (1999).

Summary of the Legal System in the United States

The legal system in the United States is characterized by the following:

1. It is a common law system.
2. More than fifty independent jurisdictions are operating simultaneously.
3. In most types of cases the right to a jury trial exists, but a jury trial can be waived.
4. It is based on the belief that justice and truth will prevail from an adversary system of legal practice.

Common Law System

Two types of legal systems govern in Western civilizations: civil law systems and common law systems. Civil law systems exist in continental Europe and in the state of Louisiana. Common law systems exist in countries tracing their legal heritage to England and in all other states in the United States.

Civil law systems are based primarily on codes and statutes. Judges and courts in these types of system interpret the law and apply it to cases; however, *the decision of a civil law judge is not law for subsequent cases.* It is very common, though, for civil law judges to follow prior decisions.

Common law systems also contain codes and statutes. In addition, they contain another category of law: **case law.** In a common law system the decisions of appellate and supreme courts (but not trial courts) are law that applies to subsequent cases containing the same facts and issues. Other names for this type of law are: *judge-made law, opinions, decisions,* and *common law.*

Multiple Independent Jurisdictions

The United States consists of fifty states or jurisdictions, which operate, for the most part, independently of one another. In addition to these fifty relatively independent states, a federal government was formed by the U.S. Constitution to operate in certain areas such as national defense, international affairs, interstate roadways, and the national park system. Since the Civil War the federal government has also been active in the area of civil rights. The federal jurisdiction is independent of the state jurisdictions, although there is overlap in some areas of law. In addition, to these fifty-one jurisdictions there are numerous other

1–3. THINK

The statement "The United States consists of fifty states or jurisdictions" is inaccurate. What other independent jurisdictions operate within the borders of the United States?

jurisdictions such as military jurisdictions and Native American jurisdictions. Puerto Rico is an independent jurisdiction within the U.S. government system.

Division of Government Power within Jurisdictions

Each state, and the federal government, has a constitution that is considered the supreme law of the land. The constitution embodies those principles of the government that should not easily be changed. This constitution also describes the powers and duties of the government.

The state and the federal governments are divided into three parts: the executive branch, the legislative branch, and the judicial branch. This is the "checks and balances" system that most grade school children study. That is, the power of the government is divided into three spheres to prevent the government from gaining too much control over the people and the market.

Today it is more accurate to state that the government is divided into four spheres: the executive branch, the legislative branch, the judicial branch, and administrative agencies.

The *legislative branch* of each jurisdiction enacts laws. Once the constitution is passed and the legislature is in session, it passes laws called *statutes*. Similar statutes may be collected together in a *code*. For example, the state legislature might enact mechanic's lien laws, family law statutes, probate statutes, and criminal statutes. All the laws relating to family law matters might be collected into the Family Law Code.

The *executive branch* of each jurisdiction carries out the laws passed by the legislature and also controls the police power of the state. Thus, the executive branch of government is the only one that can use physical force against the populace through police departments, prison systems, and the like. In the federal government the executive branch also controls the armed forces. The president of the United States is the head of the executive branch of the U.S. government. The governor is the head of the executive branch of a state government.

Because of the complexity of the government, most state and federal legislatures have set up *administrative agencies* to help the executive branch and/or the legislature carry out certain laws passed by the legislature. For example, the Internal Revenue Service (IRS) and the Equal Employment Opportunity Commission (EEOC) are two administrative agencies set up by the federal legislature to aid the executive branch in carrying out the laws relating to income tax and equal employment opportunity, respectively. Other agencies are the Occupational Safety and Health Administration (OSHA) and the Department of Transportation (DOT).

Most administrative agencies have boards that hear and resolve disputes. Matters pertaining to the agency must usually be heard within the agency before being filed in a trial court. For example, issues relating to the Social Security Administration (SSA) are first heard before an SSA administrative law judge, and if the parties are not satisfied with the outcome, they can appeal the matter to the federal district court.

The U.S. government has established the Armed Services Board of Contract Appeals and the General Services Board of Contract Appeals to handle disputes relating to government contracts.[3] Most disputes relating to government contracts are handled in this venue and not by regular federal district (trial) courts. Matters from the boards can be appealed to

---

[3] 41 U.S.C. § 607(e).

the federal circuit courts of appeal. The method of handling federal contract claims will not be further elaborated on in this text.

The *judicial branch* of each jurisdiction interprets the laws and determines whether a person or entity has engaged in activity that is criminal or that results in civil liability. Civil and criminal liability is discussed more fully in the section Civil and Criminal Law.

The judicial branch of each jurisdiction generally comprises three levels of courts, though some states have only two. The three levels are trial courts, appellate courts, and the supreme court.

Cases are filed in trial courts, and judges and juries decide the legal and factual issues presented by the parties. If one of the parties believes the trial judge made an error, that party may appeal. An **appeal** is a request to a higher court to decide whether the trial court judge made an error. The primary purpose of the appellate court system is to provide a mechanism through which the decisions of trial court judges can be reviewed for accuracy. Only very rarely do appellate courts review the decisions of juries.

Jurisdiction

Because the term **jurisdiction** is used in the legal industry in several different ways it may cause some confusion to those first encountering the term. The term can be used to describe an area that has its own, independent set of laws. For example, the state of New Mexico is its own jurisdiction and has its own set of laws. Puerto Rico is its own jurisdiction and has its own set of laws. The United States of America is its own jurisdiction (separate from each state) and has its own set of laws. This is the most common use of the term in this text.

The term jurisdiction is also commonly used in the legal industry as shorthand for the phrase jurisdiction of the court. When used in this sense jurisdiction means the power of a particular court to hear a case. For example, Michigan probate courts have jurisdiction or power over *probate* cases in Michigan. They do not have jurisdiction over *criminal* matters that occurred in Idaho or even in Michigan.

Choice of Law

Choice of Law
The determination of which jurisdiction's law applies

It is not always clear which jurisdiction's law to apply to a particular claim. Because there are more than fifty-one court jurisdictions in operation in the United States, there are more than fifty-one sets of laws. A choice must be made between which set of laws to use. The term **choice of law** refers to a determination of which jurisdiction's law applies.

For most claims that arise in the construction industry the law of the state where the project is located governs the project. If the project is a federal project, such as a U.S. Post Office construction project, federal law governs. The law usually allows the parties to choose the law that will govern.

For example, suppose a dispute arises between Owner, Inc., a corporation formed in Delaware; Architect, Inc., a corporation formed in New York; and Contractor Corporation, a corporation formed in California. The project is located in Connecticut. Which state's law will govern this transaction? If the parties in their contract have chosen no law, the law where the project is located, in Connecticut, will most likely govern.

Overlap between State and Federal Court Systems

Most students mistakenly believe that the United States Supreme Court is the supreme court of the land and that all cases can be appealed to it if the parties have the desire to do so. Rather, only very few cases originating in state courts can be appealed to the United States Supreme Court, namely, cases that involve federal law or an interpretation of the U.S. Constitution. Federal courts can overturn only state law that is contrary to the law of the United States, including the U.S. Constitution.

Much of the law regulating the construction industry is state law, so cases involving that law can never be appealed to the United States Supreme Court. In addition, most cases in the construction industry are resolved by arbitration, and the majority of arbitrated cases can never even enter any court system. Arbitrated cases, however, use the law of the particular jurisdiction in which they are located to decide cases. For this reason the law is still important in arbitration.

Right to a Jury Trial

Unlike the legal systems of many other countries, the jury system is the norm for criminal and civil trials in the United States. Some minor criminal and civil lawsuits are handled only by judges or magistrates, but the right to a jury trial applies to the majority of matters. In reality, many parties waive a jury trial, particularly when the issues are very technical and scientific. In addition, most cases in the construction industry are resolved by arbitration, which does not utilize a jury.

Many students are interested in how juries decide cases. Appendix A to this chapter contains a model jury charge that would be read to a jury. It also contains the questions a jury in that case would be asked to answer.

An Adversary System of Justice

In the United States the lawyers handling a case have a great deal of control over the case and decide, for the most part, what to present to the judge, jury, or arbitrator. In contrast, in

1-4. THINK

What is wrong and what is right with the following statement?
The state courts have superior jurisdiction to the federal courts.

1-5. THINK

When can federal courts overturn state law?

European court systems the judge retains much more control over the evidence and the handling of the case.

In the United States it is believed that truth and justice will emerge from the battle or adversary relation between the opposing sides of a claim or lawsuit. The goal of U.S. attorneys is to win the case; it is not the goal of the attorneys to promote truth or justice. The goal to win is tempered by ethical and legal requirements relating to the practice of law.

Types of Law

This section discusses the major types of law and the relative importance of each type. All law is not of equal force and effect.

Law, both federal and state, can be divided into four major types: constitutional, statutory, administrative regulation, and judge-made law.

Constitutions come about in a variety of ways. The U.S. Constitution was adopted by the states. State constitutions were adopted or passed by the state legislature. A constitution is considered the law of the land and is given great deference by the courts and by the people. Constitutions are designed to be fairly difficult to change because they embody core principles. Constitutions also contain the basic format of governmental operations and delineate the basic rights the government cannot infringe upon, such as freedom of speech and the press. An example of constitutional law:

> *Equality under the law shall not be denied or abridged because*
> *of sex, race, color, creed, or national, origin.—Texas*
> *Constitution, Art.1, Sec. 3a.*

Laws passed by the legislature are called **statutes.** These can be more easily changed and revised than constitutions. For example, state statues regulate traffic and the licensing of professionals such as engineers and architects. An example of a statute:

> *A person must bring suit for damages for a claim . . . against a*
> *person who constructs or repairs an improvement to real property*
> *not later than 10 years after the substantial completion of the*
> *improvement. . . .—Tex. Civ. Prac. & Rem. § 16.009.*

Administrative agencies pass **administrative regulations.** For example, the IRS and OSHA have passed hundreds of regulations, all of which have the force of law. An example of an administrative regulation:

> *Each employer—(1) shall furnish to each of his employees*
> *employment and a place of employment which are free from*
> *recognized hazards that are causing, or are likely to cause death,*
> *or serious physical harm to his employees . . .—29 U.S.C.S. §*
> *654 (2001)*

> **Administrative Regulation**
>
> A law or rule passed by an administrative agency

Judge-made or **case law** is law made by appellate and supreme court judges. It is generally more specific and covers *only* the specific fact situation and issue raised in a specific case. Judge-made law will apply only to cases with the same or very similar facts and issues. Case law often fills a void or prevents injustice that arises from the blanket application of the other types of law. For example, the United States Supreme Court has interpreted the Constitution as guaranteeing individuals a right of privacy; however, the words *right to privacy* do not appear in the Constitution. The courts have determined that this right exists in that document. An example of case law:

> *Architects have no duty to contractors or subcontractors and therefore cannot be sued by them for negligence.—Amazon v. British Am. Dev. Corp., 216 A.D.2d 702, 628 N.Y.S.2d 204 (1995).*

An example of case law that fills a void or clarifies a statute:

> The state legislature passed a law that requires "vehicles to have more than one passenger" in the vehicle to use the carpool lane. A man in that state was ticketed for driving alone in the carpool lane. At trial he claimed that the four frozen cadavers in the mortuary van he was driving should be counted as passengers. The trial court judge did not agree with him and said passengers must be alive. The man appealed the trial court judge's decision (that passengers must be alive) to the appellate court. In other words, the man asked the appeals court to review the trial judge's decision and determine whether the trial judge had made an error. The appellate judges (there are usually three judges on an appellate panel) affirmed the trial judge's decision.

This case produced judge-made or case law that clarified the statute passed by the legislature. The law in the state now requires vehicles to have more than one *live* passenger in order to drive in the carpool lane. A perceived ambiguity in the law was rectified. Should another similar case arise in another trial court in that same appellate district, that court must apply the above case law.

Hierarchy of Law

> **Four Types of Law in Hierarchical Order**
>
> Constitutional Law
> Statutory Law
> Administrative Regulations
> Judge-made or case Law

All laws do not have the same force and effect. The following list shows the hierarchy of laws, with the most important law listed first:

Constitution

Statutes

Administrative rules and regulations

Judge-made law

Law can be overturned by law above it. For example, statutes and administrative regulations can overturn judge-made law. The only exception to the ability of statutes and administrative regulations to overturn judge-made law is in the area of constitutional law. As part of the checks and balances of the U.S. governmental system, no statute or administrative regulation can be passed that overturns or contravenes constitutional law. The courts are given the power to overturn any statute or administrative regulation that has attempted to contravene a constitutional law.

Courts have limited power to overturn administrative regulations because administrative regulations are above judge-made law in the hierarchy. What this means is that it is extremely unlikely a court will overturn an administrative agency rule.

River of Law

People not intimately involved with the legal system often have difficulty understanding how it works. Students are taught in middle or junior high civic classes that the courts interpret the law. An analogy with a river may help clarify this statement. Cases enter the river at the bottom and travel upward if appealed to the supreme court of that jurisdiction. In the majority of cases that supreme court is the state supreme court. Few cases from the state court system can cross over to the federal system and be appealed to the United States Supreme Court. For purposes of this discussion those cases will be ignored, and the most common process will be summarized here. This process is valid for both the federal and state governments.

While the cases are making an arduous journey upriver the law is flowing downriver. In every jurisdiction several branches of law exist. Most jurisdictions have two points where law is added to the river: the appeal courts and the supreme court. However, since law flows only downriver, law placed in the river at the appellate level does not affect the supreme court. Similarly, law placed in the river by one appellate court has no effect on other appellate courts at the same level—the law flows only downriver to the trial courts below that appeal court; law does not flow sideways into other appellate courts. When making a decision a particular court *must* apply the law in its own river; however, it need not apply the law from any other river or branch of the river, though it is free to do so if it chooses. Figure 1–1 is a visual representation of this concept.

A contractor files a negligence lawsuit against an architect in the Elk City trial court. This is the first such suit filed in this state. The Elk City trial court judge dismisses the case

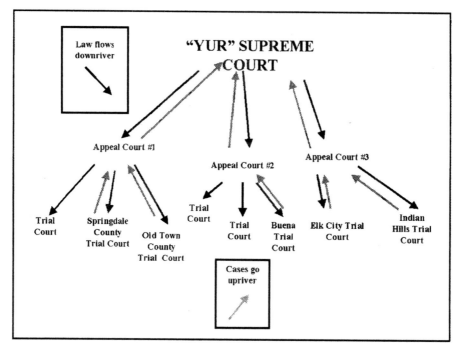

Figure 1-1   Typical organization of Court System and River of Law © 2000–2001
www.arttoday.com

because the trial judge believes that the state's architects have no duty to contractors, and the law does not allow contractors to sue architects for negligence. **Duty** is one of the basic elements of negligence, so a duty must exist between parties in order for a negligence claim to have a basis. The trial judge has not made any law because the decisions of trial judges do not become law.

The contractor appeals to Appeal Court #3. Appeal Court #3 upholds the Elk City trial court judge's decision. Now, some law exists in the state of Yur. This law states that architects have no duty to contractors and therefore cannot be sued by contractors for negligence. The state supreme court refuses to take the case, or the contractor decides not to appeal.

Several years later a similar case is filed in Buena trial court, and the trial judge dismisses the case for the same reason as the trial court judge in the Elk City court: the trial judge believes that architects have no duty to contractors, and the law does not allow contractors to sue architects for negligence. The contractor appeals to Appeal Court #2. The appellate judges (there are normally at least three appeal judges on a panel deciding an appealed case) in this court are *not* bound by the appellate judges' decision in the first case out of Appeal Court #3. The appellate court judges in Appeal Court #2 may decide that architects *do* have a duty to contractors. They **remand** (send back) the case to the trial court in Buena for trial on the matter.

The state of Yur now has different law in different areas of the state. Appeal Court #3 has said that architects have *no* duty to contractors and cannot be sued by contractors for negligence, whereas Appeal Court #2 has decided just the opposite.

It is more likely that the supreme court will now accept a case on appeal in order to determine this issue for the entire state. In this process the law is reviewed and tested prior to being solidified by the supreme court. Note that supreme courts can reverse prior supreme court decisions and change the law. This is not too common, however.

Issues of Law and Issues of Fact

"Facts are stupid things."—Ronald Reagan, misquoting John Adams in a speech to the Republican convention.

Every lawsuit contains two categories of issues: issues of fact and issues of law. An **issue of fact** exists whenever the parties do not agree on any particular fact. An **issue of law** exists whenever the parties do not agree on any part of the law. Many such issues exist in any lawsuit or claim; some are more important than others. If the parties agree on the facts and the law, no issue exists. In general, the parties tend to agree on most of the facts and on most of the law, and they concentrate on a few disagreements.

Juries decide issues of fact, and judges decide issues of law. It is possible for the parties to waive a jury. In such a case the judge will decide the issues of fact also. In arbitration the arbitrators will decide the issues of fact and law.

Issues of Fact

Issue of Fact

The parties do not agree on what the facts are, or
the parties do not agree on whether the facts support a certain law.

An issue of fact is an issue in which two (or more) parties say contradictory things, or offer contradictory evidence about what occurred. For example, assume that the issue in a particular case is: Did you run a red light? You offer your **testimony,** which is proof, that the light was green. The police officer offers testimony, which is proof, that the light was red. The jury must weigh this conflicting evidence and make a decision on the factual issue.

Issues of fact are seldom overturned. For example, in a case involving the sale of truck, a jury found that the defendant had committed fraud and breach of contract and also had violated the Unfair Trade Practices Act. The defendant appealed this decision, but the appeal court refused to overturn the jury's determination. The appeal court said, ". . . on appeal of a case tried by a jury, our scope of review extends merely to the correction of errors of law; a factual finding of the jury will not be disturbed on appeal unless a review of the record discloses that there is no evidence which reasonably supports the jury's finding. We have no power to review matters of fact . . ."[4]

We will concentrate mainly on legal issues in this text.

Students tend to believe that issues of law are more common or important than issues of fact. It is easy to see how this misconception is born, because there are many, many law classes in higher education settings. The reality of law, claims, and disputes is that issues of fact are more common and are as important as issues of law.

Only Facts Are Facts

The term **fact** has a specific meaning when applied to claims and legal disputes. In general, a fact will answer a question such as the following:

Who are the people involved in this claim?

Why did people the people act this way?

What happened?

Where did it happen?

Why did it happen?

How much did it cost to fix?

What does the contract say?

Facts are:

Contracts or contract provisions

Descriptions of what happened

Lists of injuries

Lists of damages

Descriptions of who did what and who did not do what

Facts are *not*:

Rules or laws

Issues

Conclusions of courts

Conclusions to problems

Opinions

For example, the following passage contains a mixture of facts, legal rules, legal conclusions, and opinions. The facts in this paragraph are in italics. The legal rules are not facts. The legal conclusions are not facts. The arguments made by the parties are not facts—only facts are facts.

---

[4]*York v. Conway Ford, Inc.*, 480 S.E.2d 726 (S.C. 1997).

Generally, the owner or occupier of the premises is not responsible for injuries arising from an activity being performed by an independent contractor. In order to hold Barwood (the owner) liable for his injuries arising from his work on the Barwood property, McCaughtry (injured plaintiff) must show that his case falls within an exception to this general rule of liability. *On August 17, 1993, McCaughtry ascended the top of the scaffold and proceeded to paint the top of a light standard with an aluminum extended-handle paint roller. While McCaughtry was painting the light standard, the handle of his paint roller came into contact with the high-voltage power line. McCaughtry fell over the rail of the scaffold to the ground. McCaughtry sustained personal injuries, including a fractured right ankle, third-degree burns over 60% of his body, internal injuries, a closed head injury and the amputation of his left leg below the knee.* The trial court concluded that McCaughtry's claim did not fall within an exception to the general rule of liability.

The facts are always the most important part of any legal argument or claim. Facts are discussed more fully in Chapter 4, Preparing Legal Arguments and Briefing Cases.

Issues of Law

> **Issue of Law**
>
> The parties do not agree on what the law says or means.

For the purposes of this text, issues of law are disputes about what the law says or what it covers. Trial judges and arbitrators decide issues of law. The trial judge's decisions about the law are subject to review by appeal court judges. The jury's decisions on the facts are not generally subject to review on appeal. Arbitrator's decisions on facts and law are not usually subject to review in any court.

Criminal Law and Civil Law

Law can be divided into two broad categories: criminal law and civil law. This text is concerned mainly with civil law and its application in the construction industry. Criminal law is briefly discussed as a comparison.

Criminal Law

The purpose of criminal law and the criminal justice system is to prevent and punish certain acts against the public welfare that society has deemed unacceptable. These unacceptable acts are referred to as **crimes.** Robbery and rape are examples of crimes. Punishments for crimes include incarceration.

Only government entities prosecute criminal matters. *Individuals* never prosecute, file, or handle criminal matters. The parties to a criminal trial are the government and the alleged criminal. Any victims of the crime are, at most, witnesses.

Criminal Law

Under criminal law and in the criminal justice system it is illegal to engage in certain actions.

Criminal law is designed to prevent those actions.

People are tried in criminal actions.

Civil Law

In contrast with criminal law, civil law deals *only* with the rights and duties of individuals or other entitles toward one another. Only *matters* (not people) are tried under civil law. Civil violations are not usually punished. The losing party generally has to reimburse the winning party for damages. The only exception is in the area of intentional torts, which is discussed Chapter 15, Torts and Tort Damages.

People and other entities bring civil claims against other people or entities. These claims can be negotiated, mediated, arbitrated, or tried. The various methods of dispute resolution are discussed in Chapter 18, Dispute Resolution.

Unlike criminal law, civil law and the civil law system are not designed to prevent people from doing certain acts. For example, it is not illegal to breach a contract or to delay a project or to provide faulty specifications or to make changes or to damage the work. It is illegal only to fail to pay damages that are the consequences of such actions.

For example, assume that a contractor delays a project. The contractor pays the owner the owner's losses associated with the delay. The contractor has done nothing illegal. The contractor engages in an illegal act only if it refuses to pay damages. Of course, the parties may disagree that a delay has occurred, or they may disagree as to the amount of money owed the owner. This disagreement may lead to a claim or lawsuit in which the matter of the delay or other issue is decided.

Civil law can be divided into two broad categories: contracts and torts. These categories are discussed next.

Civil Law

Under civil law it is illegal not to pay damages
for certain actions.

Civil law is designed to make people pay damages.

Matters are tried in civil actions.

Contract Law

Contract law supports and upholds *voluntary duties* between parties, duties that the parties have voluntarily agreed to in a contract. Tort law supports and upholds *duties imposed by law* between parties and is not dependent on any contract between them.

Many people believe that the proliferation of contracts in modern society is a sign of a lack of trust and/or that parties are more litigious than in previous times; however, the main purpose of a contract is not to prevent litigation or arbitration. No contract can be devised to do this. The main purpose of a contract is to aid the parties in remembering what it is they have agreed to do. No human being is capable of remembering the tremendous numbers of details involved in modern complex projects. Contracts provide a useful mechanism for recording what has been agreed on.

An example of a contract duty is an agreement between an owner and a contractor for the contractor to build the owner a barn. The contractor has voluntarily assumed the duty of barn building, and the owner has voluntarily assumed the duty of paying money for a built barn. No law requires anyone to build anyone else a barn. Should either party breach its voluntary duty (barn building or paying money for a built barn), the law will step in to help support and uphold the duties of barn building and paying money for a built barn.

Basic Premises of Contract Law

The Two Basic Premises of Contract Law

1. A party must honor its contract or respond in damages.
2. Parties are presumed to know the content of their contracts.

The two basic premises of contract law underlie a court's or arbitrator's rationale in dealing with a contract problem. Often, these premises are understood and not mentioned in the opinion because they are so basic. Many of the laws in this book are the exceptions to these rules. You should remember this: *most contracts are upheld as written.*

Tort Law

Tort duties are duties the law says people have to one another regardless of the existence of any type of contract. An example of a tort duty is the law that says drivers of automobiles have a duty to drive in a reasonable manner so as not to cause injury to pedestrians on the roadway. There is no contract between automobile drivers and pedestrians.

As with contract duties, it is not illegal to breach a tort duty. It is illegal only to fail to pay damages for the breach of a tort duty. The exception to this statement concerns an area of the law known as intentional tort. Tort law may award punitive damages to be paid by the person who committed the intentional tort to the person who was injured. Punitive damages are damages designed to punish the person who committed the tort (called the tortfeasor) and to prevent people from engaging in intentional torts.

Anatomy of a Civil Lawsuit

A civil lawsuit is a request to a court to decide a civil (that is, contract or tort) dispute between two or more entities based on the law. The terms *suit, lawsuit, case,* or *action* are all used to describe the placing of a dispute before a court for the court, and possibly a jury, to decide how the dispute is to be resolved.

Vocabulary Commonly Used in Civil Lawsuits

Plaintiff: A person or entity who files the papers with the court to begin a civil lawsuit. For example, the owner sues the general contractor for defects in the construction. The owner is the plaintiff.

Defendant: A party who answers the plaintiff's lawsuit. In the preceding example the general contractor is the defendant. The defendant may also sue the plaintiff and other entities for any claims it has related to the subject of the original litigation. If that happens, additional terms may apply to the parties, such as counterclaimant or cross-defendant. Those terms will not be used in this text.

Pleadings: The various documents filed with the court by the parties. The **complaint,** sometimes called a **petition,** is the first document filed by the plaintiff and briefly outlines the plaintiff's claims. The defendant then files an **answer,** which briefly outlines the defendant's defenses or responses to the plaintiff's claim. For the purposes of this text these are the terms with which to familiarize yourself. The defendant may also file countercomplaints against the plaintiff, or cross-complaints against other entities such as the architect or the subcontractor; however, the full nature and extent of pleadings is beyond the scope of this text.

Motions: Requests to the court for something. For example, if the plaintiff is not giving the defendant certain requested discovery (defined next) the defendant can file a motion to compel discovery. Courts will also hear motions concerning admissibility of evidence or legal theories prior to the trial date.

Discovery: The phase of the litigation, after the petition and answer are filed, during which the parties attempt to "discover" all the facts of the case, no matter who has possession of those facts. The parties are required to share *any evidence* they have and to share *any information that could lead to evidence,* with other parties.

Some of the most common discovery tools are interrogatories, requests for documents or other things, and depositions. All discovery tools include time limits. For example, parties may have thirty days to respond to interrogatories. Discovery can be very expensive, however. It can be difficult to pry needed information out of the opposing side.

Interrogatories: Written questions sent from one party to another asking general information. A sample interrogatory: "What is the name, address, and telephone number of all persons on the Construction Site on May 10, 2001?"

Request for Documents or Other Things: A request to view and copy documents related to the litigation. A sample Request for Documents: "Produce the Contract(s), General Conditions, Supplemental Conditions for the construction project _____ (identify) for review and copying on _____ (fill in date) at _____ (fill in location)."

Deposition: A face-to-face meeting between the attorneys for the parties and a potential witness or other person who may have information relevant to the issues raised in the litigation. The attorneys question the person, called a **deponent,** in a manner similar to questioning in a courtroom. A court reporter gives the same oath as in a courtroom and records the questions and responses. The questions and responses are often used at trial, particularly if the witness is unavailable. The testimony has the same force and effect as testimony in a court of law. Deponents who lie under oath can be convicted of perjury.

Motion for Summary Judgment: A request by one party asking the judge to decide the case on the issues of law because the party is of the opinion that there are no major issues of fact. This course of action has many advantages to a party seeking to end a case quickly.

Trial: The formal presentation of the evidence by the lawyers to the jury, which decides the facts; the judge decides the law.

Verdict: Decision of the jury.

Judgment: The document signed by the judge at the end of the trial or after approving a summary judgment motion. In general, the document summarizes who wins, who loses, and what relief the winner is entitled to. As a very simplified example a judgment might say: "Plaintiff is entitled to $20,000 from the defendant because defendant breached the contract."

Appeal: A request to a higher court to review the trial judge's decisions on the legal issues. Any party can make the request. Although it is possible, it is extremely rare for the appeal court to review the factual issues. It is not uncommon for an appeal court to send the matter back to the trial court.

Appellant: Party that requests the appeal; can be either the plaintiff or the defendant.

Apellee: Party responding to the appeal.

Enforcement of Judgment: The attempt by the winning party to get the loser to pay the judgment. May be longer and more time consuming than the trial. It generally takes the form of attempting to locate and liquidate the losing party's assets.

Typical Path of a Lawsuit through the Legal System

The preceding vocabulary has been presented in the order that it might be encountered in a simple lawsuit. A typical lawsuit follows the path illustrated in Figure 1–2.

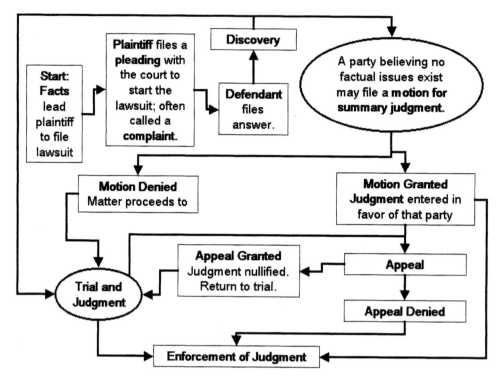

Figure 1-2 Typical Pathway of a Case in the Legal System

Anatomy of an Arbitration

A plaintiff, usually called the **complainant,** files a request for arbitration with the appropriate arbitration board. The defendant, usually called the **respondent,** files a response. Some limited amount of discovery may be allowed. If the parties do not settle the matter, they meet, usually in a conference room, with the arbitrators and present their case, both legally and factually. The arbitrators usually take an active role in the matter and may ask questions or request additional information. Eventually they come to a conclusion. Most arbitrations are binding, that is, the right to a trial has been given up. Therefore, there is no appeal of the arbitrators' decision.

It should be noted that all the law discussed in this text is valid not only in litigation but also in arbitration proceedings. Arbitrators of construction industry disputes may not be lawyers and may not understand the law or follow a legal argument in the same way as lawyers and judges would. Arbitration decisions may not be legally as consistent as cases decided in courts. On the other hand, the decision is reached much more quickly and at a substantial cost savings over a litigated claim.

A Short History of Law in Western Cultures

A brief, simplified version of the development of the law and legal systems in Western cultures may help in gaining an understanding of the law as a *process*. By *Western cultures* is meant cultures with historical and cultural roots in Ancient Greece and Rome. These cultures include those of Europe, Great Britain, the Americas, and Australia.

To understand the current U.S. legal system we will start with the Roman Empire, believed to have been founded in 753 B.C.E. (before the common era, often referred to as B.C). Although the exact dates of the Roman Empire are subject to debate, the Roman Empire was certainly a cultural force from about the fifth century B.C.E. until about the fifth century C.E. (of the common era, often referred to as A.D). Certainly, Roman law was influenced by earlier codes such as the Code of Hammurabi (1780 B.C.E.)., but we will start by looking at Roman law.

An interesting note to constructors: under a section of the Code of Hammurabi a constructor received the death penalty if his structure collapsed and killed the owner. Here are some of the codes applicable to constructors:

229. If a builder build a house for some one and does not construct it properly and the house that he built fall in and kill its owner, then that builder shall be put to death.

230. If it kills the son of the owner the son of that builder shall be put to death.

231. If it kills a slave of the owner, then he shall pay slave for slave to the owner of the house.

232. If it ruin goods, he shall make compensation for all that has been ruined and inasmuch as he did not construct properly this house which he built and it fell, he shall re-erect the house from his own means.

233. If a builder build a house for some one, even though he has not yet completed it; if then the walls seem toppling, the builder must make the walls solid from his own means.

Although the use of the death penalty is on the rise in the United States, it is not likely to rise to the past historical levels. Under present warranty law (see Chapter 13), a builder cannot be put to death for faulty construction.

Early Roman law recognized the individual rights of male Roman citizens and later the rights of male non-Romans. For example, male Roman citizens possessed the right to contract for the purchase and sale of goods, to leave property to heirs, and to own land. This was, at least by modern standards, an improvement over prior laws that tended to recognize the rights of classes of people, such as landowners or the government.

These rights developed over centuries of interaction in Roman courts. For example, under very early Roman law (circa 450 B.C.E.). only *executed* contracts for the sale of property were recognized. **Executed contracts** are those in which the transfer of the property and the payment therefore **has** already occurred. For example, assume that the buyer and the seller had agreed to the transfer of a certain amount of wool at a certain price. The parties would meet, and the transfer of the wool from the seller to the buyer would take place in a ceremony. The ceremony consisted of at least five Roman citizens of legal age who witnessed a sixth Roman citizen holding a bronze scale. The party buying the property would say (in Latin naturally), "I declare this wool is mine according to the law of my Roman clan and I purchase it with this bronze ingot and bronze scale." The buyer would then strike the scale with the ingot and give the ingot to the seller. Once the parties had completed or executed the contract the law would recognize it; however, if the seller refused to sell the wool, or the buyer refused to buy it, neither had any legal recourse against the other. The contract was an uncompleted or *executory* contract that had no status in the eyes of the law. Trade was difficult to engage in under this type of law. The law would not force the seller to sell or the buyer to buy at an agreed-on price.

By approximately 245 B.C.E. Roman law recognized *unilateral executory contracts*. A **unilateral executory contract** is one in which one of the parties has performed its part of the bargain, but the other party must still perform its part. For example, returning to the example of the sale of the wool, if the buyer appeared at the time and place for the transfer and tendered (offered) his money for the wool, but the seller refused to sell, the law would enforce the contract despite the seller's desire not to sell. Because the law would enforce such a contract, buyers and sellers were more willing to incur the costs associated with trade, knowing that if the other party refused to complete the contract, the law might offer a method of compensating the damaged party.

At some later time the law began to recognize **bilateral executory contracts**—that is, contracts in which both parties still had things to do under the contract, but one of the parties refused to perform. This allowed for complex contractual relationships to be developed between parties. In addition, Roman law recognized the formation of corporations. A **corporation** is a legal entity that is created by the law and endowed with certain rights and powers.

With the fall of Rome in the fifth century C.E. the peace and prosperity brought to the Western world by the Romans and their law began to decline. Certainly, their aqueducts and roads remained for a time, and some trade in luxury goods continued; however, with the disappearance of the Roman forces used to keep the peace and to encourage trade, the Western world slipped into feudalism and the Dark Ages. Horizons became very small, and education almost ceased. If not for the monasteries of the time, vast amounts of literature would have been lost.

Feudalism was characterized by isolated communities that were, for the most part, self-sustaining. Little trade occurred, and most of this was in luxury items for the wealthy. Towns, such as they were, and farms and all the people associated with them were "owned" by local lords or knights. Fighting among lords was common as powerful men attempted to increase their wealth and power by destroying other lords.

Feudal law was very different from Roman law. The former consisted mainly of the rules defining the relationships between lords and their vassals. All land belonged to the king and rights to use the land or benefit from it were divided by the king among lesser lords in an often-complicated hierarchical system. The vassals generally were required to perform military service to and provide farm products (and/or taxes) to the person higher up in the hierarchy. Arrangements were in the form of contracts or leases.

Even though feudalism did not completely disappear until about two hundred years ago (the Decree Abolishing the Feudal System was signed in France on August 11, 1789), it began to come under attack in the twelfth century shortly after the Crusades began. The

Crusades were attempts, generally military, to wrest the Holy Land from the Muslims, although some historians have argued that the Crusades were a convenient way to get rid of petty lords and knights who were constantly fighting among themselves for land and the wealth associated with it. Historians can argue the true cause of the Crusades; we will only briefly look at the results.

In the late eleventh century the population had grown, and the amount of land possessed by each lord had decreased through sharing with brothers. In addition, in areas where the eldest son inherited the land, the unlanded younger sons would become knights or soldiers for landed males and provide protection to the landed families. The numbers of knights grew, and the lords of these knights used them in an attempt to increase land holdings and wealth.

In 1095 the Catholic Church called the first Crusade. The knights who fought were granted homes and the right to trade in Eastern markets. These knights went home to buy trade goods to sell in the East—they changed professions from knights to merchants. They also brought back the knowledge of the advanced science of the Muslim culture they had invaded and sold it to those in the West. For example, the merchants brought back the telescope, and they learned the advanced mathematics of the Muslims—a mathematics based on the concept of zero and nine numbers. They also brought back double-entry bookkeeping, so they could drop the cumbersome Roman numeral system. These unlanded knights, now merchants, began to obtain wealth even though they owned no land! They began to form a new class, the merchants or bourgeois. Trade and the demand for trade goods increased tremendously.

The merchants needed places to live, and they did not want to live on land owned by a particular lord because they would in effect be vassals. They began to demand that the lords set up "free towns" or "charter towns" where they could live without incurring the feudal duties of a vassal. Remember, these merchants had recently been knights, so they had the skills to enforce their demands with blood if necessary. Many lords saw the value in trade and they chartered towns in exchange for taxes paid to the lord. Towns began to form.

Artisan-, craft-, and farmer vassals began to demand that they be allowed to sell part of the products of their labor to merchants in the towns for cash. They wished to buy goods other than those manufactured on the particular estate on which they lived. Soon artisans and craftspersons began wanting to live in the towns close to the merchants.

As with all change, many were against it, and in many areas the right to live in towns and be free from feudal duties to the landowners was bought with blood. The period of bloodshed was particularly long and severe for the farmer vassals. The situation of the farmers was vastly different from that of the merchants, artisans, and craftspersons. Farmers could not take their skills to a town; they needed the land to engage in their craft. The landowners did not easily give up their land, and it took many centuries and much bloodshed for farmer vassals to obtain the right to own the land they worked. That struggle will not be elaborated on here.

Trade is easier and less costly if laws exist to uphold the agreements between parties. Any person wishing to trade in a particular town's market had to agree to be bound by the decisions made by the local market court. The law employed by any particular market court was a combination of local custom and existing law, and it was often called the *Law Merchant*. Law varied widely from place to place, and there were many different sets of laws.

Roman law was rediscovered in the monasteries, where it had been sitting in old books for centuries. Since Roman law encouraged trade and commerce, it was a natural source for local courts. Other law came from feudal law, royal law, canon law, and the legal opinions of all the courts deciding cases.

Separate courts were set up for the purpose of administering each particular type of law. *Feudal law courts* resolved disputes between lords and vassals. *Canon law courts* decided cases involving the clergy, religious issues, and many nonreligious issues, as the distinction between secular and religious life was not recognized. Most courts kept records of the legal opinions and decisions made by the judges in prior cases. These decisions became a source for judges trying new matters and they eventually became known as the common law or case law.

Royal law began to develop first in England after the Norman invasion of 1066, when all of England was nominally brought under the power of one central king. Royal law evolved into what we presently call statutory law and is considered the supreme law of the land.

With the development of all this law and all these different and competing legal systems and courts, a new class of persons began to appear: the lawyers, who studied all these laws and used them to advance their clients' interests.

In Great Britain and in the United States, this system basically continues to this day and is called the common law system. The origin of the term *common law* is debatable, but one explanation is that it is another word for *custom*. The original courts based their decisions on the customs in effect in the area where the court sat. In that type of system the legal opinions (or decisions or case law) of judges became law and were typically used to decide similar cases.

A variation of this system exists in continental Europe and is the result of the takeover of much of the continent by Napoleon in the early 1800s. He simplified the law by setting up the Code Napoleon as the only law. Systems based primarily on codes are called civil law systems. Remember that civil law systems are characterized by the fact that judicial opinions are not law and they need not necessarily be followed by a subsequent court in a similar case.

Vocabulary Checklist

Law
Black letter law
Maxims of law
Clean hands doctrine
Basic premises of contract law
Common law
Civil law
Judge-made law
Adversary system of justice
Jurisdiction (two meanings)
Four types of law

Issues of fact
Issues of law
Choice of law
Criminal law
Civil law
Contract law
Tort law
Plaintiff
Defendant
Pleadings
Complaint

Motion
Discovery
Interrogatories
Deposition
Summary judgment
Motion
Trial
Verdict
Judgment
Appeal
Appellant

Complainant

Respondent

Western civilization

Petition

Answer

Request for documents

Apellee

Enforcement of judgment

Review Questions

1. What is the difference between a fact and a law?

2. What is a maxim of law? List two maxims of law.

3. What happens when parties to lawsuits do not agree on facts or laws?

4. How would you describe the following statement?

    The law is the most important aspect of a claim or legal problem.

5. Fill in the following diagram:

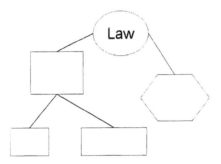

Problems

1. The State Supreme Court of Yur (see River of Law section) is getting ready to decide whether architects have a duty to contractors and therefore can be liable to the contractor for negligence. On what law, rules, opinions, and the like can the court base its decision?

2. The State of Yur (see River of Law section) is getting ready to decide this Issue: Do architects have a duty to contractors and therefore liability to the contractor for negligence? This case involves private contracts entered into in the state of Yur between The James Smith Company, owner; Samudio Contractors; and F. Downing Corporation, architects. The United States Supreme Court had a case several years earlier involving the exact same issue, but the parties to the lawsuit were different. The United States Supreme Court case involved an appeal of a federal project.

    Must the Yur State Supreme Court follow the decision of the United States Supreme Court? Why or why not?

3. Review your notes. Do they contain summaries of each section of the chapter to aid you in studying the concepts to be learned? You should each chapter summarize this way. The table of contents is detailed and provides you with this outline.

Answers to Selected Problems

1. The court may use any law, rule, principle, or other source to form the basis of its opinion. It is not required to follow any other court, unless the matter is an issue of U.S. law.

Appendix A Model Jury Charge

No. 01-123456

NATHAN WASHINGTON, individually and as guardian ad litem for TANIKA WASHINGTON, minor child of Dot Washington, deceased and	§ § § § § §	IN THE DISTRICT COURT of the 11TH JUDICIAL DISTRICT of WOODS COUNTY
for the Estate of Dot Washington, deceased	§ § §	
vs.	§ § §	
ACME SUPPLIER, SUNG LEE ELECTRICAL, GEORGE AND DEBBIE AKIMA DBA LORELEI TEA AND COFFEE ROOM, LORELEI TEA AND COFFEE, INC., CONSTRUCT CONSTRUCTION INC., DANTE, INC., SONDERN AND BLEMITH, ARCHITECTS, AND SUNSET MALL CORPORATION	§ § § § § § § § § § §	STATE OF YUR

Jury Charge

Ladies and Gentlemen of the Jury:

In any jury trial there are, in effect, two judges. I am one of the judges; the other is the jury. It is my duty to preside over the trial and to decide what evidence is proper for your consideration. It is also my duty at the end of the trial to explain to you the rules of law that you must follow and apply in arriving at your verdict.

First, I will give you some general instructions that apply in every case, for example, instructions about burden of proof and how to judge the believability of witnesses. Then I will give you some specific rules of law about this particular case, and finally I will explain to you the procedures you should follow in your deliberations.

You, as jurors, are the judges of the facts. But in determining what actually happened in this case—that is, in reaching your decision as to the facts—it is your sworn duty to follow all of the rules of law as I explain them to you.

During the trial I sustained objections to certain questions and exhibits. You must disregard those questions and exhibits entirely. Do not speculate as to what the witness would have said if permitted to answer the question, or as to the contents of an exhibit. Also, certain testimony, or other evidence, has been ordered stricken from the record, and you have been instructed to disregard this evidence. Do not consider any testimony, or other evidence, that has been stricken in reaching your decision. Your verdict must be based solely on the legally admissible evidence and testimony.

Also, do not assume from anything I may have done, or said, during the trial that I have any opinion concerning any of the issues in this case. Except for my instructions to you on the law, you should disregard anything I may have said during the trial in arriving at your own findings as to the facts.

While you should consider only the evidence, you are permitted to draw such reasonable inferences from the testimony and exhibits as you feel are justified in the light of common experience. You should not be concerned about whether the evidence is direct or circumstantial. Direct evidence is the testimony of one who asserts actual knowledge of a fact, such as an eyewitness. Circumstantial evidence is proof of a chain of facts and circumstances indicating that the defendant is guilty or not guilty. The law makes no distinction between the weights you may give to direct or circumstantial evidence. It only requires that you consider all of the evidence and be convinced of a defendant's guilt beyond a reasonable doubt before you find the defendant guilty.

This case is submitted to you on questions consisting of specific questions about the facts in this case, which are either those facts that I have instructed you to take as established in this case or facts that you must decide from the evidence you have heard at this trial. You are the sole judges of the credibility of the witnesses and the weight to be given to their testimony, but in matters of law, you must be governed by the instructions in this Charge. In discharging your responsibility on this jury, you will observe all the instructions that have previously been given you. I shall now give you additional instructions that you should carefully and strictly follow during your deliberations.

1. Do not let bias, prejudice, or sympathy play any part in your deliberations.

2. In arriving at your answers, consider only the evidence introduced here under oath and such exhibits, if any, as have been introduced for your consideration under the rulings of the Court, that is, what you have seen and heard in Court. In your deliberations, you will not consider, or discuss anything, that is not represented by the evidence in this case.

3. Since every answer that is required by the Charge is important, no juror should state or consider that any required answer is not important.

4. You must not decide who you think should win, and then try to answer the questions accordingly. Simply answer the questions, and do not discuss or concern yourselves with the effect of your answers.

5. You will not decide an issue by lot or drawing straws or by any other method of chance. Do not return a quotient verdict. A quotient verdict means that the jurors agree to abide by the result to be reached by adding together each juror's figures and dividing by the number of jurors to get an average. Do not do any trading on your

answers; that is, one juror should not agree to answer a certain question one way if others will agree to answer another question another way.

6. You may render your verdict upon the vote of ten or more members of the jury. The same ten or more of you must agree upon all of the answers made and to the entire verdict. You will not, therefore, enter into an agreement to be bound by a majority, or any other vote of less than ten jurors. If the verdict and all of the answers therein are reached by unanimous agreement, the presiding juror shall sign the verdict for the entire jury. If any juror disagrees as to any answer made by the verdict, those jurors who agree to all findings shall each sign the verdict.

These instructions are given to you because your conduct is subject to review the same as that of the witnesses, parties, attorneys, and the Judge. If it should be found that you have disregarded any of these instructions, it will be jury misconduct, and it may require another trial by another jury; then all of our time will have been wasted.

The Presiding Juror or any other who observes a violation of the Court's instructions shall immediately warn the one who is violating the same and caution the juror not to do so again.

Definitions

When words are used in this Charge in a sense that varies from the meaning commonly understood, you are given a proper legal definition, which you are bound to accept in place of any other meaning.

Negligence when used with respect to the conduct of any individual defendant, acting through its agents, servants, and employees, means a failure to use ordinary care, that is, failing to do that which another would have done under the same or similar circumstances, or doing that which another would not have done under the same or similar circumstances. A finding of negligence may not be based solely on evidence of a bad result, but said bad result may be considered by you, along with other evidence, in determining the issue of negligence; you shall be the sole judges of the weight, if any, to be given such evidence.

Proximate cause when used with respect to the conduct of any individual defendant, acting through its agents, servants, and employees, means that cause which in a natural and continuace sequence produces an event, and without such cause, such event would not have occurred. In order to be a proximate cause, the act or omission complained of must be such that another, acting through its agents, servants, and employees, using ordinary care, would have foreseen that the event or some similar event might reasonably result therefrom. There may be more than one proximate cause of an event.

Preponderance of the evidence means the greater weight and degree of credible testimony or evidence admitted in this case.

After you retire to the jury room, you will select your own Presiding Juror. The first thing the Presiding Juror will do is to have this complete Charge read aloud, and then you will deliberate upon your answers to the questions asked.

It is the duty of the Presiding Juror:

1. To preside during your deliberations;
2. To see that your deliberations are conducted in an orderly manner and in accordance with the instructions in this Charge;
3. To write out and hand to the Bailiff any communication concerning the case which you desire to have delivered to the Judge;
4. To vote on the questions;
5. To write your answers to the questions in the spaces provided; and
6. To certify to your verdict in the space provided for the Presiding Juror's signature, or to obtain the signatures of all of the jurors who agree with the verdict if your verdict is less than unanimous.

After you have retired to consider your verdict, no one has any authority to communicate with you except the Bailiff of this Court. You should not discuss the case with anyone, not even with other members of the jury, unless all of you are present and assembled in the jury room. Should anyone attempt to talk to you about the case before the verdict is returned, whether at the courthouse, at your home, or elsewhere, please inform the Judge of this fact.

Jury Questionaire

This case is submitted to you on questions about the facts which have been determined by the court, or which you must decide from the direct or circumstantial evidence, or both. In answering these specific questions, answer Yes or No to all questions unless otherwise instructed. A Yes answer must be based on a preponderance of the evidence. If you do not find that a preponderance of the evidence supports a Yes, then answer No. Whenever a question requires an answer other than Yes or No, your answer must be based on a preponderance of the evidence.

Question No. 1

Did the negligence of any individual defendant, acting through its agents, servants, and employees, proximately cause the occurrence and/or injury to Dot Washington that resulted in her death on June 1, 2000?

Answer Yes or No after the name of each defendant and indicate the percentage of negligence committed by that defendant.

Acme Supplier	_____ No	_____ Yes	_____ Percentage
Sung Lee Electrical	_____ No	_____ Yes	_____ Percentage

George and Debbie Akima
    dba Lorelei Tea and
    Coffee Room
	_____ No	_____ Yes	_____ Percentage

Lorelei Tea and Coffee, Inc.	_____ No	_____ Yes	_____ Percentage
Construct Construction Inc.	_____ No	_____ Yes	_____ Percentage
Dante, Inc.	_____ No	_____ Yes	_____ Percentage
Sondern and Blemith, Architects	_____ No	_____ Yes	_____ Percentage
Sunset Mall Corporation	_____ No	_____ Yes	_____ Percentage

If you have answered Yes to even one defendant named above, then answer the following questions Nos. 2, 3, and 4; otherwise, do not answer the following questions Nos. 2, 3, and 4.

Question No. 2: Pecuniary Loss of Nathan Washington

Consider the elements of damages listed below and none other. Consider each element separately. Do not include damages for one element in any other element. Do not include interest on any amount of damages you find.

(A) Pecuniary Loss: "Pecuniary loss" means the loss of the advice, counsel, and similar contributions of a pecuniary value that Nathan Washington, in reasonable probability, would have received from Dot Washington, had she lived.

(B) Loss of Companionship and Society: "Loss of companionship and society" means the loss of the positive benefits flowing from the love, comfort, companionship, and society that Nathan Washington, in reasonable probability, would have received from Dot Washington, had she lived.

(C) Mental Anguish: "Mental anguish" means the emotional pain, torment, and suffering experienced by Nathan Washington because of the death of Dot Washington.

In determining damages for elements (B) and (C), you may consider the relationship between Nathan Washington and Dot Washington, their living arrangements, any extended absences from one another, the harmony of their family relations, and their common interests and activities. You are reminded that elements (B) and (C), like other elements of damages, are separate, and in awarding damages for one element, you shall not include damages for the other.

What sum of money, if paid now in cash, would fairly and reasonably compensate Nathan Washington for his damages, if any, resulting from the death of Dot Washington?

Answer with respect to the elements listed above in dollars and cents for damages, if any, that were sustained in the past and in reasonable probability will be sustained in the future:

Answer: $_____

Question No. 3: Pecuniary Loss of Tanika Washington

Use the preceding questions to determine your answer.

Answer: $_____

Question No. 4: Pecuniary Loss of Dot Washington

What sum of money would have fairly and reasonably compensated Dot Washington for her:

(A) Pain and Mental Anguish: "Pain and mental anguish" means the conscious physical pain, emotional pain, torment, and suffering that Dot Washington experienced before her death as a result of the occurrence and injury in question.

Answer: $_____

(B) Funeral and Burial Expenses: "Funeral and burial expenses" means the reasonable amount of expenses for funeral and burial for Dot Washington reasonably suitable to her station in life.

Answer: $_____

(B) Medical Expenses: "Medical expenses" means the reasonable amount of expenses for medical care and treatment for Dot Washington reasonably required to sustain and attempt to save her life.

Answer: $_____

2

Applying and Using the Law

Merely learning the law is of little or no use, just like learning the rules of baseball but never playing or watching a game would be. To be useful the rules of baseball must be applied to an actual game. Similarly, the law must be applied to factual situations to be of benefit.

Applying and using the law is similar to learning how to play a sport or a musical instrument or to becoming a master craftsperson; none of these can be mastered in a few weeks. It may be possible to master a few of the basics of any of these—baseball, violin or carpentry—in a few weeks, but it is the practice, playing, or doing *over time* that allows one to be considered proficient at a particular skill. The same is true with the law. Learning the law is as frustrating as learning how to play a new musical instrument, or catch a ball, or work with wood. Everyone starts with very few skills, and it is difficult.

The tools of baseball include bats, balls, and an open area in which to play. The tools of the carpenter include wood, chisels, and saws. The tools or means by which music is played include a particular instrument, a score, and the use of hands or mouth to produce the music. The tools of law certainly include specific laws, but also logic and words. *Words and their meanings* are fundamental to law.

Some people approach the study of law as if it were a science or math course where they can learn information to protect them from legal problems. Others view law classes like psychology or sociology courses where they can learn basic principles; however, it is best to approach law as a skill to be learned.

2-1. THINK

Have you learned a sport or a musical instrument? How many hours did you have to practice before you felt comfortable playing in front of an audience?

At the ends of most of the chapters in this text you will find problems. Problem solving is commonly used to teach students how to use the law. Seeing how the law is applied to a factual situation and coming to a conclusion makes it is easier to understand how the law works.

It is advantageous to this learning process to concentrate on *why* a specific answer has been chosen. Learning or memorizing an answer because it is "right" can actually be harmful. A slight change in the facts can easily make a "right" answer wrong. By understanding *why* a particular answer is right you will gain skill in applying the law, and you can more accurately apply it when the facts are slightly different.

The problems in this text are simple situations used to illustrate various issues and laws. In the real world, situations are much more complicated, both legally and factually. In addition, the law memorized today may not be the law in existence tomorrow. Legislators, administrative agencies, and courts are constantly changing laws. Also, the law in one jurisdiction may not be the same in another jurisdiction. For example, in New York subcontractors cannot sue an architect for negligence, but in California they can. In Texas the subcontractor can sue a negligent architect only for certain types of damages, but not all the subcontractor's damages. For these reasons it is not advantageous to memorize the results of the problems studied. Rather, it is important to understand the basic and fundamental principles or rules being applied.

In summary then, when studying the law think of it as a skill to be practiced—not an academic subject to be learned.

Rules of Life and Rules of the Legal System

The process of analyzing legal problems is difficult because it involves the use of many different sets of rules and a complicated interplay of these rules. The law does not exist independently of science, ethics, and cultural attitudes. *Law is merely a part of the complex interaction between humans and their environment,* as illustrated in Figure 2–1.

Some of the very basic rules of life that can affect legal conclusions are discussed next. All the numbers are arbitrary.

Rules of Life and of the Legal System That Are the Same

> *Rule of Life and Rule of the Legal System #101: Someone always pays.*

This is one of the most fundamental principles of both life and the legal system. Life would not be possible without it.

For example, in the following scenario someone pays even though none of the people involved can really be called *liable* or *responsible* for the injury.

> *Owner, Ms. Kim, hires Tyme Contractor to clear out and scrap old machinery left on property she recently inherited from her father. The property is located in south-central Texas. Contractor's employee's (Elmer Employee) job is to*

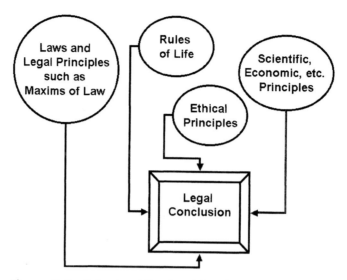

Figure 2-1   Rules that Affect Legal Conclusions.

open the foot of a very old sheepsfoot roller and remove the liquid inside it so the equipment can be refurbished. A sheepsfoot roller is a large piece of machinery used in road building (see Figure 2–2).

Water is frequently placed inside the drums of rollers such as this one, to make them heavier. This increases the compaction of the soil. In northern states, where winters are colder and longer than those of south-central Texas, kerosene was, in past decades, added to the water to prevent freezing. None of the parties knew this, or suspected it, or had any reason to suspect that this roller contained kerosene.

This roller had been placed on Ms. Kim's property approximately forty years earlier by a small corporation owned by Ms. Kim's father and two other men. Kim's father and these other men are all dead. The corporation has been out of business for forty years.

The cap on the sheepsfoot roller drum is very badly rusted and Elmer cannot remove it. Contractor's supervisor advises Elmer to use a rosetip heating element to heat the cap. If the cap is destroyed in the process a new cap can be obtained. Elmer complies; however, unknown to Elmer, Ms. Kim, and the supervisor the liquid in the roller contains kerosene, which ignites due to the heat from the rosetip heating element. Elmer Employee, who is 19 years old, suffers severe burns over 95% of his body, loses all fingers except for two stubs on one hand, requires years of skin grafts, cannot dress, clean, or otherwise take care of himself, and cannot work. At the time of trial his medical and caregiver bills amount to over $1.5 million. Estimates for future

Figure 2–2 Sheepsfoot Roller © 2000–2001 www.arttoday.com. Used with permission.

care and treatment are $3.0 million. All parties agree this is a reasonable estimate of future costs.

Elmer Employee sues Contractor and Ms. Kim for negligence.

Ms. Kim and Contractor engage in a protracted legal battle. The court determines that neither Ms. Kim nor the Contractor was negligent. Ms. Kim was not negligent because she acted reasonably, and no reason existed for her to suspect the kerosene was in the roller. In addition, Contractor was an independent contractor. The court also determines that Contractor acted reasonably, since there was no reason for it to suspect that the roller contained kerosene. Neither of these parties has to pay damages to the employee. Who pays the damages? The injured employee, Elmer, must pay the damages in this case. Someone always pays. Note: In the actual case workers' compensation paid medical bills.

Rule of Life and Rule of the Legal System #102: Every human and every process involving humans operates at a cost to someone or to something.

This rule is related to Rule #101. It arises in innumerable instances on construction projects. In order to merely exist, a human or a building project requires energy, which in most cultures can be represented in terms of the money it costs to buy the energy to operate the human or the building project. A person may just be sitting, but that person must have energy to breathe and to sit. This energy comes from food, which costs someone else to produce, package, and transport to the person.

A building, or part of a building, costs someone money every moment of its existence. Even, and probably especially, partially completed buildings or structures are costing someone money. The money may have all been paid up front, or may be paid at the end, or over time, but someone pays the cost at some time.

Rule of Life and Rule of the Legal System #103: Some people will attempt to receive a benefit without paying the cost. Most people like it when someone else pays for benefits they receive.

Human interaction would be very different if this were not a rule of life. Many problems in this text are from real cases that at first may appear to be stupid, illogical, or contrary to common sense. Many of these are the result of Rule #103 in action. This rule is handled in a variety of ways by different cultures. The discipline of economics studies this rule (among others) and its effect on human behavior.

Rule of Life and Rule of the Legal System #104: Few rules of life are universally applicable; many exceptions to any particular rule exist.

When learning the law it is common for students to apply a few laws universally but fail to recognize when the law does *not* apply. As in other areas of life, learning this rule comes only with practice and experience. One way to avoid being trapped into applying a law erroneously is to be very open minded, also listen to your feelings or intuition after reading the facts.

> *Rule of Life and Rule of the Legal System #105: Many people deny committing acts that the culture deems mistaken, bad, fraudulent, negligent, a breach of contract and/or criminal.*

Again, human interaction on this planet would be very different if this were not a valid rule; however, ***very many legal claims and actions result because people refuse to admit they have made a mistake or committed a wrongful act***. It is ironic that although many people refuse to admit to making a mistake, every person has made many, many mistakes in his or her life.

> *Rule of Life and Rule of the Legal System #106: After many years of hearing people deny or refuse to admit their mistaken, bad, fraudulent, negligent, breaches of contract and/or criminal acts, most people can tell when another person has committed such an act.*

This is one of the most basic rules by which the legal system in the United States operates—the belief that a jury can determine when people have been mistaken, bad, fraudulent, negligent, breached a contract, or committed a criminal act. Juries do this by listening to evidence and looking into the faces and/or hearing the voices of the witnesses and reviewing the proof.

> *Rule of Life #107: Many rules of life and of science are subject to change and modification.*
>
> *Rule of the Legal System #107: The rules are always subject to change.*

This is one of the most difficult rules for many humans to accept; however, it is a fundamental principle of existence. This rule is particularly applicable to the law because law changes not only over time but also over location. In other words, two or more jurisdictions can simultaneously have contradictory or different law.

Rules of Life and of the Legal System That Differ

It is also important to recognize when rules of life and the legal system differ. Some of the fundamental differences are discussed next.

2-2. THINK

As a college student, you are presently spending some time in the social institution called *college*. What are some of the rules of college life that differ from rules of real-life?

> *Rule of Life #111: Decisions need not be made.*
>
> *Rule of the Legal System #111: A decision must be made.*

In life it is often possible to get by without making decisions and instead allow circumstances and events to take their course. This is not necessarily a bad thing; however, when analyzing the legal problems in this text you *must* come to a decision and support it. Making a decision can be scary because it subjects the decision-maker to being wrong. Adults often criticize children when they make their own decisions, so many students are afraid to make a decision. Problems in the text must and can be solved. Do not be afraid of being wrong. One of the advantages of learning from this text is that you can be wrong without harming an actual person or business.

> *Rule of Life #112: Decisions and opinions can be based on faith or on very little evidence.*
>
> *Rule of the Legal System #112: Decisions and opinions must be based on a preponderance of the evidence (civil matters) or beyond a reasonable doubt (criminal matters). These terms are called* standards of proof.

This is not to say that other factors do not affect decisions of judges and juries, but for the most part decisions are based on evidence. If there is no evidence, then a party will lose. In many of the problems in this text the party seeking recovery of damages loses because that party *fails to produce the evidence needed* to prove a part of its case. In the legal system it is irrelevant whether the party was actually damaged or injured. What is relevant is that the party can *prove* it.

> *Rule of Life #113: Assumptions can be used to support opinions or decisions.*
>
> *Rule of the Legal System #113: Only evidence can be used to support an opinion or decision. If no evidence of a certain fact exists, that fact does not exist and cannot be used in a court to support a legal conclusion.*

This rule in conjunction with Rule of the Legal System #111 can produce interesting and sometimes erroneous results. Because a decision must be made (Rule #111), and only evidence (that is, only what can be proved) can be used to support a decision (Rule #113), legal reality may differ from actual reality. A fact may exist in reality but not be capable of being proved. That fact—which does exist but cannot be proved—cannot be used to reach a legal conclusion. The legal conclusion will then be wrong (see Figure 2–3).

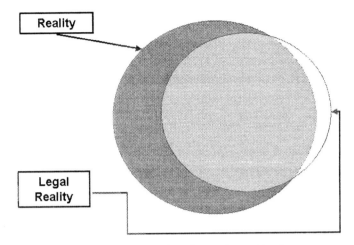

Figure 2-3 Comparison of Reality and Legal Reality

Rule of Life #114: Conflicting evidence can be ignored.

Rule of the Legal System #114: All evidence, both pro and con, must be weighed and a decision reached based on the applicable standard of proof.

The court system is designed to consider virtually all the proof, even though it is frequently contradictory. The judge or jury then weighs the proof and comes to a decision.

Rule of Life #115: The cost of energy needed to run a system is not always borne by the person or entity that benefits from the use of that system.

Rule of the Legal System #115: The law attempts to place the cost on the entity that benefits.

The history of the human race can, in some ways, be viewed as a struggle to make the person or entity that benefits from something pay for that something. Many people, businesses, and cultures are specifically operated in such a way that some people, or classes of people, reap the benefits, and other persons or classes pay the costs of those benefits. In the United States and other modern cultures the prevailing attitude is that the person who benefits should pay the cost.

Rule of Life #116: Winning is better than losing, but it is not everything.

Rule of the Legal System #116: Winning is just about everything, plus it pays more bills.

The legal system in the Unites States is characterized as an adversary system. It operates under the theory that from the battle between the lawyers or the parties, each trying to win, the truth will emerge. The pros and cons of this system will not be debated herein.

Vocabulary Checklist

Rule of life
Rule of the legal system

Review Questions

1. Why is merely learning a set of laws or legal principles of little or no use?
2. What are the tools of the law?
3. The law is similar to what other types of activities?
4. Why is it important to understand some basic rules of life in order to solve legal problems?
5. What two problems can result from trying to use memorized law to determine a conclusion to a legal question?
6. What is the first rule of life that is the same as the first rule of law?
7. What are the rules of life and the rules of the legal system that are the same?
8. What are the rules of life and the rules of the legal system that are different?
9. Fill in the following diagram comparing reality and legal reality.

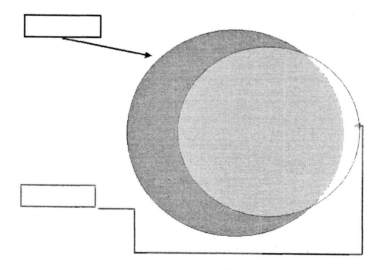

10. Fill in the elements in the following diagram of rules that are used to come to a legal conclusion.

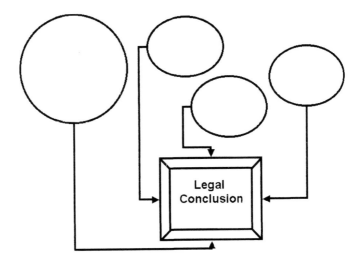

Problems

1. In the factual scenario used to illustrate Rule of Life and Rule of the Legal System #101 (*Someone always pays.*):
   a. What part did each of the following parties play?

   Ms. Kim

   Tyme Contractor

   Mr. Kim's father

   Elmer Employee

   b. Who paid for the injury to Elmer and why?

2. Using the rules of life, rules of the legal system, and/or maxims of law, come to a conclusion or solution to the following situation:

   > The general contractor has prepared a bid on a prime contract. Later that same day it notices that an error was made in its bid, making its bid approximately 30% below that of the next higher bidder. The general contractor informs the owner at the bid opening of the mistake and says it will sue the owner if the owner does not allow it to rescind its bid. No other facts can be proved by a preponderance of the evidence. Should the contractor the forced to build the project?

3. Using the rules of life, rules of the legal system, and/or maxims of law, come to a conclusion or solution to the following situation:

   > While McCaughtry was painting the light standard, the handle of his paint roller came into contact with the high-voltage power line. McCaughtry fell over the rail of the

scaffold to the ground. McCaughtry sustained personal injuries, including a fractured right ankle, third-degree burns over 60% of his body, internal injuries, and a closed head injury, and his left leg was amputated below the knee. Who pays?

4. Using the rules of life, rules of the legal system, and/or maxims of law, come to a conclusion or solution to the following situation:

> You cause injury to Peter Pedestrian by striking him with your car while running a stop sign. You were on an errand for your employer to pick up some tools and supplies needed on a particular job. Peter Pedestrian's health insurance company pays for Peter's medical bills. Can the health insurance company sue you and your employer for contribution, that is, reimbursement of the money it has paid.

5. Using the rules of life, rules of the legal system, and/or maxims of law, come to a conclusion or solution to the following situation:

> The Army Corps of Engineers had awarded a contract for demolition of two buildings to Krygoski. After contract award, the government discovered the actual quantity of asbestos in the buildings far exceeded the government's estimate. The contractor submitted a change order proposal calling for a 33% increase in the contract price. The government considered this unreasonable and elected to terminate the entire contract for convenience.[1] Should it be allowed to do so?

6. Using the rules of life, rules of the legal system, and/or maxims of law, come to a conclusion or solution to the following situation:

> The City and County of Denver (Denver) awarded a contract to Harbert to construct a terminal building at Denver International Airport. The contract contained the following provision:
>
> *"It is agreed and understood by the parties hereto that disputes regarding this contract shall be resolved by administrative hearing under procedures described in Revised Municipal Code section 56-106."*
>
> The code section referenced in the contract was promulgated to resolve disputes involving *sewer rate charges*. Under that statute the Manager of Public Works conducts a hearing and renders a decision that is reviewable by a court on questions of law or fact. Harbert sued Denver on several claims for extras relating to the airport project and a return of the retainage. The City moved to dismiss the court and compel arbitration.[2] Should the case be arbitrated?

---

[1] *Krygoski Construction Co. v. United States*, 94 F.3d 1537 (Fed.Cir. 1996).

[2] *City and County of Denver v. District Court*, 939 P.2d 1353 (Colo. 1997).

Answer to Selected Problem

2. Rule of Life #101: Someone always pays. Maxim of law: Mistakes should be fixed, not taken advantage of. Although it is true that someone must pay for this mistake, given the scenario here, the cost to the owner is minimal—it can get the next lowest contractor. Also, applying the maxim of law that mistakes should be fixed, the contractor should be able to get out of this bid, since this was a mistake.

3

Logic

As stated in the previous chapter, merely learning a set of laws is of no use. Rather, it is a person's ability to *apply* the law to situations encountered that is of value. *The application of law is emphasized in this text, not rote memorization of various laws.*

Logic
The science that evaluates arguments.

How is law applied to situations? Law is applied to situations by arguing that a particular law does or does not apply and giving reasons why the law does or does not apply. After the reasons why the law does or does not apply are provided, a conclusion is reached. This process, called **legal argumentation,** is the same as any other type of argumentation. Many people refer to the skill of making arguments as **critical thinking** or **analytical thinking.** You have no doubt come into contact with arguments, logical or not, in your life. This chapter contains a basic overview of logic, the science that evaluate arguments. Chapter 4 discusses logic as it applies specifically to legal argumentation.

The Argument

The term *argument* has several different meanings. The common definition of argument, which is not used herein, is "a highly emotional interaction between two or more people who disagree." For our purposes, an **argument** is defined as a set of premises used to support a conclusion.

Arguments can be valid or invalid. Arguments are evaluated for validity through the use of logic—that is, a *valid* argument is one that is *logical.* An invalid argument is one that is illogical. Note that validity does not mean that the argument is correct or right. Validity means only the argument is *logically* valid, not that the conclusion is right.

Arguments can be right/correct or wrong/incorrect. Arguments are *right* when their premises have been *proved to be true.* Arguments are wrong when at least one of the premises has been proved to be wrong. It is extremely difficult, if not impossible, to prove anything with 100% accuracy. In this text we are not concerned with the rightness or wrongness of the arguments. None of the arguments in this text has been proved with evidence and therefore we cannot say they are right or wrong. The arguments are, however, valid or invalid.

Logic is, by definition, the science that evaluates arguments. Arguments may be good, bad, logical, or illogical. Logic is used to evaluate all types of arguments. In this text we will concentrate on legal arguments; however, most students are familiar with nonlegal arguments, so we will spend some time on them as an introduction to legal argumentation.

The argument is one of the fundamental tools used to apply law. Other fundamental tools include command of language and writing ability. Using this tool, the argument, requires practice and skill.

Every argument consists of (1) an *issue,* (2) a least one *premise,* and (3) an *answer* or *conclusion.*

As an example of a simple argument, assume you are preparing an argument to a friend, the conclusion of which is that the two of you should study together this evening. You could organize the argument as follows:

Issue: Should we study together tonight? (Note that issues are always posited in the form of a question.)

Premise 1: Studying is good.

Premise 2: Tonight is a night we both have time to study together.

Conclusion: Yes. (Note that the conclusion is a one- or two-word answer to the issue.)

Not all passages are arguments; some are merely statements of information. If the passage does not try to prove some conclusion with premises, the passage is, by definition, not an argument. Many passages, particularly newspaper stories, are passages that *discuss* an argument or inform you of an argument; however, the newspaper story itself is not an argument. To be an argument at least one of the statements in the passage *must* be a premise.

The Issue of an Argument

The issue of an argument is what the parties want resolved. The argument may not come right out and state, "The issue here is . . ." It is very helpful when the argument informs you of the issue, but this does not always happen. It is normal to have several issues arise in any argument. In that event it is easier to come to a conclusion if all the issues are clarified.

Some examples of nonlegal issues:

Should abortion be legal?

Should children be spanked?

What should we have for dinner?

Some examples of legal issues:

Has the contractor breached the contract?

Has the subcontractor been negligent?

Has there been a constructive change to the scope of the contract?

Notice that issues are all posited as questions.

The Conclusion of an Argument

The conclusion of an argument is the answer to the issue. The conclusion should be short to make sure that no premises are included in the conclusion. In most arguments the conclusion can be stated in one or two words:

Yes

No

The owner

$3000

If your conclusion contains more than five words, be careful—you may have included a premise in your conclusion.

The Premises of the Argument

The premises are the reasons on which the arguer bases the conclusion. A passage that does not contain any premises is, by definition, not an argument.

Some examples of premises:

Doing the project my way will save time.

The law of negligence supports our conclusion.

The expenses are greater than the profit to be made.

Dissecting Arguments

One way of practicing the skill of learning how to prepare an argument is to dissect arguments made by others. This allows you to see how arguments are put together and also gives you skill in recognizing the various parts of an argument. We will start with some nonlegal arguments.

Here is a sample of a nonlegal argument and also the dissection of the argument into its component parts of issue, premises, and conclusion:

> If a work plan falls behind schedule, the standard reaction is to somehow increase the production effort in order to get back on schedule. When the production effort is increased, accidents have an increased chance of occurrence. That effect demonstrates the need for the work to progress smoothly and in an organized fashion so that the scheduled work activities take place as planned. With the many different tasks involved in most construction projects and with the large number of subcontractors that participate in the construction effort, it is clear that a great deal of coordination is required to deliver a project in the specified period of time.[1]

This argument can be dissected as follows:

Issue: Is coordination of the construction project important to safety on the project?

Premises:

1. If a work plan falls behind schedule, the standard reaction is to somehow increase the production effort in order to get back on schedule.
2. When the production effort is increased, accidents have an increased chance of occurrence.

Conclusion: Yes.

Note that the conclusion could be worded: *"Coordination and planning of the work are necessary for a safe project."* However, it is recommended that your conclusion be only one or two words. This will ensure that you do not inadvertently include a premise in the argument.

The following argument comes from *A Guide to Successful Construction: Effective Contract Administration.*[2]

> In recent years, informed opinion has reverted once again to favor the architect's traditional role of monitoring the construction contract. This has several advantages that outweigh the disadvantages. With the architect more intimately involved in the conversion from drawings and specifications to physical reality, there is a greater chance of preventing contractor misconceptions and misinterpretations in a timely manner. It also affords the architect an opportunity to correct errors and anomalies in the documents before the construction progress makes them impossible, impractical, or too costly to rectify.

---

[1] Hinze, Jimmie W., *Construction Safety,* Prentice Hall, N.J., 1997, p. 283.

[2] Arthur O'Leary, 1997, BNI Building News, p. 3.

This argument can be dissected as follows:

> *Issue:* Should the architect monitor the construction contract?
>
> *Premises:*

1. There are more advantages than disadvantages to the architect's monitoring the construction contract.
2. The architect can prevent contractor misconceptions and misinterpretations in a timely manner.
3. The architect can detect errors in the documents before the construction progress makes them impossible, impractical, or too costly to rectify.

> *Answer:* Yes.

Note that the conclusion could be worded: *"The architect should monitor the construction contract."*

3-1. THINK

The following is an argument from *Trust:*[3] Can you dissect it?

> A strong and stable family structure and durable social institutions cannot be legislated into existence the way a government can create a central bank or an army. A thriving civil society depends on a people's habits, customs, and ethics—attributes that can be shaped only indirectly through conscious political action and must otherwise be nourished through an increased awareness and respect for culture.

This argument can be dissected as follows:

Issue: How can strong, stable family structures and durable social institutions be formed?

Premises:

1. The above cannot be legislated into existence the way a government can create a central bank or an army.
2. The above depend on people's habits, customs, and ethics.
3. People's habits, customs, and ethics can be shaped only indirectly through conscious political action.

Answer: Increased awareness and respect for culture.

---

[3]Francis Fukuyama, Free Press, N.Y., 1995, p. 5:

Proof of Premises or Evidence of Premises

Notice that *the authors of the preceding arguments offer no proof that any of the premises they are making are true;* therefore, none of these arguments can be considered right or wrong. They can be considered only valid or invalid. If an argument is logical, it is valid. If an argument is illogical, it is not valid. Logical validity is not related to rightness or wrongness.

It is difficult to prove the premises of arguments. This is particularly true for political and social arguments. Most people accept the conclusion of such arguments as being right or wrong based not on proof but on emotions or experience.

Scientific and legal arguments must generally give proof of the validity of the premises. Obtaining proof of the validity of a premise can be extremely time consuming and expensive. In the legal arena failure to obtain proof of a premise can make or break a case or claim. This concept is so important to the law that it has been differentiated into two categories.

Proof of a fact or facts is demonstrated through evidence. Testimony is one of the most common forms of proof of a fact offered in a trial. Parties are sworn by a court official to "tell the truth, the whole truth, and nothing but the truth" or some similar agreement. They are then free to give evidence that can be used by the arbitrator or jury in deciding a case. Parties and witnesses can testify to the existence of facts but cannot express opinions. Only expert witnesses can give opinions in a trial. An **expert witness** is person with specialized knowledge needed to understand some issue in the case. Another common way of proving the existence of a fact is through documents or photographs. The discovery phase of litigation is designed to ensure that needed facts can be proved by evidence.

Proof of a law is accomplished through the use of a legal brief. A **legal brief** is a summary of the law that is needed to decide a particular case.

For this course you can assume that all facts and laws given to you are provable by admissible evidence or valid legal citations, unless you are told differently.

Distinguishing between Premises and Conclusions

It is sometimes difficult to tell the difference between the conclusion of an argument and a premise. For example, most students find the argument made by Francis Fukuyama in *Trust* difficult to dissect. The good news is that determining the conclusion of a legal argument is often easier than determining the conclusion of a nonlegal argument. Legal argumentation is discussed in Chapter 4.

Being able to determine the conclusion of an argument is a skill that improves with practice. Remember, the conclusion is what the arguer *wants* you to believe. Of course, this is often hard to determine, since the premises are statements the arguer *assumes* you believe. The difference between *want* and *assume* is subtle and often difficult for novices to argumentation to discern.

Very frequently, but not always, the conclusion is the first sentence in the passage. If the conclusion is not the first sentence, the next most common place to find the conclusion is in the last sentence of the passage. It is common for the arguer to give the conclusion first and then the support for the conclusion. The next most common method of presenting an argument is to present the premises first, followed by the conclusion.

Practice finding the conclusion of each of the following passages by covering up the text box containing the dissected argument.

EXAMPLE A:

The Head Start project deserves increased expenditures in the years to come. Not only does the national interest depend on it, but also the program will more than pay for itself in terms of increased worker and consumer participation in the future markets. At current funding levels the program cannot fulfill its anticipated potential.   ■   ■   ■

Argument A

Issue: Should expenditures in the Head Start project be increased?

Premises:

1. The national interest depends on the Head Start program.
2. The program will more than pay for itself in terms of increased worker and consumer participation in the market.
3. The program is not fulfilling its potential at current funding levels.

Conclusion: Yes.

EXAMPLE B:

Abortion is wrong because it is the murder of a human being. The human being comes into existence at the moment the egg is fertilized; therefore, any termination of life after that point is the taking of a human life. The taking of a human life is murder.   ■   ■   ■

Argument B

Issue: Is abortion wrong?

Premises:

1. It is the murder of a human being.
2. The human being comes into existence at the moment the egg is fertilized.
3. The taking of a human life is murder.

Conclusion: Yes.

EXAMPLE C:

Abortion is not wrong because human life does not begin until the fetus takes its first breath and is independent of the mother's body. Prior to that time the fetus is not a human being; it has only the potential of being a human being, and that potential does not outweigh the mother's right to control the use of her body. In addition, even if the fetus is a human being, no human being has the right to force another to support it, particularly when the health of the other is endangered.   ■ ■ ■

Argument C

Issue: Is abortion wrong?

Premises:

1. Human life does not begin until the fetus takes its first breath and is independent of the mother's body.
2. Prior to birth the fetus has only the potential of being a human being, and that potential does not outweigh the mother's right.
3. No human has the right to force another to support it, particularly when the health of the other is endangered.

Conclusion: No.

EXAMPLE D:

The federal court has ordered that Microsoft Corporation be divided into two different companies. The court has said this will benefit consumers and increase competition. Despite the lawsuit Microsoft has continued to bully competitors. Microsoft says the court's order is an unwarranted and unjustified intrusion into the software market, a market that has greatly benefited the United States.   ■ ■ ■

Example D is a trick question. It is not an argument; it is merely a statement. It is not attempting to convince the reader of anything but to give information only.

Emotions in Arguments

Emotion and the eliciting of emotions play an important part in trying to convince others to support a particular conclusion. It is often much easier to get another to agree with a particular conclusion by eliciting an emotion rather than by preparing a valid argument and it is certainly easier than obtaining the proof needed to prepare a correct argument! However, for our purposes an argument will be a reasoned, logical support of a conclusion through premises. Emotions are not premises and have no place in the types of arguments to be made here.

The following is an example of an argument that uses emotion-packed words such as "bulldozing," "antichrist," and "demon possession" to try to convince the reader to agree with the argument. Note that this argument does contain some premises also.

> Our bulldozing, bull, antichrist government regime says homosexuality is a third sexual preference and that it should be taught in school. God says that homosexuality is a demon possession and one of the things that he despises most and that we must not associate ourselves with it or support it. I repeat, god said that it is a demon possession, not a third sexual preference. God hated those lewd, unrepentant, disgusting, vile creatures so much that he destroyed them in the city of Sodom. This satanic one-world government now has the audacity to say that we must allow our children to be taught by homosexuals (perverts, those whom god despises) and are saying it is now lawful to teach our children that homosexuality is a third sexual choice. They want to make homosexuals out of our children and gain more revolutionists that our children and us may be destroyed with them. Misery loves company. (Full-page religious advertisement by Tony Alamo, pastor of a church in Alma, Arkansas).

This is not to say that emotions or emotional reactions have no place in the legal system or in life. Emotions play a very big role in the life of humans, and some emotions and emotional reactions are perfectly valid premises on which to base some conclusions. For example, assume the argument is, "Should we go to a horror movie tonight?" One of the parties says, "No, I hate horror movies because they scare me and I can't fall asleep for hours after." The person's emotional reaction is a valid premise on which to base the conclusion that a horror movie will not be on the evening's agenda!

Additionally, an emotional reaction to an argument's conclusion can be a hint or guide that the conclusion is invalid or even wrong. For example, assume a situation in which the contractor has entered into a contract to build a school at a certain location; however, prior to the commencement of building an earthquake strikes and the site disappears into a very deep, large hole in the ground. Should the contractor be forced to build on the site for the same amount as the original bid? The emotional reaction to the unfairness of the situation should lead the arguer to search for law and rules that will relieve the contractor from liability in this situation. (Refer to the index for a discussion of the legal doctrine of practical impossibility.)

Logical Fallacies/Fallacious Arguments

Not only is emotionalism to be avoided in argumentation, logically fallacious arguments are also to be avoided. A **logical fallacy** is a type of defect in an argument. Several schools of thought exist on the exact number and types of logical fallacies. A few of the more common fallacies are discussed here.

Fallacies of relevance—the premise has no relevance to the conclusion.

Fallacies of weak induction—the premise has some, but insufficient, relevance to or support for the conclusion.

Fallacies, other—a miscellaneous category that, however, includes the two most common fallacies students use in their writing.

Fallacies of Relevance

Appeal to Force

An argument containing the fallacy of appeal to force contains a threat of harm to the listener or reader if he or she does not accept the arguer's conclusion.

> *"I'm sure you'll want to raise my salary because I am so friendly with your husband, and I'm sure you wouldn't want him to find out what's been going on between you and that salesman from the office supply store."*

3–2. THINK

What are the issue, premises, and conclusion of the preceding argument? Notice that the premises bear no logical relevance to the conclusion. The answer is in the text box below.

Issue: Should you raise my salary?

Premises:

1. I am friendly with your husband
2. I will tell him what is going on between you and the salesman if you do not. (Notice the appeal to force as a premise to the argument).

Conclusion: Yes.

Appeal to Pity

An argument containing the fallacy of appeal to pity evokes pity in order to get the listener to support the conclusion.

> *"Professor, I admit I never handed in the written assignments on time and studied only a couple of hours before the test, but if you don't pass me, I won't be able to graduate, and I'll have to come back next semester."*

3-3. THINK

What are the issue, premises, and conclusion of the preceding argument? Notice that the premise bears no logical relevance to the conclusion.

Issue: Should the professor pass the student?

Premises:

1. If you don't pass the student the student will not be able to graduate.
2. The student will have to come back next semester.

Conclusion: Yes.

Appeal to the People

An argument containing the fallacy of appeal to the people uses the desire of the listener or reader to be loved, accepted, valued, and/or recognized to get the listener to support the conclusion.

> *"Of course you want to buy Best toothpaste. Why, 90% of America brushes with Best."*

It is not necessary that the people appealed to be all the people, but a particular subgroup. For example, "Of course you want to vote for President Connors—all good Southerners do."

3-4. THINK

What are the issue, premises, and conclusion of the preceding argument? Notice that the premise bears no logical relevance to the conclusion.

Argument against the Person

An argument containing the fallacy of argument against the person always involves at least two arguers. One of them advances a certain argument, and the other then responds by directing his or her attention not to the first person's argument, but to the first person himself. This is an extremely common fallacious argument.

> *"George W. Bush argues that a high state sales tax and no state income tax benefits the citizens of Texas. His argument should be discounted because he is a millionaire who benefits greatly from*

the fact that sales taxes place a much higher proportion of taxes on the poor, whereas income taxes spread the tax burden among the poor and wealthy more evenly."

3-5. THINK

What are the issue, premises, and conclusion of the preceding argument? Notice that the premise bears no logical relevance to the conclusion.

Issue: Should there be a high state sales tax and no state income tax?

Premise:

1. Bush is wealthy.
2. He benefits from the fact that sales taxes place a greater tax burden on the poor.

Conclusion: Yes.

"You cannot understand (whatever the topic is) because you are (fill in the blank with a word such as a college professor, a child, a man, a woman, white, black, old, young, foreign, tall, short, fat, thin)."

3-6. THINK

What are the issue, premises, and conclusion of the preceding argument? Notice that the premise bears no logical relevance to the conclusion.

Straw Man/Red Herring

A slight difference exists between the straw man and the red herring fallacies; however, both have been combined here.

In the straw man fallacy the arguer distorts an opponent's argument for the purpose of more easily attacking it, demolishes the distorted argument, and then concludes that the opponent's original argument has been demolished.

Ms. Brustein argues that people should be allowed to burn the U.S. flag because it is an expression of free speech allowed by the First Amendment to the U.S. Constitution. Obviously, Ms. Brustein advocates the overthrow of the

United States of America. Burning the flag is obviously an act of hatred, and it shows that the person does not believe that the United States should continue to exist—if the person does not want the flag to exist, she obviously does not want the United States to exist. It is common to see the enemies of the United States burning U.S. flags, and they do this because they want to see the United States go down in flames. Do we want the destruction of the United States? Of course not. Clearly, Ms. Bruestein's argument in favor of allowing the flag to be burned is nonsense.

3-7. THINK

What are the issue, premises, and conclusion of the preceding argument? Notice that the premise bears no logical relevance to the conclusion.

Issue: Should we allow people to burn the U.S. flag?

Premises:

1. Obviously, Ms. Brustein advocates the overthrow of the United States of America.
2. Burning the flag is obviously an act of hatred and shows that the person does not believe that the United States should continue to exist.
3. If the person does not want the flag to exist, she obviously does not want the United States to exist.
4. It is common to see the enemies of the United States burning U.S. flags, and they do this because they want to see the United States go down in flames.
5. We do not want the destruction of the United States.

Conclusion: No.

Notice how the original issue has been distorted from flag burning to overthrow of the government. The arguer then attacks overthrowing the government, defeats that argument, and applies the conclusion in the overthrow of the government argument to the original issue of flag burning.

In the red herring fallacy the arguer diverts the attention of the reader or listener by *totally changing the subject* to some different issue. In the straw man fallacy the *subject is the same, just distorted.* For our purposes the difference is not important.

> *"People accuse the Alpha General Corporation of contributing to the pollution of Little River, but Alpha General is the lifeblood of this community. Alpha employs thousands of people and pays millions of dollars in property taxes. These taxes support our schools and pay the salaries of our police and schoolteachers. Apparently the critics ignore these facts."*

3-8. THINK

Issue: Is Alpha General polluting the river?

Premises:

1. Alpha employs thousands of people and pays millions of dollars in property taxes
2. Alpha General taxes support our schools and pay the salaries of our police and schoolteachers.

Conclusion: No.

Notice that the premises have nothing to do with the original issue of whether Alpha General is polluting the river.

Fallacies of Weak Induction

In an argument containing a fallacy of weak induction the premises offer *some* support for the conclusion, but not enough. Because these are fallacies that draw lines between what is "enough," they can be subject to argument themselves. It is common for people using these fallacies to augment the conclusion by eliciting emotional reactions from the reader or listener to encourage agreement with the conclusion.

Post Hoc Fallacy

In an argument containing the post hoc fallacy the arguer assumes that an event A that preceded event B caused event B. Although this *might* be true, it is not necessarily true that the first event *caused* the second.

> *"The 1960s were a time of loosened morals. Today's problems*
> *with teenage, violence can be traced back to the lack of morals in*
> *the 1960s."*

3-9. THINK

Appeal to Authority

An argument containing the appeal to authority fallacy makes an appeal to the expertise of a person or thing; however, the authority is not qualified, or there is reason to believe the person or thing is mistaken, biased, or lying.

> *"1. The Rev. David has earned postgraduate degrees in philosophy and divinity. He has also studied evolution and the theories of evolution propounded by scientists. He has stated that the fossil record does not prove evolution or that the earth is in fact older than the 5000 or 6000 years accounted for in biblical records. In view of the Rev. David's expertise I conclude that this is indeed true."*

3-10. THINK

What are the issue, premises, and conclusion of the preceding argument?

What is the problem with the following evidence?

> 2. *"There must be something to the Roswell UFO incident of 1947. After all, a man who is now a doctor and a man who is now a minister both say their fathers told them, when they were children, they (the fathers) had seen the bodies of the aliens."*

Appeal to Ignorance

The premises of an argument containing the fallacy of appeal to ignorance state that nothing has been proved one way or the other on a subject. The conclusion of the argument then makes a definite assertion about the subject.

Premise: Nothing is known with certainty about X.
Conclusion: We know something definite about X.

Such an argument can prove only that we know nothing about X with certainty. It is illogical to say: We do not know for certain, but we know for certain.

> *"We have no evidence proving that the contractor caused the defect in the construction; therefore we can conclude that the contractor did not construct the project in a defective manner."*

In the preceding example all we know, for sure, is that we have no evidence. Although this is some evidence that the contractor did not perform defectively, it is not conclusive. Not only is this fallacy *extremely difficult to recognize,* much of science, and indeed most of our day-to-day activity, is based on just such thinking.

> *"People have been trying for centuries to provide conclusive*
> *evidence for the claims of (fill in the blank), and no one has ever*
> *succeeded. Therefore, we must conclude that (blank) is a lot of*
> *nonsense." Fill in the blank with the word "astrology."*

3–11. THINK

What are the issue, premises, and conclusion of the preceding argument? The premises do give some evidence for believing the conclusion. What is that evidence? What is the problem with this evidence?

Some examples of other subjects to fill in the blanks are that astrology is bunk, God exists, or God does not exist.

Hasty Generalization

The conclusion of an argument containing a fallacy of hasty generalization is based on a sample that is too small to represent the group it claims to describe.

> *"The waitress at that restaurant sure was slow this morning, and*
> *the cashiers at the drugstore don't know anything about the over-*
> *the-counter medicines they sell. The conclusion is obvious:*
> *people these days are lazy and don't care about their jobs."*

3–12. THINK

What are the issue, premises, and conclusion of the preceding argument? The premises do give some evidence for believing the conclusion. What is that evidence? What is the problem with this evidence?

False Cause

In an argument containing the fallacy of false cause, the link between premises and conclusion depends on some imagined causal connection that probably does not exist or has not been proved.

"I have been reading my horoscope almost daily for the last six months. Every time I read it and try to follow what it says I have a pretty good day, but every day that I rush through breakfast and don't have time to read it, I have a bad day and something always goes wrong. Therefore, I really need to take the time to read my horoscope in the mornings and try to follow its advice in order to have a good day."

3-13. THINK

What are the issue, premises, and conclusion of the preceding argument? The premises do give some evidence for believing the conclusion. What is that evidence? What is the problem with this evidence?

"There are more laws on the books today than ever before and more crimes are being committed than ever before. These laws actually increase the amount of illegal behavior. Therefore, to reduce crime we must eliminate the laws."

"The 1960s were a time of unrest and rebellion against the established values of the American culture. Prior to that time the country enjoyed a period of relative peace and prosperity with low crime rates. The attitudes and actions of people in the '60s destroyed that lifestyle. If people had not been so rebellious in the '60s life would be better today."

Slippery Slope

An argument containing the fallacy of slippery slope starts the listener or reader at what appears to be a reasonable starting point but quickly takes several steps down a slippery slope, leading in the end to some extremely undesirable consequence.

Immediate steps should be taken to outlaw sex education in schools once and for all. Sex education leads to an increase in sexual activity among students. This in turn increases the number of illegitimate births and single mother households. Single mothers cannot provide the same level of care for their families as both a mother and a father do, and the children raised in single-mother homes do not do as well in school and lead to the rise of an uneducated lower class of persons who go on welfare and commit crime. The increase in the numbers of people on welfare and who commit crime will destroy the United States and turn it into a welfare state where most of the population is on welfare, and not working. Eventually, the entire economic foundation of the United States will disintegrate, and the United States will collapse into a third-world country.

3-14. THINK

What are the issue, premises, and conclusion of the preceding argument? The premises do give some evidence for believing the conclusion. What is that evidence? What is the problem with this evidence?

"If the United States approves NAFTA, the giant sucking sound that we hear will be the sound of thousands of jobs and factories disappearing to Mexico."—Ross Perot.

3-15. THINK

What are the issue, premises, and conclusion of the preceding argument? The premises do give some evidence for believing the conclusion. What is that evidence? What is the problem with this evidence?

As most people know, McDonald's restaurant signs show the number of hamburgers the giant chain has sold. That number now stands at 99 billion burgers, or 99 Gigaburgers (GB). Within months, or even weeks, that number will roll over to 100 GB. McDonald's signs, however, were designed years ago, when the prospect of selling one hundred billion hamburgers seemed unthinkably remote, so the signs have only two numeric places.

This means that, after the sale of the 100 billionth burger, McDonald's signs will read "00 Billion Burgers Sold." This, experts predict, will convince the public that, in over thirty years, no McDonald's hamburgers have ever in fact been sold, causing a complete collapse of consumer confidence in McDonald's products.

The ensuing catastrophic drop in sales is seen as almost certain to force the already-troubled company into bankruptcy. This, in turn, will push the teetering American economy over the brink, which, finally, will complete the total devastation of the global economy, ending civilization, as we know it and forcing us all to live on beetles.[4]

Weak Analogy

In a fallacious argument containing a weak analogy the conclusion is based on some type of comparison claiming that two different items are in fact the same.

"Amy Carter was found innocent of trespassing charges because she was just trying to expose the atrocities that the CIA supposedly perpetrates and the false advertising it engages in

---

[4]*Earth First Journal*, http://www.earthfirstjournal.org/frontcover.cfm

*when not telling recruits about supposed attempts to destabilize
foreign governments. If she is found innocent by this type of logic,
then Lt. Col. Oliver North should also be found innocent of any
wrongdoing. He was, after all, just trying to help the people of
Nicaragua gain their freedom. If a person can plead innocence
because he or she is trying to stop a larger crime from being
committed, North should be given a medal.[5]*

3-16. THINK

What are the issue, premises, and conclusion of the preceding argument? The premises do give some evidence for believing the conclusion. What is that evidence? What is the problem with this evidence?

"There is nothing in the middle of the road except dead coyotes."

3-17. THINK

What are the issue, premises, and conclusion of the preceding argument? The premises do give some evidence for believing the conclusion. What is that evidence? What is the problem with this evidence?

Analogy is one of the primary (possibly *the* primary) methods through which courts apply the law to new cases. The courts do this by evaluating the strength of the analogy. Of course, people may differ on whether the analogy is strong or weak. In the following example the court is telling the plaintiff, McCaughtry, that its argument has committed the fallacy of weak analogy. In other words, the court is saying: "Sorry, McCaughtry, but your case is not enough like the old case to warrant that the conclusions be the same" or "McCaughtry, your case is not analogous to the old case, so the ruling is not the same."

The court's words indicating that the fallacy has been committed are set in bold type.

*McCaughtry further argues the owner Barwood is liable for his injuries
sustained while painting a light standard on Barwood's property because the
location of the power line in close proximity to the light standard was a
dangerous condition on the property, and by law Barwood had a duty to warn
McCaughtry of the dangerous condition.*

McCaughtry cites the case of Sun Oil Co. v. Massey *in support of his
conclusion above. In* Sun Oil Co., *the plaintiff, while working on a work over
crew servicing an oil well owned by Sun Oil, which was powered by
electricity from a visible high-voltage power line, received severe injuries
when he was electrocuted. There was testimony the crew had been misled by*

---

[5] *From http://www.drury.edu/faculty/Ess/Logic/Informal/Questionable_Analogy.html*

Sun Oil into believing that power in the lines had been shut off. **Sun Oil Co.**
is distinguishable from this case. *First, a Sun Oil employee had represented*
that the power line had been deenergized. Second, Sun Oil was at least
initially responsible for placing the power line so close to the well.[6]

3-18. THINK

What maxim of law supports this type of thinking by the court?

Fallacies, Other

Begging the Question
(Questionable or Arguable Premise)

Many legal arguments prepared by students suffer from this fallacy because the student
ignores, or does not recognize, an element needed to support the conclusion, and then the
student leaves out the needed element.

The next example is of an argument that begs the question, followed by the same
argument that does not beg the question:

> *A contract is considered ambiguous if it is capable of having two reasonable*
> *meanings. (Law) Riverside County believes the contract says it should pay*
> *only for excavation of rock encountered. B. Rose believes the contract states*
> *that they will be paid for all excavation from ground level to six inches below*
> *pipe. These are two meanings, and therefore the contract is, in fact,*
> *ambiguous.*

Question begged: Are both meanings reasonable? (The exact language of the contract is omitted for brevity.)

> *A contract is considered ambiguous if it is capable of having two reasonable*
> *meanings. (Law) Riverside County believes the contract says it should pay*
> *only for excavation of rock encountered. B. Rose believes the contract states*
> *that they will be paid for all excavation from ground level to six inches below*
> *pipe. These are two reasonable meanings, and therefore the contract is, in*
> *fact, ambiguous.*

(The exact language of the contract is omitted for brevity but it is helpful for deciding whether both meanings are reasonable.)

> *Murder is morally wrong. This being the case, it follows that abortion is*
> *morally wrong.*

---

[6]*McCaughtry v. Barwood Homes Association*, 981 S.W.2d 325 (Tex.App. 1998) (*emphasis*
added).

Issue: Is abortion morally wrong?

Premise: Murder is morally wrong.

Conclusion: Yes

Question begged: Is abortion murder?

Premise not argued: Abortion is murder.

3-19. THINK

Determine which question or premise is being begged in the following arguments.

> *Example A:* Contractors are entitled to compensation when the owner changes the scope of the contract. Since the owner changed the color of the walls, the contractor is entitled to additional payment.

Question begged: Has the owner changed the scope of the contract?

Premise not argued: Changing the color of the walls changes the scope of the contract.

> *Example B:* A latent ambiguity is one that is not recognizable to a reasonable contractor. The contractor did not recognize the ambiguity in the contract, and therefore it is latent.

Question begged: Is the ambiguity reasonable?

Premise not argued: A reasonable contractor would not have recognized this ambiguity.

Suppressed Evidence

An argument containing the suppressed evidence fallacy is one that ignores evidence or facts that would tend to undermine the premises. This is another common fallacy used by all persons who engage in legal arguments. People tend to ignore evidence or facts that tend to undermine their case. Do not do this. There are several ways of handling evidence that tends to undermine your claim.

- Be creative, and find a way of looking at the evidence in such a way that it actually supports your conclusion.
- Admit the negative evidence, but state that the preponderance of the evidence supports your conclusion.
- Try to find another rule.
- Test the validity of the evidence. Is it really evidence?

If nothing can be done with the evidence, the conclusion you are promoting may be invalid. It is time to settle the matter. Remember—not all arguments can be won. Many arguments are invalid or incorrect.

The Second Amendment to the U.S. Constitution states that the right of the people to keep and bear arms shall not be infringed. But a law controlling handguns would infringe on the right to keep and bear arms. Therefore, a law controlling handguns would be unconstitutional.

The Second Amendment to the U.S. Constitution actually reads: "A well regulated militia, being necessary to the security of a free state, the right of the people to keep and bear arms, shall not be infringed." The evidence tending to undermine the premise "the right of the people to keep and bear arms shall not be infringed" is that this right is related to the necessity of a well-regulated militia to ensure the security of the country. That portion of the evidence is ignored in the argument.

In the following example of an actual argument prepared by a student, the student did not discuss the fact that the contractor was uneasy about the lack of boring logs for the banks of the river (see the words in bold). This is evidence that has been suppressed; however, the opposing side will probably bring it up!

EXAMPLE

Contractor entered into contract to build a bridge. The contract provided boring logs for the banks of the river. ***The contractor was uneasy*** *about the lack of boring logs for the riverbed. The riverbed had much larger pockets of silt than had been revealed by the boring logs for the banks; however, the contractor is entitled to compensation for a differing site condition because the conditions encountered were different than the conditions he thought he would find.*

(*Note:* This is an incorrect statement of the law also. A contractor is entitled to compensation for a differing site condition when the condition at the site differs from what the contract indicates. The contractor is not entitled to compensation for a differing site condition merely because the conditions at the site are different from what he expected.)   ■ ■ ■

Restatement of Premise/Circular Reasoning

An argument containing the fallacy of circular reasoning rewords a premise so that it appears different from the conclusion. On closer inspection, however, the two are found to be the same.

The contractor is entitled to compensation for a differing site condition because the conditions at the site are different from what the contract indicated.

The definition of a differing site condition is "a condition at the site that is different than what the contract indicated." The conclusion is merely a restatement of the premise.

Homosexuals must not be allowed to hold government office. Hence any government official who is revealed to be a homosexual will lose his job. Therefore homosexuals will do anything to hide their secret and will be open to blackmail. Therefore homosexuals cannot be allowed to hold government office.[7]

False Dichotomy

The premise sets up an either/or alternative, and it claims the listener or reader must choose one or the other; however, other alternatives may actually exist.

Either you use Ultra Guard Deodorant, or you risk the chance of perspiration odor. Surely you don't want to risk the chance of perspiration odor. Therefore, you will want to use Ultra Guard Deodorant.

How to Handle a Fallacious Argument

It is often extremely difficult and frequently impossible, to get a person making a fallacious argument to change his or her mind and drop the fallacious argument and start thinking logically. One suggested method of handling the fallacious argument is to "name the game," that is, bring the fallacy to the person's attention and explain why the argument is fallacious. This requires at least some understanding of fallacies, however. An alternative is to listen to the fallacious argument and then present your own logical argument. The solution to problem 1 in Chapter 18, Dispute Resolution, is an example of how to handle fallacious arguments.

A person making a fallacious argument is often emotionally, rather than logically, tied to the particular conclusion. Perhaps a suitable alternative can be found to satisfy the fallacious arguer's emotional need and your logical need. Often, merely listening and recognizing the emotions of the fallacious arguer is sufficient for him or her to agree to a logical conclusion.

Another problem may be that the fallacious arguer is incapable of logical thinking, or at least some forms of logical thinking. Presumably, some people would not make logically fallacious arguments if they were capable of making logical ones.

(Finally, remember that the logic of your argument has nothing to do with the truth or validity of your premises. It is possible to have a logical argument yet not have the other party accept the truth or validity of your premises, so he or she will not accept your conclusion. It is often necessary to prove the truth and validity of your premises before your listener or reader will believe you.)

---

[7] http://www.infidels.org/news/atheism/logic.html#noncausa

Vocabulary Checklist

Argument
Premises
Conclusion
Logic
Facts
Law
Rules
Interpretation
Statements
Fallacy

Fallacies of Relevance
    Appeal to force
    Appeal to pity
    Appeal to the people
    Argument against the person
    Straw man/red herring
Fallacies of Weak Induction
    Posthoc fallacy
    Appeal to authority
    Appeal to ignorance

Hasty generalization
False cause
Slippery slope
Weak analogy
Fallacies—Other
    Begging the question
    Suppressed evidence
    Restatement of premise
    False dichotomy

Review Questions

1. What is a definition of the word *argument* that is invalid for arguments in this text?
2. What is the difference between a valid argument and a right argument?
3. What are the three components of an argument?
4. What is the difference between an argument and a media story about an argument?
5. How are issues and conclusions related?
6. What is the difference between premises used in courts and premises used in other arguments?
7. About how many words should your conclusion contain? Why?
8. How are facts proved in a lawsuit?
9. How is the law proved in a lawsuit?
10. Where are you most likely to find the conclusion of an argument?
11. If the conclusion of the argument is not in the place mentioned in question 10, where is the next most likely place to find it?
12. Why are emotions used in an attempt to get the listener to agree to a conclusion?
13. An emotional reaction to a conclusion can give you a hint of what?
14. What is a logical fallacy?
15. What are two ways of handling a person who is making an illogical argument?
16. Why do people make fallacious arguments?

Problems

1. Identify the fallacies of relevance in each of the following arguments. (Only fallacies of relevance are included.)
   a. This department should hire Ed Wayfield for the position and not Mary Lopez. Mr. Wayfield has three children to feed and his wife stays home and takes care of them, whereas Mary has a husband that works.
   b. Many people are arguing that something should be done about the problem of the increasing numbers of unwed mothers who abandon their babies. But most unwed mothers did not

choose to become pregnant. For many it was just a mistake. For some the pregnancy may even be the result of incest. These unwed mothers deserve our sympathy and support, not condemnation.

c. This and some other comments here make me think you would enjoy taking Steve Smith's Ph.D. seminar in Cognitive Psychology at Texas A&M University. It is not nearly as good as the one at the University of Texas, but it would broaden your shallow philosophical arsenal.

d. I know that some of you oppose the appointment of Mr. Cole as the new sales manager. Upon further consideration, however, I am confident you will change your minds. If Cole is not appointed, it may become necessary to make severe personnel cutbacks in your department.

e. Question put by Arguer 1: Did spirituality come first or did language?
  (i) Response by Arguer 2: That is a tough question. I would say language, if by language you mean any sound used to convey meaning. My dog has a primitive language, but I don't think dogs experience spirituality.
  (ii) Response by Arguer 1: Oh, you misunderstand your dog as well? Doggy communicates telepathically. The very limited vocabulary of doggy (expanded by domestic training) is basically to say "me," which is to say, "pay attention to my thoughts" or "I am here."

2. Identify the fallacies of weak induction in each of the following arguments. (Only fallacies of weak induction are included.)

a. The *Daily News* carried an article this morning about three local teenagers who were arrested on charges of drug possession. Teenagers these days are nothing but a bunch of junkies.

b. The faculty believe that adding several new courses will increase their workload even though two new faculty members are being hired; however, the assistant department head has reviewed the class schedules, and he is confident that all the new courses can be taught without an increase in the faculty's workload. The department does not see increased faculty workload as being a problem.

c. The accumulation of pressure in a society is similar to the buildup of pressure in a boiler. If the pressure in a boiler increases beyond a critical point, the boiler will explode. Accordingly, if a government represses its people beyond a certain point, the people will rise up in revolt.

d. The secretaries have asked us to provide lounge areas where they can spend their coffee breaks. This request will have to be refused. If we give them lounge areas, next they'll be asking for spas and swimming pools. Then it will be racquetball courts, tennis courts, and fitness centers. Expenditures for these facilities will drive us into bankruptcy.

e. The middle of the road is not where one drives his or her car, and therefore the middle of the road is not where one should be politically. We drive our cars on the right, so we should politically be on the right.

f. "We are the party of George Washington, of Thomas Jefferson, of John Adams and James Madison—of George Mason and of Patrick Henry. We are the only party that offers the American people the opportunity in the year 2000 to reaffirm the principles of the Declaration of Independence and the strictures of the Constitution of the United States. We are the party to which every citizen who knows and appreciates America's heritage of Christian liberty should come."[8]

---

[8]Campaign 2000 Presidential Nominee Acceptance Speech by Howard Phillips, Constitution Party Campaign 2000 Presidential Nominee, September 4, 1999, available at http://www.ustaxpayers.org/pres_accept_2000.htm

g. No one has ever been able to prove the existence of ESP. We must therefore conclude that ESP is a myth.

h. Governor Turner is prejudiced against diabetics. During her first week in office she appointed three people to important offices, and none of them is a diabetic.

i. We don't dare let the animal rights activists get their foot in the door. If they sell us on the idea that dogs, cats, and dolphins have rights, next it will be chickens and cows. That means no more McNuggets or prime rib. Next it will be worms and insects. This will lead to the decimation of our agricultural industry. The starvation of the human race will follow close behind.

j. No one has proved conclusively that America's nuclear power plants constitute a danger to people living in their immediate vicinity. Therefore, it is perfectly safe to continue to build nuclear power plants near large metropolitan centers.

k. Animals and humans are similar in many ways. Both experience sensations, fears, pleasures, and pain. Humans have a right not to be subjected to needless pain. Does it not follow that animals have a right not to be subjected to needless pain?

3. Identify the other fallacies in each of the following arguments. (Only fallacies discussed in the section "Fallacies, Other" are included.)

a. Of course, abortion is permissible. After all, a woman has a right to do as she pleases with her own body.

b. Of course, abortion is not permissible. After all, a child is being killed.

c. "In order for the law to be just and not just a manifestation of the raw power of the state, it must be rooted in the natural law." (Riley 2000)

d. "Feminism was established as to allow unattractive women easier access to the mainstream of society." (Limbaugh 1994)

e. Construction law professors are highly intelligent people, because if they weren't highly intelligent, they wouldn't be construction law professors.

4. Dissect the following argument into the issue, premises, and conclusion segments of the argument.

> A trans-Atlantic trade war over bananas? The United States abhors the European Union's unfair discrimination against banana-producing countries in Latin America. The European Union gives preferential access to member states' former colonies in Africa and the Caribbean. The policy is bad because it penalizes unfavored countries like Guatemala. These unfavored countries produce plenty of bananas, but are denied fair access to the lucrative European market. The policy also harms United States fruit companies which market bananas from unfavored Latin American countries and therefore cannot compete effectively in Europe. Right is all on the side of the United States and its Latin American co-plaintiffs. And all over bananas. Incredible.[9]

5. Dissect the following argument into the issue, premises, and conclusion segments of the argument.

> Any person should morally deserve the property holdings he has; it shouldn't be that persons have property they don't deserve. People do not morally deserve their natural assets and abilities such as physical strength or intelligence. If a person's natural

---

[9]Edited from editorial in *Dallas Morning News*, 10 December 1998.

assets partially determine the amount of property he has, and his natural assets are undeserved, then so is his property. Therefore, people's property holdings shouldn't be partially determined by their natural assets. (Rawls 1971)

6. Dissect the following argument into the issue, premises, and conclusion segments of the argument.

Property holdings ought to be distributed according to some pattern that is not arbitrary from a moral point of view. That persons have different natural assets is arbitrary from a moral point of view. Therefore, property holdings ought not to be distributed according to natural assets. (Rawls 1971)

7. Dissect the following argument into the issue, premises, and conclusion segments of the argument.

People deserve their natural assets. If people deserve their natural assets, they deserve anything that flows from their natural assets. People's property holdings flow from their natural assets. Therefore, people deserve their property holdings. (Rawls 1971)

8. Dissect the following argument into the issue, premises, and conclusion segments of the argument.

This liberalism says, in other words, that what makes the just society just is not the *telos* or purpose or end at which it aims, but precisely its refusal to choose in advance among competing purposes and ends. In its constitution and its laws, the just society seeks to provide a framework within which its citizens can pursue their own values and ends, consistent with a similar liberty for others. (Sandel 1984)

9. Dissect the following argument into the issue, premises, and conclusion segments of the argument.

"The question is not whether all men will ultimately be equal—that they certainly will not—but whether progress may not go on steadily, if slowly, till, by occupation at least every man is a gentleman. I hold that it may and that it will" (Alfred Marshall). His faith was based on the belief that the distinguishing feature of the working classes was heavy and excessive labor and that the volume of such labour could be greatly reduced. Looking round he found evidence that the skilled artisans, whose labour was not deadening and soul-destroying, were already rising towards the condition which he foresaw as the ultimate achievement of all. They are learning, he said, to value education and leisure more than "mere increase of wages and material comforts." They are "steadily developing independence and namely respect for themselves and, therefore, a courteous respect for others; they are steadily accepting the private and public duties of a citizen; steadily increasing their grasp of the truth that they are men and not producing machines. They are steadily becoming gentlemen." (T. H. Marshall 1963 quoting Alfred Marshall)

Answers to Selected Problems

1. Fallacies of relevance
   a. Pity
   c. Attack against the person
   e. Red herring

2. Weak induction
   a. Hasty generalization
   c. Analogy
   d. Slippery slope
   f. Appeal to the people
   g. Appeal to ignorance
   j. Appeal to ignorance

3. Identify the other fallacies
   a. Begging the question. Premise begged: A woman can do anything she wants with her body. Issue begged: Can a woman do as she pleases with her body?
   c. False dichotomy
   e. Suppressing evidence.
   g. Circular reasoning

4. Banana argument
   Issue: Should the European Union grant privileged access to its banana market to former European colonies in Africa and the Caribbean?
   Premises: Unfavored countries like Guatemala are penalized. These unfavored countries produce plenty of bananas, but are denied fair access to the lucrative European market. The policy also harms U.S. fruit companies that market bananas from unfavored Latin American countries and therefore cannot compete effectively in Europe.
   Conclusion: No

5. Natural assets argument
   Issue: Should a person's natural abilities and assets determine that person's property holdings?

6. Property holdings argument 1
   Issue: Should property holdings be distributed according to people's natural assets?

7. Property holdings argument 2
   Issue: Do people deserve their property holdings?

8. Just society argument
   Issue: What makes a just society just?

9. Gentlemen argument
   Issue: Will all men become gentlemen?

4

Preparing Legal Arguments and Briefing Cases

Legal argumentation, often called **legal analysis,** is merely a specialized form of the argumentation and critical thinking covered in the previous chapter. The premises of a legal argument consist of facts, laws, interpretations of facts and laws, and, to a limited extent, opinions of the person making the argument. Developing the premises of a legal argument is one of the most important skills to be learned in this class.

Legal Argument

An argument in which the premises consist of facts, laws,
interpretation of facts and laws, and opinions

In this text the method used to prepare a legal argument is called FIRPA, which is an acronym for **facts, issues, rules, premises,** and **answer/conclusion.** It is a method designed to develop legal argumentation skills more quickly. A similar and more common method used in law schools is **IRAC,** which stands for **issues, rules, analysis,** and **conclusion.** Both methods can be used for nonlegal problems, as discussed in Chapter 3 in the section on argumentation.

```
                         FIRPA
                          Facts
                         Issues
                          Rules
                         Premises
                          Answer
```

Components of a Legal Argument or Problem

In general, legal arguments contain facts, issues, rules, premises, and answers/conclusions, just like any other type of argument.

Facts

The facts are always the most important part of any legal argument or claim. Facts and proof of facts were first discussed in Chapter 3, Logic.

```
        The facts are always the most important part of a claim.
```

For our purposes the term *fact* applies to the events, or alleged events, that have led to a claim or lawsuit. For our purposes, **the contract is considered a fact.** The contract is not a rule or a law but is considered a fact because the contract is not always controlling. The courts can disregard the contract if it conflicts with the law. Rules and laws are not facts. The dictionary definition of fact is much broader than the preceding one and is not used in this text.

Even though the facts are by far the most important part of the claim, not *all* the facts are important and need to be discussed. Many facts may be irrelevant to some or all of the legal issues under discussion. For example, the following problem contains many facts, many of which are irrelevant to the issue of whether the driver was negligent:

EXAMPLE:

Facts: Driver, Tim Smyth, is driving the company truck, a 1997 red Ford, to pick up needed hardware, such as nails and screws. This hardware is needed to install cabinets at the construction site. Driver stops to have lunch—a hamburger—and has two beers with his lunch. Shortly after, Driver fails to stop at a stop sign and almost runs over a pedestrian, who is wearing a red shirt. The pedestrian is able to dodge the car without coming into contact with the car or falling. The pedestrian is scared by the incident, but is otherwise uninjured.   ■ ■ ■

It is unlikely any of the following facts will have any relevance to any of the legal issues raised in this problem:

The driver's name is Tim Smyth.

The truck is a 1997 red Ford.

The hardware needed was nails and screws.

This hardware was needed to install cabinets at the construction site.

Some of the facts might be useful to a creative person arguing this case:

It could be argued that the hamburger diluted the effect of the beers, and so the driver was not drunk.

It could be argued that the fact the pedestrian was wearing a red shirt, and still the driver did not see him, indicates the driver was drunk, since red is easy to see.

Although it is certainly good to develop the skill of creatively analyzing the facts, this skill requires much practice.

Notice that the definition of fact includes "alleged facts." For example, if one party claims or alleges its damages are $50,000, and the other party alleges the damages are only $25,000, the parties do not agree on the facts. Most legal disputes involve a disagreement as to what the facts are. Far fewer legal disputes involve a disagreement as to what the rules or laws are. Rules are discussed later in the section.

The following are examples of facts that might be given to you in a legal problem.

EXAMPLE 1:

Facts: A fire causes severe damage to the roof of a church remodel project, and the project is delayed one month. Contractor does not inform Owner; however, the architect, Ms. Maple, was on site shortly after the fire and informed the owner of the fire. The painting subcontractor states the electrical subcontractor caused the fire. Sparks from a faulty connection caught paint and paint thinner on fire. The paint was manufactured by Tru-Color Inc., and the paint thinner by Haynes Chemical. The electrical subcontractor states the painting subcontractor caused the fire. Paint thinner was spilled on the ground, touched a connection, and ignited.   ■ ■ ■

EXAMPLE 2:

Facts: The contract between the parties states: "If the Contractor is delayed at any time in progress of the Work by an act or neglect of the Owner, or Architect, or of an employee of either, or of a separate contractor employed by the Owner, or by change, ordered in the Work, or by labor disputes, fire, unusual delay in deliveries, unavoidable casualties, or other causes beyond the Contractor's control, or by delay authorized by the Owner pending arbitration, or by other cause which the Architect determines may justify delay, then the Contract Time shall be extended by Change Order for such reasonable time as the Architect may determine. Contractor must give written notice to the Architect of the cause of the delay within ten days of the event giving rise to the delay."

A fire causes severe damage to the roof, and the project is delayed one month. Contractor does not inform Owner, however, the architect was on site shortly after the fire and informed the owner of the fire.   ■ ■ ■

Notice that the facts in example 2 contain a provision of the contract. *The contract is to be considered a fact;* it is not a rule. Also notice that the facts in example 1 contain many possibly irrelevant facts. It is important to begin to recognize what facts are important to your arguments and to learn how to use facts to support your arguments.

The entire concept of facts is one about which lawyers and nonlawyers disagree. Lawyers have a different concept of facts than do other people, and this often causes tension and conflict. It is not unusual for nonlawyers to say things like "the facts are the facts." The facts are only the facts if the parties agree to them. If the parties do *not* agree on the facts, then there are no facts until the jury or arbitrator decides them.

Another way of putting this concept is to say, "It ain't a fact until the fat juror sings." Until the jury decides the facts, or the parties agree in writing to the facts, there are no facts in a legal claim. In effect, then, lawyers do not really deal with facts at all, but only with things that might, but might not, be determined to be facts by a jury or arbitrator. Of course, anticipating juries is problematical. Jury analysis and prediction are additional areas beyond the scope of this course.

To make it easier to understand this concept, we could coin the words "factals" or "factoids" to describe facts that have not yet been decided by juries or agreed to by the parties." Thus, factals are statements or representations that may or may not be accepted as true by a jury or arbitrator. Clients come to lawyers and give lawyers factals. Lawyers take those factals and try to convince the jury or arbitrator that the factals are true and that the factals should be interpreted in certain ways that support the lawyer's conclusion.

Issues

As discussed in the chapter on logic, the issue is whatever the parties are arguing about. Sometimes the issue is given in the problem; sometimes it is not. It is possible for one set of facts to contain several issues.

Issue
What the parties are arguing about

It is usually possible to word a legal issue in many different ways. Issues can generally be very broadly worded such as, Who should win? This is the ultimate issue in any legal claim, but it does not give anyone much guidance on the specific issue that may be raised by the problem or situation.

In the preceding example 2, the issue raised by that set of facts could be worded in any of the following ways:

Issue: Is the contractor entitled to delay the project?

Issue: Did the contractor breach the contract by failing to notify the owner of the fire?

Issue: Does the fact that the architect was on site when the fire occurred affect the contractor's duty to notify the owner of the fire?

Rules

When analyzing legal problems it is necessary to use at least one law. A *rule* or *law* is a general statement that can be used as a premise to support a legal conclusion in any number of cases. Laws come from several sources. Constitutions, statutes, administrative regulations, and judge-made law are all types of laws that can be used to solve legal problems. Examples of the types of law were given in Chapter 1.

Look at the following example, and try to come to a legal conclusion.

Facts: General contractor submits bid to owner using subcontractor's bid of $100,000 for the concrete. General is awarded contract. Subcontractor determines it made a mistake, and the actual cost to do the concrete work will be $125,000.

Issue: Can the subcontractor rescind (revoke) its bid without incurring any liability to the general contractor?

Given only this information you cannot come to a legal conclusion because first you need to know what the law says about mistaken bids. Only then can you prepare an argument. (See Chapter 7, Mistakes in Bidding.)

4-1. THINK

Compare and contrast *facts* and *rules.*

4-2. THINK

Using the following law, what conclusion do you come to in the preceding problem?

RULE 1:   A party must honor its contract. (basic premise of contract law)

4-3. THINK

Using both of the following laws, what conclusion do you come to in the preceding problem?

RULE 1: A party must honor its contract. (basic premise of contract law)
RULE 2: If a subcontractor makes a mistake in its bid, the loss should fall upon the subcontractor, who made the mistake, and not upon the contractor who relied in good faith upon the subcontractor's bid.[1]

Rules should always be **cited,** that is, they must inform the reader where the rule came from. Some rules are very common and so well known they might not be cited. For example, the rule "a party must honor its contract" is so common it goes uncited and perhaps even unstated. If you were to use the rule "If a subcontractor makes a mistake in its bid, the loss should fall upon the subcontractor" in an argument, your reader might want to check to make sure you have correctly stated the law by referring to the case where it came from. This rule comes from the case of *Drennan v. Star Paving Co.*

Citation

An indication of where the rule can be found. Rules should always be cited so that the reader can check to make sure the rule is accurately stated.

Any specific rule must be discussed completely. For instance, the preceding example of Tim Smyth, the truck driver, contains the following issue and rule (see p. 71):

Issue: Is the Driver negligent?

Rule: Negligence is the failure to act with reasonable care to others, which failure causes injury. (simplified rule of negligence)

A complete discussion of the cited rule involves a discussion of *both* of the following elements or issues:

1. Were the driver's actions reasonable?
2. Was there any injury to the pedestrian?

4-4. THINK

What is the difference between discussing the facts and discussing the law when doing a FIRPA?

---

[1]*Drennan v. Star Paving Co.,* 333 P.2d 757 (Cal. 1958).

Magic Words

The facetious term "magic words" is used to mean any legal situation in which certain specific words, in a specific order, are necessary to produce a certain desired result. For example, the magic words "open sesame" were needed by Aladdin to open the door to the treasure. "Sesame open" or "jingle bells" would not have accomplished the goal of opening the door. The word yes in response to a court clerk's asking, "Do you swear to tell the truth, the whole truth, and nothing but the truth?" will change a witness's words into evidence. Certain magic words need to be said over documents and contracts before they can be turned into evidence and given to the jury.

Magic Words

Certain words in a certain order that are needed in order to produce a desired
legal result

Most laws and rules are *not* composed of magic words. In this text most of the law studied will *not* contain the study of any magic words. Any words that convey the right meaning will be fine. *The meaning of the words is important—not the words themselves.* It is not necessary to memorize specific words, but to understand the concepts behind the words.

Most laws can be stated in any number of different ways and still convey the same meaning. For example, the simplified rule of negligence can be stated in the following ways, all of which are acceptable:

- A person must act in a reasonable manner so as not to cause harm to others.
- Negligence is the failure to act reasonably in one's actions toward others resulting in jury.
- A person is negligent if he or she had acted unreasonably and injured someone.

Assumptions versus Proof of Facts and Law

Be careful when making an assumption in your legal argument. The law assumes very little; facts and law must be proved to the court or arbitrator. An assumption is often a hole in a legal claim—a hole the opposing side may be able to slip through.

Assumption

The statement of a fact or law without proof of its existence. In a legal matter
assumptions are often holes through which the opponent can slip and
defeat your claim.

4–5. THINK

A man jumps off a 60-foot ladder but is unhurt. How can this be?

4-6. THINK

A man and his son are in a car accident, and the son is badly injured. They arrive at the hospital, and the hospital administrator refuses to allow the doctor to operate on the boy because the boy is the doctor's son. How is this possible?

4-7. THINK

A woman looks through a window on the 60th story. She is depressed. She opens the window and steps through it but is unhurt. How is this possible?

4-8. THINK

Compare and contrast *facts* and *assumptions*.

For example, suppose an employee of a painting subcontractor sues the masonry subcontractor because a pallet of bricks stacked on a scaffold fell off and broke the painting subcontractor's leg. One of the employees of the masonry subcontractor (Sam) told the foreman that the painting employee had hit the scaffold with a wheelbarrow, causing the bricks to fall. (This allegation tends to indicate the painting employee was at least contributorily negligent, that is, partially at fault for her injuries.) All the parties go to court, and they begin to testify; however, the employee of the masonry subcontractor, Sam, has moved to another state.

4-9. THINK

What assumption has been made in the scenario of the falling bricks?

4-10. THINK

What discovery tool can prevent the preceding from being a problem?

The Premises of a Legal Argument

The premises can come from several different sources. The most common type of premise in a legal argument is a law or rule of some type. For example, in all arguments involving contracts the primary or basic premise is *a party must honor its contract.* The maxims of law discussed in Chapter 1 are used in very simple legal arguments. This text will introduce you to many other laws that can be used as premises in legal arguments.

Simple Premises

This text emphasizes the use of **simple premises** to solve the legal problems presented at the ends of the chapters. A simple premise is the application of a specific rule to the facts of the problem. Only the following two simple premises exist.

Simple Premises

1. Rule = Facts; rule applies.
2. Rule ≠ Facts; rule does not apply.

The following is an example of a legal argument in outline form using simple premises only.

Facts: A drunken driver hit and injured a pedestrian who was walking across the street. The pedestrian was wearing a chicken suit at the time. It was daylight.

Issue: Was the driver negligent?

Rule: A person who acts unreasonably and causes harm to another is negligent. (simplified negligence rule)

Premise 1: acts unreasonably (rule) = driving while drunk (fact)

Premise 2: causes harm to another (rule) = pedestrian was injured (fact)

Answer: Yes

Using the preceding outline gives the writer an outline of the argument. The next step is to put the outline into complete sentences and paragraphs. The argument might read as follows:

> In this claim, the issue is whether the driver was negligent. Negligence is acting unreasonably and thereby causing harm to another person. In this matter the driver was drunk. Driving while drunk is unreasonable. In addition, the law requires that the person suing be injured. The facts state that the pedestrian was injured. Therefore the driver was negligent because he acted unreasonably and caused an injury to another person.

Premises Based on Opinion and Creative Thinking

Opinion and creative interpretation of the facts are extremely important in legal argumentation, because many legal opinions come down to the judge's or the jury's opinion. Creative use of facts can help support an argument.

In the preceding example the facts that the pedestrian was wearing a chicken suit and it was daylight can be used creatively to bolster the argument that the driver was negligent. For example:

> In this claim, the issue is whether the driver was negligent. Negligence is acting unreasonably and thereby causing harm to another person. In this

matter the driver was drunk. Driving while drunk is unreasonable. *It is certainly reasonable to assume that a person who was watching the road, and who was driving in a reasonable manner, would have noticed a person in a chicken suit crossing the road, especially since this accident occurred in daylight.* The driver was not paying attention and was not driving in a reasonable manner; therefore, the driver was negligent.

In addition, the law requires that the person suing be injured. The facts state that the person was injured; therefore, the driver was negligent because he acted unreasonably and caused an injury to another person.

It is often the interpretation of the facts, not the facts themselves, that are important in a legal claim. Nonlawyers have a tendency to think, the facts are the facts; however, facts are not so simple. Facts can easily be used to misrepresent any situation. As any child knows, one of the easiest ways to lie is to withhold certain critical facts while admitting only certain, carefully selected facts.

An analogy may be useful here. Think of any situation or claim as a picture puzzle with several pieces missing. When all the pieces are in place it is easy to see the picture, but if many of the puzzle pieces are missing, it becomes more difficult to determine what the picture is. It is more likely that the interpretation of that picture will contain errors.

For example, assume the following fact and rule:

Fact: Chris killed Antonie.

Rule: Killing is wrong and should be punished.

Conclusion: Chris should be punished.

But what if the following additional facts come to light? Antonie was beating up a small child, Chris pushed Antonie away, Antonie hit his head on the corner of a marble table and died. Is your conclusion the same?

Instead, assume the following additional facts come to light: Chris is a French soldier in World War II, and Antonie is a German soldier attacking Chris's position. Again, is the conclusion the same? No, of course not. The conclusion changes as additional information comes to light.

Another analogy may prove useful and encourage you to look at facts more critically and creatively. Think of the facts as being like a photograph. Many people have the mistaken belief photographs do not lie, but photographs lie all the time. They lie by giving only a part of the entire reality—only part of the facts. The photographer can take a photo of 10 foreigners burning an American flag but may choose not to photograph the 100 foreigners walking by and shaking their heads in disgust. The picture leads the viewer to believe that foreigners do not support the United States. The photo has misrepresented the situation by being selective with the content of the picture.

People who are skilled at interpreting the facts can take a few facts and correctly interpret the reality behind them. Of course, other equally skilled people can take a few facts and misinterpret the reality behind them.

4–11. THINK

Come up with an example, real or imagined, in which only parts of the facts are given and thereby someone is deceived.

Answer or Conclusion: The answer or conclusion is a one- or two-word answer to the issue. Answers should be very short so you will not include any premises in the answer.

How to FIRPA

FIRPA is a tool for helping you organize a comprehensible argument. The parts of the FIRPA are Facts, Issues, Rules, Premises, and Answer/Conclusion. This section contains a detailed methodology designed to produce a completed argument that is understandable to a reader. Appendix A contains a sample FIRPA prepared by a student.

The following problem will be used in explaining how to FIRPA. Figure 4–1 shows the relationships among the parties.

Facts: Mr. and Mrs. Wright are the owners of a home recently built by Reveille Contractors. The Wrights have a performance/payment bond with Slow Pay Insurance Co. guaranteeing Reveille Contractor's indebtedness for all "labor and material furnished" in connection with the work. Shortly after the work on the house is completed, Best Hardware sends the Wrights a copy of an invoice for hammers, pliers, and screwdrivers that Best claims were purchased by Reveille for the Wright job, and in fact Reveille did use these items on that job site. Reveille did not, however, pay Best. The Wrights turn the claim over to Slow Pay to pay pursuant to the performance/payment bond.

Issue: Is Slow Pay required to pay the invoice of Best pursuant to its bond with the Wrights?

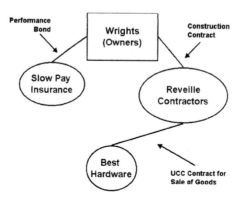

Figure 4–1 Relationships Among Parties in Sample Problem

Rule: The surety on a performance bond must pay for all materials and equipment actually consumed in performing a construction contract.

Premises:

Answer:

Outline the Facts, Issue(s), and Rule

For problems in this text the facts and issues are usually given to you. This is not common in real life; however, it is necessary for learning purposes.

You must choose a legal rule or rules. The choice of rule is very critical, and this skill can take years to develop. In this text the rule or a hint as to which rule is applicable is frequently given. For this problem the rule has been given to you.

Prepare the Simple Premises

Without a doubt preparing the premises of your argument is the most difficult part of the FIRPA. To solve the problems in this text you should concentrate on the simple premises.

Review the Rule

Circle or highlight all the elements or important words in the rule that the parties are arguing over or that you think the parties can argue over. These circled or highlighted words *must* appear in your argument. Parties can argue over the applicability of any and all words in the rule. It is unlikely they will argue over every word in the rule, however.

In this example the rule words the parties are likely to argue over are

- materials/equipment
- actually consumed

Put each of the bulleted items into a separate premise. Do not combine these two items in one premise.

The following outline of the argument is starting to appear:

Facts: The Wrights have been sued on a performance bond because the contractor failed to pay a supplier for hammers, pliers, and similar types of items.

Issue 1:
Rule 1: Surety must pay for all materials and equipment actually consumed.
Premise(s)1: materials/equipment
Answer/Conclusion 1:

Issue 2:
Rule 2: Surety must pay for all materials and equipment actually consumed. (For this example the rule happens to be the same as rule 1. This is not always true.)

Premise(s) 2: actually consumed
Answer/Conclusion 2:

Review the Facts

Circle or highlight all the facts dealing with the rule words chosen, and place them in the premise next to the rule words. Also place the fact words in the issue section of the FIRPA.

In this example the following fact words deal with material/equipment: *hammers, pliers, and screwdrivers.* The closest or most similar word to the rule word *actually consumed* is *use.*

At this point the FIRPA outline looks like this:

Facts: The Wrights have been sued on a performance bond because the contractor failed to pay a supplier for hammers, pliers, and similar types of items.

Issue 1: materials/equipment (rule words)   hammers, pliers, and screwdrivers
                                                (fact words)
Rule 1: Surety must pay for all materials and equipment actually consumed.
Premise(s) 1: materials/equipment (rule words)   hammers, pliers, and
                                                     screwdrivers (fact words)
Answer/Conclusion 1:

Issue 2: actually consumed   used
Rule 2: (For this example it happens to be the same as rule 1.)
Premise(s) 2: actually consumed (rule words)   used (fact words)
Answer/Conclusion 2:

Next, put an equal sign [=] or a not equal [≠] sign between the rule words and the fact words in only the premise section of the FIRPA.

At this point the FIRPA outline looks like this:

Facts: The Wrights have been sued on a performance bond because the contractor failed to pay a supplier for hammers, pliers, and similar types of items.

Issue 1: materials/equipment   hammers, pliers, and screwdrivers
Rule 1: Surety must pay for all materials and equipment actually consumed.
Premise(s) 1: materials/equipment (rule words) ≠ hammers, pliers, and
screwdrivers (fact words)
Answer/Conclusion 1:

Issue 2: actually consumed   used
Rule 2: (For this example it happens to be the same)
Premise(s) 2: actually consumed (rule words) ≠ used (fact words)
Answer/Conclusion 2:

Determine the Issue and Conclusion

Wording the issue is often difficult, especially if more than one legal issue exists. The following are two acceptable ways of writing the issue:

- Is Slow Pay responsible for paying Best for the hammers, pliers, and screwdrivers pursuant to the performance bond it has with the Wrights?
- Are hammers, pliers, and screwdrivers materials/equipment?

The second statement of the issue is the more specific wording of the issue. Finally, answer the issue, and add the answer to the outline.

At this point the FIRPA outline looks like this:

Facts: The Wrights have been sued on a performance bond because the contractor failed to pay a supplier for hammers, pliers, and similar types of items.

Issue 1: Are hammers, pliers, and screwdrivers materials/equipment?
Rule 1: Surety must pay for all materials and equipment actually consumed.
Premise(s) 1: materials/equipment (law or rule words) ≠ hammers, pliers, and screwdrivers (fact words)
Answer 1: No

Issue 2: Is using the hammers, pliers, and screwdrivers the same as actually consuming the hammers etc?
Rule 2: (For this example it happens to be the same as rule 1.)
Premise(s) 2: actually consumed (rule words) ≠ used (fact words)
Answer 2: No

You now have an outline that will help you in preparing a complete and comprehensible memo discussing this topic. Turn the outline into complete sentences and paragraphs. Also give the reader some general background on the law. A finished argument regarding this scenario would be:

> Mr. and Mrs. Wright are the owners of a home recently built by Reveille Contractors. The Wrights have a performance/payment bond with Slow Pay Insurance Co. guaranteeing Reveille Contractor's indebtedness for all "labor and material furnished" in connection with the work. Shortly after the work on the house is completed, Best Hardware sends the Wrights a copy of an invoice for hammers, pliers, and screwdrivers that Best claims were purchased by Reveille for the Wright job, and in fact Reveille did use these items on that job site. Reveille did not, however, pay Best. The Wrights turn the claim over to Slow Pay to pay pursuant to the performance/payment bond.
>
> (Discussion of performance bonds and the law behind this scenario is omitted for brevity.)

The issue in this case is whether Slow Pay must pay for the hammers, pliers, and screwdrivers purchased by Reveille Construction for use on the Wrights' construction project. These tools were supplied by Best Hardware and used by Reveille on the Wrights' project; however, Reveille did not pay Best for them. Best has submitted the invoice to the Wrights for payment. The Wrights have turned over the invoice to Slow Pay, the bonding company, to pay because they have a performance/payment bond with Slow Pay.

The law requires Slow Pay to pay for all materials and equipment actually consumed in the project. (*Notice that this sentence is a restatement of the rule. It is a good introductory sentence for your paragraph because you reader does not know what the rule is.*) However, hammers, pliers, and screwdrivers are not materials or equipment. (*This sentence is a premise of your argument. Notice how it applies the facts to the law.*) In the construction industry materials are such things as paint and wood that are used in a particular construction job and cannot be reused. (*This sentence is a premise of your argument. It falls into the category of creative thinking.*) Since the hammers, pliers, and screwdrivers are not material or equipment, Slow Pay does not have to pay for them. (*This sentence is a statement of the Answer/Conclusion relating to this part of the rule.*)

In addition, the rule requires Slow Pay to pay for items "actually consumed" in the construction. (*This sentence is a restatement of another part or element of the rule.*) The facts indicate that the hammers, pliers, and screwdrivers were not consumed but were merely used in the construction. (*This sentence is a premise of your argument. Notice how the premise applies the rule to the facts.*) Slow Pay is not required to pay for items merely used. (*This sentence is a statement of the Answer/Conclusion: relating to this part of the rule.*)

In this matter Slow Pay is not required to pay Best's invoice. This is because Best's invoice is not for materials or equipment, and the items were not consumed on the Wrights' project. (*These sentences are a restatement of your entire Answer/Conclusion: It is OK to repeat. Sometimes your ideas get across better if you repeat them.*)

Checklist for Arguments

Once your argument is finished, complete the following checklist to make sure your argument is comprehensible:

1. **Change your answer/conclusion to the opposite of what you reached.** For example, if your conclusion was yes change it to no. You should be able to change just a few words in your argument to support the opposite conclusion. Your argument should sound or feel unethical, immoral, or laughable. If it does not, examine *your* argument to make sure it is not unethical, immoral, or laughable.

2. **Does your argument stand alone?** That is, can the reader understand what you are saying without having to refer to the facts, issues, rules, and conclusion given in the

problem? Assume that the reader does not have the problem. The reader has only what you have given to him or to her.

3. **Can you pick out the premises(s) of the argument?** If not, you may not have any in there. In that case you have not made an argument.

4. **Have you completely discussed the entire rule?** Beginners might discuss *only* whether hammers are material/equipment and fail to discuss the "using is not the same as consuming" issue.

Common Problem Areas

The following is a list of some of the more common problems that appear in arguments:

1. **Argument does not stand alone.** This problem is discussed in the preceding "Checklist" section.

2. **Student cannot tell which facts are important or relevant and puts all facts into the premise section of the FIRPA.** Discuss only the facts relevant to a particular element of your issue. For example, if the issue involves someone's reasonable actions, do not throw in facts about the proper notice given. If notice is an issue in the problem, discuss it separately.

3. **Student needs to improve writing skills.** Brush up on your skills by consulting appropriate texts. The following are some suggestions for improving your writing:

Get to the point. Use short sentences.

Start your sentences with nouns:

> The contractor . . .
>
> The owner . . .
>
> The court . . .
>
> The issue here . . . (These are magic words! Use them!)
>
> The rule says . . . (These are magic words! Use them!)
>
> The rule applies to the contractor because . . . (These are magic words! Use them!)
>
> The rule does not apply to the owner because . . . (These are magic words! Use them!)

Check sentence structure.

> *Poor sentence:* This should be based off of the ambiguity of the contract specifications.
> *Better:* The contract specifications were ambiguous.
>
> *Poor sentence:* There are several rules that can subject the owner to liability.
> *Better:* Several rules can subject the owner to liability.

Poor sentence: Being that B. Rose is a pipeline company, their main line of work is civil engineering.

Better: B. Rose Company is a pipeline company, and their main line of work is civil engineering.

Check paragraph structure.

Many students are unsure how to divide the argument into paragraphs. The following is a recommended structure for simple arguments:

Paragraph 1: Facts

Paragraph 2: Issue and Rules, including background discussion of relevant law. This may require more than one paragraph.

Paragraph 3: Premises and Conclusion

Briefing Cases: Trips down the Rabbit Hole

To **brief a case** is to dissect it into its component parts. Briefing cases should not be confused with **briefing a legal issue.** Whereas a case brief is brief, a brief of a legal issue can be hundreds or even thousands of pages long. A brief of a legal issue is a comprehensive discussion of the law relating to an issue.

Many, but not all, of these components of a case brief have already been discussed, namely, facts, issues, rules, premises, and conclusion/answer. The following is a more complete list of the items that appear in a typical case brief:

Name of case with complete citation

Facts

Procedural posture (discussed next)

Issues

Rules

Premises (often labeled Analysis)

Conclusion

Disposition (discussed later in this section)

A brief should be brief and attempt to *summarize* the case or part of a case in a few words. For example, the fact section of a brief of *Blinderman Construction Co., Inc. v. United States,* included in the appendix to Chapter 9, Scope, could read as follows:[2]

Contractor entered into contract with Navy to replace meters and other similar items in over 600 apartments on a Naval base. The contractor

---

[2]695 F.2d 552 (Fed. Cir. 1982)

> *encountered difficulties in obtaining access to many of the apartments,*
> *causing a delay in the completion of the contract.*

The facts of *McCaughtry v. Barwood Homes Association,* included in the appendix to Chapter 15, Torts, can be summarized in the following two sentences:[3]

> *Employee of independent contractor (employed by owner to refurbish tennis*
> *courts) was injured when his painting tool came into contact with an*
> *overhead powerline. Utility company owned the powerline.*

The preceding summary could even be shorter. It is not really important that the independent contractor was employed to refurbish tennis courts; however, a detail like this may help you remember the case at a later time when you are referring to your brief.

Procedural Posture

Information in the case telling the reader where the case is in the legal process is called **procedural posture.** Some examples of procedural posture follow.

- This case is an appeal from a jury trial in favor of . . .
- This case is an appeal sustaining the defendant's motion for summary judgment and dismissing the plaintiff's case.
- This case is an appeal to the State Supreme Court . . .
- This case is a federal district (trial) judge's opinion . . .
- This case is on appeal from the Federal Board of Contract Appeals in favor of . . .
- This case is on appeal from an administrative hearing before the Occupational Health and Safety Administration in favor of . . .

The following is an example of the procedural posture of the *Blinderman* case:

> *"Pursuant to the Contract Disputes Act of 1978, 41 USC §§ 601,*
> *et seq., the appellant (contractor) appeals from a decision of the*
> *Armed Services Board of Contract Appeals (Board) which denied,*
> *in part, the contractor's claim in the amount of $45,312 and its*
> *request for a time extension of 13 days for the completion of the*
> *contract."*

The procedural posture of a case is not a fact. Because the events in the preceding quotation occurred after the filing of the lawsuit, they are, by definition, not facts.

---

[3]981 S.W.2d 325 (Tex. App. 1998)

Recognizing Rules

Finding the rules and laws in a case takes practice. The following is an example of a judge-made law as written by the judge.

> *"When the mistake is so fundamental in character that the minds*
> *of the parties have not, in fact, met, or where an unconscionable*
> *advantage has been gained by mere mistake, equity will intervene*
> *to prevent intolerable injustice where there has been no failure to*
> *exercise reasonable care on the part of the [general contractor]*
> *and where no intervening rights have been accrued."[4]*

This rule could be reworded as follows: "The law will prevent one party from taking advantage of another's mistake when (a) the mistake is fundamental to the nature of the contract or (b) the nonmistaking party would have an unconscionable advantage over the mistaken party. This rule applies only if the mistaken party has exercised reasonable care to avoid the mistake, and no intervening rights have accrued."

Analysis and Conclusions

The bulk of the opinion consists of the premises and conclusions of the judge. Many judges and lawyers refer to this section of the case as **analysis.** The arguments contain the premises on which the judge based the conclusion. The arguments are usually fairly long and complicated, involving many rules and facts.

The conclusions are usually part of the argument. Sometimes the judge will identify the conclusion, and sometimes you must discover the conclusion.

The following are two examples of conclusions determined by the judges in the *Blinderman* case:

> *"We conclude"* . . . *the rule enunciated in Worthington Pump*
> should be applied here." This is the judge's conclusion
> concerning the issue of law: What law applies to this case? The
> conclusion is the rule enunciated in another case entitled
> *Worthington Pump*. The parties had a disagreement as to which
> law applied.

After reviewing the facts and the law, the judge made the following decision:

> *"After the contractor notified the project manager that the*
> *contractor's reasonable efforts had not resulted in gaining entry*

---

[4]*School District of Scottsbluff v. Olson Constr. Co.*, 45 N.W.2d 164 (Neb. 1950)

> *to certain apartments, the Navy was under an implied obligation*
> *to provide such access so that the contractor could complete the*
> *contract within the time required by its terms."*

The preceding is the conclusion to the major issue raised in the case: Did the Navy have an implied obligation to provide access to the contractor? The conclusion or answer was yes.

Disposition of the Case

The final element of the brief is called the **disposition.** It tells the reader what should happen to the case in the future given the particular conclusions reached in the opinion. Recall that the procedural posture told the reader how the case got to this point. The disposition tells the reader where the matter goes from here, if anywhere. The following are some examples of the disposition of a case:

- Remanded for trial. (*Translation:* the case is returned to the trial court, where it is to be tried.)
- Upheld. (*Translation:* The trial judge did not make any mistakes. If you want to appeal to a higher court, go ahead. Of course, if the Supreme Court makes this disposition, there is no higher court to appeal to.)
- Overruled. (*Translation:* The trial judge did make a mistake. Usually, additional verbiage will explain what needs to happen.)
- Overruled and dismissed. (*Translation:* The trial judge made a mistake in not dismissing this case, and we are going to dismiss it.)
- Returned to the trial court to issue orders in conformity with this opinion. (*Translation:* We decided the legal issues here. Certain orders need to be made by the trial judge to tie up the loose ends.)

The case of *Grace Community Church v. Gonzales* appears in Appendix B, on pp. 99. A brief of the case is shown on p. 94. In addition, the case of *Erlich v. Menezes,* which appears in Appendix C, p. 102, is given to you to brief on your own.

Vocabulary Checklist

FIRPA
Rule
Magic words
Basis premise of
  contract law

Legal maxims
Simple premises
Case brief

Legal brief
Procedural posture
Disposition of a case

Review Questions

1. The premises of a legal argument can consist of what?
2. What is FIRPA, and what is it *used* for?
3. A solution to a problem is what element of an argument?
4. Order the following elements of a problem from easiest to most difficult to determine
   a. Facts
   b. Issue
   c. Rule
5. Why do students get an unrealistic picture of problem solving?
6. What is a *brief?*
7. Why is briefing helpful?
8. What two different meanings are given to the term *brief?*
9. What is a *fact?*
10. What part of the argument are the terms of the contract?
11. Are all facts of equal importance?
12. Why is the following statement false to a lawyer?

   "The facts are the facts."

13. What is a *factal?*
14. What is an *issue?*
15. What is a *rule?*
16. What types of rules are usually used in legal argumentation?
17. What does it mean to *cite* a case or statute?
18. What is the difference between the need to discuss all the facts and the need to discuss all of the rule?
19. By failing to discuss all of the rule, what fallacy of logic will the arguer make?
20. Each element or issue should be discussed in its own separate what?
21. What are "magic words"?
22. What magic words are necessary to change a witness's words into evidence?
23. What is the most important part of any legal claim?
24. What is the basic premise or starting point from which all legal argumentation concerning contracts starts?
25. How would our society be different if the answer to question 24 were not the basic premise?
26. Why is it important to have an understanding of the maxims of law?
27. What is the most difficult part of preparing an argument?
28. What are the *simple premises?*
29. Fill in the following blank:

   "It is often the _____ of the facts, not the facts themselves, that are important in a legal claim."

30. What was the purpose of the analogy to the picture puzzle?

Problems

1. Dissect the following argument using FIRPA.

   Errin Architect ordered the contractor to change the roof pitch of the building. The contractor changed the roof pitch, but the owner refused to pay the contractor for the change and insisted the contractor redo the pitch according to the original plans and specifications, which the contractor did. The contractor is now seeking reimbursement from the owner for its costs associated with redoing the pitch according to the original plans and specifications.

   Legally, the owner is responsible for all actions of his agent taken within the confines of the power given by the owner to its agent. (See Chapter 6, Relationships among the Parties on the Project.) According to the contract between Errin Architect and the owner, the architect is the agent of the owner. The contract also gives the architect the power to make minor changes in the scope of the work without the owner's approval.

   The question here is whether changing the pitch of the roof is a minor change and therefore within the scope of the owner–architect agreement. If the change in pitch of the roof is minor, then the owner must pay for it, but if it is not, then the architect acted outside her authority in the owner–architect agreement, and the owner is not liable for those actions. In my opinion changing the pitch of the roof is not a minor change. The architect has acted outside the authority given her by the contract between the architect and the owner. The owner is therefore not responsible to the contractor.

2. Dissect the following argument using FIRPA.

   Pike, the general contractor, and Bat, the masonry subcontractor, entered into a contract. A time line of the contract negotiations between the parties is helpful in analyzing the legal issue here.

   1 June 1985 Pike provided Bat with drawings of the project and the general parameters of the masonry work to be performed.

   1 July 1985 Bat submitted a bid and heard nothing from Pike for several months.

   December 1985 Pike contacted Bat, informed Bat that the scope of the project had changed, and requested that Bat resubmit a bid. Bat resubmitted a bid in the amount of $1.1 million.

   January 1986 Pike sent Bat a letter of intent stating it intended to award Bat the masonry subcontract. Pike also sent a subcontract agreement.

   January–May 1986 Discussions between Pike and Bat were held to discuss the scope of the contract.

   May 1986 Bat returned the signed subcontract agreement.

   The law says a contract is formed if there has been an offer by a party, acceptance by the other, and consideration. Pike argued that a contract between Pike and Bat was formed in January 1986. Bat stated that no contract was entered into until the subcontract was signed and returned in May 1986.

   Pike argued that Bat's bid [given on 1 July] was an offer that Pike accepted with the letter of intent [sent in January 1986]. Bat argued that the contract was not formed until May 1986 when it signed and returned the subcontract. This trial court found that the contract was entered into in May 1986 when the subcontract was signed.

   "Regardless of the specific reason or reasons that Bat delayed in executing the contract, it is clear from the evidence presented at the trial that the parties were still in the process of negotiation throughout the Spring of 1986 and that a final agreement had not been reached.

The letter of intent was, at most, an agreement to agree. 'An agreement to agree is not a contract; just as a proposal to contract is not a contract.' [citing Showcase Woodworking Ltd, v. Fluor Daniel, Inc., (E.D.Va. 1990)].[5]"

3. Dissect the following argument using FIRPA.

The masonry subcontract between Pike and Bat contained the following language:

> *"Subcontractor shall proceed with the work according to a progress*
> *schedule furnished by Contractor."*

A CPM (critical path method) schedule was submitted to Bat in April 1986 with indications for the masonry work to begin in mid-August and be completed by mid-November. Bat based its bid to do the work on this schedule.

However, due to delays in the project, all caused by Pike, the masonry could not be done until late November, and it had to be carried out in winter weather conditions. In addition, due to the delays Pike resequenced the work so that Bat had to do the masonry in small bits and pieces, and work originally scheduled for the winter was rescheduled for the summer. All these changes were conveyed to Bat through updated progress schedules.

Pike argued that it was understood by all parties that the CPM schedule was to be updated monthly and, therefore, was not a document that was "set in stone." Pike also argued that Bat should have been aware it might have to complete the project later than expected, and Bat should have included a contingency for this in its bid.

"The Court finds, however, that although the CPM schedule was subject to modification, Bat was justified in the assumption that Pike would not radically depart from the schedule, i.e., Bat could reasonably assume that Pike would not completely resequence the project. The court finds that Pike breached the express terms of its contact with Bat.— (Bat, p. 178.)

4. Dissect the following argument using FIRPA. Note there are *three* issues here. Discuss each separately.

Pike alleged that Bat breached the subcontract by delaying performance (issue 1) and by failing to clean up the job site (issue 2.) In addition, Pike claimed it was entitled to reimbursement for winter protection it provided to Bat (issue 3.)

"The Court finds no credible evidence that Bat was responsible for any material delay in the project. The evidence did show that Bat was late in constructing the sample panel and tendering other submittals. The evidence also showed, however, that these delays did not delay the start of the masonry work. The court finds that Bat made every reasonable effort to work on walls as soon as Pike made them available to Bat. William Ryals, the witness that the Court determines to be the most credible and independent, testified that Bat did not delay the CPM schedule in any manner.

Regarding the clean up costs, the photographs of the job site strongly suggest that Bat may have been the only subcontractor on the job that did consistently clean up its worksite. Pike is not entitled to recover clean up costs from Bat.

As for the winter protection, the Court finds that Pike has a legitimate claim for a portion of the costs of the winter protection it provided for Bat. The contract expressly obligated

---

[5]Argument from the case of *Bat Masonry v. Pike-Paschen Joint Venture III*, 842 F.Supp. 174, 176 (E.Md. 1993)

Bat to provide enclosures and heaters for the interior masonry work which was scheduled to be completed under winter conditions. Therefore, Pike is entitled to recover Pike's costs for the winter protection it provided to Bat for those interior walls."— (Bat, pp. 181–182.)

5. Brief the case of *Grace Community Church*, which appears in Appendix B, p. 99. The solution appears on p. 94.

6. Brief the case of *Erlich v. Menezes*, which appears in Appendix C on p. 102.

Answers to Selected Problems

1. *Facts:* The contract between architect and owner gives architect power to make minor changes in the plans and specifications. Architect orders contractor to change the roof pitch of the building. The owner refuses to pay the contractor for the change, and owner insists the contractor redo the pitch according to the original plans and specifications. The contractor complies.

   The architect is the agent of the owner. The contract also gives the architect the power to make minor changes in the scope of the work without the owner's approval. (See contract. Contract terms are always facts.)

   Issue: Must the owner pay the contractor for redoing the work? *Alternative wording:* Is changing the roof pitch a major or minor change in the specifications?

   Rule: The owner is responsible for all actions of his agent taken within the confines of the power given by the owner to his agent. (See Chapter 6, Relationship among the Parties on the Project.)

   Premises:

   - The owner is responsible for all actions of his agent taken within the confines of the power given by the owner to his agent. (rule)
   - The contract gives the architect the power to make minor changes in the scope of the work without the owner's approval. (fact)
   - Changing the pitch of the roof (fact) is not a minor change (rule.) (simple premise facts ≠ rule)

   Answer: No. Owner does not have to pay. *Alternative answer:* Changing the pitch of the roof is a major change.

5. BRIEF OF *GRACE COMMUNITY CHURCH v. GONZALES*

Grace Community Church v. Gonzales, 853 S.W.2d 678 (Tex. App.—Houston 1993)

Procedural Posture: On appeal from trial court judgment in favor of Gonzales for monetary damages.

Facts: Grace Community Church (Grace) hired R. L. Gould as a general contractor to build a church. Gould, in turn, entered into a contract with Fred Gonzales, d/b/a Alamo Contractors (Gonzales), to install a new roof on the church. Grace did not sign the contract between Gould and Gonzales.

When the roof was 90% complete, a hurricane hit the area. Gonzales did not do any more work on the roof. Grace's insurance company reimbursed Grace for damages to the church, including the damage to the roof. Gould and Grace refused to pay Gonzales for the work he had completed on the roof before the hurricane.

Gould had been hired as a general contractor to supervise the construction of the project. Gould was given the authority to hire subcontractors such as Gonzales and to direct their work.

Issue 1: Was there a contract between Grace and Gonzales?

Summary of rule(s) used in Argument 1: If there is more than a scintilla of evidence to support the findings, the "no evidence" challenge cannot be sustained.

An *agent* is one who is authorized by another to transact business or manage some affair. The agency relationship does not depend on express appointment or assent by the principal; rather, it may be implied from the conduct of the parties under the circumstances. An agent acting within the scope of his apparent authority binds the principal as though the principal itself had performed the action taken.

Argument 1: The associate pastor's evidence was sufficient to support the finding of a contract, namely, Gould was the agent of Grace, and Gould could legally obligate Grace to the contract with Gonzales. This evidence supports the finding that Gould was the agent for Grace and authorized by Grace to hire Gonzales. Grace is responsible for the contracts entered into by its agent, Gould.

Conclusion 1: Yes. Principals who have given agents the power to enter into contracts are responsible for those contracts.

Issue 2: Is the evidence factually sufficient to support the judgment? (*Note:* This issue is almost always raised on appeal and almost never wins.)

Rule(s) used in Argument 2: When factual insufficiency of the evidence is alleged, this court must examine and weigh all the evidence. We will set aside the verdict only if it is so contrary to the overwhelming weight of the evidence that it is clearly wrong and unjust.

Argument 2: The associate pastor's evidence was sufficient to support the finding of a contract; that is, Gould had been hired as a general contractor to supervise the construction of the project. Gould was given the authority to hire subcontractors such as Gonzales and to direct their work.

Conclusion 2: Yes.

Disposition: Trial court's judgment affirmed.   ■ ■ ■

Appendix A Sample Problem with Student FIRPA

Memorandum

TO: Student

FROM: Prof. Nancy J. White

RE: Homework Assignment—FIRPA

Instructions: Solve the following problem using FIRPA. Your answer must be in paragraph form with complete sentences.

A couple of weeks ago your boss informed you that there was a *big* problem on that government project on the naval base. You are told to review the file, assess the problem, do a preliminary legal analysis, and make suggestions for how to proceed. You review the file and you come up with the following facts and legal issues. You are now ready to begin drafting the memo in response to your boss's instructions.

You review the section "How to FIRPA" from your old construction law class text before preparing the memo. Your assignment: prepare a memo to your boss analyzing the legal problems presented by the following facts.

Facts: By contract dated March 31, 1997, the contractor was required to furnish and install electrical meters, gas meters, hot-water meters, hot-water heating meters, and condensate meters in the apartments housing naval personnel at a military base. The contract was to have been completed by September 12, 1997, but was not completed until October 3, 1997. One hundred thirty-nine (139) buildings and 656 individual apartments were involved in the work to be performed.

The contract contained the following provision:

> *"Scheduling of Work: The contractor shall notify the occupants of the housing unit at least 3 days prior to commencing any work in a housing unit. The contractor shall perform his work between the hours of 8:00 A.M and 5:00 P.M. and having once started work in a housing unit shall work to completion in consecutive work days . . . . In no case shall a unit be left overnight without a completed meter installation, including testing and resumption of gas service."*

The Navy had, at the site of the work, a project manager who represented the contracting officer in the administration of the contract, and most of the contractor's dealings were with this project manager.

The contractor experienced considerable difficulty and delays in gaining access to approximately 60 apartments. After the contractor had prepared and delivered to the Navy a progress chart showing when the contractor required access to the buildings, the contractor's quality control manager had the responsibility for notifying the occupants of the time when the work in their apartments was to be performed. The specifications stipulates that this notice be given 3 days before work was to commence, so contractor's quality control manager attempted to notify the occupants personally at least 3 but usually 7 days before the work was to begin.

Notices to the occupants were given in the morning, during the noon hour, or in the afternoon. If the manager could not reach the occupants during the day, he tried to see them in the evening. If all these efforts failed, the manager would, in accordance with a suggestion made by the Navy's project manager, leave a yellow card on the doorknob of the apartment, indicating when the work in that unit would begin.

In some instances, the occupants refused to permit the contractor's workers to enter their apartments, even after notice was received by them. At times, the contractor was unable to serve personal notice because occupants were on military leave for periods of as long as 2 weeks. In other instances, the occupants would go out during the lunch hour while the work was being performed, leaving their doors locked, with the workers tools inside. On most of the occasions complained of by the contractor, the occupants were not at home when the work was scheduled despite notice given to them in person or by the card left on the doorknob.

Whenever the contractor or the subs were unable to gain access to an apartment for any of the reasons mentioned above, they would call on the project manager to provide the access they needed. If the occupants could be contacted by telephone, the project manager would ask them to return home and permit entry into their apartments. If the occupants were absent from the apartment on vacation, the project manager first telephoned them to get permission to enter their apartments. Then he obtained keys from the Housing Section at the base to admit the workers. On occasion, the workers could not obtain access until several days after the scheduled date for commencing work.

The workers were carpenters, plumbers, pipefitters, electricians, and laborers, and their work had to be coordinated and performed in a planned sequence. Because of the delays, they would have to leave buildings with work unfinished in several apartments and work in another building. To complete the contract, they would have to backtrack to those apartments that they were unable to enter during the time previously scheduled for the work.

Shortly after experiencing delays for lack of access to the apartments, the contractor notified the project manager that the contractor's responsibilities ended after it had notified the occupants in the manner described above, that a record would be kept of the delays, and that a claim would be submitted later for the increased costs incurred as a result of such delays. The contractor did this and presented an accurate claim for its delay damages.

The contracting officer (superior in rank to the project manager) responded that the Navy had no responsibility for assisting the contractor in obtaining access to the apartments. She stated that, in fact, the Navy had no right to access the apartments unless there was an emergency such as a fire or flood. In her opinion the contract provision obligated the contractor to give notice to the occupants and that the contractor was obligated to obtain an agreement with each occupant for performance of work in that particular apartment. If the tenant refused access, no agreement had been reached, and the contractor had breached its contract with the Navy.

The contractor argued that an implied term of the contract was that the Navy would make the apartments available to the contractor as long as the contractor had taken reasonable steps to properly notify the occupant per the contract provision. Approximately 1.5 years before this contract was entered into, the contractor had completed a project involving some of the same buildings on the same base. The work involved an overhauling of the kitchens. In that instance, when the contractor was unable to notify the individual occupants, the Navy was informed to that effect and promptly provided access to the apartments.[2]

Issue 1: Is the contract ambiguous?

Issue 2: Is the ambiguity, if any, patent or latent?

Issue 3: In whose favor should the court rule?

Rules: The court used the following rules in interpreting the contract in the contractor's favor: Ordinary meaning, Clear expression of intention, Conduct of the parties during construction.

Re-create the court's argument.

Memorandum

TO: Prof. Nancy J. White

FROM: David C. Student

RE: Homework Assignment—FIRPA

In response to your inquiry about the naval base renovation project, I composed the following memo in which I assessed the problem, did a preliminary legal analysis, and made suggestions as to how to proceed. The issues in this case are whether the agreement between the contractor and the Navy is ambiguous, whether the ambiguity (if any) is patent or latent, and in whose favor should the court rule.

By the contract dated March 31, 1997, the contractor was required to furnish and install electrical meters, gas meters, hot-water meters, hot-water heating meters, and condensate meters in the apartments housing naval personnel at a military base. The contract was to have been completed by September 12, 1997, but was not completed until October 3, 1997. One hundred thirty-nine (139) buildings and 656 individual apartments were involved in the work to be performed. The contractor experienced considerable difficulty and delays in gaining access to approximately 60 apartments. The contractor submitted a claim for the increased costs incurred as a result of the delays. The contract contained a provision

---

[2]*Blinderman Construction Co. v. U.S.*, 695 F.2d 552 (1983).

stating " . . . the contractor shall notify the occupants of the housing unit at least 3 days prior to commencing any work in a housing unit."

Issue 1: Is the Contract Ambiguous?

Is the contract ambiguous? A contract is *ambiguous* if it is capable of having two relatively reasonable meanings. In this situation, the Navy said that the agreement implied that the contractor was obligated to obtain an agreement with each occupant for performance of the work in that particular apartment, and if the tenant refused access, no agreement had been reached and the contractor had breached its contract with the Navy. The contractor argued that an implied term of the contract was that the Navy would make the apartments available to the contractor as long as the contractor had taken the reasonable steps to properly notify the occupant at least 3 days prior to commencing work in that housing unit. Since there are two relatively reasonable meanings to this contract, it is considered ambiguous.

Issue 2: Is the ambiguity, If Any, Patent or Latent?

Is the ambiguity, if any, patent or latent? A *patent ambiguity* is one that would not be obvious to a reasonable contractor given the circumstances of the situation. A *latent ambiguity* would not be obvious to a reasonable contractor given the circumstances of the situation. In this case, the ambiguity is latent because the contractor was reasonable in assuming that the Navy would assist in gaining access to the apartments. This assumption was based on a past project in which the Navy promptly provided access to the apartments that the contractor was unable to gain access.

Issue 3: In Whose Favor Should the Court Rule?

Subissue A: Ordinary Meaning   The law requires that the ordinary meaning of words be used and technical or industry-specific terms be given their normal interpretation, unless the intent is clearly stated otherwise. It was stated in the provisions of the contract that the contractor shall notify the occupants of the housing unit at least 3 days prior to commencing any work in a housing unit. That is exactly what the contractor did. The Navy said that the agreement implied that the contractor was obligated to obtain an agreement with each occupant for performance of the work in that particular apartment. The ordinary meaning of the contract provision was simply to notify the occupants 3 days prior, not obtain an agreement with them.

Subissue B: Clear Expression of Intention   The law also requires that the drafter of the document has an obligation to express its intention with clarity, however, the Navy said that the agreement implied that the contractor was obligated to obtain an agreement with each occupant for performance of the work in that particular apartment, and if the tenant refused access, no agreement had been reached and the contractor had breached its contract with the Navy. The contract stated only that the contractor must notify the occupants of the housing unit at least 3 days prior to commencing work, the contract did not state what the contractor was to do in the event access could not be obtained. Because the Navy was not clear in its expression of intention, the contractor did not know the extent to which it was to be responsible in gaining access to the apartments.

Subissue C: Conduct of the Parties during Construction   In addition, the law states that the conduct of parties helps to interpret or to imply a contract and can modify or suspend portions of an agreement. The Navy stated that they had no right to access the apartments unless there was an emergency such as a fire or flood. Since the project manager, a representative of the Navy, provided access to apartments that the contractor or subcontractors were unable to access, the agreement was modified.

In this matter, the agreement between the Navy and the contractor was ambiguous, and the ambiguity was latent, so the court should rule in favor of the contractor, for the following reasons the ordinary meaning of the terms "3 days prior notification," the Navy's lack of clear expression of intention of the contractor's obligation to obtain an agreement with each occupant for the performance of work in the particular apartment, and the modification of the agreement by the Navy's conduct during the construction in gaining access to apartments for the contractor and subcontractors.

Appendix B

CASE: GRACE COMMUNITY CHURCH v. GONZALES[3]

853 S.W.2d 678 (Tex. App.—Houston 1993)

OPINION BY: GARY C. BOWERS

> Appellant, Grace Community Church, appeals from a judgment in favor of appellee, Fred Gonzales, d/b/a Alamo Contractors Co., in the amount of $8,350.00 plus prejudgment interest in the amount of $1,628.25.
> [*Procedural posture—how the case came to be here.*]

> In two points of error, appellant complains the trial court erred in rendering judgment against appellant because there is no evidence of a contractual relationship between appellant and appellee, and because the evidence is insufficient to support the judgment. We affirm. [*Issue raised by Grace: Is there sufficient evidence of a contractual relationship?*]

> Neither party provided this court with a summary of the statement of facts in their briefs. In addition, findings of fact or conclusions of law were not filed. This complicated our addressing appellant's contentions. When findings of fact and conclusions of law are not properly requested, and none are filed, the judgment of the trial court must be affirmed if it can be upheld on any legal theory that finds support in the evidence. *Schoeffler v. Denton,* 813 S.W.2d 742, 744–45 (Tex. App.—Houston [14th Dist.] 1991, no writ.) We,

therefore, place this case in its proper context by setting forth a summary of the statement of facts.
[*Here the court is berating the parties for not doing what they should have done. If I had to categorize this, I would say this is procedural posture.*]

Grace Community Church (Grace) hired R. L. Gould as a general contractor to build a church. Gould, in turn, entered into a contract with appellee, Fred Gonzales, d/b/a Alamo Contractors (Gonzales), to build a new roof for the church. Gonzales and Gould agreed upon $18,500.00 as the contract price. Grace did not sign the contract between Gould and Gonzales.
[*Facts*]

Gonzales began working on the roof on June 2, 1989. On June 30, 1989, Gould began doing other work in the roof area and asked Gonzales to stop working on the roof. At that time, the roof was 90% complete, and the only work Gonzales needed to do was lay down gravel and pour asphalt on top.
[*Facts*]

Gould made two payments to Gonzales. The first payment, in the amount of $1,700.00 was made on June 30, 1989. The second payment, in the amount of $7,500.00, was made on July 21, 1989. The balance due on the contract was $9,300.00
[*Facts*]

On August 2, 1989, a hurricane hit the area. The back church wall and a section of scaffolding were destroyed. The front part of the roof was rolled back and there was wind damage. Gonzales did not do any more work on the roof. Grace's insurance company reimbursed Grace for damages to the church, including the damage to the roof. Gould and Grace refused to pay Gonzales for the work he had completed on the roof before the hurricane. The trial court found Grace and Gould jointly and severally liable for 90% of the balance due on the contract. Grace appeals the trial court's judgment.
[*Facts*]

In its first point of error, Grace contends that there was no evidence of a contractual relationship between Grace and Gonzales.
[*Appeal court's summary of Grace's view of trial court's error.*]

Appellant argues it did not sign the contract, nor was it a party to any oral agreement between Gould and Gonzales. Appellant argues it cannot be held liable unless Gonzales proves privity of contract, or establishes other circumstances that would render Grace liable. Grace then contends that Gonzales can only prevail if Gould was acting as an agent for Grace.

[*Related issues raised by Grace at this point: 1A. Did evidence exist to prove a contract between Grace and Gonzales? 1B. Was Gould the agent for Grace?*]

In deciding a "no evidence" point of error, this court will consider only the evidence, and inferences that support the challenged findings, and will disregard all evidence, and inferences to the contrary. *Davis v. City of San Antonio,* 752 S.W.2d 518, 522 (Tex. 1988.) If there is more than a scintilla of evidence to support the findings, the "no evidence" challenge cannot be sustained. *Stafford v. Stafford,* 726 S.W.2d 14, 16 (Tex. 1987.)

[*Law governing Issue 1A*]

The associate pastor for Grace testified that Gould had been hired as a general contractor to supervise the construction of the project. The total cost of the land and construction of the building was approximately four million dollars. Gould was paid a salary of $80,000.00 and was not paid a portion of the total cost of the project. The associate pastor further testified that Gould was given the authority to hire subcontractors, direct their work, and negotiate the contract with Gonzales.

[*Facts governing Issue 1 (both parts)*]

An "agent" is one who is authorized by another to transact business or manage some affair. *Augusta Development Co. v. Fish Oil Well Servicing Co., Inc.,* 761 S.W.2d 538, 543 (Tex. App.—Corpus Christi 1988, no writ.) The agency relationship does not depend on express appointment or assent by the principle; rather it may be implied from the conduct of the parties under the circumstances. *Jorgensen v. Stuart Place Water Supply Corp.,* 676 S.W.2d 191, 194 (Tex. App.—Corpus Christi 1984, no writ.) An agent acting within the scope of his apparent authority binds the principal as though the principal itself had preformed the action taken. *Ames v. Great Southern Bank,* 672 S.W.2d 447, 450 (Tex. 1984.)

[*Law governing Issue 1B*]

Gould was an agent for Grace. Grace gave Gould actual authority to hire Gonzales. Gould contracted with Gonzales to install a roof on the church for $18,500.00, thereby binding Grace to the contractual agreement. We find there is evidence that a contractual relationship

between Grace and Gonzales existed. We overrule appellant's first point of error.
[*Conclusion to Issue 1B*]

In its second point of error, Grace argues that the evidence is factually insufficient to support the judgment.
[*Grace is claiming the trial court made a second error—that Gonzales did not prove enough facts to support the trial court's decision. This point of error almost* never *succeeds.*]

When factual insufficiency of the evidence is alleged, this court must examine and weigh all of the evidence. *Lofton v. Texas Brine Corp.,* 720 S.W.2d 804, 805 (Tex. 1986.) We will set aside the verdict only if it is so contrary to the overwhelming weight of the evidence that it is clearly wrong and unjust. *Cain v. Bain,* 709 S.W.2d 175, 176 (Tex. 1986.)
[*The Law regarding this issue is given here.*]

Appellant argues that the trial court must have implicitly found the existence of an agency relationship between appellant and Gould, and that in examining all of the evidence in the record, it is clear that no such agency relationship existed. We disagree. As discussed in appellant's first point of error, we find that an agency relationship between Gould and Grace existed. We overrule appellant's second point of error.
[*Conclusion to Issue 1B*]

Accordingly, we affirm the judgment of the trial court.
[*Disposition of the appeal. Trial Court desicion upheld. Gonzales wins.*]

■ ■ ■

Appendix C

CASE: ERLICH v. MENEZES

21 Cal. 4th 543, 981 P.2d 978, 87 Cal. Rptr. 2d 886; (Ca. 1999) (This is not the complete text of the opinion.)

OPINION BY: BROWN

OPINION: We granted review in this case to determine whether emotional distress damages are recoverable for the negligent breach of a contract to construct a house.

I. Factual and Procedural Background

Both parties agree with the facts as ascertained by the Court of Appeal. Barry and Sandra Erlich contracted with John Menezes, a licensed general contractor, to build a "dream house" on their ocean-view lot. The Erlichs moved into their house in December 1990. In February 1991, the rains came. "The house leaked from every conceivable location. Walls were saturated in [an upstairs bedroom], two bedrooms downstairs, and the poolroom. Nearly every window in the house leaked. The living room filled with three inches of standing water. In several locations water 'poured in streams' from the ceilings and walls. The ceiling in the garage became so saturated . . . the plaster liquefied and fell in chunks to the floor."

Menezes' attempts to stop the leaks proved ineffectual. Caulking placed around the windows melted, "'ran down [the] windows, and stained them, and ran across the driveway, and ran down the house [until it] . . . looked like someone threw balloons with paint in them at the house.'" Despite several repair efforts, which included using sledgehammers and jackhammers to cut holes in the exterior walls and ceilings, application of new waterproofing materials on portions of the roof and exterior walls, and more caulk, the house continued to leak—from the windows, from the roofs, and water seeped between the floors. Fluorescent light fixtures in the garage filled with water and had to be removed.

"The Erlichs eventually had their home inspected by another general contractor and a structural engineer. In addition to confirming defects in the roof, exterior stucco, windows, and waterproofing, the inspection revealed serious errors in the construction of the home's structural components. None of the 20 shear or load-bearing walls specified in the plans were properly installed. The three turrets on the roof were inadequately connected to the roof beams and, as a result, had begun to collapse. Other connections in the roof framing were also improperly constructed. Three decks were in danger of 'catastrophic collapse' because they had been finished with mortar and ceramic tile, rather than with the light-weight roofing material originally specified. Finally, the foundation of the main beam for the two-story living room was poured by digging a shallow hole, dumping in 'two sacks of dry concrete mix, putting some water in the hole and mixing it up with a shovel.' " This foundation, required to carry a load of 12,000 pounds, could only support about 2,000. The beam is settling and the surrounding concrete is cracking. According to the Erlichs' expert, problems were major and pervasive, concerning everything "related to a window or waterproofing, everywhere that there was something related to framing," stucco, or the walking deck.

Both of the Erlichs testified that they suffered emotional distress as a result of the defective condition of the house and Menezes' invasive and unsuccessful repair attempts. Barry Erlich testified he felt "absolutely sick" and had to be "carted away in an ambulance" when he learned the full extent of the structural problems. He has a permanent heart condition, known as superventricular tachyarrhythmia, attributable, in part, to excessive stress. Although the condition can be controlled with medication, it has forced him to resign his positions as athletic director, department head, and track coach.

Sandra Erlich feared the house would collapse in an earthquake and feared for her daughter's safety. Stickers were placed on her bedroom windows, and alarms and emergency lights installed so rescue crews would find her room first in an emergency.

Plaintiffs sought recovery on several theories, including breach of contract, fraud, negligent misrepresentation, and negligent construction. Both the breach of contract claim and the negligence claim alleged numerous construction defects.

Menezes prevailed on the fraud and negligent misrepresentation claims. The jury found he breached his contract with the Erlichs by negligently constructing their home and awarded $406,700 as the cost of repairs. Each spouse was awarded $50,000 for emotional distress, and Barry Erlich received an additional $50,000 for physical pain and suffering, and $15,000 for lost earnings.

By a two-to-one majority, the Court of Appeal affirmed the judgment, including the emotional distress award. The majority noted the breach of a contractual duty may support an action in tort. The jury found Menezes was negligent. Since his negligence exposed the Erlichs to "intolerable living conditions and a constant, justifiable fear about the safety of their home," the majority decided the Erlichs were properly compensated for their emotional distress.

The dissent pointed out that no reported California case has upheld an award of emotional distress damages based upon simple breach of a contract to build a house. Since Menezes' negligence directly caused only economic injury and property damage, the Erlichs were not entitled to recover damages for their emotional distress.

We granted review to resolve the question.

II. Discussion

A.

In an action for breach of contract, the measure of damages is "the amount which will compensate the party aggrieved for all the detriment proximately caused thereby, or which, in the ordinary course of things, would be likely to result therefrom" (Civ. Code, § 3300), provided the damages are "clearly ascertainable in both their nature and origin" (Civ. Code, § 3301). In an action not arising from contract, the measure of damages is "the amount which will compensate for all the detriment proximately caused thereby, whether it could have been anticipated or not" (Civ. Code, § 3333).

"Contract damages are generally limited to those within the contemplation of the parties when the contract was entered into, or at least reasonably foreseeable by them at that time; consequential damages beyond the expectation of the parties are not recoverable.

"'The distinction between tort and contract is well grounded in common law, and divergent objectives underlie the remedies created in the two areas. Whereas contract actions are created to enforce the intentions of the parties to the agreement, tort law is primarily designed to vindicate "social policy." (*Hunter v. Up-Right, Inc.* (1993) 6 Cal. 4th 1174, 1180, 864 P.2d 88, quoting *Foley v. Interactive Data Corp.* (1988) 47 Cal. 3d 654, 683, 254 Cal. Rptr. 211)

B.

In concluding emotional distress damages were properly awarded, the Court of Appeal correctly observed that "the same wrongful act may constitute both a breach of contract and an invasion of an interest protected by the law of torts." (*North American Chemical Co. v. Superior Court* (1997) 59 Cal. App. 4th 764, 774, citing 3 Witkin, Cal. Procedure (4th ed. 1996) Actions, § 139, pp. 203–204.) Here, the court permitted plaintiffs to recover both full repair costs as normal contract damages and emotional distress damages as a tort remedy.

The Court of Appeal also noted that "[a] contractual obligation may create a legal duty and the breach of that duty may support an action in tort." This is true; however, conduct amounting to a breach of contract becomes tortious only when it also violates a duty independent of the contract arising from principles of tort law. (*Applied Equipment,* supra, 7 Cal. 4th at p. 515.)

Plaintiff's theory of tort recovery is that mental distress is a foreseeable consequence of negligent breaches of standard commercial contracts; however, foreseeability alone is not sufficient to create an independent tort duty. (Citations omitted.) In short, foreseeability is not synonymous with duty; nor is it a substitute.

The question thus remains: is the mere negligent breach of a contract sufficient? The answer is no. It may admittedly be difficult to categorize the cases, but to state the rule succinctly: "Courts will generally enforce the breach of a contractual promise through contract law, except when the actions that constitute the breach violate a social policy that merits the imposition of tort remedies."

Our previous decisions detail the reasons for denying tort recovery in contract breach cases: the different objectives underlying tort and contract breach; the importance of predictability in assuring commercial stability in contractual dealings; the potential for converting every contract breach into a tort, with accompanying punitive damage recovery and the preference for legislative action in affording appropriate remedies. (Freeman & Mills, supra, 11 Cal. 4th at p. 98, citing approvingly *Harris v. Atlantic Richfield Co.* (1993) 14 Cal. App. 4th 70, 81–82.) The same concerns support a cautious approach here. Restrictions on contract remedies serve to protect the "'freedom to bargain over special risks, and [to] promote contract formation by limiting liability to the value of the promise.'" (11 Cal. 4th at p. 98, quoting *Harris*, supra, 14 Cal. App. 4th at p. 77.)

Generally, outside the insurance context, "a tortious breach of contract . . . may be found when (1) the breach is accompanied by a traditional common law tort, such as fraud or conversion; (2) the means used to breach the contract are tortious, involving deceit, or undue coercion; or (3) one party intentionally breaches the contract intending or knowing that such a breach will cause severe, unmitigable harm in the form of mental anguish, personal hardship or substantial consequential damages." (Freeman & Mills, supra, 11 Cal. 4th at p. 105 (conc. and dis. opn. of Mosk, J.) Focusing on intentional conduct gives substance to the proposition that a breach of contract is tortious only when some independent duty arising from tort law is violated. (*Applied Equipment*, supra, 7 Cal. 4th at p. 515.) If every negligent breach of a contract gives rise to tort damages the limitation would be meaningless, as would the statutory distinction between tort and contract remedies.

In this case, the jury concluded Menezes did not act intentionally; nor was he guilty of fraud or misrepresentation. This is a claim for negligent breach of a contract, which is not sufficient to support tortious damages for violation of an independent tort duty.

Here, the breach—the negligent construction of the Erlichs' house—did not cause physical injury. No one was hit by a falling beam. Although the Erlichs state they feared the house was structurally unsafe and might collapse in an earthquake, they lived in it for five years. The only physical injury alleged is Barry Erlich's heart disease, which flowed from the emotional distress and not directly from the negligent construction.

The Erlichs may have hoped to build their dream home and live happily ever after, but there is a reason that tag line belongs only in fairy tales. Building a house may turn out to be a stress-free project; it is much more likely to be the stuff of urban legends—the cause of bankruptcy, marital dissolution, hypertension, and fleeting fantasies ranging from homicide to suicide. As Justice Yegan noted below, "No reasonable homeowner can embark on a building project with certainty that the project will be completed to perfection. Indeed, errors are so likely to occur that few if any homeowners would be justified in resting their peace of mind on [its] timely or correct completion . . . ." The connection between the service sought and the aggravation and distress resulting from incompetence may be somewhat less tenuous than in a malpractice case, but the emotional suffering still derives from an inherently economic concern.

D.

Having concluded tort damages are not available, we finally consider whether damages for emotional distress should be included as conse-quential or special damages in a contract claim. "Contract damages are generally limited to those within the contemplation of the parties when the contract was entered into, or at least reasonably foreseeable by them at the time; consequential damages beyond the expectations of the parties are not recoverable. [Citations omitted.] This limitation on available damages serves to encourage contractual relations and commercial activity by enabling parties to estimate in advance the financial risks of their enterprise." (*Applied Equipment*, supra, 7 Cal. 4th at p. 515.)

" 'When two parties make a contract, they agree upon the rules and regulations which will govern their relationship; the risks inherent in the agreement and the likelihood of its breach. The parties to the contract in essence create a mini-universe for themselves, in which each voluntarily chooses his contracting partner, each trusts the other's willingness to keep his word, and honor his commitments, and in which they define their respective obligations, rewards and risks. Under such a scenario, it is appropriate to enforce only such obligations as each party voluntarily assumed and to give him only such benefits as he expected to receive; this is the function of contract law.' " (*Applied Equipment*, supra, 7 Cal. 4th at p. 517.)

Accordingly, damages for mental suffering and emotional distress are generally not recoverable in an action for breach of an ordinary commercial contract in California. [*Kwan v. Mercedes-Benz of North America, Inc.* (1994) 23 Cal. App. 4th 174, 188 (*Kwan*).]

Plaintiffs argue strenuously that a broader notion of damages is appropriate when the contract is for the construction of a home. Amicus curiae urge us to permit emotional distress damages in cases of negligent construction of a personal residence when the negligent con-struction causes gross interference with the normal use and habitability of the residence.

Such a rule would make the financial risks of construction agree-ments difficult to predict. Contract damages must be clearly ascertainable in both nature and, origin. (Civ. Code, § 3301.) A contracting party cannot be required to assume limitless responsibility for all consequences of a breach and must be advised of any special harm that might result in order to determine whether or not to accept the risk of contracting. (1 Witkin, Summary of Cal. Law, supra, Contracts, § 815, p. 733.)

Moreover, adding an emotional distress component to recovery for construction defects could increase the already prohibitively high cost of housing in California, affect the availability of insurance for builders and greatly diminish the supply of affordable housing. The potential for such broad-ranging economic consequences—costs likely to be paid by the public generally—means the task of fashioning appropriate limits on the availability of emotional distress claims should be left to the Legislature. [See Tex. Prop. Code Ann., § 27.001 et seq. (1999); Hawaii Rev. Stat., § 663-8.9 (1998.)]

Permitting damages for emotional distress on the theory that certain contracts carry a lot of emotional freight provides no useful guidance. Courts have carved out a narrow range of exceptions to the general rule of exclusion where emotional tranquillity is the contract's essence. Refusal to broaden the bases for recovery reflects a fundamental policy choice. A rule which focuses not on the risks contracting parties voluntarily assume but on one party's reaction to inadequate performance, cannot provide any principled limit on liability.

We agree. The available damages for defective construction are limited to the cost of repairing the home, including lost use, or relocation expenses, or the diminution in value. (*Orndorff v. Christiana Community Builders*, (1990) 217 Cal. App. 3d 683, 266 Cal. Rptr. 193.) The Erlichs received more than $400,000 in traditional contract damages to correct the defects in their home. While their distress was undoubtedly real and serious, we conclude the balance of policy onsiderations—the potential for significant increases in liability in amounts disproportionate to culpability, the court's inability to formulate appropriate limits on the availability of claims, and the magnitude of the impact on stability, and predictability in commercial affairs—counsel against expanding contract damages to include mental claims in negligent construction cases.

Disposition

The judgment of the Court of Appeal is reversed, and the matter is remanded for further proceedings consistent with this opinion.

BROWN, J.

WE C ONCUR: GEORGE, C. J., KENNARD, J., BAXTER, J., CHIN, J.

Concurring and Dissenting Opinion by Werdegar, J. (omitted)

n1 At oral argument, plaintiff cited *Sloane v. Southern Cal. Ry. Co.* (1896) 111 Cal. 668, 44 P. 320, a case involving a passenger wrongly ejected from a train, for the proposition that emotional distress damages arising out of breach of contract have been permitted in California for many years. In fact, Sloane specifically recognized the distinction between contract and tort remedies, and held plaintiff could either "bring an action simply for the breach of . . . contract, or she could sue . . . in tort" for the carrier's violation of the duty, as a common carrier, which it assumed upon entering into the contract. (Id. at p. 677.) ■ ■ ■

5

Law, Ethics, and Morality

Why Has Ethics Become So Important?

In recent years the number of U.S. professions and businesses adopting and enforcing written codes of ethics has risen dramatically. Not only have the numbers of codes increased but also they are sometimes enforced in a quasi-legal manner with hearings and appeals. Punishments from professional boards established to monitor the ethics of the profession are often harsher, from a financial standpoint, than any court would impose. For example, an attorney or architect accused of ethical violations must attend hearings before a panel of peers and is subject to loss of license, which in effect is loss of livelihood.

Ethics is one of the topics historically studied as part of a philosophy course. With the decline in liberal arts education and the rise in study of more specialized fields such as engineering and computer science, fewer students study philosophy and ethics. Ethics is now frequently taught in a law course. This chapter briefly discusses ethics and business in general.

Why ethics is becoming more important in the business arena is the subject of debate. Many Americans believe it is because the moral climate is deteriorating, and the family structure is breaking down.

A more likely alternative explanation is that the need for raising the ethical standards is a necessary outgrowth of the historical ethic of business, which has been "it is OK to do anything to make a profit, as long as it is not illegal." The natural outcome of this ethic has been the accumulation of actions and behaviors not acceptable to society. Sufficient societal pressure has built up to force or to encourage businesses to operate more ethically.

5–1. THINK

What other activities, in addition to making a profit, do you think U.S. society believes are important? How do these activities conflict with one another?

Improving ethical practices in business is an idea whose time has come. Like other social problems such as slavery, religious repression, child abuse, war, animal abuse, and the oppression of women, poor business ethics has been around for centuries. At the present time U.S. society and culture have developed to a point where this problem can be resolved.

Free-market forces encourage unethical behavior because it can be lucrative, particularly in the short run, in an isolated incident, or in a situation in which the consumer of the product or service has little control or knowledge. In the United States, making a profit has long been one of the most highly prized and revered activities of people and businesses; however, society has now begun to set limits on how far businesses can go in order to make profits. Profit making, when taken to extremes or set as the sole goal of existence, hinders or prevents the realization of other important social goals such as raising a family, having increased leisure time, and participating in volunteer work. A balance of potentially conflicting goals is necessary for a healthy life and society.

In addition to the effect of free-market forces, the increased size of businesses and the anonymity of the individual employee also tend to encourage unethical behavior. It is easy to believe that ethics is someone else's job, or that an unethical behavior will have a minimal effect. In an enterprise with large numbers of people and a specialized workforce the consequences of unethical behavior may not be seen or felt by the person engaging in the unethical behavior. For example, the consequences of allowing defective parts to be used in the production of automobiles are going to be felt more at the dealership level rather than at the production level.

Highly ethical behavior is important in the construction industry because the construction industry is one of the most complex in the marketplace. The maze of competing interests, complexity of laws and regulations controlling the various aspects of the construction process, and the detail of the contracts seems to be impossible to successfully negotiate. However, one of the most effective tools constructors and other professionals have to help them is a strong commitment to highly ethical behavior and highly ethical operation of their company.

Definitions of Law, Ethics, Morality, and Values

As used herein, **law** is the constitutions statutes, administrative regulations, and case law of the United States or other appropriate government entity. **Ethics** is a system or code of behavior adopted by a particular profession or other group and is a characteristic of that particular group. Every group of persons has an ethical system or code. **Morality** is the system or code of behavior adopted by a particular person and is a characteristic of that individual. Every person has a morality.

Law is the legal standard of behavior and is generally the lowest level of acceptable behavior in society. Basically, laws are enacted to place limits on acceptable human behavior and to increase the amount of certainty in human interactions. Behavior below the acceptable legal level is punished either criminally, civilly, or both. Criminal punishments include fines, imprisonment, or even death in some jurisdictions. Civil punishments are generally limited to the payment of monetary damages, although a person may be required to do something, such as remove a fence from a neighbor's property.

People who routinely engage in behavior violating criminal statutes are often referred to as **criminals.** The deterrence of criminal behavior is enforced by the police power of the jurisdiction in which the behavior occurs. Persons who engage in illegal activity are subject to being arrested and detained by the police. Criminals frequently are sent to prisons or to other institutions to attempt to force them to conform to the law, to prevent them from interacting with others in the society, and/or to punish them. They may even be killed through the state's police power.

Ethical standards are the standards of behavior demanded of a particular group. Most groups require adherence to the law as a requirement of their ethical code. Some groups, such as gangs and criminal organizations, require just the opposite. Frequently, ethical standards require a higher level of behavior than the law. For example, refusing to hire someone because they are short is not illegal; however, a particular employer may believe it is unethical to do so. Persons who engage in behavior outside of ethical standards are said to be **unethical,** although such behavior may not be illegal. On the other hand, a person found negligent in one car accident would not generally be considered unethical; a person found negligent in several car accidents might, however.

Traffic regulations are another example of ethics that require a lesser standard than the law. It is generally accepted by society, and therefore ethical, that persons may, if the road conditions permit, drive up to 10 miles per hour over the speed limit. This behavior, driving 10 miles per hour over the speed limit, is illegal but ethical. Such a driver would not be considered a criminal by the vast majority of persons, although technically he would be. Similarly, few would label a person who rolls through a stop sign on a country road with nary another car or cow in sight, unethical or criminal.

Morality for our purposes is limited to the personal, subjective standards a person sets for him- or herself. These standards may be higher than, lower than, different from, or the same as the ethical and/or legal standards. For example, a person whose morality can be summed up as "get the other guy before he gets you" has a morality, although one not necessarily considered ethical or moral by the majority of people.

Values are the judgments of "good" or "bad" relating to the worth or importance of any particular behavior. Globalization has caused a clash in values between world cultures. For example, an ethical behavior in some societies is to kill female rape victims (the rapist is also severely punished in these cultures.) Many of the people in that society believe this is an acceptable activity because the rape victim brings shame on the family. The value placed on the victim is not as high as the value placed on the avoidance of shame.

The definitions of law, ethics, morality, and values vary widely; however, there is an agreement over the fundamental concepts behind the words. The definitions used in this text do not involve any value judgments such as "good," "bad," "high," or "low" of a particular ethic or morality.

5-2. THINK

Compare and contrast the meanings of the following sentences:

- She has a morality peculiar to her place of birth.
- She is moral.
- His ethics is not my ethics.
- His morality is not my morality.
- Being ethical is not the same as being moral.
- Ethics and morality mean acting with integrity.

Frequently, the terms *ethics* or *morality* are used to indicate behavior deemed "good" or "acceptable." For example, the statements "He is ethical" and "That company is moral" mean that the person and the company operate in a way determined to be good and/or valuable by the culture. Those definitions of ethical and moral are not used in this book; however, the term *highly ethical* is used to mean a company that operates at a level that is considered good by the culture within which it operates.

Theories of Law, Ethics, and Morality

Several theories of law, ethics, and morality exist and are the subject of philosophical debate. Several different views are presented here: two objective and two subjective theories. **Objective theories** are theories holding that laws, ethics, and morality can be judged against a standard that is right or correct. Actions contrary to the standard are wrong or incorrect. **Subjective theories** are theories holding that no law, ethic, or morality is true or correct according to any outside standard but rather according to internal beliefs. All the theories, except nihilism, support acting highly ethically in business.

Objective Theory 1: Law and Ethics Evolved Out of Human Social Interaction

Law, and Ethics Are Designed to Ease Interpersonal Relations

The forces of law, ethics, and morality have arisen out of humans' interactions with one another. If each of us existed alone and apart from all other persons, there would be no need for law, ethics, or morality; however, just as certain processes have evolved that allow us to digest our food and engage in other physical functions, certain other mental processes have evolved that allow us to live and to coexist with others. Action contrary to these processes, particularly long-term action, may produce illness or even death of the individual or culture.

Group or community activity allows for specialization and increased production of goods and services, which in turn leads to greater personal satisfaction. The increased personal satisfaction achieved while acting within a group or community setting encourages persons to engage in activities that enable the group or community to operate. Persons will operate in ways to protect and encourage group or community activity. This does not mean that all areas of life are better when controlled by the group or community. In fact, political disagreements often occur over the precise demarcations between group/community control and personal/individual control. This subject is beyond the scope of this text.

Law and ethics as well as other forces also encourage cooperative behavior. Religious institutions, educational institutions, and the institution of the family have evolved to encourage cooperative behavior and interaction among persons. Law and ethics also attempt to prevent persons from harming one another. In addition, law and ethics offset or curb the desire of individuals to maximize personal wealth or benefit in the following situations:

- When one person forcibly or negligently takes wealth or benefits from another person against the second person's will. (Benefits are defined very broadly here. For example, good health would be a benefit.)
- When one person attempts to take wealth or benefits from another person but at a cost that does not adequately compensate the second for the wealth or benefit taken. (This is the concept that law and ethics, together with other social forces, contribute to the fair distribution of the increased benefits that result from social cooperation.)

As social creatures, humans exist together in societies where individuals are closely tied by common needs and wants. As a result, humans have developed complex systems in which individuals rely not only on the work of their own bodies and minds to provide for the necessities and pleasures of life but also on the work of the bodies and minds of others. By specializing, a person can do one thing very well and make more than she needs. The excess production can be traded for necessities or luxuries. Increased specialization over the centuries has increased the amount and variety of goods and services, and the standard of living.

However, once an individual makes more of something than she wants to use personally, she must have a system, usually called a **market,** whereby she can trade her product or service to obtain things she does not have the time or desire to make for herself. Laws and ethical standards are part of the system that encourages this trading of labor and capital. Law and ethical standards also encourage personal interaction that does not necessarily result in the trading of a good or service.

Laws and ethical standards encourage trade and personal interaction because they offer some protection and some certainty in trade and personal interaction. The protection and certainty are not total, as people can disobey the law or the ethical standard; however, the existence of the laws and ethics provides more protection and certainty than a system without them. For example, if you knew that someone could just come in and steal your extra crop of potatoes, and the law would do nothing about it, you would not be as likely grow that extra crop. If you knew that the law would not uphold the contract you and the buyer entered into for the sale of those potatoes, you would not be as likely to grow that extra crop. Laws and ethics encourage you to grow that extra crop of potatoes.

The desire to maximize personal well-being or individual satisfaction is a fundamental characteristic of the human race. It is not a problem unless individuals maximize their personal satisfaction by decreasing someone else's satisfaction. Historically this has tended to be extremely common—that is, increasing one's satisfaction at a cost to another. Those persons whose satisfaction was decreased did not support and encourage the laws and ethics that allowed such interaction and often worked to change them, particularly if they could do so without being killed or punished by the people who wanted to maintain the status quo. For example, slavery is the ultimate example of how one person's satisfaction (the slaveowner's) was increased and the other party's satisfaction (the slave's) was decreased. Property crimes of all types are examples of this concept as well. The thief's satisfaction is increased, and the victim's satisfaction is decreased.

The economic system of capitalism uses the innate human desire to maximize personal well-being in such a way that the personal well-being of the parties involved in a transaction is increased. This encourages trade and cooperation, which in turn increases the personal well-being of all parties involved. For example, when John sells Mary his used CD, the satisfaction of both parties increases. John has money, which he values more than the CD, and Mary has a CD, which she values more than the money she paid. The interaction of the two parties causes an increase of satisfaction for both parties. If Mary were to decide to increase her satisfaction by stealing the CD rather than paying for it, her satisfaction would be increased to a greater extent than if she had to pay for the CD; however, John's satisfaction would be decreased. Laws and ethics have been developed to prevent Mary from stealing the CD.

Figures 5–1 through 5–5 illustrate the preceding concept.

Figure 5-1 Both parties have dissatisfaction

Figure 5-2 Parties exchange dissatisfaction for desire

Figure 5-3 Dissatisfaction disappears in mutual exchange

Figure 5-4 CD is stolen

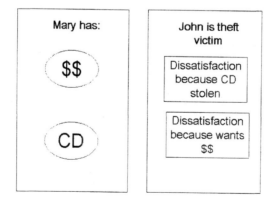

Figure 5-5 Thief has increased satisfaction; victim has increased dissatisfaction

Law and Ethics Affect Fair Distribution of Benefits from Social Cooperation

Besides being a mechanism for combating the desire for self-maximization at a cost to another, laws and ethics discourage taking wealth or benefits from another person for inadequate compensation. What is "inadequate" is subject to debate and beyond the scope of this text.

Another way of saying this is that laws and ethical standards contribute to the fair distribution of the increased benefits that result from social cooperation. Social cooperation is the process humans have developed that allows them to specialize and exchange their labor and capital with others. By cooperating, humans increase the amount and quality of goods and services available for each individual. Working together, humans make more than they would alone. The excess they make over what they would have made individually can be called **social income.**

For example, assume that each of six people, A, B, and C, and D, E, and F lives alone, on separate plots of land. None knows of the others' existence. Each can produce enough to live, with a little left over for emergencies. Each person can build a shelter, grow food, and make clothing. Let us arbitrarily put a value of $100 on Person A's shelter, food, and clothing; $110 on Person B's shelter, food, and clothing because his is of higher quality or greater amount, and $120 on Person C's shelter, food, and clothing because hers is of the highest quality, or greatest amount. The total value of all the goods and services produced by A, B, and C is $330. For the sake of simplicity we will put a value of $110 each on the services of D, E, and F. This example assumes that A, B, and C have different abilities to produce.

Now, assume that A, B, and C begin working together. Because A has the most ability, she handles the money and manages the work for the group and is in sales. C produces most of the goods, and services for the group, and B maintains the property and engages in tasks that are necessary to keep the production running smoothly, such as cleaning and preparing meals. D, E, and F are impressed with the quality of B's workmanship, so they trade C for some of B's production. (This assumes that D, E and F have organized and produce excess product desired by A, B, and C for trade.) The total value of the goods and services produced by A, B, and C because of their specialization is $600, or $270 more than the sum of what each could produce individually. This number is completely arbitrary; however, if the value was less than $330, we could assume that A, B, and C would not work together very long.

How and to whom is the $270, or the social income, to be distributed? Is it fair to distribute it equally among A, B, and C? Is it fair to distribute in proportion to their original ability to produce? This would mean that A would get 10% more than B, and C would get 10% more than A. What happens when these persons set up governments to help coordinate the trade of the various groups? C takes some of her money and buys health insurance but gives money to government officials to pass laws saying the group does not have to buy health insurance for B because, after all, B's contribution is "menial." C does this because of her innate desire to increase her own well-being, and she can do so by paying B as little as possible. At any rate, the interactions of the people become more complex, and the connections and interactions multiply. Laws and ethical standards help regulate how the social income is distributed. Figures 5–6 and 5–7 illustrate these concepts.

Unfair distributions tend to discourage production of goods and services, which decreases the amount of profit in the system. The decrease or lack of profits decreases satisfaction with the system and encourages people to do something to change the system. One of the best ways to increase satisfaction is to divide the social income more fairly. This encourages people to work, which contributes more profits to the system, which increases satisfaction.

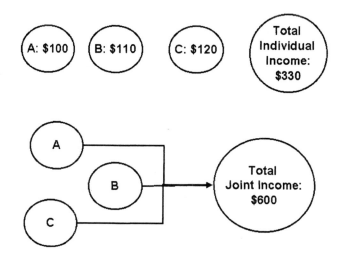

Figure 5-6   Individual v. joint production

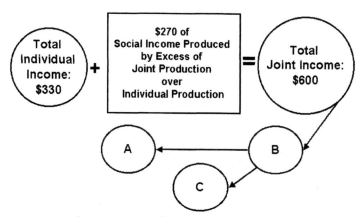

Arrows represent flow of money to individuals.

How much should each receive of Joint Production? Notice that
B controls the flow of money to A and C in this example.

Figure 5-7   Distribution of joint production to contributors to joint production

Objective Theory 2: Divine Command Theory

The **divine command theory** states that law and ethics are based on the dictates of the group's particular deity. Because Christianity is the predominant religion of the West, this means to most Westerners a belief that the Bible is the basis for God's law and rules, the rules that need to be applied both ethically and legally. According to the divine command theory the true standard of legal and ethical right and wrong is God's law.

This theory offers many advantages over other theories. One is that people who adhere to God's law, or certain parts of it, are assured an eternal life of bliss and happiness after they die. This is an excellent incentive for encouraging legal and ethical behavior, an incentive that is missing from other theories.

Subjectivist Theories: Nihilism and Relativism

Subjectivism, nihilism, and relativism are theories of morality and ethics holding that no moral or ethical claims and principles are true and others false but that the truth or falsity of any moral/ethical claim is subjective. By **subjectivism** is meant that truth or falsity depends on what the person or group says or believes is true or false, not on some outside standard.

Nihilism is the belief that there is no correct or incorrect moral or ethical code, that there is no right or wrong. Consequently, no behavior can be prohibited or required.

Relativism is the belief that moral or ethical standards are relative to a particular culture and only moral or ethical in relation to that particular culture. For example, in some Middle Eastern cultures it is ethical to kill rape victims for bringing shame to the family. In Western countries this would be considered unethical and illegal. To state this belief another way, whatever a society or culture *says* is right or wrong is right or wrong.

Business Ethics

In recent times different types of business enterprises have begun to develop very detailed ethical standards.

One of the fundamental maxims of business ethics is that actions must comply with current law. In fact, a great deal of business ethics deals with encouraging people and businesses to uphold the law even when it is unlikely they will be prosecuted or punished for failure to do so.

In the construction industry both architects and engineers have fairly detailed codes of ethics, whereas constructors are guided mainly by very informal ethical standards such as the following:

- Do not accept a late bid.
- Do not hide nonconforming work from the owner.
- Do not bid-shop. (This ethical principle may have anti–trust law implications.)
- Treat employees and subcontractors fairly.

5-3. THINK

Can you name other ethical standards of the construction industry?

How to Determine Whether an Action is Highly Ethical

Most people want to know how to determine whether an action is highly ethical. Few clear-cut answers exist, and the rules are always changing. Historically, the answer to this question when related to business activities was simple: if the act was legal and it made a profit, the activity was ethical. In recent decades, however, this historical ethical rule has lost its appeal and no longer has widespread acceptance in Western culture. Social pressure has forced business to change its ethics and several different philosophies have emerged.

When confronted with an ethical dilemma it is suggested that a person look at it from at least one of the following viewpoints and make a decision:

1. *The Golden Rule:* Do unto others as you would have done unto you.
2. *Code of Ethics:* Refer to your profession's code of ethics for guidance.
3. *Utilitarianism:* The proper behavior is the one that will produce the greatest good or the least harm for the greatest number of people.
4. *Categorical Imperative* (Kant 1724–1804): Similar to the golden rule. Act in such a way that your actions (or the actions of your company) could be "universal law"—that is, if all people or organizations were to act in that manner, would it be proper?
5. *Veil of Ignorance* (Rawls 1989): The proper action is the one the affected group of people or organizations, behind a veil of ignorance, would recommend. That is, assume that all the people to be affected by the action (or lack of action) are put into a room, and their memories of their role in the situation are erased. The people are to come up with a solution all of them will be willing to live with once their memories of their role are given back to them.
6. *Front Page of Newspaper Test:* Act in such a way that would not embarrass you if your acts were to appear on the front page of the local newspaper.

Why People Are Unethical

A person may act unethically for any number of reasons: ignorance, greed, need, or because the cost of acting ethically is too high. All except ignorance can be summarized by the concept that humans are self-regulating systems that seek to maintain optimal levels of well-being. If acting ethically will lessen an individual's well-being, it becomes difficult for an individual to act ethically and the less likely that he or she will do so. At some point, though, the value of the particular human involved should outweigh mere rules and standards, and perhaps an individual should not follow an abstract law or ethic if the cost to the individual is too high. (This is a very Western concept and subject to much debate. Are the rules or the people involved more important?) Of course, people will disagree on when the cost is "too high." Several answers to the question, Why are people unethical? are more fully discussed next.

Ignorance

Many people behave unethically out of ignorance of the law, so many ethical dilemmas could be avoided if people realized their actions were illegal. The majority of people will obey the law if they know what it is.

Greed

The majority of people desire pleasures and benefits, and work to increase those pleasures and benefits. Most people also accept legal, ethical, and/or religious limits on what behaviors are an acceptable means to gaining individual pleasure and benefit. Fundamentally, a person who is unethical because of greed desires to maximize his or her individual benefit at a cost to another.

Need

Some philosophers would argue that a person who engages in an "unethical" or even "illegal" act out of extreme need has actually not acted unethically or illegally. This viewpoint places the value of individuals above law and ethical standards that prevent persons from obtaining what they need in order to survive. For example, suppose that a person is starving and steals food to eat. Many philosophers would say that this behavior is not unethical.

The Cost of Acting Ethically Is Too High

Probably the most common reason that ethical standards are not upheld in the construction industry is that the cost of doing so is considered too high. Acting ethically, just like every other act, has a cost associated with it. If participants in the construction process want the construction process to be run ethically, they are going to have to be willing to pay for it. However, because of the extremely low profit margins in the industry, it is very tempting to operate unethically.

Physical and/or Neurological Defects

The effect of physical and/or neurological defects on ethical and moral behavior is little understood at present but is the subject of study. The brain develops according to the use to which it is put and the experience it receives. During childhood such things as trauma affect the development of the brain. The brain of a child is malleable, and in the process of growth it develops according to the use to which it is put, and the experience to which it is exposed.

Events that might affect an adult emotionally affect a child physiologically and can cause the brain to form in a certain way that is incompatible with later ethical and moral behavior. For example, children who are subjected to trauma in childhood develop a certain type of brain that has lost a certain capacity for empathy. This capacity for empathy has proven difficult, if not impossible, to regain. The ability of such a person to develop high ethical and moral standards is affected by these early childhood experiences (Perry 1995a, 1995b, 1996).

Other Factors Influencing Moral and Ethical Standards

Many factors influence moral and ethical standards. Family degree of dysfunction (or function), parents' moral background, location of upbringing, socioeconomic status, type of religion, personal involvement in religion, and education all play a part in the creation of ethical and moral standards. In addition, having good ethics and high morals are like learning to play an instrument: the more you practice, the better you get.

Differences between International Ethics and Domestic Ethics

In the international arena, most businesses recognize the necessity of spending at least some time attempting to understand the cultural values and local customs of the place where they are doing business. Ethical dilemmas can arise when the standard of behavior in the home country is different from the standard of behavior in the host country.

International ethics can be more problematic than domestic ethics because the underlying values of the two (or more) conflicting groups may be different, and this difference causes discomfort. In general, when persons come into contact with a new or different idea, particularly one related to some fundamental value they hold, some amount of mental dissonance and discomfort occurs. The more contrary a new idea or value is to a person's existing belief or value system, the more discomfort experienced. Persons dealing with other cultures must recognize these phenomena and learn to deal with the discomfort (Payne 1998).

Discomfort with new and different ideas and values is greater for people who believe in an objective theory of law, ethics, and morality—that is, that some behaviors are right and others wrong—than it is for people who believe in one of the subjective theories of law, ethics, and morality—that is, that behavior is relative, not absolute.

The concept of cultural relativism is common when approaching ethical situations in the international arena. **Cultural relativism** is the belief that parties must adapt to the host country's culture. If it is acceptable to employ children to carry heavy loads of brick around the construction site, then American companies in that country can do this in the host country. Such behavior is unacceptable and illegal in the United States. Cultural relativism is criticized by people who believe in objective theories of law and ethics (Smeltzer and Jennings 1998).

International companies that attempt to have one ethical standard for domestic operations and another for foreign operations, however, are likely to have trouble maintaining the higher standard. For example, Johnson and Johnson has the following credo: "We are responsible to our employees, the men, and women who work with us throughout the world. Everyone must be considered an individual. We must respect their dignity and recognize their merit . . ." This credo does not allow for drastically different codes of ethics depending on the location of the particular employee.[1]

It is important for international companies that operate by different ethical standards in the home-base country and in the host country to reinforce the higher ethic in the home-base country on a regular basis. Likewise, international companies operating with the same ethical standards at the home base and in the host country need to reinforce the company ethics in the host country. Otherwise, host-country managers may fall into the "everyone else is doing it" attitude, and the ethic will erode.

A suggested method of handling ethical dilemmas in international arenas is to categorize them as Type 1 or Type 2. A **Type 1 ethical dilemma** is characterized by a fundamental difference in values between the host country and the home-base country. A **Type 2 ethical dilemma** is one in which the fundamental values of the home-base company and the host country are the same, but the approach is different.

A Type 1 ethical dilemma is one that causes demoralization or cynicism in the workers as a whole—for example, the payment of bribes or the hiring of twelve-year-olds to work on a construction job site. When confronted with this type of problem a company taking the highly ethical course of action should refuse to engage in the behavior that is considered ethical in the host country. For example, in the 1990s Levi Straus decided not to do business in mainland China because of human rights abuses by the government and the extensive use of child labor. The loss of business to the company was estimated to be in the billions of dollars (Smeltzer and Jennings 1998).

A Type 2 ethical dilemma is a problem in which the fundamental values of the home-base company and the host country are the same, but the approach is different. For example, in India it is common for a company to guarantee a job to one child of each employee. This action is linked to the value that "the family unit should be protected and valued." Western culture also protects and values the family unit; however, many Western firms, particularly American firms, have policies against hiring family members, so an ethical dilemma arises.

When a company is confronted with a Type 2 ethical dilemma it should explore the underlying values with all parties and agree on an alternative means of supporting them. In the preceding example, perhaps a scholarship could be given to one family member if the international firm believes it is necessary to uphold the company policy against hiring family members.

The following basic ethical standards are helpful for operating in another country (Smeltzer and Jennings 1998):

- Obey local laws.
- Do not interfere in intergovernmental relationships.
- Do not engage in improper political actions.
- Do not take or give bribes.

---

[1]Read about Johnson and Johnson's commitment at http://www.jnj.com/who_is_jnj/cr index.html

Foreign Corrupt Trade Practices Act

Congress has passed a law designed to prevent U.S. firms from paying bribes to foreign officials to secure work. This law, the Foreign Corrupt Trade Practices Act (FCPA), also requires proper accounting methods for payments to foreign officials.[2] Passed in 1977, and amended in 1988, the act applies to all "domestic concerns" whether or not doing business overseas and whether or not registered with the Securities and Exchange Commission.

The FCPA was enacted because Congress considered corporate bribes to foreign officials to be

1. unethical;
2. harmful to our relations with foreign governments (Korean and Japanese officials were forced to resign after disclosure of payments from American-based multinational corporations); and
3. unnecessary to American companies doing business overseas.

The FCPA prohibits business from offering or authorizing corrupt payments or bribes to

1. a foreign official (or someone acting in an official capacity for a foreign government);
2. a foreign political party official or a foreign political party;
3. a candidate for political office in a foreign country; or
4. any person if the party making the payment knows that the money will be passed along, directly or indirectly, to any of the above.

A payment is *corrupt* if its purpose is to get the recipient to act or to refrain from acting so that a U.S. firm can retain or get business. The act does not prohibit "facilitating or expediting payments" to foreign officials to expedite or ensure performance of a routine governmental action such as to get goods through customs or to secure a visa; however, such payments must be truthfully listed in accounting records.

Competitors who lose business as a result of corrupt payments might be able to bring suit for their damages. In the case of *W. S. Kirkpatrick & Co. v. Environmental Tectonics Corp.*, the United States Supreme Court allowed a suit by a business that had lost a contract due to a bribe paid by another.[3] In that case the plaintiff, Environmental Tectonics, and the defendant, W. S. Kirkpatrick, were competing for a military procurement contract for the government of Nigeria. After Environmental Tectonics lost the bid, it discovered that W. S. Kirkpatrick had paid a bribe to Nigerian officials of 20% of the contract price. Nigerian law prohibited such payments. The trial court had dismissed the case but the United States Supreme Court reinstated the case and sent it back for trial.

---

[2] 15 U.S.C. § 78a, 78dd-1, 78dd-2, 78ff (2000)

[3] 110 S.Ct. 701 (1990)

The Origin of Our Ethics

Ethics in Western culture (Europe, the Americas, Australia) is a specialized topic within the study of philosophy. Two of the foundation stones of present-day Western culture are ancient Greek philosophy, which emphasized the *importance of the individual* and Christian philosophy, which centers on how individuals should relate to God.

Greek philosophy started to develop around 600 B.C.E. and was primarily interested in defining "what it means to be a human individual in a human community" (Ashby 1997). The major Greek philosophers were Socrates, Plato, and Aristotle.

The Greeks established a primitive democracy at about that time and recognized the worth of the individual, or at least the worth of individuals who where free, white, and male. The four basic elements of Greek philosophy can be summarized as follows (Ashby 1997):

1. All things, including humans, have a purpose or goal.
2. Humans should live in harmony.
3. Humans are superior to other life forms because of their ability to think rationally and logically.
4. Humans are interdependent with their community.

One of the unique contributions of the Greek philosophers was the conviction that *ethical questions are the most important questions, and failing to ask and answer those ethical questions means a person has failed to become as fully human as possible.* This concept is starting to regain recognition in present times.

Of course, Greek philosophy is much more complex than this summary indicates. For example, Plato taught that humans must go through stages of growth and knowledge toward a higher good, and Aristotle taught that the good person has a strong passion for knowledge; a love of wisdom and truth will raise a person above the love of money and physical pleasure.

An extremely simple statement of the basic principle of Christian philosophy is that humans should believe that Jesus is their savior and behave in accordance with the divine laws and principles set down in the Bible. Christian philosophy developed about 250 C.E. to 325 C.E.

After the fall of Rome, 476 C.E., Greek philosophy retreated to the monasteries during the Dark Ages (approximately 500 C.E.–700 C.E.) and the feudal period (approximately 700 C.E.–1300 C.E.), and Christian philosophy in the form of the Catholic Church became dominant. As feudalism fell under pressure for a more commercial culture, beginning in approximately 1000 C.E., Greek philosophy, together with Roman law, emerged from the monasteries and again was studied and applied. The two philosophies, Greek and Christian, have both been influential since that time, with Christian philosophy declining in importance in most Western countries other than the United States.

The period following feudalism is called the Renaissance or Reformation (1400–1600 C.E.) During this time major changes occurred in the organization of societies and in the relationships among people. The traditional social order (Catholic clergy, noble, serf) was changing and being transformed by merchants. This reorganization was primarily due to the increase in the importance of commerce and trade to societies. During the Reformation the Western world was characterized by the growth of commerce, the decline in the power of the Catholic Church, and the rise of many Protestant denominations. The fundamental philosophy of the Renaissance/Reformation can be characterized as follows: humans are individuals who are actively seeking the meaning of life.

The next period in Western culture can be called the Rise of Science (1600–1700 C.E.) Supporting the rise of science was a strong commitment to Greek logic and reason. There was extreme conflict between the Christian and Greek philosophies during this time, as beliefs established by science and reason conflicted with some Christian beliefs. This conflict is still present in the West, though more noticeably in the United States, where Christianity is still a major force.

Although science certainly continued to expand, and continues to expand, a new period emerged called, from a philosophical standpoint, the Age of Enlightenment (1700s C.E.) The form of government that characterizes Western cultures was developed at that time. The U.S. Constitution was drafted, and it became a model for governing documents of other Western countries.

The basic philosophy of the Enlightenment was that people can be self-reliant and self-governing. Basic to the philosophy was the importance of individual freedom. Additionally, the philosophy held that through rational thought humans could provide all that was necessary for a just moral life and a just society.

Following the Age of Enlightenment the period called Romanticism (late 1700s–mid-1800s C.E.) arose in response to the rationality of the Enlightenment. Romantic philosophy taught that humans and human institutions are not rational, scientific, machinelike entities. Instead, humans and human activity are dynamic, interrelated, and often irrational. The concept of friendship was highly thought of at this time. The philosophy taught that humans could, and must, rise to a higher nature, a nature beyond mere rationality and reason.

Modernism was the period from the mid-800s to the late 1900s C.E. It was characterized by a change from rural societies to urban societies, and the rise of capitalism and the importance of the free market. In addition, the concept of evolution played a major role in the philosophy and ethics of the time. This concept proclaimed that humans compete for all things, and the strongest and best are the most highly rewarded by the marketplace and society.

The present era is generally referred to as postmodern, and its philosophy is attempting to integrate many diverse and challenging concepts, including the following (Ashby 1997):

1. To what extent is human life to be controlled by capitalism and the profit motive?

2. Can science and religion be reconciled?

3. How can humans with diverse cultural heritages cooperate?

Vocabulary Checklist

Law
Ethics
Morality
Criminals
Values
Objective theory of ethics
Subjective theory of ethics
Market

Social income
Divine command theory
Subjectivism
Nihilism
Relativism
Cultural relativism
Type 1 ethical dilemma
Type 2 ethical dilemma

Feudal period
Renaissance
Reformation
Rise of Science
Enlightenment
Romanticism
Modernism
Postmodernism

Review Questions

1. Why do fewer and fewer people study ethics?
2. What are two reasons given in the text for the increased interest in ethics in business in recent years?
3. The text mentions several situations in which unethical behavior can be expected to occur. What are they?
4. A construction project can be one of the most complicated process humans and businesses undertake. What is one of the easiest ways to successfully navigate through this complicated process?
5. What is the definition of *law?*
6. According to the text, what are the two purposes of law?
7. In general, what establishes the lowest level of acceptable behavior in a society?
8. What happens to people who operate below this level of acceptable behavior?
9. What types of punishments are possible for criminal acts?
10. What types of punishments are typical for civil wrongs?
11. Why are people put into prison?
12. What is the definition of *ethics?*
13. Compare law and ethics as a standard of behavior.
14. What is the definition of *morality?*
15. What is the definition of *values?*
16. According to objective theory 1, why did law and ethics evolve?
17. Why do the law and ethical standards encourage trade and personal interaction?
18. What is a fundamental characteristic of the human race?
19. When is the answer to question 18 a problem?
20. What is one of the principal achievements of capitalism?
21. How are humans tied to each other?
22. What is meant by the statement in the text that "laws and ethical standards contribute to the fair distribution of the increased benefits that result from social cooperation"?

23. What is social income?

24. What is the divine command theory?

25. What advantages does the divine command theory have over other theories?

26. What is nihilism?

27. What is relativism?

28. Which of the preceding theories supports business ethics?

29. Why can a nihilist not support acting highly ethically in business?

30. Find the codes of ethics of the American Institute of Architects, National Society of Professional Engineers, and the American Institute of Constructors at the following Web sites.

American Institute of Constructors: http://www.aicnet.org/ethics.htm

National Society of Professional Engineers: http://www.nspe.org/ethics/eh1-code.asp

American Institute of Architects: http://www.aiamidtn.org/members/codeofethics.htm

31. Which of the preceding codes contains the *least* detail?

32. Which fundamental maxim of business ethics is mentioned in the chapter?

33. What are the five approaches the text recommends using to decide how to act highly ethically in a given situation?

34. What is the Golden Rule approach to deciding which acts are highly ethical?

35. What is utilitarianism approach to deciding which acts are highly ethical?

36. What is the categorical imperative approach to deciding which acts are highly ethical?

37. What is the veil of ignorance approach to deciding which acts are highly ethical?

38. Give three reasons why people are unethical?

39. Why are international ethics different from domestic ethics?

40. Discomfort with new and different ideas and values is greater for people who believe in what type of theory of law, ethics, and morality?

41. What is meant by the concept of cultural relativism?

42. What problem will companies that have two different ethical standards, one for home-base operations and one for host-country operations, run into?

43. An international company that decides to operate by different ethical standards in the home-base country and the host country must do what?

44. An international company that decides to operate by the same ethical standards in the home-base country and the host country must do what?

45. What is a Type 1 ethical dilemma?

46. How is a Type 1 ethical dilemma to be resolved?

47. What is a Type 2 ethical dilemma?

48. How is a Type 2 ethical dilemma to be resolved?

49. What four basic ethical standards are given in the text for operations in foreign countries?

50. What was the Foreign Corrupt Trade Practices Act designed to do?

Historical Questions

51. What is meant by the West?

52. What is the basic principle of Greek philosophy?

53. What makes a human a human according to Greek philosophy?

54. Which of the following people could most accurately be called the Founder of Western culture?

  a. Moses

  b. Siddhartha Gautama

  c. Socrates

  d. George Washington

  e. Margaret Chase Smith

  f. Walt Disney

  g. Madonna

55. What are the basic principles of Christian philosophy?

56. The fall of Rome ushered in what period in Western history?

57. What characterized the Renaissance or Reformation period in Western history?

58. The Rise of Science period supported a strong commitment to what?

59. What happened in the United States during the Age of Enlightenment?

60. What did the Romantic period emphasize and what did it deemphasize?

61. What were the characteristics of the Modern period?

62. What is the name of the current philosophical period?

63. What are some of the issues of postmodernism?

Questions Relating to Business Ethics in General

64. Imagine that you lost your thumb because of your own carelessness with a power saw. If you knew you could collect a lot of money even though the accident was your fault, would you sue the manufacturer? What if you knew that to win the suit you would have to lie under oath?

65. Should there be a limit to the personal wealth one individual is allowed to amass? If so, how much is "too much"?

66. Should there be a limit on the activities a person can engage in to amass personal wealth? What types of limits would you set?

Problems

Answer the issue in each of the following problems:

1. Pearson Construction, a general contractor, has a long-standing relationship with Turk Electrical, a subcontractor. On a particular job to build a five-story building at a community college,

the total amount of the electrical subcontract was $125,000. During the course of the project there were four change orders in the following amounts:

a. $11,234

b. $2,345

c. $5,400

d. $3,555

All the changes were approved by the Owner and Architect, and Pearson was paid for all. For some reason, unknown to Pearson, Turk never submitted the paperwork to be paid for change (a), though Turk did do the work. Pearson suspects that the paperwork "fell through the cracks" someplace at Turk's office. It is now five months after substantial completion of the project.

Issue: Should Pearson inform Turk that the paperwork has not been completed on change order (a)?

2. McCarren Memorial Hospital advertised for bids to erect a new wing for the hospital. The bid proposal stated, "The owner reserves the right to reject any or all bids." The following four bids were received:

   a. Edmondson Construction $1.2 million

   b. Brett Construction $1.5 million

   c. Klatt Construction $1.55 million

   d. Riley Construction $1.3 million

   After opening the bids McCarren elected to review the bids prior to awarding the contract. Before the contract was awarded, Riley Construction called McCarren and informed it that Riley had made a $150,000 error on its bid and that it was actually supposed to be $1.05 million. This made Riley the low bidder.

   Issue: Should McCarren award the project to Riley?

3. You are an employee for a midsize construction company. Late one night you see the project foreman taking a truckload of materials. The next morning you check, and they were not delivered to the site. What should you do?

4. You are an employee for a midsize construction company. Late one night you see the project foreman taking a truckload of materials. The next morning you check, and they were not delivered to the site. You know that this particular foreman is working two jobs to pay for medical care for his daughter who has a rare genetic disorder. The insurance benefits at the company are limited to $1 million, and you know that he has exhausted those benefits and is paying for all the care from his two jobs and the two jobs his wife is working. You suspect the foreman is selling the materials to make extra money for bills and medical debts.

   Issue: What should you do?

5. Goodrum Contracting has been working with Shane Development for five months on a small shopping center project. Two months ago it was discovered that 2 of the 10 acres lie in an "environmentally sensitive" area. This threatened to scuttle the entire development. Shane hired the brother of the chairman of the planning commission as a consultant, and, amazingly, the problem went away.

   It is time to start the paperwork for the building permit. Goodrum is now intimately knowledgeable about the site and the regulations governing the situation. Goodrum believes the project will, indeed, destroy a sensitive natural area and should not be built.

   Issue: What should Goodrum do?

6. Talon Enterprises, the owner of a multimillion project, wanted and expected Flint, Inc., the design/build firm, to assign its very best people to a project in phase one, which was the conceptual and preliminary design phase. Flint expected to be given the subsequent phases of the project, but Talon was not willing to make any commitment to Flint. It became apparent to Flint that Talon was keeping the door open so they could take the project from the contractor at the end of phase one; however, the owner's representatives very subtly built the expectation with Flint that Flint would do the next phase. Talon's attitude when pushed was, "We're big, we're tough buyers, and people are lining up to do our work. We can behave any way we choose, and they will be back the next time we have a job."

Issues:

a. What, if anything, should be Flint's approach?

b. Is it possible for Flint to change Talon's approach?

7. Dario Contractors was bidding a lump-sum project and had a bid cutoff time to its potential subcontractors of 10:00 A.M. The contractor's bid to the owner was due at 10:30 A.M. The contractor developed its total bid from the subcontractor and supplier bids turned in prior to 10:00 A.M. and turned in its number at 10:15 A.M. The bid used for the electrical was from Timely Electrical. At 10:20 A.M. Dario received a bid from Lately Electrical. This bid was $50,000 lower than Timely's bid. Dario was awarded the job by the owner.

Issue: Should Dario award the electrical subcontract to Timely or to Lately and why?

Answer to Selected Problem

1. Yes, Pearson should inform Turk that the paperwork has not been completed. The long-standing relationship of the parties will be enhanced if Pearson does so, and the amount of trust between the parties will increase. Using the Golden Rule (do unto others as you would have done unto you) or Kant's Categorical imperative (act in such a way that your actions could be "universal law") would dictate this result.

6

Relationships Among the Parties on the Project

A construction project frequently has many, many people, and legal entities, such as corporations and partnerships, working together in complex contractual and noncontractual relationships. As a general statement, the law allows the parties to determine how they will interact with one another, who will do what, and who will bear the risk for what. These decisions are made by **contracts,** which are promises or agreements that the law will uphold. Contracts do not have to be *written* to be valid, though written contracts offer many advantages.

First, we will briefly review the major legal entities encountered in the construction industry. Second, we will look at the fundamental contractual relationships on a construction project. Finally, we will look at the most common forms in which the fundamental contractual relationships are combined to make the delivery of a construction project to an owner possible.

Legal Entities Commonly Involved in the Construction Industry

The major legal entities encountered in the construction industry are the following:

Sole proprietorships

Partnerships or Joint ventures

Limited partnerships

Corporations

Government entities

Sole Proprietorship

A **sole proprietorship** is a business owned by one person only. In a community property or marital property state this type of business is, for many family law purposes, considered owned by two people, the husband and wife. California, New Mexico, Arizona, and Texas are community property states. Maine is a marital property state. For all other purposes the business is considered a sole proprietorship. No special legal formalities are required to form this type of business operation, and it is the default form of business operation when one person starts doing business.

> *Tax implications:* All deductions are taken on the person's individual state (if any) and federal income tax returns. The business does not file a separate income tax form.
>
> *Liability:* The individual and his or her property are liable for all contracts, debts, and torts of the business.
>
> *Death/Termination:* The business automatically ends when the sole proprietor dies. The business and its assets will be distributed to the heirs of the sole proprietor, either by the terms of a will or by the terms of law if there is no will. A sole proprietorship may have little value on the death of the sole proprietor, however.

Partnership/Joint Venture

A **partnership** is the doing of business by two or more people. Unlike a sole proprietorship, a partnership is a legal entity separate and apart from the two or more people who operate the business.

A **joint venture** is a form of partnership. A joint venture is usually for a limited undertaking or for a limited time, whereas a partnership is usually designed to operate indefinitely. Legally there is little if any difference between a partnership and a joint venture.

Any legal entity can enter into a partnership with another person or entity. For example, two people can enter into a partnership, or a corporation and a person can form a partnership, or two partnerships can form a joint venture.

No special forms are needed to form partnerships, and the partnership is the default type of business when two or more entities join forces for any commercial purpose. Parties attempting to form a corporation or other legal entity but failing for some reason are usually considered to be partners.

> *Tax implications:* Income and deductions are split among the partners and taken on each individual entity's tax return, either individual or corporate. No partnership tax return need be filed.
>
> *Liability:* Partners are jointly and severally liable for all contracts, debts, and torts of the business and its employees. This means that each partner is held *individually* responsible for all the contracts, debts, and torts of the partnership. For example, you and your friend enter into a partnership to do home remodeling. One of your employees severely injures a pedestrian while speeding through a traffic light on his

way to buy paint for a certain job. Your personal assets and the assets of your partner are subject to seizure to pay any judgment received by the pedestrian. If your partner takes off for Tahiti, you alone are still responsible for all the damages suffered by the pedestrian.

Death/Termination: A partnership is automatically terminated on the death of any partner, unless there is a partnership agreement to the contrary. If the partnership terminates, the assets must be liquidated and distributed to the heirs and the remaining partners. This can be a tremendous problem for any remaining partners who would like to continue the operation of the partnership.

Limited Partnership/Limited Liability Partnership

Many states recognize limited partnerships or limited liability partnerships. In fact, some states recognize several different types of limited partnerships such as family or farm limited partnerships. **Limited partnerships** are designed to give the limited partners the tax advantages of partnerships but the limitation of personal liability afforded by corporations.

Limited partnerships require formal written agreements and registration with the state. State law varies widely and must be followed for a valid limited partnership to be formed.

A limited partnership must usually have a general partner who is liable for the debts, contracts, and torts of the limited partnership. This entity is frequently a corporation, as no individual is likely to want to expose personal assets to the liability that attaches to doing the business.

The limited partners invest money into the project. The limited partnership may require them to pay additional sums into the limited partnership. This type of partnership was common for land purchases in the 1970s and 1980s.

Limited partnership interests are often difficult or impossible to sell. In fact, the agreement may require the holder of the limited partnership interest to sell at a reduced sum to the remaining limited partners.

Tax implications: The limited partnership must file an informational tax return; however, the income and deductions of the limited partnership flow through to the individual partners and are added to their own tax returns.

Liability: The limited partners are not liable for the partnership contracts, debts, or torts. The general partner of the limited partnership is liable for these.

Death: A limited partnership interest is treated as an asset and transferred by will or by law if there is no will. The limited partnership does not terminate on the death of a limited partner; however, many limited partnership agreements contain provisions allowing the remaining limited partners or the general partner to purchase the share of a deceased limited partner.

Termination: Some states allow limited partnerships to exist indefinitely, and others allow them to exist only for a certain period of time.

Corporation

A **corporation** is an independent legal entity created by a state. A corporation has many of the rights and duties of individuals and is often defined as a person for the purposes of some law. Corporations can be set up as profit-making ventures to operate a business. Non-profit corporations can also be set up to operate for charitable, educational, and similar purposes as established by the state's nonprofit corporation laws. Corporations carry out their functions through officers elected by shareholders, who are the owners of the corporation. Corporations come in all sizes, from large publicly held corporations to small corporations held by only a few people.

The requirements for forming a corporation vary from state to state, but in general, the parties desiring to form a corporation must file certain forms with the secretary of state. All corporations are formed under state law—there is no such thing as a "federal corporation." Once the corporation is formed, it is considered an entity separate and apart from the officers who operate it or the shareholders who own it.

A **publicly traded corporation** or **publicly held corporation** is one whose stock is bought and sold on a public stock exchange, such as the New York Stock Exchange. For example, Xerox is a publicly traded corporation; Al's Construction Corporation is not.

A **closely held corporation** is one whose stock is held by a small group of people, often related. The stock is not publicly traded.

A **Subchapter S corporation** is not a separate *type* of corporation; it is a tax status only. Corporations may register as a Subchapter S corporation for federal government taxation purposes only. When a corporation becomes a Subchapter S corporation, the income and deductions of the corporation flow through to the individual tax returns of the shareholders, just as in a partnership. Subchapter S status does not affect state tax liability.

Tax: The corporation is a legal entity and must get its own state and federal tax ID number and pay its own taxes. The corporation must pay income tax just like any other person. If the corporation pays out funds to shareholders in the form of dividends, the dividends are taxed as income to the shareholders. Because of this, corporate income is taxed twice—once when received by the corporation, and once when received by the shareholders. Corporations require bookkeeping and tax filings that are generally beyond the capability of the average person. Corporations usually retain professionals to make sure that the corporation is in compliance with state and federal laws.

Liability: The corporation alone is responsible for its own contracts, debts, and torts. Neither the officers nor the shareholders are responsible for the contracts, debts, or torts of the corporation or of its employees. One drawback to this feature is that few lending institutions will lend small corporations money or extend them credit without a personal guarantee by some individual involved in the corporation. If a shareholder gives a personal guarantee to a lending institution for a loan to a corporation, that shareholder is personally responsible for the debt.

Death: The shares of the corporation are an asset distributed by will or if there is no will, by law. The corporation continues unimpeded by the death of any shareholder. Note that it is very common, and highly recommended, for shareholders of small corporations to have a **shareholder agreement** that outlines what is to happen with the shares of stock upon the death of the shareholder. In a typical shareholder agreement the parties agree that the surviving shareholders or the corporation will purchase the shares of the deceased shareholder. This type of agreement is often referred to as a **buy–sell agreement.**

Termination: The corporation does not terminate naturally and can go on indefinitely until dissolved by the shareholders or by the government.

Government Entities

Government entities include such entities as the U.S. government, state governments, cities, counties, school districts, highway departments, the U.S. Postal Service, and the U.S. Army. Government entities are frequently the purchasers of construction projects and construction services.

The main difference between a government entity–owner, and a private entity–owner is the **doctrine of sovereign immunity.** This is a very old common-law doctrine that essentially held that "the king could not be sued." This doctrine eventually got translated into "the government cannot be sued." Most states and the federal government have passed laws that allow the governments to be sued in many circumstances; however, some states still apply this doctrine and prevent private parties from suing the state on at least some types of contracts and for some torts.

For example, in the case of *Federal Sign v. Texas Southern University,*[1] the Supreme Court of Texas said,

> *"The issue in this case is whether the sovereign immunity*
> *doctrine precludes Federal Sign, a private party, from suing Texas*
> *Southern University (TSU), a state institution, for breach of*
> *contract without legislative permission."*

The court said yes. In 1988 TSU began accepting bids for the construction and delivery of basketball scoreboards for its new Health and Physical Education facility, and Federal Sign submitted a bid for the contract. In early 1989 TSU accepted Federal Sign's bid and instructed Federal Sign to begin building the scoreboards. However, shortly after, TSU notified Federal Sign that Federal Sign's bid was unacceptable and told Federal Sign that TSU intended to pursue other avenues to secure the scoreboards. Later, TSU contracted with Spectrum Scoreboards for the building of the scoreboards. Federal Sign was not allowed to sue for breach of contract.

6-1. THINK

You are planning on starting your own construction, or subcontracting business. Which legal entity would you choose, and why?

---

[1]951 S.W.2d 401 (Tex. 1997).

Fundamental Contractual Relationships

The entities described in the preceding sections enter into the following types of fundamental contractual relationships in order to produce a construction product:

Owner–Builder contracts. These contracts involve the complex interplay of a number of the following types of contracts and are discussed in the section "Project Delivery Methods."

Employer–Employee contracts

General contractor–Subcontractor contracts

Principal–Agent contracts

Principal–Independent Contractor contracts

Sales of Goods or Uniform Commercial Code contracts

Employer (Principal)–Employee Contracts

The **employer–employee contract** is a contractual relationship between two parties: the employer and the employee. The employer, occasionally called the **principal,** hires another, the employee, to perform some task the employer wants completed. Generally, the employee is hired by the employer to perform certain work, such as typing, or making cabinets, and the employer (generally through other employees) closely manages the performance of the work.

As a general rule, employer–employee relationships are controlled by the **at-will employment doctrine.** The at-will employment doctrine is a legal doctrine holding that the employer can terminate the employee for any reason or for no reason without incurring any legal liability to the employee. Also, the employee can quit the employment for any reason or for no reason without incurring any legal liability to the employer. In recent years some laws have been passed that have modified the at-will employment doctrine. For example, federal law prohibits terminating people from employment if the termination is based on race. Neither the at-will employment doctrine nor the exceptions to it are covered in this text.

As a general rule, employees do not have the authority to enter into contracts on behalf of the employer. The employee cannot bind the employer to third parties.

The employer is liable for personal injuries, also called torts, caused by the employee *when committed within the scope of the employment.* For example, if the employee drives negligently while delivering the employer's product to a job site and injures a pedestrian, the employer is liable for all the damages to the pedestrian. Note that the employee is also personally liable; however, the pedestrian is more likely to obtain damages from the employer than from the employee. Tort liability is discussed in detail in Chapter 15, Torts and Tort Damages.

6-2. THINK

Why might the injured pedestrian be more likely to obtain his or her damages from the employer rather than from the employee?

Corporations and other business entities employ many people. People employed by corporations and business entities have an employer–employee relationship with the corporation or business entity. For example, if Driver Delivery, Inc., employs Denise Driver, she is an employee of the corporation. She may also be the major stockholder and/or an officer of the corporation, but she is also an employee.

The General Contractor–Subcontractor Contract Relationship

The **general contractor–subcontractor contract** is in essence a temporary employer–employee contract. The general contractor hires the subcontractor to perform a portion of the work on the project. Some general contractor–subcontractor relationships may be principal–independent contractor relationships (discussed later in the section.)

Principal–Agent

Often, people, including employers, will entrust others with the power to act on their behalf and bind them to contracts. This type of relationship is controlled by a **principal–agent contract.**

The main difference between the principal–agent relationship and the employer–employee relationship is that the agent (who may or may not be an employee) is generally given power to bind the principal to contractual agreements with others. For example, a secretary may be authorized by his employer to make purchases of up to $100/month at a local office supply store. The secretary is also the agent of the employer.

It is common for one party, such as an architectural firm, to have several ongoing agency relationships with several owners. It is more common for employees to work in only one employer–employee relationship. Employees who have two or more employment relationships are often referred to as *moonlighting.*

The owner principal is responsible for the actions and torts of the designer agent *committed within the scope of the agency agreement.* The opposite is also true: the owner–principal is *not* responsible for the actions of the designer-agent committed *outside the scope of the agency agreement.* In other words, if the contract between the owner and the architect does not give the architect the power to make major changes to the project, the architect does not have the power to obligate the owner to pay for major changes on the project. Should a party—for example, a contractor—undertake a major change on a project at the architect's request, the owner is not liable to the contractor to pay for the changed work. In fact, the owner can demand that the contractor redo the work in accordance with the original plans at the contractor's expense.

The principal–agent relationship is characterized by high levels of trust and legal accountability between the principal and the agent. This type of relationship is often called a **fiduciary relationship.** A person in a fiduciary relationship with another is expected to act in the best interests of the other, not in his or her own best interest.

The opposite of a fiduciary relationship is an arm's-length relationship. In an arm's-length relationship the parties are expected to act in their own best interests within the bounds of the law and ethics. Arm's-length relationships include principal–independent contractor and buyer–seller relationships, discussed in the next section.

Fiduciary relationships are found in many areas of the law. Spouses have a fiduciary relationship to each another. Partners have a fiduciary relationship to one another. Lawyers have a fiduciary relationship with their clients. Architects and engineers have a fiduciary relationship with the owner. Contractors generally have an arm's-length relationship.

The Owner–Designer Contract

The most common principal–agent contractual relationship encountered in the construction industry is between the project owner as principal and the designer as agent. The owner hires a designer, either an architect or an engineer, or both an architect and an engineer to design a construction project. On many projects the designer manages or is heavily involved in the construction of the project.

The Owner–Construction Manager Contract

Because of the complexity of modern construction projects many owners hire a **construction manager** to oversee the construction of the project instead of giving this responsibility to the designer. The term *CM* or *construction manager,* usually refers to a construction manager who is the agent or employee of the owner, not a person who is the agent or employee of the contractor.

The CM may be either the agent or employee of the owner. For example, a city or government agency may hire construction managers as employees to oversee the various construction projects that are being undertaken by the city. The owner of a hospital project may hire a CM through an agency contract rather than hire the CM as an employee.

Principal–Independent Contractor

The relationship between the owner and the general or prime contractor on a construction project is usually that of principal–independent contractor. This is an arm's-length relationship, not a fiduciary relationship.

As a very general statement only, in the principal–independent contractor relationship *the principal does not control the means and methods of accomplishing the task.* It is very common to see words such as "the contractor shall have the sole responsibility for the means, methods, techniques, and sequences, and coordination of the work" in a contract. These words are included to establish the relationship between the owner and the general/prime contractor as that of principal–independent contractor.

This relationship *protects the owner* from the actions of the independent contractor. The owner is not responsible for the torts or contracts of the independent contractor. For example, if one of the *contractor's* employees is injured on the job, the owner is not responsible to the contractor's employee. If one of the *designer's* employees is injured on the

6-3. THINK

Compare and contrast the relationship to the owner of the architect and the construction manager.

job, the owner *is* responsible to the employee. In addition, the owner need not pay state and federal employment taxes for an independent contractor.

Because of the advantages of this type of relationship, owners and business people often attempt to characterize employer–employee relationships as principal–independent contractor relationships. This is illegal.

It is possible for the owner to destroy the principal–independent contractor relationship *by instructing the general contractor on the means and methods of construction.* This can have devastating legal and financial repercussions for the owner. Most owners are aware of this and carefully maintain the principal–independent contractor relationship.

Sales of Goods or Uniform Commercial Code Contracts

A Uniform Commercial Code relationship involves the seller of goods and the buyer of those goods. Goods are such things as pencils, lumber, and nails. Land and improvements on land such as dams and buildings are not goods. This is an arm's-length relationship in which both parties are expected to operate in their own best interests within the boundaries of law and ethics.

This relationship is governed by the form of the **Uniform Commercial Code** (UCC) adopted by the particular jurisdiction. The UCC is a set of laws developed by experts designed to make the law of the sales of goods more consistent among the various jurisdictions in the United States. It has been adopted in every jurisdiction, although many jurisdictions have made slight modifications to the code. Sales of services are generally governed by case law in most jurisdictions in the United States, and codes and statutes govern some service industries such as businesses selling ballroom dance lessons and providing hairdressing services.

Project Delivery Methods

Completed construction projects are delivered to owners in a variety of ways. The three most common methods of construction project delivery are the following:

 Traditional form

 Construction Management or CM

 Design–build

Traditional Form

In the **traditional form** of construction project delivery, the owner enters into an agency relationship with a designer—either an architect or an engineer, or both—to design the project and to oversee the construction of the project. The owner enters into a principal-independent contractor relationship with the contractor to build the project. A diagram of this relationship is shown in Figure 6–1.

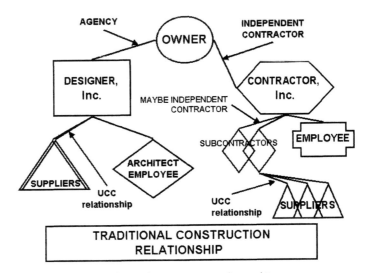

Figure 6-1 Traditional construction relationship

Construction Management or CM

Figure 6–2 illustrates the **construction management** project delivery method. This is a relatively new type of relationship that has developed due to several factors in the industry. One factor is the increased complexity of projects, which requires specialized training of those who manage projects. Another factor is the unwillingness of architects to manage the construction as they have historically done. The owner hires a specific person or firm to manage the construction. It is not uncommon for the construction manager to enter into

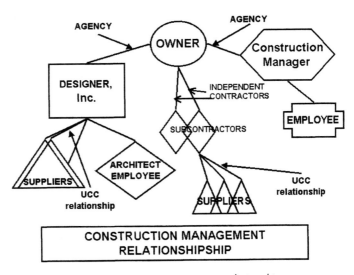

Figure 6-2 Construction management relationship

prime and/or subcontracts on behalf of the owner. On many CM projects the general or prime contractor is eliminated. The owner retains more control over the construction while still maintaining the advantages of the principal–independent contractor relationship with those entities doing the work.

Design–Build

Figure 6–3 illustrates the **design–build** project delivery method. This is also a relatively new type of relationship that has developed due to several factors in the industry. It has proved to be a very economical form of project delivery. The owner enters into one contract with a company to both design and build the project. The design–build firm then enters into contracts with designers, contractors, subcontractors, and suppliers as needed to complete the project. Several variations of this method exist.

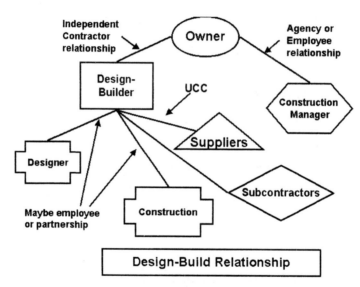

Figure 6–3 Design–build relationship

Vocabulary Checklist

Contract	Subchapter S corporation	General contractor–subcontractor contract
Sole proprietorship	Buy–sell agreement	Principal–agent contract.
Partnership	Shareholder agreement	Principal
Joint venture	Government entities	Agent
Limited partnership	Sovereign immunity	Fiduciary relationship
Corporation	Employer–employee contract	Construction manager
Government entity	Employer	Uniform Commercial Code
Publicly traded corporation	Employee	Traditional form project delivery method
Closely held corporation	At-will employment doctrine	

Review Questions

1. Which legal entity affords an individual the most protection of individual assets from creditors of the business?

2. Which form(s) of legal entity never dies or terminates naturally?

3. Which form of legal entity exposes the personal assets of a person to pay for actions (torts) of *other* people involved in the business?

4. If two or more people form a corporation to do business, but the proper paperwork is never filed, what form of business operation will the law say they are engaging in?

5. True or False: Only corporations can have employees.

6. Which business entities can have employees?

7. Which business entities can hire agents?

8. Which business entities can hire independent contractors?

9. Which business entities can enter into contracts to buy and sell goods or services?

10. An owner of a construction project can be what type of legal entity?

11. A contractor on a construction project can be what type of legal entity?

12. You and your friend Lynn Humble decide to form a small corporation that will manufacture and install cabinets. Each of you is to own 50% of the stock. Although you have been friends with Lynn for over fifteen years, you do not get along very well with Lynn's spouse or children. You are afraid that should Lynn die you will not be able to get along with Lynn's spouse should Lynn's spouse want to get involved in the business. What can you do to protect yourself from this problem?

13. Diagram the relationships among the following for the traditional, CM, and design–build forms of construction project delivery:

Owner

Designer

Contractor

Construction manager

Problems

Answer the issue in each of the following problems by making a legal argument, including premises, in support of your answer.

1. Owner hires Chapin Architect, Inc., to do a design–build project. The parties' contract states that the architect is an independent contractor and is responsible for all means and methods of construction. Chapin Architect, Inc., hires a construction manager, plumbing subcontractor, and all other needed subcontractors. All relationships between Chapin Architect, Inc. and these entities are independent contractor relationships. The plumbing subcontractor installs defective plumbing.

Issue: Is Chapin Architect, Inc., liable to the owner for the defective plumbing?

Rule: With regard to the employment of independent consultants/contractors, the prime professional is legally responsible to the owner for errors in judgment by his/her consultants/contractors.[2]

Premises:

Answer: Yes

2. The contract between Ken Robson Owner and Aceland Constructors states that Ken Robson must approve all changes in color of tiles for the project. Ken Robson has chosen type A, which is available, but at a slightly greater price than type B. Ken Robson's architect approves a tile change to type B, which Aceland installs. A few days later Ken Robson is walking through the area and notices the type B tile. Ken Robson orders the contractor to remove the type B tile and install the type A tile. Mr. Robson refuses to pay for the cost of installing and removing the type B tile.

Issue: Must Ken Robson pay the contractor for the installation and removal of the type B tile?

Rule:

Premises:

Answer: No

Note: The tort liability of the architect to the contractor in this problem is discussed in Chapter 15, Torts and Tort Damages.

3. The engineer, Mr. Holz, is given power to interpret the plans and specs in a contract between the owner, Mr. Gysler, and the engineer on a certain construction job. Mr. Holz tells Emanuel Construction it is not necessary to prepare a written change order, but to go ahead and upgrade the fill that will be used on the site. This upgrade increases the project cost $5000.

Issue: Must Mr. Gysler pay Emanuel Construction for the upgraded fill?

Rule:

Premises:

Answer: No

4. Ms. Bisharat, the owner of a certain project, tells Ms. Werth, the engineer, to "get other bids" for certain work that must be done on the project relating to the chemical plant. Ms. Werth hires Lance Contractors to do the work. Lance was the lowest bidder.

Issue: Is there a contract between Ms. Bisharat and Lance?

Rule:

Premises:

Answer: No

---

[2]*Johnson v. Salem Title Co.*, 246, or. 409, 425 P.2d 519 (1967).

5. Frost Contractors builds according to the plans and specs, but a stairwell collapses and must be redesigned and rebuilt. Frost's costs for rebuilding the stairwell are $20,000. Negligence on the part of the architect in the design of the stairwell has been established and is not an issue. Prior to paying Frost, Deep Sea, Inc., the owner of the project, goes bankrupt and cannot pay Frost.

Issue: Is Frost Contractors entitled to damages for breach of contract from the architect?

Rule:

Premises:

Answer: No

Note: The tort liability of the architect to the contractor in this problem is discussed in Chapter 15, Torts and Tort Damages.

6. The contract between the architect and Fox Industries, owner, gives the architect power to make minor changes in the plans and specs. The architect orders Bledsoe Construction to change the roof pitch of the building. This results in an increase in cost to the contractor of $10,000. Fox Industries' construction manager visits the site one day and insists that the new roof be removed and the contractor rebuild according to the plans and specifications. This costs the contractor another $15,000.

Issue: Is Fox Industries, the owner, liable to the contractor for any of the $25,000?

Rule:

Premises:

Answer: No

7. The contract between the architect and Hound Industries, owner, gives the architect power to make minor changes in the plans and specs. The architect orders Sloe Construction to add a rain gutter to a certain section of the roof. The cost of the rain gutter is $200. Fox Industries' construction manager visits the site one day and insists that the rain gutter be removed and refuses to pay for the gutter. It costs the contractor $5 to remove the gutter.

Issue: Is Fox Industries, the owner, liable to the contractor for any of the $205?

Rule:

Premises:

Answer: Yes, all of it.

Answer to Selected Problem

2. *Issue:* Must Ken Robson pay the contractor for the installation and removal of the type B tile?

Rule: The owner-principal is responsible for the actions and torts of the designer-agent committed within the scope of the agency agreement.

Premises: The owner is not responsible because the designer's act is outside of the scope of the owner–designer contract. The contract between the designer and the owner states that the owner must approve all changes in the color of tiles. The architect is given no power to approve such changes, so when the architect does approve a change, the architect is acting *outside* of his authority. The owner is not responsible for acts of the designer that are outside of the authority the owner has given the designer. The contractor should obtain owner approval for this change.

Answer: No

7

Mistakes in Bidding

What happens when a general contractor or a subcontractor makes a mistake in its bid? The law of mistakes is part of contract formation law, and that law is outlined here first before we go into the specific law of mistakes as applied to the construction industry. A *contract* has previously been defined as a promise that the law will enforce.

Contract Formation

The major elements needed to form a valid contract from a promise are as follows:

- An offer is made.
- The offer is accepted.
- Consideration is received.
- The parties have the legal capacity to enter into a contract.
- The Contract must be for a legal purpose.
- No fraud or force is involved.

An **offer** is the expression of a willingness to enter into a contract. The law considers a construction bid to be an offer. Offers may be withdrawn at any time prior to acceptance; however, once accepted, a contract is formed (assuming all the following other elements also exist).

An **acceptance** is the expression of a willingness to abide by the terms of the offer or bid. The acceptance must mirror the terms of the bid. A party is not allowed to make changes in the bid and then to accept the changed bid. If this occurs, the original bid is terminated, and the changed bid is considered a counteroffer. The parties may go back and forth with counteroffers until an agreement is reached.

Consideration is what each party gives up and what each party receives from the transaction. In order for a promise to be a contract, *both* parties must negotiate to give up something of value, and *both* parties must receive something of value from the negotiation. If this does not occur, then any promises made are not contracts and will not be enforced by the law.

The one area where contract formation law plays a major role in the construction industry is in the area of changes to an existing contract. In general, the law does *not* allow the parties to change a contract, but since changes to the contract are so common in the construction industry, the law allows them. However, the law considers a change to be the formation of a new contract, and therefore the change must be supported by consideration. This aspect of the law of consideration is further discussed in Chapter 10, Changes and Additions to the Contract.

Parties must have the **legal capacity** to form a contract. In general, this means they must be over the age of majority, which is 18 in most states.

The law will uphold only contracts that have been entered into for a **legal purpose.** For example, the law will not uphold contracts for murder or for the purchase of illegal imports.

The law will not uphold contracts that have been entered into by fraud or force. **Fraud** is sometimes called deceit or misrepresentation. The elements of fraud are as follows:

1. There is false representation or nondisclosure of material fact(s).
2. It is made with the intent to deceive.
3. The statement has been relied on by the complaining party.
4. There is actual damage.

Force is the use of a wrongful act or the threat of a wrongful act to force a party to sign an agreement. For example, assume the parties have a contract for the delivery of lumber at a price of $10,000. The lumber supplier threatens not to deliver the lumber unless the buyer promises to buy an additional $10,000 of lumber. The buyer agrees to buy an additional $10,000 of lumber and signs a "contract." The second lumber sale "contract" is not a contract, as it was entered into through the use of force. The law will not enforce this promise.

Not every contract that has failed to satisfy one of the listed elements makes the contract unenforceable. For example, if a minor enters into a contract, the contract is voidable at the minor's election. By **voidable** is meant that one or both parties can get out of or **rescind** the contract if they want to. A **void** contract is one that the law refuses to uphold. Illegal contracts are void.

It should be noted that even if a contract is formed, and one of the parties refuses to perform the contract or otherwise breaches the contract, the court will not order the breaching party to actually *perform* the contract. The court will order only that the breaching party pay damages to the nonbreaching party. This concept comes under the law of remedies—

that is, what the court will order parties who have breached a duty to do or pay. Remedies and damages are discussed in more detail in Chapter 14, Termination of the Contract and Contract Damages.

Claims and disagreements concerning contract formation are rare in the construction industry and therefore will not be further elaborated on here; however, because of the complexity of construction projects, it is unlikely any project is designed and bid without some mistakes, so this area of the law is important in the construction industry.

Mistakes

The law of mistakes can be divided into three areas:

- Unilateral mistakes
- Mutual mistakes
- Mistakes in transcription

A **unilateral mistake** is a mistake made by one party to the contract. For example, if the general contractor forgets to add in the cost of removing old flooring in its bid on a remodeling project, that is a unilateral mistake. The legal rule is that unilateral mistakes do not alter the existing contract, and the parties must perform the contract. In the preceding example, the contractor must still remove the flooring but cannot charge the owner.

One major exception to this rule is that if the nonmistaken party knows or should have known of the mistake, that part of the contract is voidable. This rule has been slightly modified for the construction industry in some circumstances. See the sections "Contractor Mistakes: Rescission of the Contract" and "Contractor Mistakes: Reformation of the Contract."

Unilateral Mistake

Rule: A unilateral mistake has no effect on the contract. Both parties must perform the contract as written.

Exception to this rule: If the nonmistaken party knew of or should have realized a mistake had been made, that part of the contract is voidable by the mistaken party.

A **mutual mistake** is a mistake of law or fact by both of the parties. A mutual mistake makes the contract voidable by either party. For example, assume that Ms. Capano believed she had inherited a lot on the northwest corner of Highway 21 and 17, and she and the contractor, Schuette Construction, entered into an agreement to build a house on that lot. However, it was later discovered that the land was actually located on the southwest corner of the intersection. The contract is voidable.

Mutual Mistake

Rule: A mutual mistake makes the contract, or that portion of the contract, voidable at the election of either party.

A **mistake in transcription** is a mistake made when an oral agreement is put into writing. For example, the parties may agree on a price of $5000 to build a deck, but the contract contains the price of $6000, and neither party notices this error until after the contract is signed. A mistake in transcription can be **reformed,** that is, changed by the court; however, the standard of proof is higher than for other facts. In most civil trials and arbitrations a fact must be proved by a *preponderance of the evidence;* that is, there must be slightly more evidence proving a certain fact than disproving a certain fact. However, the evidence to prove a mistake in transcription cannot be proved merely by a preponderance of the evidence but must be proved by *clear and convincing evidence,* which is a higher standard. Standards of proof are very technical legal concepts that are normally only of importance to lawyers and judges.

Whether a mistake in transcription has occurred is an issue of fact. For example, in the preceding example the buyer of the deck would have to introduce clear and convincing evidence to prove that the actual agreed-on price was $5000 not $6000. Perhaps the contractor told Mr. Rodger, a neighbor, that the contract had been for $5000. Mr. Rodger's testimony would be proof that an arbitrator or jury could use to decide the case.

Mistake in Transcription

Rule: A mistake in transcription can be reformed, but only on clear and
convincing evidence.

Mistakes in Bids

A mistake in a bid is a mistake made by the contractor in its bid to the owner, or a mistake by a subcontractor in its bid to the contractor. The law treats these two types of mistakes differently. In addition, the law for federal projects is slightly different from the law for projects governed by state law. Figure 7–1 illustrates the major divisions in the law that will be discussed here.

In this area of the law, the concept of "choice of law" is very important. By **choice of law** is meant the law chosen or that governs the particular transaction. The law has its own laws for determining this issue! For purposes of this chapter, the law chosen or applied to a specific case will be the law of the state where the claim or lawsuit arose. If the claim relates to a federal project, federal law will control.

Contractor Mistakes

Contractor mistakes in bids can be divided into two categories: state law and federal law. The federal law, but not state law, will allow the contractor to reform the contract in some circumstances. Note that many states have specifically enacted legislation to cover this situation, and it is always necessary to review your specific state's law before making a legal argument. Appendix A to this chapter contains a summary of state law covering this area.

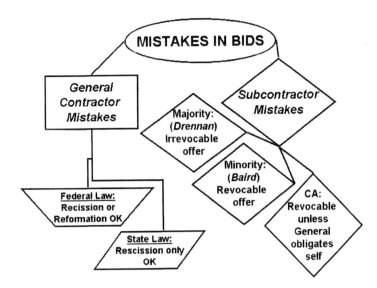

Figure 7-1 Summary of mistakes in bid law

Rescission of the Contract (State Law and Federal Law)

In general, state and federal law allows the contractor to rescind (that is, revoke) a bid or contract that has a *major mistake* in it if work on the project *has not yet begun* (simplified rule). The American Institute of Architects Form A701—1997, *Instructions to Bidders* contains the following language that attempts to nullify this rule:

> § *4.2.1 Should the Bidder refuse to enter into such Contract . . . the amount of the bid security shall be forfeited to the Owner as liquidated damages, not as a penalty.*
>
> § *4.4.1 A bid may not be modified, withdrawn, or canceled by the bidder during the stipulated time period following the time and date designated for the receipt of Bids.*

However, the law prevails, not the above contract language.

Mistake in General Contractor's Bid

Rule: The general contractor may rescind its bid, or the contract entered
into based on that bid, if the mistake in the bid is major,
and work has not yet begun. (*simplified rule*)

This simplified rule is the one we will use to gain a basic understanding of the principles of law surrounding mistakes. Realize, however, that in a real case, in a court of law or arbitration, the following more complex rule will be used, and the conclusion may be different from the conclusion obtained using the simplified rule.

The actual law regarding bid mistakes as established by the majority of state courts is similar to the following rule outlined in *Kenneth E. Curran, Inc. v. State:*[1]

> A bid or contract can be rescinded for a contractor mistake if the contractor can prove each of the following elements:
>
> 1. The mistake is of so great a consequence that to enforce the contract as made would be unconscionable; and
> 2. the mistake relates to a material feature of the contract; and
> 3. the mistake was made regardless of the exercise of ordinary care; and
> 4. the parties can be placed in status quo (neither party will be prejudiced, except the owner has lost the bargain).

EXAMPLE:

The bids are being opened, and Ace Contractor's representative at the bid opening notices that Ace's bid is much lower than all the other bids. Ace's representative quickly reviews the bid and notices that part A does not contain any value for the cost of the concrete, which the representative estimates to be at least $1 million. Ace does have several in-house review procedures for bids, but this error slipped by despite those procedures. Ace Contractor's representative wants to rescind Ace's bid at the bid opening, because if Ace is awarded the contract, Ace will lose a substantial amount of money and may even be forced into bankruptcy. The owner, however, wants to award the contract to Ace, attempt to collect on Ace's bid bond, and then give the project to the next higher bidder. Assume the bids are as follows:

	Ace's Bid	*Accurate Contractor's Bid*
Part A	$0.1 million	$1.2 million
Part B	$2.1 million	$2.1 million
Part C	$1.8 million	$1.9 million
Total	$4.0 million	$5.2 million

All the legal elements are supported by facts and the contractor can rescind this bid.   ■ ■ ■

---

[1] *Kenneth E. Curran, Inc. v. State,* 215 A. 2d 702 (N.H. 1965).

The following legal argument using simple premises can be made:

Issue: Can Ace rescind its bid?

Premises:

1. The mistake is of so great a consequence that to enforce the contract as made would be unconscionable (law) = The mistake is 25% of the total value of the entire bid, and forcing Ace to perform the work would result in bankruptcy (fact)

2. The mistake relates to a material feature of the contract (law) = The concrete is a material feature of the contract, and the mistake is almost all of Part A of the bid (fact)

3. The mistake was made regardless of the exercise of ordinary care (law) = Ace has several in-house review procedures for bids, but this error slipped by despite those procedures (fact)

4. The parties can be placed in status quo (neither party will be prejudiced, except the owner has lost the bargain (law) = The owner can award the project to Accurate and has lost nothing except the windfall on Ace's error (fact)

Answer: Yes.

Frequently, mistaken bid cases result when the owner attempts to collect on the bid bond after the contract has been awarded to another contractor. In those cases state courts generally allow the mistaken contractor to rescind the bid or contract without incurring any legal liability to the owner, as in the following example:

> The bids are being opened on a school project, and the contractor notices that its bid is much lower than all the other bids. The contractor tells the school project representative it wants to rescind its bid at that point; however, the school project representative awards the contractor the bid. The contractor refuses to do the work. The bid is awarded to the next bidder, and the school administration makes a claim on the bid bond.

Issue: Can the contractor rescind its bid?

Answer: Yes.

In this case, the owner tried to make a windfall on the contractor's error by collecting the amount of the bond.[2] The court said:

> No contractual obligations existed between a school board and a contractor where the contractor had submitted a bid, there was a mistake in the bid which created a <u>significant disparity</u> in the bid figure and the actual cost of construction, the mistake was caused by a clerical error, the defendant told the school board at the meeting at which the bids were to be accepted that

---

[2]*Fraser Public Schools District v. Kolon,* 35 Mich. App. 441, 193 N.W. 2d 64 (1971 Mich. App.).

there was an error and that the bid as originally made was withdrawn, and the school board, twelve days after the bid had been withdrawn, accepted the bid; equity prevents the school board from recovering the difference between the erroneous bid and the second lowest bid, because the bidder's mistake was not result of gross negligence, no rights had accrued, and to allow recovery would be unconscionable.

Reformation of the Contract (Federal Law Only)

Federal law goes further than state law to protect the contractor from a mistake in a bid. Under federal law a bid can actually be reformed as long as the mistaken bid *does not displace another bid*, and the *intended bid is ascertainable from the bid documents*. Under federal law the government agent or officer in charge of the bidding is required to examine all bids for mistakes.[3] Indications of mistakes can be a substantial disparity between the low bid and other bids, a dealer underbidding a manufacturer, or a bid out of line with government estimate or even past experience.[4] If the officer believes a mistake might have been made, the officer must request the bidder to verify its bid, calling the bidder's attention to the possible error. If the officer fails to verify the bid, and the error is one that should have been discovered, the contractor can rescind or reform its bid. This rule developed under federal law and is not generally applicable to state law–governed projects, but many states have similar rules for state-government projects.

7.1 THINK

Why is the law so different for federal and state cases?
Who is the *owner* in the federal cases?
Who is the *owner* in most state law cases?

EXAMPLE:

Ace Construction made a mistake in adding five subtotals on the bid form on a proposed federal project. The bids were as follows:

	Ace's Bid	*Accurate's Bid*
Part A	$1.1 million	$1.2 million
Part B	$2.1 million	$2.1 million
Part C	$1.8 million	$1.9 million
Bid	$5.3 million	$5.2 million
Correct total	$5.0 million	

---

[3]FAR 14.406-1.

[4]*M.K.B. Mf. Corp.*, 59 Comp. Gen. 195, 80-1 CPD ¶34 (1980).

The intended, correct amount could be determined from the face of the bid itself, so Ace was allowed to correct its mistake and displace Accurate Construction, the "apparent" low bidder. Ace could reform its bid to $5 million at the bid opening and be awarded the job, as long as it met all other requirements. ■ ■ ■

In addition to the preceding rule regarding reformation, the Comptroller General is fairly liberal and allows withdrawal of bids "wherever it reasonably appears that an error was made."[5] This is despite FAR 14.406-39b, which states that bids can be withdrawn only after permission and when the evidence is *clear and convincing that a mistake has been made.* The benefit of the doubt is to be given to the contractor. For example, Trafalgar House Construction, Inc., was the apparent low bidder on a U.S. government project. It requested permission to increase its bid by $643,545, still leaving it as low bidder. The contractor had made an error when a handwritten subcontractor's quotation was erroneously entered into the contractor's computer. This was proved by bid preparation worksheets and affidavits. The Comptroller General said:

> The question for our review is whether the VA [Veterans Administration, a federal agency] reasonably concluded that Trafalgar had submitted clear and convincing evidence of the mistake and of the intended bid, not whether Trafalgar was negligent in preparing its bid. Thus, even if the error was caused by Trafalgar's negligence, as the protester contends, the VA may properly consider Trafalgar's request for bid correction.[6]

Mistake in General Contractor's Bid (Federal Law)

Rule: The general contractor may reform its bid, or the contract entered into based upon that bid, if it can prove it made a mistake in the bid and the reformed bid is still less than the next higher bidder. (*simplified rule*)

Subcontractor Mistakes

State law relating to mistakes made by *subcontractors* is *very* different from the law relating to mistakes by contractors. The difference is primarily due to the fact that the *contractor depends on the subcontractor's bid* in its bid to the owner, and the contractor cannot request more money from the owner if the subcontractor claims a mistake has been made. No federal law exists in regard to subcontracts because state law governs all subcontracts.

The states are not consistent in their treatment of subcontractor mistakes. Three different rules have emerged: the majority rule, which is also called the ***Drennan rule***,[7] the

---

[5]*Murphy Bros.*, 58 Comp. Gen. 185, 78-2 CPD ¶440 (1978).

[6]*Matter of Huber, Hunt & Nichols, Inc.*, Comp. Gen. No. B-271112 (May 21, 1996).

[7]*Drennan v. Star Paving Co.*, 333 P. 2d 757 (Cal. 1958).

minority rule, which is also called the ***James Baird*** ***rule***,[8] and the ***California*** ***rule***.[9] This area of the law is not totally settled, and different jurisdictions, even within a single state may have different law. Notice that the *Drennan* rule and the California rule are both from California cases.

Drennan is the rule in the majority of jurisdictions. This rule states that a subcontractor's bid is *irrevocable* for a reasonable time after the award of the prime contract if the general contractor has *relied* on that bid in its bid to the owner. This rule is based on the principle of **promissory estoppel**, which is defined as follows:

> A promise which the promisor [*promisor is the party making the promise, subcontractor in this case*] should reasonably expect to induce action or forbearance on the part of the promisee [*promisee is the party receiving the promise, the contractor in this case*] . . . and which does induce such action or forbearance is binding if injustice can be avoided only by enforcement of the promise.[10]

Mistake in Subcontractor's Bid (Majority Rule)

Rule: The subcontractor's bid is *irrevocable* for a reasonable time after the award of the prime contract, but only if the general contractor relied on that bid in the general contractor's bid to the owner.

Notice that *Drennan* changes the general contractual legal principle that *an offer may be withdrawn at any time prior to acceptance.* Naturally, in the construction industry the contractor will not accept the subcontractor's bid until it knows it has the prime contract. Accepting the subcontractor's bid prior to being awarded the prime contract would obligate the general contractor to the subcontractor even if the general contractor were not to be awarded the prime contract.

The major drawback with the *Drennan* rule is that it is unfair. Whereas the subcontractor is obligated to the prime contractor, the prime contractor is *not* obligated to the subcontractor. Once the prime contractor is awarded the prime contract, the prime contractor can legally give the subcontract to another subcontractor. In the industry this practice is called **bid shopping** and is considered unethical; however, the practice is common.

7–2. THINK

What are the two legal elements the contractor must prove in order to recover damages from a subcontractor under the *Drennan* rule?

---

[8]*James Baird Company v. Gimbell Bros.*, 64 F. 2d 344 (2nd Cir. 1933).

[9]*Southern Cal. Acoustic Co. v. C.V. Holder*, 71 Cal. 2d 719, 79 Cal. Rptr. 319, 456 P. 2d 975 (1969).

[10]*Restatement (2nd) of Contracts* (1981).

Bid shopping can be detrimental to the prime contractor who attempts to enforce a low subcontractor's bid. Some jurisdictions hold that bid shopping is proof the general contractor *did not rely* on the subcontractor's bid. The contractor cannot prove both of the elements *Drennan* rule and is therefore not entitled to damages.

EXAMPLE:

Doffing General Contractor submits a project to build a wing of a hospital. Doffing uses Subcontractor Hill's bid of $135,000 to do the electrical work. Doffing has obtained several bids for the concrete as follows:

Subcontractor Piskun	$150K
Subcontractor Johnston	$142K
Subcontractor Perez	$145K
Subcontractor Hill	$135K

After award of the prime contract to Doffing, Doffing contacts several other subcontractors in an attempt to obtain a contract for the electrical at $130,000. Subcontractor Hill informs Doffing it made a mistake in its bid and is rescinding the bid of $135,000. Doffing is forced to hire Subcontractor Johnston to do the work. Assuming that Subcontractor Hill can prove that Doffing did in fact contact other subcontractors, Subcontractor Hill need not pay damages to Doffing. ■ ■ ■

James Baird is the minority rule. Under this rule the subcontractor's bid is an offer revocable at any time prior to acceptance by the contractor. This rule is consistent with general contract law. In jurisdictions using this rule the general contractor has no assurance that the subcontractors will perform at the price quoted. Contractors must include this risk in bidding contracts. As with the *Drennan* rule the prime contractor is not obligated to award the subcontract to any particular subcontractor.

7–3. THINK

> In what position does this place the contractor? What risk is the contractor taking in these jurisdictions? How does this rule affect bid shopping? Who is obligated here?

Some California courts use the California rule, which balances the obligations of the contractor and the subcontractor. This rule also discourages bid shopping. Under this rule the subcontractor's bid is revocable at any time prior to acceptance *unless* the general contractor has stated in writing it will accept the subcontractor's bid if awarded the prime contract. Under this rule both the general contractor and the subcontractor are obligated to perform. The general is obligated to give the subcontract to the subcontractor, and the subcontractor is obligated to perform the work. If the contractor bid shops or otherwise fails to give the job to the subcontractor, the contractor is in breach and liable to the subcontractor for damages. (Remember that the court will not order either party to do either of these things. The court will order only that one party pay damages to the other party.)

7-4. THINK

What are the two legal elements the contractor must prove in order to recover damages from a subcontractor under the California rule?

7-5. THINK

Under the California rule when can the subcontractor recover damages from the contractor?

EXAMPLE:

V. Maa General Contractor submits a prime bid to an owner using Subcontractor Ross's bid of $135,000 to do the concrete work. V. Maa informs Subcontractor Ross by letter it has used Subcontractor Ross's bid in its bid to the prime contractor, and V. Maa will award the subcontract to Subcontractor Ross if it gets the prime contract. V. Maa has obtained several bids for the concrete as follows:

Subcontractor Williams	$150K
Subcontractor Davis	$142K
Subcontractor Smith	$145K
Subcontractor Ross	$135K

After award of the prime contract to V. Maa, Subcontractor Ross informs V. Maa it made a mistake. V. Maa gives the subcontract to Subcontractor Davis. Subcontractor Ross is liable for $7000 damages. ■ ■ ▦

As mentioned previously, a subcontractor is not entitled to reform its bid, even on a federal job; however, it is possible for a prime contractor to get its subcontractor additional money. The prime can do this by *reforming the prime bid* and paying the subcontractor the additional sum. For example, assume the following two bids were made on a federal job: Carsey Construction $5.3 million, and Ballard Construction $5.4 million. Carsey submitted its prime bid based including Subcontractor Griffin's bid of $135,000 to do the concrete work. Subcontractor Griffin informs Carsey it made an error in its original bid and can do the job only if it is paid $140,000. Carsey can seek to reform its prime bid to $5.305 million and pay Subcontractor Griffin the additional $5000.

Telephone Bids

It is not uncommon for subcontractors to give bids over the telephone minutes before a prime bid is due. Unless the bid is one for goods, such as lumber or refrigerators, and valued at over $500, the telephone bid is a valid offer. The bid can be accepted by the contractor either in writing or by return call. It is not necessary to have a writing of any type.

The Uniform Commercial Code in most states requires a writing in order to enforce a contract for the sale of goods valued at over $500. Some states will allow the contractor to use the doctrine of promissory estoppel to recover damages even if there has been no writing, however. Under this doctrine the contractor must prove a promise made by the supplier, that the supplier intended or should reasonably have expected that the contractor would have relied on the promise, and contractor did in fact rely on the promise by using the supplier's bid in the prime bid.

Vocabulary Checklist

Choice of law
Rescission of contract
Reformation of contract

Majority rule
Minority rule
Drennan rule

James Baird rule
California rule

Review Questions

1. Legally, what are the contractor's options when it makes a mistake in its bid?
2. Will the court order a contractor to perform a construction contract?
3. When can a contractor rescind its contract?
4. What is the simplified rule regarding contractor's mistakes? Compare this with the actual rule.
5. When can the contractor reform its contract?
6. Is your state listed in Appendix A, State Laws Regarding General Contractor Mistakes in Bids? What is the law in your state?
7. Why are there three different rules for subcontractors who make mistakes?

Problems

Answer the issue in each of the following problems by making a legal argument, including premises in support of your answer.

1. The general contractor has prepared a bid on a prime contract. Later that same day it notices that an error was made in its bid, making its bid approximately 30% below that of the next higher bidder. The general contractor informs the owner at the bid opening of the mistake and says it will sue the owner if the owner does not allow it to rescind its bid. No other facts can be proved by a preponderance of the evidence.

   Issue: Can the general contractor rescind its bid without incurring any liability to owner?

   Rule: (*Hint:* Use the simplified rule.)

   Premises:

   Answer: Yes

   Question (can be answered only if Chapter 3, Logic, has been studied): The contractor stated in its argument that it would sue the owner if the owner did not allow it to rescind the bid. Which logical fallacy does this argument contain?

2. Gutierrez Construction sends in a bid for a federal government contract to build a federal courthouse in Denver, Colorado. Later that same day it notices an error in its bid, making its bid approximately 30% below that of the next higher bidder. The error is due to a list of numbers incorrectly added and can easily be fixed by putting the correct total in the space provided. If the contractor can "fix" the error, it will still be the lowest bidder. Gutierrez Construction informs the officer at the bid opening of the mistake. No other facts can be proved by a preponderance of the evidence.

   Issue: Can Gutierrez Construction reform its bid?

   Rule:

   Premises:

   Answer: Yes

3. Compton General Contracting, Inc., submits a bid to the owner on a prime contracting project to build a waterpark. Compton uses Molkentine Concrete's bid of $100,000 to pour concrete. Compton is awarded the prime contract. Meanwhile, Molkentine determines that it made a mistake, and the actual cost to pour the concrete will be $125,000. Molkentine informs Compton immediately; however, Compton was awarded the prime contract a few hours previously. No other facts can be proved by a preponderance of the evidence.

   Issue: Can the subcontractor rescind its bid without incurring any liability to the general contractor?

   Rule: (*Hint:* This issue must be discussed in three different ways using the three different rules.)

   Premises:

   Answer:

4. Zayas and Spalten General Contracting submits a bid to an owner on a prime contract. Zayas has obtained several bids for the concrete, as follows:

Fryas Concrete	$150,000
Millner Concrete	$142,000
Bradley Concrete	$145,000
Williams Concrete	$90,000

After being awarded the contract, Zayas and Spalten General Contracting contacts Woodley Concrete and Quintana Concrete in an effort to get a bid for the concrete that is even lower than Williams Concrete's bid. Neither Woodley nor Quintana will do the job for less than $90,000.

Williams Concrete realizes it made an error in its calculations and informs Zayas and Spalten General Contracting that it will not perform the subcontract, saying its business will probably fold if it is required to perform the contract for $90,000. No other facts can be proved by a preponderance of the evidence.

Issue: Can Williams Concrete rescind its bid without incurring any liability to Zayas and Spalten General Contracting?

Rule: Detrimental reliance by the prime on the sub's bid is the cornerstone on which the courts have based their decisions in holding subcontractors to their bids. It is important that after receipt of the contract the prime not cast doubt on the existence of that reliance. The courts have construed prime contractor bid shopping after contract award to reflect that the prime did not rely on the original subbid but merely used the subbids to ascertain the approximate prices it should bid on each item.

Premises: (*Hint:* Use the preceding rule.)

Answer: Yes

Question (can be answered only if Chapter 3, Logic, has been studied): In this problem the subcontractor commits a logical fallacy in its argument that the contractor must allow it to rescind its bid. Which logical fallacy does this argument contain?

5. Hunt and Rios General Contracting submits a bid to an owner on a prime contract to build a strip mall in California. Hunt has obtained several bids for the electrical, as follows:

Peterson Electrical	$150,000
Millner Electrical	$142,000
Cunningham Electrical	$145,000
Montes Electrical	$140,000

Hunt sends a letter to Montes Electrical informing it that should Hunt and Rios General Contracting be awarded the prime contract to build the strip mall, Hunt and Rios will award the contract to Montes. Montes receives this letter; however, after being awarded the prime contract, Hunt awards the electrical subcontract to Kotz Electrical at $138,000.

Shortly after the project is completed Hunt and Rios dissolve Hunt and Rios General Contracting, and Hunt moves to Canada. Montes discovers that the electrical contract was awarded to Kotz and sues Rios in a California court for breach of contract.

Issue 1: Did Hunt and Rios General Contracting breach the subcontract with Montes?

Rule: (*Hint:* California)

Premises:

Answer: Yes

Issue 2: Is Rios liable for the damages to Montes?

Rule: (*Hint:* See Chapter 6 on forms of businesses.)

Premises:

Answer: Yes

6. Exeter Construction entered into a contract with the State of Massachusetts Department of Transportation (DOT). Five days after receiving a notice to proceed on the contract, Exeter informed DOT of its bid error, which had been caused by an employee's erroneous transcription of a telephone quote. Exeter requested that DOT increase the amount of the contract price, even though Exeter would no longer be the lowest bidder. The error amounted to approximately 18% of the contract price. DOT refused. Exeter commenced work and later sued for the increased amount. No other facts can be proved by a preponderance of the evidence.

Issue: Can Exeter reform its bid?

Rule:

Premises:

Answer: (*Hint:* Either a yes or a no conclusion can be supported depending on your opinion on whether the facts equal or do not equal a part of the rule. If this were a real case, you might research Massachusetts law to see if a court had decided this issue, but for our purposes you can assume no other law exists to help you make this decision.)

7. In a federal contract Daisy Dealer, dealer of manufactured sheds, underbids the Manny Corporation, the manufacturer of the sheds, on a project to erect the sheds.
The bids look like this:

Daisy		**Manny**	
Sheds	$150,000	Sheds	$200,000
Erection of sheds	$150,000	Erection of sheds	$200,000
Total bid	$300,000	*Total bid*	$400,000

After the contracting officer accepts Daisy Dealer's bid, Daisy claims it made a mistake in its bid and that it can get the sheds only for $200,000 from Manny. You can assume Manny will not sell the sheds for less than $200,000. Daisy's employee files an affidavit stating he had had a conversation with an employee of Manny's and that he thought the employee had told him the cost for the sheds would be $150,000. The employee from Manny claims she said the cost of the sheds would be $200,000. Daisy requests that its bid be raised to that of Manny Corporation's on that portion of the job. No other facts can be proved by a preponderance of the evidence.

Issue: Can Daisy's contract be reformed?

Rule: (*Hint:* Federal)

Premises:

Answer: Yes.

8. Workman Electrical, a subcontractor, determines it made an error in the amount of $10,000 on its bid on a federal project. Assume this error can be proved by competent evidence. The subcontractor informs the general contractor, Jennyth Construction, and it asks for the additional $10,000. Jennyth's bid (and now the contract price) to the owner, the U.S. government, was $1.2 million. The next highest bid on the project, $1.35 million, was from Holiday Contracting. The project has been underway for approximately six months.

   What argument can Jennyth make to the federal government to get Workman the additional $10,000? (*Hint:* Federal)

9. Rangel Construction has prepared a bid of $1 million for the construction of an addition to a privately owned hospital. The date to begin construction is August 1, six months after the date scheduled for the bid opening. The profit margin is typical for that of the industry, approximately 3%. Rangel has provided a bid bond of $50,000, as required by the bid package. The Bonding Company is Excalibur Insurance Company.

   The bid package includes AIA A701—1997 (see p. 151).

   At the bid opening the following five bids come in:

Overman Construction:	$1.34 million
Sloan Construction:	$1.33 million
Lebow Construction:	$1.40 million
Beshara Construction:	$1.38 million
Rangel Construction:	$1.0 million

   Rangel finds an error in the amount of $350,000 in its bid. The next day Mr. Flores, an employee of Rangel, informs the owner its bid is rescinded. The owner contacts Excalibur, and tells it to mail the $50,000 check because Rangel has refused to enter into the contract. The owner awards the project to Sloan Construction.

   Issue: Must Excalibur pay the owner the value of the bid bond?

   Rule: (*Hint:* Compare this problem with problem 1. They are the same.)

   Premises:

   Answer: No

10. On a fast-track project Mobil awarded a contract to R&S Company for construction of a phosphate beneficiation plant. R&S negotiated a subcontract with Hardaway for fabrication and installation of above-ground piping. R&S and Hardaway had several communications regarding which of them was responsible for pipe supports that were *not* shown in the drawings but that the parties knew would have to be installed. Hardaway submitted a subcontract to R&S that *excluded* the pipe supports. This subcontract was signed by R&S.

    Later, prior to the commencement of the work, R&S sent a letter to Hardaway rescinding the contract, claiming a mistake. R&S had a subcontract review process whereby a project team first reviewed all subcontract documents; however, in this case the subcontract was erroneously sent to the president without the review and approval of the project team.

Issue: Can R&S rescind the contract?

Rule:

Premises: (*Hint:* Word your answer like this, "If the arbitrator determines . . . ." This problem tests whether you understand the elements or factors of the law. Insufficient evidence exists to come to a definitive conclusion.)

Answer:

Answer to Selected Problem

1. *Facts:* Contractor makes a bid that is 30% below that of next bidder.

   Issue: Can the general contractor rescind its bid without incurring any liability?

   Rule: A contractor can rescind its bid if the mistake is large and work has not yet begun (*simplified rule*). *Note:* Be sure to cite the page number where the rule was found.

   Premises: The law in all jurisdictions allows the general contractor to rescind its bid if the mistake is large and work has not yet begun. In this case the mistake is large, amounting to 30% of the bid. In addition, the mistake is noticed on the same day of the opening, and we have no facts to indicate that work has yet begun. It is unlikely that work begins on the same day as the bid opening. Therefore, both elements of the rule have been satisfied by the facts.

   Answer: Yes

   Question: Appeal to force

Appendix A State Laws Regarding Contractor Mistakes in Bids

Some states have enacted special legislation to cover this situation. For example, in California, the contractor may also reform the bid if the owner is the state of California,[11] but not if the owner is a private person or business entity.[12] In Florida the bid can be rescinded if the mistake is made by an employee of the bidder,[13] but not if actually made by the bidder.[14] In Illinois see *Santucci Constr. Co. v. County of Cook*.[15] In Massachusetts relief is governed by statute,[16] and the bid deposit can be returned in case of "death, disability, bona fide clerical or mechanical error of a substantial nature, or other similar unforeseen circumstances affecting the general bidder." In Michigan see *Kutsche v.*

---

[11]"Relief of Bidders," Cal. Pub. Cont. Code § 5100 *et seq.*

[12]*M. F. Kemper Constr. Co. v. City of Los Angeles,* 37 Cal. 2d 696, 235 P. 2d 7 (1951).

[13]*State Bd. of Control v. Clutter Constr. Corp,* 139 So. 2d 153 Fla. Dist. Ct. App., *cert denied* 146 S. 2d 374 (Fla. 1962).

[14]*Lassiter Constr. Co. v. School Bd.,* 395 So. 567 (Fla. Dist. Ct. App. 1981).

[15]*Santucci Constr. Co. v. County of Cook,* 21 Ill. App. 3d 527, 315 N.E. 2d 565 (1974).

[16]Mass. Gen. Laws. Ann. ch. 149 § 44B.

Ford.[17] In Nebraska see *School District of Scottsbluff v. Olson Construc. Co.*[18] In New Jersey see *Intertech Assocs., Inc. v. City of Patterson.*[19] In New York see *Buffalo Mun. Hous. Auth. v. Gross Plumbing & Heating Co.*[20] In Ohio[21] and Pennsylvania[22] relief is also governed by statute. In Texas see *James T. Taylor & Son, Inc. v. Arlington Indep. School Dist.*[23]

States with law that does not allow the contractor to rescind its bid include Alaska[24] and Kansas.[25] In Alaska a state agency resolved a conflict between a dollar figure printed in numerals and words by following the state regulations, even though this produced a result obviously out of proportion with other bids. The state action was upheld because proper agency regulations had been followed. In Kansas, case law had held that a bid cannot be withdrawn after bid opening, only before. This was despite the fact the bidder had attempted to withdraw its bid shortly after bid opening and before the bids were even considered.

Another alternative method of getting the bid or contract rescinded when the mistake is very large is through the legal doctrine of mistake, summarized by a court as follows:

> *"Where there is a mistake that on its face is so palpable as to place a person of reasonable intelligence upon his guard, there is not a meeting of the minds of the parties and consequently there can be no contract."*[26]

A wide range between the low bid and the other bids puts the owner on notice of possible error.[27] If there is a wide range between the low bid and the other bids, the owner must inquire as to the accuracy of the bid before accepting it.[28]

[17]*Kutsche v. Ford*, 222 Mich. 442, 192 N.W. 714 (1923).

[18]*School District of Scottsbluff v. Olson Constr. Co.*, 45 N.W. 2d 164 (Neb. 1950).

[19]*Intertech Assocs. Inc. v. City of Patterson*, 255 N.J. Super. 52, 604 A. 2d 628 (App. Div. 1992).

[20]*Buffalo Mun. Hous. Auth. v. Gross Plumbing & Heating Co.*, 172 A.D. 2d 1030, 569 N.Y.S. 2d 289 (1991).

[21]Ohio Rev. Code Ann. § 9.31.

[22]Pa. Stat. Ann. tit. 73 § 1601 *et seq.*

[23]*James T. Taylor & Son, Inc. v. Arlington Indep. School Dist.*, 160 Tex. 617, 335 S.W. 2d 371 (1960).

[24]*Alaska International Constr. Inc. v. Earthmovers of Fairbanks, Inc.*, 697 P. 2d 626 (Alaska 1985).

[25]*Anco Constr. Co., Ltd. v. City of Wichita*, 660 P. 2d 560 (Kan. 1983).

[26]*Ex parte Perusini Construction Co.*, 7 So. 2d 576 (Ala. 1942). See also *M. F. Kemper Construction Co. v. City of Los Angeles*, 235 P. 2d 7 (Calif. 1951).

[27]*Moffett, Hodgkins and Clark Co., v. Rochester*, 178 U.S. 373 (1899).

[28]*Hudson Structural Steel Co. v. Smith & Rumery Co.*, 85 A. 384 (Me. 1912).

8

Specifications and Plans

Plans and/or specifications are often the subject of disputes and claims. The ability to perform according to a particular plan or specification, the extent to which a particular plan or specification has been adequately performed, or the party that pays when the construction proves defective are areas where disputes may arise.

Because of the complexity of building specifications, some specifications may be inadequate or may contain errors. Specifications are often "boilerplate." **Boilerplate** is a common term in the law and refers to standard provisions included in similar types of documents. For example, simple wills are often merely boilerplate clauses with only the names changed. In the construction industry many specifications are now boilerplate, that is, taken from a reference book and used in any number of similar sets of specifications. These boilerplate specifications may not be adequate for the particular job and may lead to claims.

When defects in the construction develop, it is not uncommon for everyone to try and lay the responsibility at the door of the "other guy." Architects and engineers may claim that the poor quality of the contractor's construction caused the defect. The contractor may claim that the poor quality of the design caused the construction defect. To further complicate matters, it may be some combination of the two. The owner is often stuck in the middle of this finger-pointing. When the parties cannot agree on where the responsibility lies, issues relating to joint liability and indemnity arise. These topics are discussed in Chapter 16, Joint Liability and Indemnity. This chapter covers law directly relating to plans and specifications.

Defective Construction Caused by Faulty Construction Practices

In determining who is responsible for a construction defect it is necessary to determine whether the defect is caused by faulty construction practices or faulty plans and/or specifications. This may not be easy, but expert witnesses can be employed by the parties to give opinions. An **expert witness** is a witness with specialized knowledge, usually related to a scientific or technical matter. *Only expert witnesses are allowed to give opinion testimony at trial.* In arbitration proceedings the rules of evidence are not as stringent and it is possible that parties involved in the claim will be entitled to give opinions. Of course, the arbitrators are not required to accept those opinions.

Defective Construction Caused by Faulty Construction Practices

Rule: The contractor is responsible to the owner for defective construction caused by faulty construction practices.

If the defect is caused by faulty construction practices, the liability rests with the contractor, and the contractor must remedy the defect or be in breach of the contract. The contractor usually remedies this type of contract breach by fixing the defect or being paid less than the agreed-on price for the project. The owner cannot generally terminate the contract for defective construction unless the defective construction amounts to a material breach. The concept of material breach is discussed in more detail in Chapter 14, Termination of the Contract and Contract Damages.

Defective Construction Caused by Defective Plans or Specifications

Liability for defects in the construction caused by defective plans and/or specifications depends on the relationship of the parties involved. From the contractor's standpoint the liability rests with the owner if the owner's designer has prepared the plans and specifications. Unless the designer has agreed to guarantee the plans and specifications, the liability will rest with the owner unless the defect arises to the level of a malpractice.

In recent years, however, more and more design responsibility has been placed on the general contractor and the specialty subcontractors. With the increase in complexity of systems, it is more likely, for example, that the HVAC (heating, ventilation, and air conditioning) subcontractor is better able than the architect to design an adequate HVAC system for a particular project. If the contractor or subcontractor is responsible for designing a portion of the project, such as the HVAC system, the contractor or subcontractor will be responsible for assuring that the design is adequate to perform the job.

It is not uncommon for contracts to define the responsibility and liability of architect, contractor, and subcontractor for the design of specific systems. For example, the following provisions put the responsibility for the design of a wastewater filtration system on the subcontractor:

> *1.3.C.1 Hydro Engineering, Manufacturer and supplier of the wastewater filtration system shall be solely responsible for the performance of the wastewater filtration system as specified and shall modify, add to, or alter the equipment as necessary, without any additional cost to Government to provide a satisfactory performance.*

The advantage to the contractor in the preceding contractual relationship is that should the wastewater system fail, the owner has agreed that only the subcontractor, not the contractor, is responsible.

If the contract fails to place liability for a specific system on a particular party, the law will do so. In general, the owner is responsible for performance of *design specifications,* and the contractor is responsible for the performance of *performance specifications.* In addition to design and performance specifications, there are *combination* and *or-equal specifications.* Each of these categories of specifications is discussed more fully in this section.

Design Specifications

Liability for Design Specifications

A **design specification** tells the contractor what to do and does not leave anything to the contractor to design. Historically, this has been the most common type of specification prepared by design professionals.

> *Design specifications explicitly state how the contract is to be performed and permit no deviation . . . Detailed design specifications contain an implied warranty that if they are followed, an acceptable result will be produced . . . Performance specifications, on the other hand, specify the results to be obtained and leave it to the contractor to determine how to achieve those results.*[1]

Defective Construction Caused by Faulty Design Specifications

Rule: The owner is responsible to the contractor for defective construction caused by faulty *design* specifications.

The designer does not warrant that the plans and specifications will be free from defects, so the designer is generally not liable to the owner.

---

[1] *Stuyvesant Dredging Co. v. US.,* 834 F.3d 1576, 1582 (1987).

The following are examples of design specifications:

    a. Provide welded-wire units prefabricated into straight lengths of not less than 10 feet coverage on exterior exposures and 1/2 inch elsewhere. Wire sizes: Side rod diameter: 0.1483 inch. Cross rod diameter: 0.1483 inch.

    b. Provide waterstops at all construction joints and other joints in all foundations walls below grade and where shown on the drawings.

Liability for the performance of a design specification is on the owner. In other words, if the construction proves to be faulty, the contractor is not responsible for paying to fix the problem—the owner is responsible. This concept has been called the **Spearin warranty** or **Spearin doctrine** from the United States Supreme Court case *United States v. Spearin*.[2] Although *Spearin* is not applicable to the states, but only to federal construction projects, a similar warranty has been adopted in many state jurisdictions.

8-1. THINK

Why is the *Spearin* warranty not state law unless the state adopts it?
Hint: Refer to the River of Law in Chapter 1.

Claims between the Owner and the Design Professional

If the plans and specifications prove to be defective, the owner may seek reimbursement from the design professional for any sums it pays to remedy the defects. This is difficult to do, and the owner is not likely to be entitled to relief from the design professional for minor faults and defects in the plans and specifications. The reason for this is that unless the designer has specifically guaranteed or warranted that the plans and specifications will conform to the owner's desires or intentions or be perfect, *the designer is not an insurer of perfect plans.* If the designer has conformed to the prevailing standard of professional care, then the liability for the defective plans stays with the owner.

For example, if the designer has made an error that costs $200 to fix, the designer has probably acted within the "prevailing standard of professional care," and the owner, not the designer, must pay the $200 to the contractor. The designer is not liable to the owner for reimbursement.[3,4] Of course, the owner may decide not to hire a designer in the future based on such occurrences, but that is not a legal issue.

The designer's relationship to the owner is discussed in Chapter 6, Relationships Among the Parties on the Project. This relationship is usually one of principal–agent, with

---

[2]*United States v. Spearin*, 248 U.S. 132, 39 S. Ct. 59, 63 L. Ed. 166 (1918).

[3]*Gravely v. Providence Partnership*, 549, F.2d 958 (4th Cir. 1977).

[4]*First National Bank v. Cann*, 503 F. Supp. 419 (N.D. Ohio), *aff'd.* 669 F.2d 415 (6th Cir. 1982).

the designer being the agent of the owner. A principal–agent relationship is more similar to an employer–employee relationship. In an employer–employee relationship the employer generally absorbs the cost of employee mistakes.

Claims between the Contractor and the Design Professional

Because the contractor and the design professional are not in **privity of contract,** that is, there is no contractual relationship between them, neither can sue the other for breach of contract. The only duties that exist between contractors and design professionals are those established by law. Duties established by law are tort duties and are discussed in Chapter 15, Torts and Tort Damages.

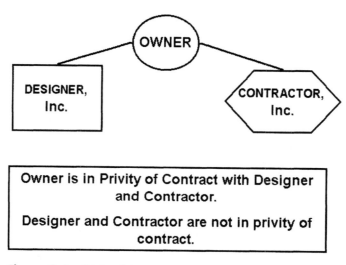

Figure 8-1 Privity of contract

In general, most jurisdictions do not recognize any tort duty between the design professional and the contractor relating to the design of the plans and specifications. This lack of a legally recognized duty between the design professional and the contractor prevents the contractor from collecting damages from the design professional for extra or changed work caused by defective plans and specifications. The contractor can collect only from the owner.

Application of *Spearin* to Availability of Materials or Fixtures

What happens when the plans or specifications call for a particular fixture, but the fixture is not available when needed by the contractor? Can the contractor claim that the *Spearin* doctrine warrants the availability of the fixture? The courts have consistently held no. The *Spearin* warranty warrants only that the particular fixture will be available, it does not warrant that the fixture will be available at any certain time. The contractor must ascertain whether the materials and fixtures it needs to complete the project are available in accordance with the project's schedule.

Availability of Materials or Fixtures

Rule: The contractor is responsible for making sure that all materials and fixtures are supplied to the project when needed to complete the work.

The owner warrants only that the specified materials and fixtures will be available, not when they will be available.

Of course, if the fixture is no longer available, or the delay in obtaining the fixture reaches the point of practical impossibility or commercial senselessness, the contractor may be excused from obtaining a particular fixture. The contractor could seek protection under doctrines of impossibility of performance or the commercial senselessness discussed later in this chapter.

Performance Specifications

If the specification tells the contractor only what the final performance of the system is to be but allows the contractor latitude in how to achieve that performance, the specification is called a **performance specification.** Liability for performance specifications rests with the contractor.

Defective Construction Caused by Faulty Performance Specifications

Rule: The contractor is responsible to the owner for defective construction caused by faulty performance specifications.

Examples of performance specifications follow:

> *a. Thoroughly clean forms and adjacent surfaces to receive concrete. Remove chips, wood, sawdust, dirt, and all other debris just prior to concrete placement. Retighten forms and bracing prior to concrete placement as required to prevent mortar leaks and maintain proper alignment.*

Notice that this specification does not tell the contractor how to clean the forms, how to remove the debris, or how to retighten the forms. The contractor is free to develop its own methods to do this work. Should a problem later develop because the forms were not clean or because the mortar leaked, the contractor is responsible for the damage.

> *b. Furnish, install, operate, and maintain all necessary pumping for dewatering the various parts of the work and for maintaining free of water the foundations, and such other parts of the work as required for construction operations.*

Notice that this specification gives the contractor only the results to be achieved: dewatering. The method for dewatering is left to the contractor or subcontractor. Should the dewatering prove to be inadequate, the contractor, not the owner or architect, will be responsible for damages.

Combination Specifications

Of course, many, if not most, specifications contain both design and performance characteristics. This type of specification is called a **combination specification.** For example, the first example of a design specification (on p. 169) states,

> *Provide welded-wire units prefabricated into straight lengths of not less than 10 feet coverage on exterior exposures, and 1/2 inch elsewhere.*

It could be argued that this specification has some performance specification characteristics because it does not tell the contractor *how* to place the welded-wire units. If we assume no other specification instructs the contractor how or where to place the wire-welded units, then the specification is a combination specification. Should a problem develop because of defective placement of the welded-wire units, the contractor is responsible.

Defective Construction Caused by Faulty Combination Specifications

Rule: The contractor is responsible to the owner for defective construction caused by the performance part of the specification, and the owner is responsible for the faulty part of the design specification.

The following are additional examples of combination specifications:

> a. *Pitch new roofing surfaces, and shape "crickets" to provide continuous runoff and drainage to locations of roof drains* (performance.) *Set drains at 1 inch above deck level on new roofs* (design). *Gradually taper foam approximately 12-inch radius from roof drains down to minimum 1 inch thick at drain ring; build into drain* (design).
>
> b. *Silicone rubber coating shall be applied* (performance) *in three separate and distinct coats* (design). *Materials shall be applied to horizontal surfaces in three coats* (design) *of contrasting colors to ensure complete coverage and uniformity* (performance).

Determining liability for a problem related to a combination specification requires the arbitrator, court, or jury to determine whether the specific problem is related to design (liability falls on owner/design professional) or performance (liability falls on contractor). It is likely that the parties will employ expert witnesses to help the arbitrator, judge, or jury decide this issue.

Or-Equal Specifications

An **or-equal specification** is generally a design specification, but with the terms *or equal* or *approved substitution* after it. Such specifications are particularly common in government contracts, where they are often mandated by law. Because it is a design specification the designer is responsible for performance of the specification. If the contractor substitutes an or-equal or obtains an approved substitution, the specification becomes a performance specification, and the contractor becomes responsible for performance. *Once the specification becomes a performance specification, designer approval will not change it back into a design specification.* In other words, just because the designer approves the substitution does not mean that the designer is responsible for the contractor's substitution. Most contracts make this concept clear. (See the maxim of law, "liability follows responsibility.")

Examples of or-equal specifications are the following:

a. *White LCS Writing Surface or equal with 24-gauge porcelain enameled steel face on 3/8-inch foil-backed particleboard.*

b. *Floor-supported, overhead-braced, Sanymetal "Normandie" model, or approved substitution, minimum 58 inches high.*

**Defective Construction Caused by Faulty Or-Equal Specification:
No Substitution Made by Contractor**

Rule: The owner is responsible for defective construction caused by an or-equal specification if the contractor does not substitute an or-equal into the specification.

A question can arise as to liability when the original system required by the specification would not have performed adequately and neither does the system substituted by the contractor. Who is responsible? Since the contractor is responsible only for performance as required by the contract specifications, the contractor should not be not responsible for the damages. This area is, however, under legal development and not settled in all jurisdictions.

**Defective Construction Caused by Faulty Or-Equal Specification:
Made Substitution by Contractor**

Rule: The contractor is responsible for defective construction caused by contractor's substitution, unless the original specification was also defective.

Note: This rule is not yet well established.

8-2. THINK

Fill in the following table. Do *not* assume defective or shoddy work on the contractor's part except in the last column.

Type of Specification	Party Responsible to Owner When Design Will Not Perform As the Owner Wants It To	Is Contractor Able to Apply Own Methods or Design?	Does the Spearin Doctrine Apply?	Party Responsible to Owner When Product Fails to Perform because of Shoddy Installation
Design				
Performance				
Combination				
Or-equal				

Other Concepts Relevant to Specifications

Strict Compliance vs. Substantial Compliance/Completion/Performance

Owners and/or designers often believe that the contractor must build the project in strict conformance with the plans and specifications in order to be entitled to payment or final payment; however, the *law requires only that the contractor "substantially comply" with the plans and specifications in order to be entitled to payment.* If the contractor's failures are relatively minor, the owner may deduct a reasonable cost to repair the items from the final payment.

**Performance Required by Contractor and
Payment Required by Owner**

Rule: The contractor is required to substantially comply with the plans
and specifications.

Upon substantial completion of the plans and specifications the owner is
required to pay the contractor minus a reasonable sum to fix any minor defects
in the work.

The law generally states that the contractor is entitled to final payment, minus reasonable deductions for defective or incomplete work, when the project has been substantially completed. The contract documents may state otherwise, but the law controls. For example, assume that on a certain project an air conditioning chiller unit was wired incorrectly, but the unit can be operated on another circuit.[5] The contractor is entitled to payment. Of course, if the facts are even slightly different, the result may be different. Assume that on another project the chiller unit was wired incorrectly, and the building cannot be used because of the temperature. Substantial completion has not occurred.[6] As you can see, substantial completion will depend on the facts of each situation.

As a general rule, substantial completion is measured by the ability of the project to perform; however, if aesthetics is an important part of the project, failure to complete that aspect may prevent substantial performance. For example, assume that the owner of a casino facility awarded a contract for renovation of the rooms and erection of a new glass facade. The facade, although nonfunctional, was intended to attract customers to the renovated property. The project will not be substantially completed until the facade is constructed. This is true even though the interior work has been finished.[7]

Causation

The concept of **causation** is, for many, difficult to grasp at first. People unfamiliar with the law have a tendency to think that a mistake or breach of contract means that the mistaken party must pay for *any* problem that exists. For example, assume the contractor has breached the contract by installing the incorrect type of roof tiles, and a heavy rain causes rain damage to the interior of the structure. Many people, even contractors, erroneously believe that the contractor must pay for the damage to the interior of the structure. Legally, however, the contractor is not required to pay for the damage because no evidence exists that installing the incorrect type of roof tiles *caused* the interior damage. The interior damage may have been caused by a faulty design specification. The owner must prove causation, and if the owner cannot do so, the contractor is not liable for the damages.

> **Causation**
>
> *Rule:* Even if the contractor breaches the contract, the contractor is liable only for damage the owner can prove the contractor caused, not for all damage that exists.

---

[5] See *Appeal of Hill Construction Corp.*, ASBCA No. 43615 (March 29, 1993); CCM June 1993, p. 4.

[6] *O & M Construction, Inc. v. State of Louisiana*, 576 So. 2d 1030 (La. App. 1991); CCM July 1991, p. 6.

[7] *Perini Corp. v. Greate Bay Hotel & Casino, Inc.*, 610 A.2d 364 (N.J. 1992); CCM November 1992, p. 2.

In the following examples no proof of causation exists, therefore the contractor is not liable for the damages.

EXAMPLES:

1. Contractor paints the kitchen white instead of pale yellow as called for in the specifications. Cracks develop in the foundation. It costs the owner $30,000 to fix the foundation. Contractor is not required to pay the owner $30,000 to fix the foundation. There is no evidence that failing to paint the walls white instead of pale yellow caused the cracks to develop in the foundation.

2. Contractor is hired to put an addition, including a new roof, onto a retail store. After the project is completed the roof leaks over the new addition. Owner incurs $10,000 in damage to carpets and furniture. Assuming that the owner can prove nothing other than these facts, the contractor is not required to pay $10,000 for damage to the carpets and furniture. In this example not only is there no evidence of causation, there is no evidence the contractor breached the contract.

3. Contractor is hired to put an addition onto an existing structure. The plans and specifications call for the removal of a certain section of concrete and the placement of rebar in the existing and in the new concrete to attach the old slab to the new slab. Several months after the job is finished the owner notices cracking in the walls and ceiling. Excavation is completed, and it is determined that the contractor never removed the section of old concrete, as required by the plans and specifications. The contractor did attach rebar between the old and new slabs, but not in the place indicated in the plans. It costs the owner $25,000 to fix the cracking in the walls and ceiling. Assuming that the owner can prove nothing other than these facts, the contractor is not required to pay $25,000 to repair the cracking in the walls and ceiling. There is no evidence that failing to put the rebar in the slab at the indicated points caused the cracks in the walls and ceiling.   ■ ■ ■

The case of *Doyle Wilson Homebuilder, Inc. v. Pickens* is a good example of a court's refusing to assume causation.[8] Pickens, the homeowner, sued the general contractor and the electrical subcontractor for damages to his home caused by a fire. Pickens's expert ruled out all other causes of the fire except for a problem with the wiring. The defendant's expert testified that the wiring had been inspected and approved. He also testified, "there were a number of tradespersons . . . such as plumbers, carpenters, and air conditioning

---

[8]*Doyle Wilson Homebuilder, Inc. v. Pickens*, 996 S. W. 2d 876 (Tex. App. 1999).

installers. After the electrical installation was performed, [the electrical subcontractor] had no control over who was allowed to work around the electrical lines." The court stated, "While numerous witnesses testified in the present case, the record reveals a lack of evidence of the fire's cause . . . causation may not be presumed."

Objective Impossibility

The law does not always require a contractor to perform the contract. In other words, there are times when the basic maxim of contract law "a party must perform its contract or respond in damages" is *not* upheld.

A contractor who cannot perform a contract or some portion of the contract is not required to perform or pay damages if performance is *objectively impossible.* By **objective impossibility** is meant that the specification is impossible for a disinterested third party, called an *objective third party,* to perform. For example, if the contract requires the contractor to install Ace Manufacturer Fixture #23A, but Ace does not, and never did, manufacture a fixture #23A, it is impossible for the contractor to install that fixture. Has the contractor breached the contract? Technically yes, however, the law will relieve the contractor from liability for breach of contract under the doctrine of objective impossibility.

Objective Impossibility

Rule: A contractor is not required to perform a specification or plan that is objectively impossible to perform. A specification or plan is objectively impossible to perform if a disinterested third party (not the contractor) could not perform the plan or specification.

EXAMPLE:

The contract between the owner and the contractor requires the contractor to install a government-furnished boiler so that it attains a certain level of efficiency detailed in the specifications. However, after installation, problems develop. The government sues the contractor, claiming it has breached the contract. The claimed breach is the contractor's failure to attain the level of efficiency prescribed in the contract. Experts testify that the boiler is incapable of attaining the level of efficiency prescribed under the contract for its operation and maintenance. The contractor is excused from performance under the doctrine of "impossibility of performance." Since the government was required to furnish the boiler to be used, the contractor is excused from its breach of the contract.[9] ■ ■ ■

---

[9]*American Hydrotherm Corp.* ASBCA 5678, 60-1 BCA ¶ 2617 (1960), 2. G.C. ¶352.

If the performance is merely *subjectively impossible* to perform, the law will still require the contractor to perform the contract or pay damages. **Subjective impossibility** is personal impossibility or impossibility because the subject or person under discussion cannot perform for some personal reason—for example, if the contractor lacks the experience or the ability to perform or has some internal problem that prevents it from complying with the specification.

If the contractor takes a calculated risk as to its ability to perform, it must bear the consequences.[10] In other words, the objective impossibility doctrine is a shield to prevent unfairness, but it cannot be used by a contractor who knowingly accepts a risk.

Practical Impossibility/Commercial Senselessness

Much more common than the problem of objective impossibility is the problem of **practical impossibility,** also referred to as **commercial senselessness.** In the construction industry it is usually possible to achieve almost any result as long as enough money is poured into the project—and if it is the contractor's money getting poured into the project, the owner does not care about the difficulty of performing a specification. The owner wants the contractor to "just do it," and for most specifications that is what the contractor must do.

However, courts do not like the idea of waste, particularly when some unforeseen intervening event or condition has occurred, making the contract more expensive to perform than the contractor had originally contemplated. At some point a court is going to give the contractor relief, meaning the contractor may not have to comply with a certain specification, if the specification is impractical due to extreme expense.

Practical Impossibility

Rule: A contractor is not required to perform a specification or plan if performance of the specification is impractical due to extreme expense.

Figure 8–2 illustrates the concept of practical impossibility or commercial senselessness. At point A on the chart (inside the circle) the contractor must perform the contract, even if it costs more (or less) to do so than it anticipated at the point it entered into the contract. However, if an event occurs that causes the project cost to rise beyond that circle, the court will grant the contractor relief. The exact point at which a court will grant relief depends on the facts of the particular case.

Notice that some event must occur to trigger this doctrine. For example, assume that the contractor enters into a contract to install solid gold fixtures in a bathroom. The contractor cannot be relieved from liability for performing this contract simply because it is a lot less expensive to use brass fixtures. The contractor must perform the contract and install solid gold fixtures. However, if under the same contract the price of gold goes up tenfold, the court or arbitrator might grant the contractor relief under the doctrine of practical impossibility.

---

[10] *Natus Corporation v. United States,* 371 F.2d 450 (Ct. Cl. 1967).

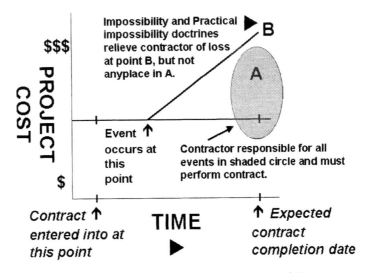

Figure 8-2 Contractor relief from practical impossibility event

As with objective impossibility, the practical impossibility must be objective, that is, practically impossible for an objective, third-party contractor. If the practical impossibility is only subjectively impossible, that is, impossible due to the contractor's shortcomings, incompetence, lack of diligence, lack of proper equipment, or inadequate financing, the contractor is still liable for damages to the owner. As with the doctrine of impossibility, if the contractor takes a calculated risk as to its ability to perform, it must bear the consequences.

Approval of Shop Drawings

Owner or architect/engineer approval of shop drawings does not relieve the contractor from compliance with the plans and specifications. In addition, designer approval of shop drawings or other submittals pertaining to a performance specification or an or-equal specification does not change the specification into a design specification.

Designer Approval of Shop Drawings

Rule: Designer approval of submittals or shop drawings does not change the contractor's responsibility to perform according to the original plans and specifications.

EXAMPLE:

For example, the plans and specifications contain explicit detail outlining how the fire alarm system is to be wired. The subcontractor, Sharp, submits shop drawings that change the wiring, and the designer approves the shop drawings. The owner subsequently directs Sharp to tear out and replace the fire alarm wiring because it deviates from the specifications. Sharp is not entitled to any payment for tearing out and replacing the wiring because designer approval of a shop drawing does not relieve the contractor or subcontractor from performing according to the original plans and specifications. Perhaps if the shop drawing submittal expressly called the change in the wiring to the designer's attention, the theory of waiver, discussed in a later section, might be applicable.   ■ ■ ■

Open, Obvious, and Apparent Defects in the Plans and Specifications

What if the contractor knows or should have known that a specification would cause a problem? In that case *the contractor must warn the owner or designer of the potential problem.* Failure to do so could require the contractor to correct the defect at its cost. Many contracts contain a provision stating that the contractor has this duty. Although this issue has not been litigated in every jurisdiction, many courts have upheld the duty of the contractor to inform the owner of a defect.

Open, Obvious, and Apparent Defects in the Plans and Specifications

Rule: A contractor is required to inform the owner of open, obvious, or apparent defects in the plans and specifications. Failure to do so could result in contractor liability for damages.

8-3. THINK

What is the factual issue that always arises when this topic becomes an issue?

Open, Obvious, and Apparent Defects in the Work

In general, the owner is precluded from later attempting to collect for open, obvious, and apparent defects in the work. That is, if the owner or the owner's agent does not complain about a defect at or near the time the defective work is completed, the owner cannot later claim damages. At or near substantial completion of the project, when the time has come to pay the contractor the retainage, the owner may go around the project and try to find defects in order to subtract the cost of repair from the retainage to be paid to the contractor. This list of defects is commonly called the **punch list.** The use of the punch list is so common in the industry it is likely that an arbitrator or judge will require the contractor to fix or repair items on the punch list or to pay damages. The only time the law might step in is if the owner attempts to abuse the privilege.

Waiver and Acceptance

A **waiver** is the knowing relinquishment of a known right. A waiver requires proof of facts showing that the parties acted differently than required by the contract. Often the real issue in a waiver case is whether the evidence is sufficient to prove that a waiver has occurred. Ultimately the arbitrator, judge, or jury will weigh the evidence and come to a decision.

Waiver

Rule: Any plan, specification or clause of a contract can be waived, despite language attempting to nullify this right in the contract.
A waiver is the knowing relinquishment of a known right.

Any plan, specification, or clause of a contract can be waived despite contract language requiring all waivers or modifications to the contract to be in writing. A provision requiring all waivers and modifications to be in writing can be waived. A waiver is generally *proved by evidence of conduct* showing that a party has waived its right to receive some benefit to which it is entitled. If the contractor installs a different fixture than the one called for in the contract, and the architect is aware of this, then the architect (and the owner, assuming that the architect is the owner's agent) by never complaining or ordering the contractor to install the fixture called for in the specification, waives the requirement of the original fixture.

EXAMPLE:

For example, in the case of *Consolidated Electrical Distributors of El Paso v. Peinado* a supplier to a plumbing contractor sued the general contractor for failing to issue joint checks pursuant to a joint-check agreement between the supplier, the plumbing subcontractor, and the general contractor.[11] The joint-check agreement stated that the general contractor would issue only joint checks payable to the plumbing subcontractor and the plumbing supplier, and deliver the checks to the supplier. The parties then acted contrary to this joint-check agreement— the general contractor issued checks for the plumbing work directly to the subcontractor. The checks contained only the plumbing subcontractor's name as the payee. The supplier never made any objection until late in the contract when the subcontractor failed to pay the supplier for a large amount of supplies. The supplier sued the general contractor for breach of the joint-check agreement. The court determined that the supplier had waived the provisions of the joint-check agreement.

---

[11]*Consolidated Electrical Distributors of El Paso v. Peinado,* 478 S.W.2d 565 (Tex. App. 1972), *no writ*).

Acceptance is a form of waiver. **Acceptance** occurs in the specific situation in which the owner has accepted work with the knowledge of patent (obvious) defects. The owner cannot require the contractor to repair or replace patently defective work once the owner has accepted the project. Occupancy itself is not always acceptance under the AIA A201, which reads "entire use or occupancy of the Project by the Owner shall not constitute acceptance of Work not in accordance with the Contract Documents." This provision has been upheld, but certainly at some point the owner must be considered to have accepted the project. The acceptance doctrine never applies to latent (not obvious) defects.   ■ ■ ■

Acceptance

Rule: The owner is not entitled to damages or compensation for patent defects
in work it has accepted.

It is typical for the owner to be very happy when a project is completed and to accept the work. However, several months later, after the honeymoon is over, some owners want the contractor to return and repair items that were defective or left out of the project. This rule prevents the contractor from having to do this.

Exculpatory or Onerous Clauses

Parties to contracts may attempt to insert clauses in the contract that attempt to nullify important or fundamental legal rights. These types of clauses are called **exculpatory clauses** or **onerous clauses.** Another description used is to that these clauses **violate public policy.** Such clauses are not upheld by the courts.

Exculpatory or Onerous Clauses or Clauses that Violate Public Policy

Rule: An exculpatory or onerous clause, or a clause that violates public policy,
is a clause that attempts to nullify important or fundamental legal rights.
The law will not uphold these types of clauses, but the law uses this
doctrine sparingly.

For example, it is possible to find U.S. government contracts with the following language, which attempts to negate the *Spearin* warranty or *Spearin* doctrine:

The government does not warrant the plans and specifications.
or
The Owner is not responsible for the adequacy of the plans and specifications.

or

If either party retains an attorney to advise or enforce this contract, the contract is null and void.

It is unlikely that a court will uphold such provisions, because they are exculpatory or onerous.

As another example of an exculpatory clause, the contractor may include a clause that attempts to void or waive the implied warranty of habitability and/or implied warranty to build in a good and workmanlike manner. These warranties are discussed in Chapter 13, Warranties. Clauses attempting to negate warranties are routinely considered unenforceable by the courts.[12]

The attitude of the courts toward such clauses is expressed in *People ex rel. Department of Pub. Works & Bldgs. v. South East Natl. Bank of Chicago:*[13]

> *"Where the conditions requisite to relief are present, equity will act* in spite of a contract *to avoid the unconscionable result."* (emphasis added)

A word of caution is warranted here however. Courts use this theory only in extreme cases, and not all jurisdictions draw the same lines. For example, a contract might contain a provision that states that a party to the contract agrees not to oppose a Motion for Relief from Automatic Stay should one of the parties file a bankruptcy. This automatic stay precludes creditors from engaging in activity to collect on their debt once the bankruptcy is filed. Some courts have upheld this contract provision, whereas others have refused to uphold it. The automatic stay in bankruptcy is discussed in Chapter 17, Bankruptcy.

Vocabulary Checklist

Boilerplate	Causation	Open, obvious, and apparent defects
Design specifications	Objective impossibility	in construction
Spearin doctrine or warranty	Subjective impossibility	Punch list
Performance specifications	Practical impossibility aka	Waiver
Combination specifications	commercial senselessness	Acceptance
Or-equal specifications	Designer approval of shop	Exculpatory clauses
Strict compliance vs.	drawings	
substantial compliance	Obvious defects in specifications	

Review Questions

1. Name some problems that can arise with plans and specifications.

2. When the construction is defective, and the defect is caused by faulty construction practices, who is responsible?

---

[12]See *Melody Home Mfg. Co. v. Barnes,* 741 S.W.2d 349 (Tex. 1987).

[13] 131 Ill. App. 2d 238; 266 N.E.2d 778 (1971).

3. When the construction is defective, and the defect is caused by faulty plans and specifications, who is responsible?

4. How has responsibility for the design of a project changed recently?

5. Why is it important to know the type of specification?

6. What happens when the plans or specifications call for a particular fixture, but the fixture is not available *when needed* by the contractor?

7. According to the maxims of law, what follows responsibility?

8. Does the law require the contractor to build exactly according to the plans and specifications?

9. What is correct, and what is incorrect with this statement:

> "The contractor must pay for all problems exhibited by the construction."

10. On rare occasions, it is possible for the contractor to legally be excused from performing (get out of) a part of the contract, even though it is possible for the contractor to do the work. When can this occur?

11. What does the law say about an open, obvious defect in the work?

12. What does the law say about an obvious error in the plans and specifications?

13. How is the waiver doctrine or rule relevant to plans and specifications?

14. How is the onerous doctrine or rule relevant to plans and specifications?

Problems

1. Identify the type of specification each of the following represents:

    a. *Install drainage course on horizontal and vertical surfaces in accordance with the manufacturer's recommendations.*

    b. *Fabric Placement: Position the fabric over the insulation as follows: Overlap the edges a minimum of 1 foot. Install the fabric so that no joints will exist between the sheets parallel to and within 6 feet of the roof perimeter.*

    c. *Install steel overhead coiling doors designed to withstand a windload of 20 psf.*

    d. *Store materials inside under cover, stack flat, off floor. Stack wallboard so that long lengths are not over short lengths. Avoid overloading floor systems. Store adhesives in a dry area. Provide protection against freezing.*

    In each of the remaining problems, answer the issue in each problem by making a legal argument, including premises, in support of your answer.

2. The following specification exists in a certain construction contract between Kevin Construction and the owner:

    e. *Install drainage course on horizontal and vertical surfaces in accordance with the manufacturer's recommendations.*

After completion of the project, a storm hits the area. The drainage course proves inadequate to handle the runoff and causes leakage that causes some damage to ceiling and flooring tiles amounting to $10,000. The owner makes a claim against the contractor for those damages, claiming the contractor did not install the drainage course per the manufacturer's recommendations. The owner argues that any decent contractor would have installed the drainage course properly or would at least pay the damages. The drainage course extended for approximately 137 feet, and two screws were found to be lacking. No other facts can be proved by a preponderance of the evidence.

Issue: Is Kevin Construction liable to the owner for the damage to the ceiling and flooring?

Issue: (*Hint:* Causation)

Rule: (*Hint:* Causation)

Premises:

Answer: No

Question (can be answered only if Chapter 3, Logic, has been studied): In this problem the owner argues that any decent contractor would have installed the drainage course properly or would at least pay the damages. Which logical fallacy does this argument contain?

3. Owner and Ace Construction entered into a construction agreement for a paddock to be constructed on owner's property at a cost of $25,000. The paddock is attached to an existing barn. Ace gave the owner a one-year-warranty, and Ace agreed to repair or replace defects should the paddock prove defective. During that same year the owner notices that the barn, to which the paddock is attached, has developed some cracks and sags. The owner employs Pace Contracting to remedy the cracks and sags in the barn, and it sends the bill to Ace, requesting that Ace pay it. Pace's charge is reasonable and, in fact, is lower than Ace would have charged to do similar work. The amount of the bill is $5000. Ace refuses to pay the bill. The owner argues that Ace is responsible for the damage to the barn because the cracks appeared after Ace attached the paddock to it.

   The owner claims that Ace Construction is liable to owner for damages because the barn did not sag prior to the installation of the paddock and therefore the installation of the paddock caused the barn to sag.

Issue: Is Ace liable for the damage to the barn?

Alternative wording of *Issue:* Is there proof of causation?

Rule: (*Hint:* Causation)

Premises:

Answer: No

Question (can be answered only if Chapter 3, Logic, has been studied): In this problem the owner argues that Ace is responsible for the damage to the barn because the cracks appeared after Ace attached the paddock to it. Which logical fallacy does this argument contain?

4. A masonry subcontract required Milton Masonry, the subcontractor, to parge the inner face of a brick wall and to use Z brand galvanized ties. The subcontractor did not use the specified ties and did not parge the walls. The prime contractor's project manager, Ms. Pallanca, never objected, though she saw the work being done in this manner over a one-month period. The owner's representative, Mr. Rosen, never objected, even though he was on site, and he saw the

work being done in this manner on at least one occasion. The prime contractor withheld Milton's payment of $25,000 because the owner refused to pay for the work.

Issue: Is the subcontractor entitled to payment from the contractor?

Rule: (*Hint:* Waiver). You also may use this rule: Parties are presumed to know the contents of their contracts.

Premises:

Answer: Yes

5. Campos Contracting agreed to install a 50' × 72' steel building for $11,000. Prior to occupying the building the owner made the following complaints to the contractor: cracked concrete ramp, leaks at the base of wall panels, and sliding door problems. Campos admitted the defects, calculated the cost of repair to be $1225, and asked the owner to pay $9775. The owner countered that the basic premise of contract law states that a party must perform its contract, and since Campos did not perform, Campos is not entitled to payment. No other facts can be proved by a preponderance of the evidence.

Issue 1: Is the owner liable to Campos for any amount of money?

Issue: (*Hint:* Substantial completion, performance)

Rule: (*Hint:* Substantial completion, performance)

Premises:

Answer: Yes

Question (can be answered only if Chapter 3, Logic, has been studied): In this problem the owner counters that the basic premise of contract law states that a party must perform its contract, and since Campos did not perform, Campos is not entitled to payment. Which logical fallacy does this argument contain?

6. The contract contains the following clauses:

> 7.1 *The contractor may be granted an extension of time because of changes ordered in the Contract or because of strikes, lockouts, fire, unusual delay in transportation, unavoidable casualties, unusual inclement weather, or any cause beyond the Contractor's control that constitutes a justifiable delay.*
>
> 7.2 *The contractor shall not be granted an extension of time or other damages because of hindrance or interference of the contractor by the owner or its agents, delay caused by owner, delayed or restricted site access, owner's failure to coordinate several prime contractors, defective plans and specifications, delay in approvals, or failure to make timely progress payments.*

The owner causes a delay by failing to turn over the site on time. Damages to the contractor are $50,000.

Issue: Is clause 7.2 enforceable?

Rule: (*Hint:* Onerous)

Premises:

Answer: No

7. The Met Transit Authority awarded a contract to Atkinson Construction Co. for construction of earth tunnels as part of a rapid rail transit system. The specification called for the final tunnel liner to be able to withstand a load $2\frac{1}{2}$ times greater than the actual estimated load. Soon after the contract award, Atkinson submitted a change request proposing a different design for the tunnel liner. Atkinson estimated that the change would save Atkinson $1 million. After extensive technical investigation and negotiation, the change was accepted by the owner and approved by the owner's engineer; however, because of a slight misalignment of the tunnel, the final tunnel liner was thinner in some areas and had to be reinforced with steel in order to achieve the specified load bearing capacity of $2\frac{1}{2}$ times the actual estimated load. Atkinson filed a claim for additional work for reinforcing the liner. Atkinson also claimed that since the owner's engineer approved the change in the design of the tunnel liner, the owner is required to pay for the reinforcing steel.

Issue 1: Is Atkinson entitled to compensation for the steel reinforcement?

Rule: (*Hint:* Performance specification)

Premises:

Answer: No

Issue 2: Does the approval of the specification by the owner's designer absolve the contractor of responsibility for the performance of the specification?

Rule: (*Hint:* Designer approval of performance specification)

Premises:

Answer:

Question (can be answered only if Chapter 3, Logic, has been studied): In this problem Atkinson claimed that since the owner's engineer approved the change, the owner is responsible for the performance of the specification. Besides being legally incorrect, which logical fallacy does this argument contain?

8. Reeves Construction constructed a concrete water slide at Acioma River Rapids Park owned by Acioma, Inc. There were cracks in the slide, but they did not interfere with the use of the slide, and the contractor did not perform in an unworkmanlike manner. The owner refuses to pay the contractor. No other facts can be proved by a preponderance of the evidence.

Issue: Is the contractor entitled to payment?

Rule: (*Hint:* Substantial compliance)

Premises:

Answer: Yes

9. A contract entered into between the State of Colorado, owner, and Keanu Construction calls for "approved Colorado marble" and it tells the contractor to put in an allowance of $125,000 in the contract for the price of the marble. However, the owner refused to approve *any* of the *available* Colorado marble. Keanu could get satisfactory marble from Tennessee at a cost of $125,000, but it would cost an additional amount ($25,000) to transport the marble from

---

[14]*Appeal of Guy F. Atkinson Construction Co.* ENG BCA No. 6145 (December 29, 1997).

Tennessee to Colorado. The owner approved the Tennessee marble as long as it did not have to pay any additional costs for the marble from Tennessee. The owner argued that the only choices available to it were use of Colorado marble or Tennessee marble if it did not have to pay transportation costs. Keanu objected to this. No other facts can be proved by a preponderance of the evidence.

Issue: Is the contractor entitled to the $25,000?

Rule: (*Hint:* Objective impossibility)

Premises:

Answer: Yes

Question (can be answered only if Chapter 3, Logic, has been studied): In this problem the owner argued that the only choices available to it were (1) use of Colorado marble or (2) Tennessee marble if it did not have to pay transportation costs. Which logical fallacy does this argument contain?

10. Turk Construction has been hired to put an addition onto a house for the owners. Turk fails to put four pieces of rebar into the old slab and attach it to the new slab. This work was required by the plans and specifications. The house develops some cracks, and the owner hires New Construction Company to level the house and put in piers to stabilize the structure. The cost to do this is $10,000. Do not assume any other facts.

Issue 1: Has Turk Construction breached the contract?

Rule: Failing to perform the contract is by definition a breach of the contract.

Premises:

Answer: Yes

Issue 2: Is Turk Construction liable to owner for the $10,000 to stabilize the structure?

Rule: (*Hint:* Causation)

Premises:

Answer: No

11. Roth Steel entered into a contract dated February 1, 2000, with Sharon Steel Corporation to purchase approximately 200 tons of hot-rolled pickled steel each month for 24 months, for $148.00 per ton. Shortly after the contract was entered into, the complexion of the steel industry changed. Federal price controls discouraged foreign producers from importing steel; domestic producers began exporting steel in an effort to avoid federal price controls. Therefore, the domestic steel supply was sharply reduced. Demand also rose in the domestic market, and the costs for labor, raw material, and energy rose. These factors compelled domestic steel producers to increase prices.

Sharon began to deliver the steel to Roth very late. Sharon claimed the delayed deliveries were due to the preceding factors (increased costs for labor, raw materials, energy). Roth accepted the late deliveries and agreed to an increased price for the steel of $170/ton, or approximately 15% more than the contract price.

In March 2001, Roth discovered the following facts: Sharon was selling substantial amounts of rolled steel to one of its subsidiary companies, Ohi Metal Processing Company.

Ohi Metal Processing was operating as a warehouse and selling steel at premium prices. By selling through its warehouse-subsidiary, Sharon was able to obtain higher prices than federal price controls otherwise permitted. Roth immediately sent a letter dated March 21, 2001, to Sharon objecting to the delays it was experiencing and to the increased price it was paying. Roth told Sharon to supply it pursuant to the February 1, 2000, contract (at $148.00/ton) before supplying Ohi Metal. Sharon refused to do so. Roth could not obtain another supplier with better prices and delivery dates than Sharon's.

After the end of the two-year contract Roth sued Sharon for the 15% difference between the price in the February 1, 2000, contract and what it actually paid. This difference amounted to $897,000.

Note: The Uniform Commercial Code governs this case. For the purposes of this problem assume the UCC contains the same law as the common law for the issues indicated.[15]

Issue 1: Does the doctrine of objective impossibility protect Sharon from being liable for breaching its contract with Roth?

Rule: (Hint: Impossibility)

Premises:

Answer: No

Issue 2: Does the doctrine of practical impossibility protect Sharon from being liable for breaching its contract with Roth?

Rule: (Hint: Practical impossibility or commercial senselessness)

Premises:

Answer: No

Issue 3: Has Roth waived the provisions of the March 1, 2001, contract?

Rule: (Hint: Waiver)

Premises:

Answer: No

12. Kuhlke Construction Company contracted with Mobley, Inc., to expand Mobley's restaurant building. Following completion of the expansion project, several problems arose relating to the quality of the workmanship. The contract price was $42,328.00, of which Mobley has paid $13,117.00.

    Mobley admitted occupying the premises following the completion of construction in November 2000. The evidence showed leaks in the roof that were caused by faulty construction and that resulted in damage to the ceiling and puddles of water on the floor of the restaurant. In addition, the rocks making up the exterior facing of the building had fallen off in several places, and the repairs made to the facing gave the walls the appearance of having been patched. Mobley notified Kuhlke of all these problems as they were discovered, sometime after November 2000.

---

[15]Facts simplified from *Roth Steel v. Sharon Steel Corp.*, 705 F.2D 134 (6th Cir. 1983).

[16] Facts simplified from *Kuhlke Construction Co. v. Mobley*, 285 S.E.2d 236, 159 Ga. App. (1981).

Issue: Is Mobley entitled to damages?

Rule: (*Hint*: Acceptance)

Premises:

Answer: Yes

13. In the following dispute the owner is suing the contractor for damages caused by the movement of two precast concrete planks. The damage was caused because the two planks were not grouted together.

    Assume that the evidence proves each of the following items:

    a. *Detail:*

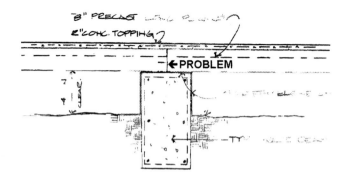

SECTION UNDER FOUNDATION

Figure 8–3   Drawing detail

b. *Question and answer in addendum:*
   Is there a void between the precast planks to be grouted?

   Answer: No

c. *Contractor's knowledge:*
   There has to be grout or something to hold the two precast planks together or the topping will crack because the planks below it will move independently of each other.

d. *Additional facts proved:*
   Contractor builds exactly according to the plans and specifications, and *it does not grout the planks together*. Later the owner sues the contractor for damages related to the movement of the two planks. The contractor claims that it is not responsible for the damages because the designer made a mistake.

Questions:

   a. Who made the error in the plans and specifications?

   b. Who made the error in the addendum?

Issue: Is the contractor responsible for the owner's damages?

Rule: (*Hint:* Open, obvious, defects in the plans and specifications)

Premises: (*Hint:* Be sure to discuss the question and answer in the addendum and how it affects your conclusion.)

Answer: Yes

Question: Would your answer be different if the contractor did not actually know that grout was needed to bind the two precast planks together? What factual issue is then raised?

Question (can be answered only if Chapter 3, Logic, has been studied): In this problem the contractor argues that it is not responsible because the architect made the mistakes. Which logical fallacy does this argument contain?

Note: This example comes from a case arbitrated by M. L. "Skip" Coody, Assistant Professor, Texas A&M University, 1998. He ordered the contractor to pay the damages because the contractor knew, or should have known, there had to be grout or the problem would arise. The question asked in the addendum, "Is there a void between the precast planks to be grouted? Answer: No," did not relieve the contractor of responsibility. The contractor should have been more specific in informing the owner of the error. The law requires a contractor who knows of an error in the plans and specifications to inform the owner.

14. Trent, president of West Racquet Club, negotiated with Republic Floors to resurface tennis courts for West Racquet Club. Republic Floors made a site visit to the courts and examined them. Republic wanted to use ChemTurf, a polyurethane material manufactured by Chem-Turf, Inc., to resurface the courts. Republic performed adhesion tests to determine whether ChemTurf would be appropriate for the courts. Various employees of the three companies (West, the owner; Republic, the contractor; and ChemTurf, Inc., the material supplier) had extensive conversations regarding the bondability of the ChemTurf to the existing concrete surface. Trent was not convinced that the ChemTurf would bond to the existing surface and insisted that a two-year warranty be included in the contract (see Section 15 following) if ChemTurf was to be used.

    A contract, dated September 1, was entered into between West Racquet Club and Republic Floors for resurfacing of the tennis courts. The cost of the project was $150,000. Although West paid Republic $100,000 for some of the work, it refused to make the final payment of $50,000 because the new surface, ChemTurf, began to bubble up shortly after the final coat was applied. The parties could not agree on how to handle the problem, and eventually West redid the surface with another contractor at a cost to it of $100,000. West sued Republic and ChemTurf for the return of the $100,000 paid to Republic.

    Republic countersued West for the $50,000 still due it under the contract. Republic claimed the doctrines of impossibility and practical impossibility precluded it from being liable to West Racquet Club because it was impossible for the ChemTurf to bond to the existing surface. All the expert witnesses, even those employed by West Racquet Club, testified that this was in fact the case.

    The following provisions existed in the contract:

    Section 15: ChemTurf, Inc. and Republic will guarantee the ChemTurf installation at West for a period of two years with respect to the suitability of the performance characteristics of the material and with respect to all workmanship and performance of the surface, both indoors, and outdoors, and against such problems as de-bonding, de-lamination, separation, bubbles, crazing, cracks, discoloration and dead spots. In the occurrences, ChemTurf, Inc./Republic will restore the surface or any portion thereof to original form, function, and performance characteristics.

Issue 1: Is Republic responsible to West for the cost of removing the ChemTurf and installing a suitable surface?

Alternate wording of issue: Who is responsible for the performance of the specification?

Rule: (*Hint:* Performance specification versus design specification)

Premises:

Answer: Yes

Answer to alternatively worded issue: Contractor

Issue 2: Is Republic excused from liability for performance of the specification by the doctrine of objective impossibility?

Rule:

Premises:

Answer: No

Issue 3: Is Republic excused from liability for performance of the specification by the doctrine of practical impossibility?

Rule: Practical impossibility.

Premises:

Answer: No

Question (can be answered only if Chapter 3, Logic, has been studied): In this problem Republic raised two legal theories and then proceeded to use them incorrectly. Which logical fallacy has it committed? *Hint:* Little fish.

Answers to Selected Problems

2. The following specification exists in a certain construction contract between Kevin Construction and the owner:

    a. *Install drainage course on horizontal and vertical surfaces in accordance with the manufacturer's recommendations.*

   Issue: Is Kevin Construction liable to the owner for the damage to the ceiling and flooring?

   Rule: Causation: parties are responsible only for damages they cause, even if they have breached a contract. The party claiming damages has the burden of proof.

   (*Note:* Be sure to cite the page number where the rule was found.)

   Premises: Even assuming that omitting two screws is a breach of the contract, there is no proof that omitting the two screws caused the leakage and damage to the ceiling and floor tiles. The owner has failed in its burden of proof of causation.

   Answer: No

3. Owner and Ace Construction entered into a construction agreement for a paddock to be constructed on owner's property at a cost of $25,000. The paddock is attached to an existing barn. . . .

Issue 1: Is Ace liable for the damage to the barn?

Alternative wording of issue: Is there proof of causation?

Rule: Causation. Parties are responsible only for damages they cause, even if they have breached a contract. Party claiming damages has the burden of proof.

Premises: There is no proof that the paddock or the construction of the paddock caused the barn to sag. The owner has failed in its burden of proof of causation. The warranty is not relevant, as it affects only the construction of the paddock, not the barn. The contractor did not warrant the barn for anything. There is no evidence that the warranty was to cover the barn. Without this evidence the law will assume it does not.

Answer: No

Answer to alternatively worded issue: No

4. A masonry subcontract required Milton Masonry, the subcontractor, to parge the inner face of a brick wall and to use Z brand galvanized ties . . . .

Issue 1: Is the subcontractor entitled to payment from the contractor?

Alternative wording of issue: Has the contractor waived performance of the subcontract?

Rule: A waiver is the knowing relinquishment of a known right.

Premises: It is likely a jury or arbitrator will find that the contractor has waived the subcontract provisions requiring the parging and the specified tiles because it observed the subcontractor's failure to parge the inner face of the brick and use the specified brand of tiles over a one-month period. By failing to say anything about the way the work was done the contractor has waived compliance with the specifications.

Answer to Issue 1: Yes

Answer to alternatively worded issue: Yes

Issue 2: Is the prime contractor entitled to payment?

Alternative wording of issue: Has the owner waived performance of the contract?

Rule: Waiver. A waiver is the knowing relinquishment of a known right. Parties are also presumed to know the contents of their contracts. Basic maxim of contract law: a party must honor its contract or pay damages.

Premises: It is not as likely a jury or arbitrator will find that the owner has waived the contract provisions requiring the parging and the specified ties. The owner's representative saw the subcontractor's failure only on occasion—perhaps only once. It is not likely that seeing something once leads to a waiver. Other realities of the construction process would probably be taken into consideration by the court. These include the fact that it is not usually the owner's representative's job to determine that the subcontractors are complying with the contracts. The contractor is liable for breach of the contract and is liable to the owner for damages.

Answer: No

Answer to alternatively worded issue: No

9

Scope

Scope issues, often referred to as *ambiguity, contract ambiguity,* or *contract interpretation* issues, arise when the parties to a contract disagree on what the contract says or means. Think of scope issues as a battle between two conflicting interpretations.

For example, in a subcontract between a prime contractor and the heating, ventilation, air conditioning subcontractor (HVAC), the prime contractor interprets the scope of the subcontract as including 5 miles of wire necessary to hook up the air conditioning system to outside wiring. The HVAC subcontractor disagrees and is of the opinion that the 5 miles of wire are to be placed by the electrician.

As another example, assume that the contract between the owner and the contractor states that rollover protective devices *"shall be installed on crawler and rubber-tire tractors such as dozers, push-and-pull tractors, winch tractors, mowers, off-the-highway self-propelled pneumatic-tire earth movers such as trucks, pans, scrapers, bottom dumps, and end dumps, motor graders."* The contractor is planning on using a certain type of trenching machine to perform the work. After the contract is entered into, a dispute arises as to whether the contractor must put the rollover protective device on the trencher. The contractor says the contract does not require him to put the rollover protective device on the trencher, and the owner says the contract requires the rollover protective device. This is a contract interpretation or scope issue.

Scope issues are among the most difficult to analyze because they may go unnoticed and because they can involve any aspect of the contract. For example, if the parties disagree about whether the contract allows the contractor additional time for inclement weather, the issue is a scope issue, not a delay issue. If the parties disagree about whether the subcontractor is to supply wiring, the issue is a scope issue, not a changes issue. *Whenever the issue between the parties involves a question about what the contract says, a scope issue exists.*

Simplified Approach to Scope Issues

Courts generally approach a scope issue with caution and look at it from several different viewpoints before finally deciding which of the two competing interpretations will win. This chapter uses a simplified two-step approach to scope issues. Each step consists of a legal issue and legal rules used to come to a conclusion. The first step asks the question, Is the contract ambiguous? If the answer to issue 1 is yes, move onto the second step. The second step asks the question, Which rules can be applied and how? See Figure 9–1.

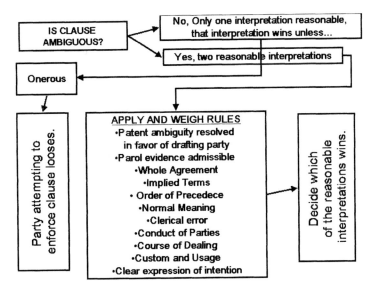

Figure 9–1 Solving scope issues

Step 1, Issue 1: Is the Contract Ambiguous?

The first step in solving a scope issue is to ask the question, Is the contract ambiguous? The rule to be applied is: *A contract is ambiguous if it is capable of having two relatively reasonable meanings.*[1] At this point in the analysis it is necessary to look *only* at the meaning each party is giving to the contract.

Always clearly state each party's meaning and what provisions, if any, of the contract support that party's interpretation. At this step *do not use parol evidence.* **Parol evidence** is evidence outside the actual contract; only the words in the contract should be discussed here. For example, if the parties exchanged letters or had conversations about

---

[1]*Edward R. Marden Corp. v. United States,* 803 F.2d 701, 705 (Fed. Cir. 1986); *Highway Prods., Inc. v. United States,* 530 F.2d 911, 917 (Ct. Cl. 1976); *Sun Shipbuilding & Dry Dock Co. v. Unites States,* 183 Ct. Cl. 358, 393 F.2d 807, 815–16 (Ct. Cl. 1968).

the contract, that evidence is parol evidence and cannot be used at this point to determine if the contract is ambiguous.

It is *very important to have a clear picture of what each party is claiming* the contract says. This point cannot be emphasized enough. It is impossible to intelligently analyze a scope issue if you do not clearly see the two competing contract interpretations. It is not always possible to support each of the parties' interpretation with specific clauses from the contract, but if possible, do so. For example, if the meaning of some particular word or phrase is being argued over, be sure to clearly state that in your legal argument. It is *not* uncommon for one party to propose an interpretation of the contract that is not in the contract in black and white.

If the answer to the first issue is yes, move on to issue 2. If the answer is no, then it is likely an arbitrator or judge will rule in favor of the party propounding the only reasonable meaning. The only exception to this is that the court will not enforce a reasonable meaning if the clause is onerous. Onerous clauses are discussed later in the section.

The following is an example of an unambiguous contract.

EXAMPLE:

Facts: Cassie Contractor is to install a wastewater filtration system for the state of Yur. The system is manufactured and designed by the subcontractor/supplier Hydro Engineering. The following two provisions are in the contract between the contractor and the owner, State of Yur:

3.3.D. Contractor is to provide a one-year service contract to the Owner.

3.3.E. Contractor is to provide one-year warranty to Owner.

1.3.C.1 Hydro Engineering, supplier of the wastewater filtration system, shall be solely responsible for the performance of the wastewater filtration system as specified and shall modify, add to, or alter the equipment as necessary, without any additional cost to Government, to provide a satisfactory performance.

Six months after the system is installed an employee of Yur calls Cassie Contractor, and asks her come out and service the wastewater filtration system. Contractor says she is not obligated to do so; Hydro Engineering is responsible. Hydro refuses to come out either, and the owner calls the contractor back and says contractor must service the system or get someone out there to do it.

Issue: Is the contract ambiguous? *Alternative wording of issue:* Is the contractor required to service the equipment?

Rule: The contract is ambiguous if it is capable of having two relatively reasonable meanings.

Premises: The owner is giving the following meaning to the contract: *The contractor is required to service the equipment or provide service to the owner for one year.* The owner is basing its interpretation on the clause *"3.3.D. Provide one-year service contract to Owner."* Since no outside service contract has been provided to the owner, the contractor is liable for the performance of this provision.

The contractor is giving the following meaning to the contract: *Contractor is not responsible for the service; Hydro Engineering is responsible for the service.* The contractor is basing its interpretation on the following provision: *"1.3.C.1 Hydro Engineering, supplier of the wastewater filtration system, shall be solely responsible for the performance of the wastewater filtration system as specified and shall modify, add to, or alter the equipment as necessary, without any additional cost to Government, to provide a satisfactory performance."*

The contractor's interpretation is not reasonable, however. The provision quoted by the contractor states only that the subcontractor, Hydro, is responsible for making sure that the system performs as specified in the contract. This provision is separate and apart from the duty to service the equipment for one year. The contractor agreed in the original contract to provide a one-year service contract to the owner, and that is what the contractor must do. The contractor can satisfy this contract by either providing service itself or purchasing a service contract. For example, the contractor could have entered into a service contract with Hydro whereby Hydro would provide service for one year. Failure to provide service to the owner is a breach of the contract, and the contractor is liable for damages.

Answer: The contract is not ambiguous. The contractor must provide the requested service. ■ ■ ■

Strained or Absurd Interpretations

If one party's interpretation is strained or absurd, the court will not uphold it. For example, suppose the contract says the contractor shall install rollover protective devices *"on crawler and rubber-tire tractors such as dozers, push-and-pull tractors, winch tractors, mowers, off-the-highway self-propelled pneumatic-tire earth movers such as trucks, pans, scrapers, bottom dumps, and end dumps, motor graders."* The owner says that the contractor is required to install a rollover protective device on any vehicle that enters the project, including the company truck that is used to visit the site and run errands. The owner's interpretation is strained, absurd and/or unreasonable.

Onerous or Unconscionable Clauses

On very rare occasions a court may not enforce an unambiguous clause. This will occur only when the unambiguous clause is so unfair that the judge cannot in good conscience enforce it. For example, a clause that attempts to violate a maxim of law is not likely to be upheld. The law terms such clauses **onerous** or **unconscionable** or **exculpatory** and will not enforce them. Another term used in such cases is that the clause **violates public policy.** Often the judge does not define what the public policy is—the judge just decides the clause is against it. For purposes of this text all these terms—onerous clauses, unconscionable clauses, exculpatory clauses, and clauses that violate public policy—are the same and are defined as clauses that the law will not enforce because the law cannot in good conscience do so.

The following rule is applied by many jurisdictions to determine whether a clause is onerous. A clause is onerous if

1. it was drafted by a party with significantly superior bargaining power; and
2. is not in accordance with industry practice; and
3. the contract reallocates a risk to the nondrafting party that the drafting party has more control over; and
4. serious financial loss will result to the nondrafting party.

Onerous clauses are generally encountered in contracts between parties with unequal bargaining power or knowledge. Although such clauses *may* serve the narrow, short-term interests of the party preparing them, they prevent a partnering relationship between the parties and are detrimental to the health of the industry. They may be circumscribed by a well-argued presentation before a sympathetic arbitration panel or jury.

It is possible to put *anything* into a contract. It is not possible, however, to have the law enforce *everything*. The following is a slightly modified example of an actual proposed provision between Party A and Party B:

> *47. Party A shall be deemed aligned with the Forces of Light and Party B shall be deemed allied with the Powers of Darkness for all litigation or arbitration of this contract and Party A shall therefore win all litigation or arbitration.*

It is unlikely a court or arbitrator would enforce such a clause.

Step 2, Issue 2: Which Rules Can Be Applied and How?

If the answer to issue 1 is, Yes, the contract has two relatively reasonable meanings, the next step of the analysis is to solve issue 2: Which rules can be applied and how? Some of the most important and common rules used at this stage of the analysis to help determine who wins are the following:

- Parol evidence rule
- Patent/latent rule
- Custom and usage rule
- Course of dealing rule
- Conduct rule
- Normal meaning/ordinary meaning rule
- Implied terms rule
- Whole-agreement rule
- Order of precedence rule
- Clear expression of intention rule
- Clerical errors rule

Each of these will be discussed more fully. The two rules used most frequently by the law to resolve scope issues are the parol evidence rule and the patent ambiguity rule. Figure 9–1 illustrates the paths for solving scope issues.

Parol Evidence Rule

Parol evidence is evidence outside the contract such as conversations or letters. Parol evidence can be used only to aid the court or arbitrator in determining which of the two competing reasonable meanings wins; it cannot be used to determine if there are two reasonable meanings. The parol evidence rule states that parol evidence can be used only to clarify *ambiguous* terms of the contract. Parol evidence cannot be used to change an unambiguous term of a contract.

Parol Evidence Rule

Parol evidence is evidence extrinsic to the actual contract and can be used only to clarify *ambiguous* terms of the contract. It cannot be used to change an unambiguous term of a contract.

The parol evidence rule bars any evidence of *oral representations that differ from the written words in the contract.* For example, assume that the completion date in the contract is May 1. Prior to signing the contract, the contractor and the owner have a discussion during which the owner tells the contractor that the May 1 date is not really that important, and as long as the project is completed before the summer holidays there will be no problem. Later, when the project is completed on May 15 the owner back-charges the contractor for delay damages. (Damages are discussed in the Chapter 14, Termination of the Contract and Contract Damages.) The contractor is obligated to pay damages to the owner. The contract is unambiguous, and the conversation between the owner and the contractor regarding the later completion date is barred by the parol evidence rule.

As a further example, assume the contract says that the contractor is to install aluminum sprinkler heads. Figure 9–2 illustrates the production of this unambiguous contract. At a prebid meeting the contractor tells the owner's representative that plastic sprinkler heads will be used, and the owner's representative does not disagree. After the work on the contract has begun a dispute arises as to whether aluminum or plastic sprinkler heads are required. The contract is *unambiguous* on this point because it specifies aluminum sprinkler heads. The conversation between the contractor and the owner's representative about the plastic sprinkler heads is parol evidence and cannot be used to change the unambiguous term of the contract. Figure 9–3 illustrates that the court or arbitrator will look only at the contract to decide the issue.

Compare the preceding example with this one: The contract says that the contractor is to install sprinkler heads. This contract is ambiguous (see Figure 9–4). At a prebid meeting the contractor tells the owner's representative that plastic sprinkler heads will be used, and the owner's representative does not disagree. After the work on the contract has begun a dispute arises as to whether aluminum or plastic sprinkler heads are required. The contract is ambiguous on this point because it does not specify the type of sprinkler heads. The conversation between the contractor and the owner's representative about the plastic sprinkler heads is parol evidence and can be used to clarify the *ambiguous* term of the contract. Figure 9–5 illustrates that the judge or arbitrator may look at parol evidence to determine this issue. Note that the arbitrator, judge, or jury does not have to believe the evidence; this rule only allows the evidence in.

Patent Ambiguity Rule

Another frequently used rule for determining the meaning of a contract is the **patent ambiguity rule.** The word *patent* means "open or obvious." The opposite of patent is *latent*, which means "hidden or unobvious." A simplified version of the patent ambiguity rule states that a patent ambiguity is resolved in favor of the party who drafted the document.

The following are equivalent statements of this rule:

- A patent ambiguity is resolved against the nondrafting party.
- A latent ambiguity is resolved against the drafting party.
- A latent ambiguity is resolved in favor of the nondrafting party.

Since the owner is usually the drafting party of the construction contract, this means that patent or obvious ambiguities are resolved in the owner's favor. The case of *Community Heating & Plumbing Co. v. Kelso* at the end of the chapter contains a discussion by a judge of the terms *patent* and *latent*. In a contract between a general contractor and a subcontractor, the general contractor is usually the drafting party, and therefore patent ambiguities are resolved in the subcontractor's favor.

9–1. THINK

Why does the law prevent people from taking advantage of patent ambiguities?

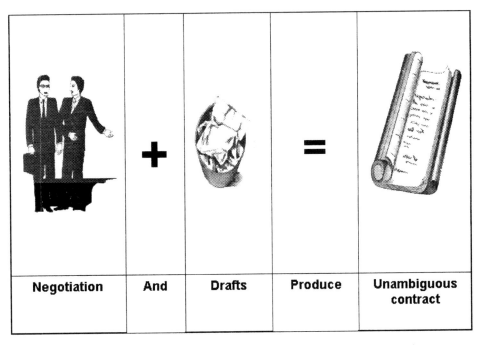

Negotiation	And	Drafts	Produce	Unambiguous contract

Figure 9–2 Production of unambiguous contract © 2000–2001 www.arttoday.com

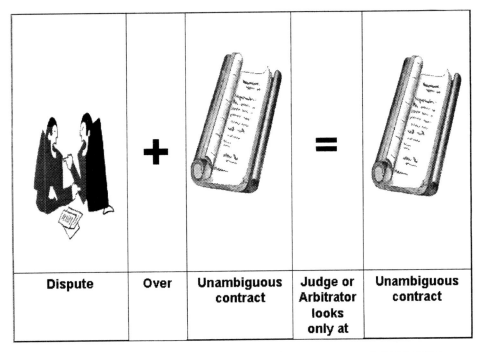

Dispute	Over	Unambiguous contract	Judge or Arbitrator looks only at	Unambiguous contract

Figure 9–3 Court or arbitrator looks only at unambiguous contract © 2000–2001 www.arttoday.com

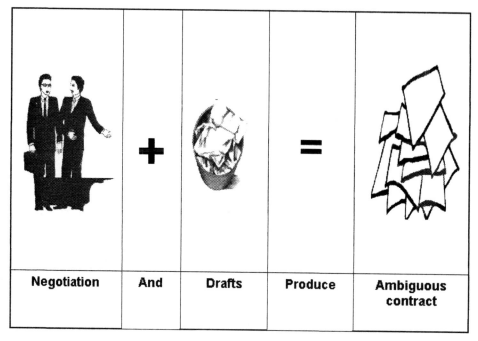

Figure 9–4 Production of ambiguous contract © 2000–2001 www.arttoday.com

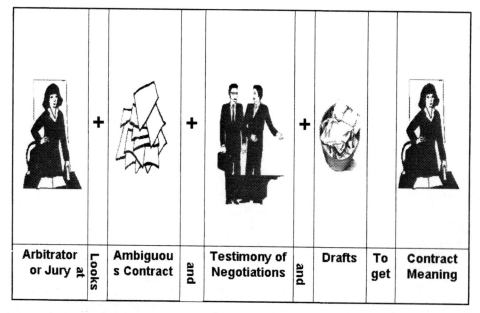

Figure 9–5 Evidence that can be used to determine meaning of ambiguous contract © 2000–2001 www.arttoday.com

The patent/latent rule is consistent with the rule of open and obvious errors discussed in Chapter 8, Specifications and Plans. It is also consistent with the maxim of law that mistakes should be fixed and not taken advantage of. When a person encounters a mistake, and an obvious or patent ambiguity is really a mistake, the law wants that person to attempt fix the mistake, not take advantage of it. If the person does not attempt to fix the mistake but instead attempts to take advantage of it, courts will prevent that from occurring.

EXAMPLE 1:

Owner awarded a contract for building a small convenience store. The drawings and specifications were accompanied by a statement that the "Contractor is responsible for furnishing all the labor and materials to produce a complete, functioning project." This type of project is also called a **turnkey project.** In a turnkey project the owner has only to insert her key and open the door to begin operation of the business. The owner prepared the contract and the contractor signed it.

When originally estimating the job the contractor had noticed that a necessary transformer box had been omitted from the drawings. The contractor said nothing to the owner and bid the job *without* the transformer box. The contractor was awarded the job. After being awarded the contract the contractor called the omission of the transformer box to the owner's attention and then sought additional sums in a change order. The contractor is not entitled to an additional sum to install the necessary transformer box, since the contract required the contractor to produce a complete, functioning project. The omission of the box was a patent, or obvious, ambiguity and is resolved against the contractor, the nondrafting party. ■ ■ ■

9-2. THINK

The owner may negotiate to pay a sum to the contractor in the preceding situation. What ethical values is the contractor exhibiting in doing this?

EXAMPLE 2:

The U.S. government contracted with Wickham Contracting to provide manholes, ductwork, and underground cable work. Wickham Contracting was low bidder at $44,000, and the other bids were as follows: $52,000, $63,000, and $85,000. The drawings contained a scale error. On the left-hand side of the documents the scale was indicated as $1'' = 200'$; however, in the middle section of the drawing the scale indicated was $1' = 200'$. This was an error made by the drafter of the document. The contractor based its bid on the $1' = 200'$ scale. The contractor was not entitled to additional costs of performance because the error was patent.[2]   ■ ■ ■

EXAMPLE 3:

The Public Housing Administration (owner) contracted with Beacon Construction to construct a defense housing project. The specifications required weather stripping, but the drawings made no mention of weather stripping. Beacon based its bid on a lack of weather stripping. Later the government representative ordered Beacon to install the weather stripping, which it did. Beacon filed a claim for additional costs. Beacon was not entitled to extra costs because the error in the documents was patent.[3]   ■ ■ ■

Miscellaneous Rules of Contract Interpretation

The following are many of the rules that courts and arbitrators can use to help them determine which of two competing meanings should prevail in a dispute. Different courts in different jurisdictions will have slightly different rules. Also, the names used here are for your convenience only. An arbitrator or judge may not say "I am using the custom and usage rule to decide this matter." See the *Blinderman* case at end of this chapter for an example of how a court analyzes a scope problem using several of the following rules without actually calling them by any specific name.

Custom and Usage.   **Custom and usage** in the industry can be used to interpret language having a specific industry meaning. For example, it is the custom in the construction industry that a $2'' \times 4''$ is not actually two inches by four inches. If an owner were to sue a contractor for failing to use boards that were exactly $2'' \times 4''$, the owner would lose because the custom and usage of the industry controls the size of a $2'' \times 4''$. However, custom and usage *cannot* be used to change an expressly unambiguous term. For example, it may be the custom in the industry to allow for a $1/2''$ tolerance, but if a particular contract calls for $1/4''$ tolerance, the contractor must bid the $1/4''$ tolerance.

Custom and usage can be a problem because craftspersons have a tendency to do things the way they have always done them and not necessarily in accordance with the plans and specifications; however, craftspersons are supposed to follow the plans and specifications agreed to. Custom and usage is not a valid excuse for failing to fulfill the contract requirements unless the term is ambiguous.

Another problem with this rule is that it must be introduced through expert witness testimony, since it is unlikely a judge or jury will know the custom and usage of the particular industry. In arbitration the arbitrators may substitute their own knowledge for this item.

---

[2]Example slightly modified from *Wickham Contracting Co. Inc., v. United States*, 546 F.2d 395 (1976).

[3]See *Beacon Constr. Co. v. United States*, 314 F.2d 501 (1963).

9-3. THINK

Course of Dealing or Conduct of the Parties. The party's dealings can be used to interpret a present dispute. If the parties have acted in a certain way, the law assumes that, all things being equal, the prior actions are still accepted.

For example, assume that the contract between the owner and the contractor states that rollover protective devices *"shall be installed on crawler and rubber-tire tractors such as dozers, push-and-pull tractors, winch tractors, mowers, off-the-highway self-propelled pneumatic-tire earth movers such as trucks, pans, scrapers, bottom dumps, and end dumps, motor graders."* The contractor has had several similar contracts with the owner. For each job the contractor used a certain type of trencher to do the job, and at no time did the owner request that a rollover protective device be attached to the trencher. On this job, however, the owner has a different construction manager who demands that a rollover protective device be added to the trencher. The court will not require the rollover protective device because the parties' **course of dealing** shows that they did not intend the trencher to have a rollover protective device.

Normal Meaning/Ordinary Meaning. The **ordinary meaning of words** is used by the law unless some other meaning has been indicated for the word. Technical or industry-specific terms are given their normal interpretation as used in that industry, unless the intent is clearly otherwise.

Implied Terms. The **implied terms** necessary to comply with the *explicit terms* become part of the contract. For example, the contract may merely state "place concrete." The contractor cannot get additional money for placing the forms, as they are essential to the placing of the concrete.

For example, assume First contractor entered into a contract to build a house for the owner. The project was taking a very long time to complete, and finally the contractor just stopped coming to the site. The owner terminated the contractor and hired Second contractor to finish the job. Owner sued First contractor for delays and breach of contract. First contractor claims it cannot be sued for delay because the contract did not state a specific date by which the project had to be completed. The court will imply a reasonable date to the contract, and if First contractor went beyond this implied date, it can be liable for damages.

Warning! This theory is very popular with nonlawyers because it is very easy to dream up an implied provision that one would like the law to add to the contract. Arbitrators and judges use this theory very, very carefully.

9-4. THINK

Whole Agreement.   Words and phrases must be interpreted within the context of the **whole agreement** with all parts given equal weight. The interpretation must be consistent with the entire contract. This rule is often the basis for an argument that says, "No, the contract does not say what you claim." The person using this argument is, in essence, saying, "The meaning of the entire contract, when read as a whole, supports my interpretation. Your interpretation is out of context."

Order of Precedence.   It is possible that a contract will contain conflicting provisions. For example, a completion date of April 1 may be handwritten near the beginning of the contract but typed as February 1 in a later provision. The following **order of precedence** rules apply when this happens:

- Special conditions prevail over general conditions.
- Handwritten terms prevail over typewritten or preprinted provisions.
- Typewritten provisions prevail over preprinted provisions.
- Words prevail over figures.

Clear Expression of Intention.   The **clear expression of intention** rule states that the drafter of the document has an obligation to express its intention with clarity.

Clerical errors.   The **clerical errors** rule states that clerical errors are discounted or ignored unless relied on by the nondrafting party.

Vocabulary Checklist

Scope
Onerous clause
Unconscionable clause
Exculpatory clause
Clause that violates public
  policy
Parol evidence
Parol evidence rule

Patent ambiguity
Latent ambiguity
Patent/latent rule
Turnkey project
Custom and usage
Course of dealing
Conduct of the parties

Normal meaning or ordinary
  meaning
Implied terms
Whole agreement
Order of precedence
Clear expression of intention
Clerical errors

Review Questions:

1. What are the two issues that are always analyzed in a scope problem?
2. What is wrong with the statement of the following issue?
   Issue: Is the contractor's interpretation of the contract reasonable?
3. What is the parol evidence rule?
4. What is an onerous or unconscionable clause?
5. What are the two primary rules of contract interpretation?

Problems

Answer the issue in each of the following problems by making a legal argument, including premises in support of your answer.

1. Sanchez Construction was awarded a fixed-price contract with the U.S. Army in connection with the construction of an artificial battlefield. A safety manual was provided by the army and was incorporated as one of the contract documents. The contract required the installation of several electrical systems including interior wiring and an underground electrical distribution system. The contractor intended to use a particular *trenching machine* to dig the trenches required by the contract.

   After contract performance had begun, the Army required the contractor to install a rollover protective structure (ROPS) on the trencher. The contractor had performed similar contracts for the army in the recent past and had not been told to install ROPS on trenchers of the type used here.

   The safety manual provided by the army (on this and prior jobs) stated that ROPS *"shall be installed on crawler and rubber-tire tractors such as dozers, push-and-pull tractors, winch tractors, mowers, off-the-highway self-propelled pneumatic-tire earth movers such as trucks, pans, scrapers, bottom dumps, and end dumps, motor graders."* No other facts can be proved by a preponderance of the evidence.

   The authorized government representative said that the contract was not ambiguous and required the contractor to install a ROPS. The contractor did so and filed a claim for the additional cost of the equipment with a ROPS.

   Issue: Is Sanchez entitled to payment for the ROPS?

   > *Subissue 1:* Is the contract ambiguous?
   >
   > *Rule:*
   >
   > *Premises:* Be sure to clearly state what each party wants the contract to say and where in the contract, if anywhere, each party has support for its interpretation.
   >
   > *Answer:* Yes

   > *Subissue 2:* Which rules can be applied and how?
   >
   > *Rule:* (*Hint:* Course of dealing)
   >
   > *Premises:*
   >
   > *Answer:*

   Answer: Yes, Sanchez is entitled to payment.

2. (Note the difference in facts here.) Sanchez Construction was awarded a fixed-price contract with the U.S. Army in connection with the construction of an artificial battlefield. A safety manual was provided by the army and was incorporated as one of the contract documents. The contract required the installation of several electrical systems including interior wiring and an underground electrical distribution system. The contractor intended to use a particular *trenching machine* to dig the trenches required by the contract.

   Prior to the bid the contractor had a conversation with an authorized representative of the owner during which he mentioned he intended to use a particular *trenching machine* to dig the trenches required by the contract, and he asked if a ROPS would be required to be installed on that trenching machine. The representative said no. The contract was bid accordingly.

After contract performance had begun, the army required the contractor to install a ROPS on the trencher. The contractor complied and filed a claim for additional funds.

The safety manual provided by the army (on this and prior jobs) stated that ROPS *"shall be installed on crawler and rubber tire tractors such as dozers, push and pull tractors, winch tractors, mowers, off-the-highway self-propelled pneumatic-tire earth movers such as trucks, pans, scrapers, bottom dumps, and end dumps, motor graders."* No other facts can be proved by a preponderance of the evidence.

Another authorized government representative said that the contract was not ambiguous and required the contractor to install a ROPS. The contractor did so and filed a claim for the additional cost of the equipment with a ROPS.

Issue: Is Sanchez entitled to payment for the ROPS?

    Subissue 1: Is the contract ambiguous?

    Rule:

    Premises: Be sure to clearly state what each party wants the contract to say and where in the contract, if anywhere, each party has support for its interpretation.

    Answer: Yes

    Subissue 2: Which rules can be applied?

    Rule: (*Hint:* parol evidence rule)

    Premises:

    Answer: Sanchez prevails.

Answer: Yes, Sanchez is entitled to payment.

3. The owner awarded a contract for construction of an industrial facility. As work progressed the engineer realized that soggy soil conditions made it desirable to upgrade the design of the drainage system around the foundation. The engineer discussed the matter with the contractor's on-site supervisor, informing the contractor that there would be an increase in both the diameter of the drainage pipe and the quantity of gravel backfill. The contractor pointed out that the original design did not call for any drainage system along one side of the building. The engineer said that aspect of the design would remain unchanged.

The contractor received a change order calling for the contractor to "upgrade the drainage system around the perimeter of the foundation by installing 4″ pipe and higher quality gravel backfill." The parties agreed on a price. The contractor installed the upgraded drainage system on the three sides of the building *only* and not along the side that had no drainage system in the original plans.

A dispute later developed as to whether the contractor was required to install the improved/changed drainage system on all four sides of the building. The owner claimed that the change order required the upgraded drainage system all around the building, and the contractor claimed the upgraded drainage system was to be on only three sides of the building. No other facts can be proved by a preponderance of the evidence.[4]

Issue: Was the change order for upgraded drainage system on all four sides of the building, or for only the three sides as per the original design?

---

[4]Facts slightly modified from *Appeal of J. W. Bateson Co., Inc., VABCA No. 1883.*

Subissue 1: Is the change, order ambiguous?

Rule:

Premises:

Answer: No. Owner wins.

Alternative Approach: Approach this problem as if it were a problem relating to the plans or specifications. (Refer to Chapter 8, Specifications and Plans.)

Issue: Is there an "open, obvious defect" in the specification?

Rule:

Premises:

Answer: Yes, contractor is responsible.

Questions:

a. Is this an argument about an ambiguity in the contract between the parties?

b. Why is the discussion between the engineer and the contractor's on-site supervisor irrelevant?

4. The contract documents between the government and the contractor required removal and replacement of existing sections of raised flooring. No mention was made of removal of existing air conditioning units and closet walls permanently bolted to the floor. The contract required contractor to make a prebid site inspection, which the contractor did. The contractor removed and replaced the raised flooring, and it filed a claim for additional sums to remove the existing air conditioning units and closet walls. No other facts can be proved by a preponderance of the evidence.

Issue: Is contractor entitled to be paid extra costs of removing the air conditioners and closet walls? Be sure to argue both legal issues needed to analyze a scope issue.

Rule: (*Hint:* Latent/patent)

Premises:

Answer: No, contractor is not entitled to payment.

5. (Note the slight change in facts.) The contract documents between the government and the contractor required removal and replacement of existing sections of raised flooring. No mention was made of the need to remove ducts and pipe attached to the flooring, underneath the flooring. These ducts and pipe were attached to the flooring, but were not visible on a visual inspection of the site. The contract required contractor to make a prebid site inspection, which the contractor did. The contractor had done several other similar jobs and was aware that there were concealed ducts and pipe; however, on all other jobs another contractor had been hired by the government to remove the ducts and pipe. No other facts can be proved by a preponderance of the evidence.

Issue: Is contractor entitled to be paid extra costs of removing the air conditioners and closet walls? Be sure to argue both legal issues needed to analyze a scope issue.

Rule: (*Hint:* Conduct of the Parties)

Premises:

Answer: Yes, contractor is entitled to payment.

6. Lokal Retirement Community issued an invitation to bids for building a retirement community to include various buildings housing retirees, food service, tennis courts, swimming pools, parking, and other amenities. Drawings and specifications for the work to be done were supplied by King Architects and Engineers. Tops Construction submitted its bid price and subsequently was awarded the contract.

The contract documents required many clarifications, and the files contain many letters, faxes, and other documentation among Lokal, King, and Tops concerning the various clarifications of the plans and specifications needed in order to bid the project.

Tops' low bid was $1.2 million. There were several bids with variances of about $200,000. Tops' bid was $150,000 lower than the next higher bid, with the third from the bottom being about $200,000 above that.

Paragraphs 4, 5, and 6 of the technical specifications described, respectively, buildings 4, 5, 6. Each paragraph contained a brief description of the work. These paragraphs mentioned that each building was to have two stories. Each paragraph referenced pages 23 (first floor) and 45 (second floor) of the drawings. The caption block on page 23 of the drawings indicated that it described work for all three buildings—4, 5, and 6—and contained drawings regarding the first floor; however, page 45 of the drawings referred to the second floor and indicated that it described work for only buildings 4 and 5. Tops Construction never inquired about this discrepancy. (What is the discrepancy?)

As a consequence, Tops Construction included in its bid the cost of constructing a second floor only on buildings 4 and 5. Shortly after construction had begun, the parties realized that a discrepancy existed between what Lokal Retirement Community intended and what Tops construed the drawings as intending. The difference in the scope of the work amounted to about $245,000.

Tops submitted a claim requesting a change to the contract agreement for time and additional compensation to construct the second floor on building 6. King rejected this request. King wrote a letter to Tops denying the request because ". . . this was an issue of patent ambiguity, and, therefore, you are not entitled any additional time, or money. Please perform the contract as required by law." No other facts can be proved by a preponderance of the evidence.

Question: Why can't Tops rescind the contract for mistake? (Refer to Chapter 7, Mistakes in Bidding.)

Issue: Is Tops entitled to additional compensation for building the second floor onto building 6?

Subissue 1: Is the contract ambiguous? Be sure to clearly state what each party wants the contract to say.

Rule:

Premises:

Answer: Yes, the contract is ambiguous.

Subissue 2: Is the ambiguity latent, and therefore contractor is entitled to payment for the second floor on building 6?

Rule:

Argument:

Answer: Yes, the ambiguity is latent.

Answer: Tops is entitled to additional compensation.

7. Hawker, Inc. was the design / build contractor on a cogeneration power plant in Roanoke Rapids. As the general contractor, Hawker subcontracted with plaintiff Sergeant Constructors, Inc. for construction of the power plant. In turn, Sergeant subcontracted for specialized work with Clare County Electrical and Clare County Concrete. Because all the designs for the plant were not complete prior to the commencement of the construction the project was called *fast track.*

Pursuant to its contract with Sergeant, Hawker was responsible for engineering design drawings and procurement of major equipment items. The contract had an inflexible completion date of October 30, 1998, and in contract negotiations and in the contract, Hawker promised to issue drawings at a pace that would allow Sergeant to finish its work on time. The contract further provided that Sergeant would receive a bonus of $9000 per day for early completion.

[Those who want to know procedurally what happens in cases like this should read the following paragraph; however, this paragraph has no effect on the conclusion of the legal issues related to scope of the contract.] To recover their expenses and losses Sergeant and the Clare County companies filed a lien on the property and brought suit against the owner to foreclose on the lien. As is typical in the industry, the owner had a payment bond protecting the property. A *payment bond* protects the owner from the contractor's failure to pay the subcontractors. If the contractor fails to pay the subcontractors, the bonding company will do so and remove the liens from the property. The insurance company bonded around the lien and proceeded with the lawsuit, stepping into the shoes of the owner. **Bonding around the lien** means that the insurance company puts money into the court's bank account to pay the liens or agrees to pay any judgment. This removes the liens from the owner's property and allows the owner to sell or mortgage the property. The bonding company sued Hawker for any damages owner would have to pay to the Clare County companies pursuant to the lien. This is the normal way these suits are handled.

The lien and the suit included the following damages to the following entities:

Sergeant: $2 million

Clare County Concrete: $2 million

Clare County Electrical: $2 million

The total damages were therefore over $6 million including attorney fees and interest. (Eventually the total was $7,615,863.) *In this problem we are concerned only with the $4 million claim of the Clare County companies.*

Hawker answered claiming (among other things) that pursuant to the contract it owed nothing to the Clare County companies and could *not* be sued for any damages due the Clare County companies.

Hawker based its argument that it did not owe the Clare County companies any money on the following contract provisions:

4. Insurance provisions:

4.2.1 All proposed Lower Tier Subcontracts must be submitted to Hawker for written approval. If so approved, subcontractor shall bind all Lower Tier Subcontractors to the provisions of the Subcontract Documents. **Neither this Subcontract nor any Lower Tier Subcontract shall create any contractual relationship between any Lower Tier Subcontractor and Hawker nor any obligation of Hawker to Lower Tier Subcontractor.** *Notwithstanding the existence of any Lower Tier Subcontract, Subcontractor shall be liable to Hawker for performance hereunder as if no Lower Tier Subcontractor exists (emphasis added).*

Pursuant to the boldfaced language of Section 4.2.1, Hawker argued that *it had no contractual obligation to the Clare County companies* because they were Lower Tier Subcontractors. Hawker claimed that pursuant to the wording in 4.2.1 provision it could, *under no circumstances,* be liable to the Clare County companies for damages.

Issue: Are Clare County Electrical and Clare County Concrete entitled to payment from Hawker?

> *Subissue 1:* Is the contract ambiguous?
>
> *Rule:*
>
> *Premises:*
>
> *Answer:* No

> *Subissue 2:* Is the provision enforceable?
>
> *Rule:* (*Hint:* onerous)
>
> *Premises:*
>
> *Answer:* No

Answer: Hawker must pay the Clare County companies' damages.

Question: What maxims of law can be used to support a conclusion in support of the subcontractors? (Refer to maxims of law in the index.)

8. Riverside County entered into an agreement with B. Rose Pipeline, Inc. to install underground pipes for a sewer project. Contract provision § 2.09 specified that B. Rose would be "paid $30/per cubic yard for the excavation of an estimated 7,000 cubic yards of rock; and that the rock excavation shall be measured for payment from centerline profile down to a depth six (6) inches below the bottom of the pipe barrel. . ." (*Note:* This is one of the contract terms disputed here.)

   The contract also contained a provision that read:

   > *1.07(f) "Solid rock shall consist of such materials in their original bed or well-defined ledges; which in the opinion of the Engineer, cannot be removed with pick and shovel, ditching machine, backhoe, or other similar devices and which require drilling and blasting or use of jackhammers or bullpoints."* (*Note:* This is the other section of the contract in dispute.)

   The drawings entitled Plan and Profile, which were incorporated by reference in the contract, showed a vertical measurement for excavation down from the current roadbed grade or ground surface. Riverside County drafted this contract.

   B. Rose submitted two payments for removal of rock measured from ground level to 6 inches below the pipe. (*Note:* You should make a drawing of these details.) Riverside paid both invoices. However, prior to the third payment, Riverside County officials learned from officials from another state agency that this other agency paid for excavation only from the centerline of rock, not from the centerline of the street.

   Thereafter, Riverside refused to pay for excavation work that included charges from the centerline profile of the ground or street. Riverside agreed to pay for excavation only from the centerline profile of the actual rock encountered—that is, it refused to pay for excavation of dirt between the rock and the street. (Add this information to your drawing.) Riverside claimed that the contract clearly required it to pay only for excavation of rock and not dirt or "overburden" based on § 1.07 of the contract. (Reread this section of the contract.)

Centerline profile is a common engineering term used to indicate ground surface or street level. *Centerline* is defined by the U.S. Department of Interior as "[a] line marked on the roof of a roadway . . ." In the *Dictionary of Mining, Mineral, and Related Terms, profile* is defined as "[a] drawing used in civil engineering to show a vertical section of the ground along a surveyed line or graded work." The engineering supervisor of the project, an employee of Riverside County, testified in a deposition that the "the term 'centerline profile' in the contract means ground or street level."

B. Rose testified during its deposition that at a meeting immediately prior to the execution of the contract, and at a meeting held nine days thereafter, Riverside County informed B. Rose that it intended to pay for removal of material measured from ground level to 6 inches below the pipe. Riverside County disputed that any such conversations took place.

B. Rose excavated 6,353.1 cubic yards of rock and gravel (10% less than the amount, originally estimated in the contract) and sought payment of $190,563. Riverside paid $94,133.40. Riverside stipulated in a Request for Admission that the amount of excavation performed by B. Rose was accurately measured, if the measurement was taken from the centerline of the street.

Issue: Does Riverside owe B. Rose for the excavated material from the level of the street down to the level of the rock?

Subissue 1: Is the contract ambiguous?

Rule:

Argument:

Answer: Yes

Subissue 2:

Rule: (*Hint:* parol evidence rule)

Premises:

Answer: Yes

Subissue 3:

Rule: (*Hint:* course of dealing)

Premises:

Answer: Yes

Answer: Riverside owes B. Rose for all excavated material.

Answers to Selected Problems

1. *Subissue 1:* Is the contract ambiguous?

   Rule: A contract is ambiguous if it is capable of two relatively reasonable meanings.

   (*Note:* Be sure to cite the page number where the rule was found.)

   Premises: The two meanings being advocated by the parties are:

   a. *Contractor's meaning:* Contractor need not install a ROPS on the trenching machine.

   b. *Owner's meaning:* Contractor must install a ROPS on the trenching machine.

The contractor is claiming that the trencher is not one of the types of machines that require a ROPS. The safety manual states that ROPS are required on *"crawler and rubber-tire tractors such as dozers, push-and-pull tractors, winch tractors, mowers, off-the-highway self-propelled pneumatic-tire earth movers such as trucks, pans, scrapers, bottom dumps, and end dumps, motor graders.* The owner is claiming that the trencher is covered by the list. Both of these meanings are reasonable given the vagueness of the language and the fact the trencher is not specifically mentioned in the list.

Answer: Yes

Subissue 2: Which rules can be applied and how?

Rule: The party's prior dealings can be used to interpret a present dispute. If the parties have on prior occasions acted in a certain way, the law assumes that, all things being equal, the prior actions are still accepted. *Note:* Be sure to cite the page number where the rule was found.

Premises: The facts state that the contractor had performed similar contracts for Lindco in the recent past and had *not* been told to install ROPS on trenchers of the type used here. This is a prior dealing between the parties and can be used by the court to clarify the ambiguity in the contract.

Answer: Sanchez prevails.

2. *Subissue 1:* Is the contract ambiguous?

   Rule: Same as above

   Premises: Same as above

   Answer: Yes

   Subissue 2: Which rules can be applied?

   Issue: Can the conversation between the authorized representative of the owner and the contractor be used to clarify the ambiguity in the contractor's favor?

   Rule: The parol evidence rule states that extrinsic evidence *can* be used to explain or clarify an *ambiguous* term of a contract.

   Premises: Since this contract has been determined to be ambiguous (see subissue 1) the court can use the conversation to clarify the ambiguity and impart to the contract the meaning the contractor has presented. The parol evidence rule prevents extrinsic evidence from being used only when the contract is *unambiguous*. If a contract is ambiguous, extrinsic evidence, such as the conversation here, can be used by the court to aid it in determining which of two competing meanings it should give to the contract; therefore, this conversation can be used to decide which of the two competing meanings the court should uphold. This conversation supports the contractor, and no other competing evidence exists.

   Answer: Sanchez prevails.

Appendix A

CASE: BLINDERMAN CONSTRUCTION CO. v. U.S.

695 F.2d 552 (Fed. Cir. 1982)

DECISION OF THE COURT DELIVERED BY THE HONORABLE JUDGE COWEN
(The opinion has been condensed for student use.)

The claim grows out of a contract entered into between the contractor and the Department of the Navy (Navy) for installation of permanent improvements in multifamily housing at the Great Lakes, Illinois, Naval Base (Base.)

The claim of $45,312 includes three separate items. (*Note:* We are interested in only one of the claims, that is, the contractor's claim for delay damages caused by the Navy.)

I. Factual Background and Prior Proceedings

By contract dated March 31, 1978, the contractor was required to furnish and install electrical meters, gas meters, hot water meters, hot water heating meters, and condensate meters in [656] apartments housing Naval personnel at the Base. The contract was to have been completed by September 12, 1978, but the completion date was extended by a change order to October 3, 1978.

Since the work was not completed until October 20, 1978, the contractor was charged by the Navy with liquidated damages of $2,975 for 17 days of inexcusable delays.

III. The Claim for Delays in Obtaining Access to the Apartments

This claim presents the only difficult issue in this appeal, because its resolution involves an *interpretation* of the following provisions of the contract [emphasis added]:

[*The italicized word* interpretation *tells you this is a scope problem or issue.*]

SCHEDULING OF WORK: Work shall be scheduled to issue [*sic*]

[*The word* sic *means the text has quoted the contract exactly, and the grammatical or spelling errors appear in the original text*]

minimum description [*sic*] of service to the housing units. The contractor shall notify the occupants of the housing unit at least 3 days prior to commencing any work in a housing unit. The contractor shall perform his work between the hours of 8:00 A.M. and 5:00 A.M., and having once started work in a housing unit shall work to completion in consecutive work days. . . .

In no case shall a unit be left overnight without a completed meter installation, including testing and resumption of gas service.

METHODS and SCHEDULES OF PROCEDURES: The work shall be executed in a manner and at such times that will cause the least practicable disturbance to the occupants of the buildings and normal activities of the station. Before starting any work, the sequence of operations and the methods of conducting the work shall have been approved by the Contracting Officer.

The facts as found by the Board, or which are otherwise established by undisputed evidence, show that the contractor experienced considerable difficulty and delays in gaining access to approximately 60 apartments. After the contractor had prepared and delivered to the Navy a progress chart showing when the contractor required access to the buildings, the contractor's quality control manager had the responsibility for notifying the occupants of the time when the work in their apartments was to be performed. The specifications required that this notice be given 3 days before work was to be commenced, and the CQC attempted to notify them personally at least 3 but usually 7 days before the work was to begin.

Notices to the occupants were given in the morning, during the noon-hour, or in the afternoon. If CQC could not reach the occupants during the day, he tried to see them in the evening. If all of these efforts failed, the CQC would, in accordance with a *suggestion made by the Navy's project manager, leave a yellow card on the doorknob of the apartment, indicating when the work in that unit would begin* [emphasis added]. The Navy had, at the site of the work, a project manager who represented the contracting officer in the administration of the contract, and most of the contractor's dealings were with this project manager.

In some instances, the occupants refused to permit the contractor's workmen to enter their apartments, even after notice was received by them. At times, the contractor was unable to serve personal notice because the occupants were on military leave for periods for as long as 2 weeks. In other instances, the occupants would go out during the lunch hour while the work was being performed, leaving their doors locked with the tools of the workmen inside. On most of the occasions complained of by the contractor, the occupants were not at home when the work was scheduled despite notice given to them in person or by a card left on the doorknob.

Whenever the contractor or the subcontractors were unable to gain access to an apartment for any of the reasons mentioned above, they would call on the [government's] project manager to provide the access they needed.

[*What the government's project manager did do to help the contractor gain access:*]

If the occupants could be contacted by telephone, the project manager would ask them to return home and permit entry into their apartments. If the occupants were absent from the apartment on vacation, the project manager first telephoned them to get permission to enter their apartments. Then he would obtain keys from the Housing Section at the Base to admit the workmen. Thus on occasion, access by the workmen could not be obtained until several days after the scheduled date for commencing work.

Shortly after experiencing delays for lack of access to the apartments, the contractor notified the project manager that the contractor's responsibilities ended after it had notified the occupants in the manner described above [*in the section of the contract entitled "Scheduling of Work"*]; that a record would be kept of the delays, and that a claim would be submitted later for the increased costs incurred as a result of such delays. [*Procedural note: The claim for delay was submitted by the contractor to the Navy and denied. This opinion is the result of an appeal of that decision*].

[*According to the contractor, what were its duties under the contract regarding access?*]

The project manager, by letter of December 22, 1978, took a position that was inconsistent

[*Use of the word* inconsistent *should alert you to a problem. Courts do not like inconsistency.*]

with his conduct during the performance of the contract. He stated that the claimed delays were due to the failure of the contractor to notify the occupants as required by the specifications, and that placing cards on doorknobs of the housing units did not constitute notification, because the occupants could have been on leave at the time. He also denied that the Navy had any responsibility for assisting the contractor to obtain access to the apartments.

During his testimony before the Board, the project manager gave his interpretation of the provisions of the specifications which have been quoted above.

[*What does the Navy say the contract says about the Navy helping the contractor gain access?*]

He testified that the "Scheduling of Work" provision required the contractor to give actual notice to the individual occupants, and that the contractor was obligated to obtain an agreement with each occupant for the performance of work in that particular apartment. It also was his view that if the tenant refused access, no agreement had been reached, and the contractor had not complied with the specifications. He further stated that the contractor's responsibility to gain access to each apartment never terminated.

On appeal, the contractor argued before the Board that the 150-day completion schedule, the provision for liquidated damages, the specification limiting work hours, and the requirement for the contracting officer's approval of the construction schedule and sequence of the work implied a duty on the part of the Navy to make the apartments in the buildings available in accordance with the schedule and sequence of work which had been approved by the project manager.

[Issue 1 raised: Is the contract ambiguous?]

The answer to the question is not free of doubt; however, after considering the language of the specifications, and other pertinent facts, and circumstances, we conclude that [the Navy had a contractual duty to aid the contractor in gaining access to the apartments.]

Therefore, we hold that the contractor complied with the "Scheduling of Work" provision by giving as much notice as was reasonably required by that provision. After the contractor notified the project manager that the contractor's reasonable efforts had not resulted in gaining entry to certain apartments, the Navy was under an implied obligation to provide such access so that the contractor could complete the contract within the time required by its terms.

[Implied terms rule introduced.]

Consequently, if any part of the contractor's work was thereafter delayed for an unreasonable period of time because of the Navy's failure to provide access to the apartments, the contractor is, under the "Suspension of Work" clause, entitled to an increase in the cost of performing the contract. We have reached this conclusion on several grounds.

[The preceding is the court's argument in support of its conclusion.]

We find that if their ordinary meaning

[The ordinary meaning rule is introduced.]

is attributed to the words used in the "Scheduling of Work" provision, there is simply nothing in that specification or elsewhere which states that the contractor is required to make an arrangement with or obtain an agreement from each apartment occupant as the Board decided.

[The preceding is the court's argument in support of its conclusion.]

It was reasonable for the contractor to interpret this provision of the specifications to relieve it of further responsibility to notify the occupants after reasonable efforts to give the notice had been exhausted. If the Government had intended the specifications to convey an intent

[The clear expression of intent rule is introduced.]

to require the contractor to make an agreement covering the matters found by the Board with each of the 656 occupants, the drafters of the specifications wholly failed to convey this meaning. Therefore, the provision must be construed against the Government. *Troup Bros., Inc. v. United States*, 224 Ct. Cl. 594, 643 F.2d 719 (1980); *Singer-General Precision, Inc. v. United States*, 192 Ct. Cl. 435, 427 F.2d 1187 (1970); *Jefferson Constr. Co. v. United States*, 151 Ct. Cl. 75 (1960.)

The conduct

[The conduct of the parties' rule is introduced.]

of both parties during construction and before the contractor's claim was submitted to the project manager provides persuasive evidence that the contract should be construed as urged by the contractor. Although the Board refers to the assistance given by the project manager as "cooperation," our study of the record reveals that the project manager recognized the obligation of the Navy to provide access to the apartments when it could not be obtained by the contractor. The Navy knew when the contract was entered into that it would be impossible for the contractor to gain access when the occupants refused to admit the workmen or when the occupants were on leave and their whereabouts were unknown to the contractor. The record supports the conclusion that the project manager realized that in such circumstances, it would be necessary for the Navy to provide the necessary access in order to enable the contractor to complete the work within the time required by the Navy. It is a familiar principle of contract law that the parties' contemporaneous construction of an agreement, before it has become the subject of a dispute, is entitled to great weight in its interpretation. *State of Arizona v. United States*, 216 Ct. Cl. 221, 575 F.2d 855 (Ct. Cl. 1978.)

The record shows that approximately 1-1/2 years before this contract was entered into, the contractor had completed a project involving some of the same buildings on the same Base.

[*The course of dealing rule is introduced.*]

The work involved an overhauling of the kitchens. In that instance, when the contractor was unable to notify the individual occupants, the Navy was informed to that effect and promptly provided access to the apartments.

We do not hold that the contractor was justified in believing that it would encounter no difficulty in notifying the occupants when the work would begin; however, the evidence shows that in view of the contractor's previous experience on the same base, it believed the Navy would provide access to the apartments when such difficulties arose.

Appendix B

CASE: COMMUNITY HEATING & PLUMBING CO. v. KELSO

987 F.2d 1575, 1582 (Fed. Cir. 1993)

(The opinion has been abbreviated, and some footnotes have been omitted.)

This is an appeal from a decision of the Armed Services Board of Contract Appeals (board) denying the claims brought by Community Heating and Plumbing Co., Inc. (Community) against the Secretary of the United States Navy (Navy.) The claims arose out of a contract to remove and replace the condensate and steam system located at the Marine Corps Air Station, Cherry Point, North Carolina. Community seeks compensation for: (1) the costs associated with the installation of conduit sleeves in existing manholes and . . . *(other claim omitted).*

The Conduit Sleeve Claim

On May 18, 1982, Community submitted a bid in response to the Navy's Invitation for Bids. On May 19, Navy Contract Specialist Rosalind D. Rogers replied by mail informing Community that although it was the apparent low bidder, its bid appeared "somewhat out of line" as compared to the Navy's estimate and the other bids received. In fact, Community's estimate for the project was 14% below the Navy estimate and 5% below the second lowest bid received. Accordingly, Ms. Roger's letter instructed Community to check its proposal and confirm its bid price in writing. In addition, Navy officials decided that if the bid were confirmed, Community should also be required to meet with the Navy officials to reverify the project's scope.

[*Why did the Navy officials meet with Community to reverify the project's scope?*]

On June 1, 1982, Community confirmed its bid, and on June 3 a bid confirmation meeting was held at the Navy's offices.

On June 4, 1982, the day after the meeting, Mr. Levy [employee of Community] wrote a letter to the Navy referencing the meeting and stating in part:

The items listed below were discussed and approved during our June 3, 1982, conference.

3. The conduit sleeves shown on Sheet M-5 in the lower righthand corner are for the new manholes only for both condensate and steam.

The Navy responded to Community's June 4 communication with a letter dated June 21, 1982. That letter made no express objection to Community's contract interpretation regarding the conduit sleeves, but it did state in part:

The meeting referred to in your letter was held as part of the bid confirmation process in order to insure that you had considered all components of the job in preparing your bid. Contract awards on formally advertised procurements must be made in strict accordance with the terms of the Invitation for Bids.

It is requested that you verify in writing the correctness of your bid in accordance with the Invitation for Bids.

On June 30, 1982, the bid was confirmed in writing, and on July 15, 1982, the contract, No. N62470-81-C-1345, was awarded to Community.

After the contract was awarded, the Navy directed Community to furnish conduit sleeves in *new and existing manholes where needed.* Community then brought a claim for additional compensation, ASBCA No. 38167, arguing that the contract required installation of conduit sleeves at *new manholes only.*

[*What are the two conflicting interpretations of the contract?*]

Upon consideration of the evidence, the board ruled in favor of the Navy in a final decision dated February 24, 1992. The board held that the contract was unambiguous since there was "no way" the contract could be construed in the manner advocated by Community. Community now appeals.

Community argues that the contract contained latent ambiguity and, because the June 4 letter gave notice of Community's contract interpretation, the Navy is bound to that interpretation by its failure to object (citations omitted). However, Community's alternate contract interpretation cannot be adopted if the present contract is unambiguous (citations omitted).

Community asserts that the contract, as it pertains to the conduit sleeves, is ambiguous. It contests the Navy's reading of the contract, which was adopted by the board, and argues in favor of an alternative contract interpretation based upon its own reading of the contract language, specifications and drawings; however, *contracts are not necessarily rendered ambiguous by the mere fact that the parties disagree as to the meaning of their provisions* (citations omitted, emphasis added).

[*The italicized words preceding and following are what part of the FIRPA?*]

That the parties disagree with a specification, or that a contractor's interpretation thereof is conceivable, does not necessarily render that specification ambiguous so as to require that it be construed against the drafter (citations omitted). *A contract is ambiguous if it is susceptible of two different and reasonable interpretations, each of which is found to be consistent with the contract language* (citations omitted, emphasis added).

Here, Community's contract interpretation, based on its reading of the contract drawings and specifications, is not reasonable. First, there is substantial evidence in the drawings to support the board's finding that conduit sleeves are required in new and existing manholes. Second, the M-6 project drawings are entitled "Typical Detail Showing Penetration of Existing Manholes, or Bldg. Pit Wall for Condensate Line." Finally, other bidders interpreted the drawings to mean that the conduit sleeves are required in new and existing manholes. (*Footnote:* For example, the Sheet M-6 drawings indicate that the existing manhole wall must be patched with concrete; however, if conduit sleeves were required in new manholes only, the concrete around existing manholes would not need to be broken and patched up to install the sleeve. . . .)

[*The preceding is the court's argument concerning the issue: Are both interpretations reasonable? What conclusion does the court make?*]

Accordingly, the contract is unambiguous, and Community's conduit sleeve claim must be rejected (emphasis added).

[*The preceding italicized words are what part of the FIRPA?*]

If a contract contains a patent ambiguity, the contractor is under a duty to inquire and must seek clarification of the proper contract interpretation (citations omitted).

In addition, where a discrepancy exists in the contract drawings, as Community here alleges, a contractor may be required to seek clarification (citations omitted). The court considered this discrepancy obvious and held that the contractor should have asked for clarification. . . .

However, it is not enough under the duty to inquire that a contractor merely make an initial inquiry (citation omitted). Also instructive on this point is *Construction Service Co.,* ASBCA No. 4998, 59-1 BCA P 2077 at 8838, where a contractor requested clarification of a contract but received an addendum which did not alleviate the confusion. The board found that the duty to inquire had not been met. "If after receiving the addendum, the intended meaning was still not clear to appellant, it should have requested a further clarification."

This holding was reiterated in *Southside Plumbing Co.,* ASBCA No. 8120, 64 BCA P 4314 at 20,860. In that case, a contractor became aware of an ambiguity prior to bidding, sought and received an addendum that was expected to furnish clarification and later realized that the addendum failed to resolve the ambiguity. Without seeking further clarification, the contractor bid on the basis of its own interpretation, which, under the circumstances, was more favorable to the contractor. The board held that the contractor had not met its burden under the duty to inquire. "Here, the appellant not only recognized the ambiguity but made inquiry. This circumstance, in our opinion, brings the case within the principle in *Construction Service Company,* that the inquiry should have been pursued to clarification" (citations omitted).

The Navy's response to the June 4 letter expressly failed to address the issue of the conduit sleeves and thus provided a strong indication to Community that confusion still existed between the parties. Community was therefore obligated to request further clarification regarding the proper installation of the conduit sleeves. While it troubles this court that the Navy did not directly and timely object to Community's contract interpretation, Community nevertheless failed to satisfy its own obligations under the duty to inquire and thus acted at its own risk when it proceeded to perform on the contract.

10

Changes and Additions to the Contract

Parties to the construction contract often make changes and additions to the contract, which are frequently covered by contract provisions that should be followed. In addition to recovery under contract law, parties may be entitled to additional compensation under the theories of promissory estoppel and waiver when a change or addition has been made to the contract.

Changes

The changes clause in a construction contract allows the owner to make changes in the contract without affecting the validity of the contract. This type of change—one that is made by only one party to a contract—is called a **unilateral change.** Unilateral changes are *not* favored in the law, and the general rule regarding unilateral changes is, they are forbidden; however, changes in the plans and specifications are such a normal part of the construction industry that this rule has been modified for the industry—the law allows unilateral changes to the contract as long as the owner pays the contractor for the change. In many contracts the parties agree in advance on certain items, such as overhead and profit, to be paid the contractor for changes. If the parties do not agree in advance, the law will require the owner to pay a reasonable amount, including an amount for overhead and profit.

Changes are of two types: *changes to the scope of the project* and *changes in the amount of time allowed for completion of a project.* For example, if the owner requests a different type of roofing than what is outlined in the plans and specifications, the owner has made a **change in the scope of the contract** by ordering different or additional work (see

Figure 10–1). This chapter covers only changes to the scope of the project. Changes to the amount of time to complete a project are discussed in Chapter 11, Delays and Acceleration.

Changes to the Contract

Rule: The owner may make changes to the contract as long as the owner pays the contractor for the change. The parties may agree in advance on the amount to be paid, but if they do not, a reasonable amount, including overhead and profit, will be paid to the contractor.

Most claims related to change orders concern only a dispute between the owner and the contractor related to the cost of the change. For example, the contractor estimates that the cost to install the changed roofing is $5000, and the owner estimates the cost should be only $3500. If the parties disagree about whether the owner has changed the contract, the issue is one of scope. Interpretation of the contract and scope issues are discussed in Chapter 9, Scope.

Change Orders

Changes to contracts are handled by **change orders.** Most contracts contain detailed instructions on how changes and change orders are to be handled. Failure to follow these instructions can result in delays in payment or in a denial of payment.

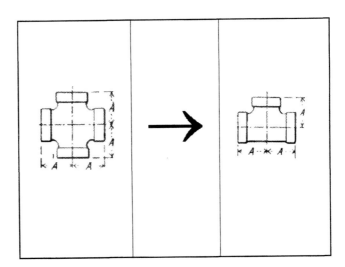

Figure 10-1 Change in scope © 2000–2001
www.arttoday. com

Contract Provisions Regarding Changes Orders

Rule: Contract provisions regarding change orders will be upheld.

Exceptions to this rule: Waiver, promissory estoppel

Courts will uphold provisions in contracts requiring written change orders. For example, in the case of *Bibeau Cons. Co. v. Hauser Brothers, Inc.*, the contract between Bibeau and the plumbing subcontractor, Hauser, contained the following clause:[1]

> *"Please do not do any extra work on the . . . project unless you have a written order from us. If you do, it will be your responsibility, not ours."*

In this case Bibeau Construction Co. was one of several prime contractors on a project. Hauser was a subcontractor for Bibeau. Hauser performed additional and *necessary* grading of the site, and it then sued Bibeau for payment. The additional grading was required because another prime contractor on the job, who was *not* a party to the suit, failed to *grade* the site according to the specifications. The court upheld the contractual provision and ruled that Hauser was *not* entitled to any additional payment for the grading it had performed.

In another case, *Hunter Brothers Systems v. Brantley Const. Co.*, the prime contractor was required to prepare a progress schedule for the construction of a warehouse.[2] According to the schedule, *the roof was to be completed by May 2, and immediately thereafter, the electrical subcontractor was to begin installation of electrical conduit.* The contract between the owner and the prime contractor contained a contractual requirement that the owner approve all changes in the contract schedule. The roof was *not completed* on May 2; however, the prime contractor requested that the electrical subcontractor begin the electrical work immediately. The electrical subcontractor refused to begin work, and it did not do so until the roof was completed in July. The prime contractor withheld the subcontractor's payment, claiming the subcontractor had breached the contract by failing to begin installation of the electrical work on May 2, the date in the contract. Although the prime contractor insisted on the immediate commencement of the work, rather than waiting until the roof was completed as stated in the contract, the prime contractor never had a change order to that effect executed by the owner.

10-1. THINK

The prime contractor in the preceding example could have won the lawsuit or arbitration if it had had a written change order signed by the owner. What should the change order have said?

---

[1]*Bibeau Cons. Co. v. Hauser Brothers, Inc.*, 39 A.D.2d 855, 333 N.Y.S.2d 459 (1972).

[2]*Hunter Brothers Systems v. Brantley Const. Co.*, 332 S.E.2d 206 (S.C. 1985).

In the case *Dehnert v. Arrow Sprinklers, Inc.* the court denied Arrow's claim for additional compensation because it had failed to follow the procedures prescribed in the contract when it changed the type of sprinkler heads on a project.[3] At the bid opening, Arrow, the contractor, informed the school board it intended to use plastic sprinkler heads instead of the aluminum sprinkler heads called for in the specifications. The board awarded Arrow the contract as low bidder. One week later, Arrow met with the architect, presented its layouts, and discussed the use of the plastic sprinkler heads. The architect verbally approved their use. Later, the architect accepted in writing Arrow's layouts, which contained specific references to the plastic sprinkler heads.

After the project was 80% complete, a dispute arose concerning the use of the plastic sprinkler heads. The architect ordered Arrow to replace the plastic sprinkler heads with aluminum sprinkler heads. When Arrow refused, the architect recommended to the school board that it terminate Arrow's contract, which it did. The state supreme court denied Arrow relief; that is, the court agreed that the architect's actions were acceptable. The court stated that Arrow had not followed the procedure under the contract for obtaining change orders, and therefore the owner was within its rights under the contract to terminate the contract for a material breach.

The court stated that the architect's preliminary approval of the layouts could not substitute for the contract change procedure that required an order signed by the school board. Since the substitution of plastic sprinkler heads was never effectively approved, the work was nonconforming, and the architect had a duty to reject nonconforming work.

This case was very much on the borderline. Another court might have found that the owner had *waived* the use of the aluminum sprinkler heads given the facts; however, contractors cannot depend on the waiver doctrine to save them from their failure to obtain a written change order. *It is critical that contractors follow the procedures prescribed in the contract for changed work.*

Guidelines for Owner-Ordered Changed Work

Following the listed simple guidelines will decrease the number of claims related to change orders:

1. Document the change to be made; and
2. Estimate all expected costs to be incurred including additional costs for labor, material, overhead, delivery, storage, and any other costs; and
3. Estimate the time increase needed to comply with the change, if any; and
4. Send the preceding, in written form, to the owner or the owner's representative depending on the instructions in the contract. Most contracts contain a specific format to be followed in the event of a change. *Read the contract, and follow the prescribed procedures for changes.*

Major changes in the construction project should not be undertaken without some type of authorization *from the owner.* The design professional is not the owner. It is

---

[3]*Dehnert v. Arrow Sprinklers, Inc.*, 705 P.2d 846 (Wyo. 1985).

unlikely that the design professional has authorization from the owner to make major changes. For a more complete discussion of the authority of the architect or engineer to order changes see Chapter 6, Relationships among the Parties on the Project.

If there is no time to obtain the owner's authorization prior to initiating the change, the contractor should *immediately* follow up the change with documentation outlining the change and explaining why there was no time to obtain authorization from the owner. A change without prior authorization of the owner is called a **field change.** Field changes should be documented as soon as possible after the designer orders the change.

If the field change is major, the contractor must place a great deal of trust in the owner. Trust plays a very important part in the construction industry, but it is usually outside the realm of law. Trust is discussed in Chapter 5, Law, Ethics, and Morality. One reason laws are passed and enforced is so parties need *not* trust one another but can depend on the power of the government to enforce certain duties and behaviors. It is a testament to the integrity of the parties in this industry that only a few of the many, many field changes lead to arbitration or litigation.

Construction Change Directive

AIA Document A201-1997 §7.2.1 defines a change order as follows:

> "A Change Order is a written instrument prepared by the Architect and signed by the Owner, Contractor and Architect, stating their agreement upon all of the following:
>
> 1. change in the Work;
> 2. the amount of the adjustment, if any, in the Contract Sum; and
> 3. the extent of the adjustment, if any, in the Contract Time.

By contract definition, then, a change order involves agreement by all the parties to the change.

If the contractor does not agree to one of the preceding elements, for example, the contractor believes the change will cost more or take more time than the architect estimates, no change order is made; instead the architect issues a **construction change directive.** The construction change directive requires the contractor to perform the work as instructed by the owner and architect, and the contractor may file a claim. The amount due the contractor will then be determined through the claims procedure outlined in the contract.

Constructive Change

The concept of *constructive change* (this concept is *not* related to the concept of construction change directive discussed above) has developed in federal law to help resolve a situation that contains both a scope issue and a change issue. A **constructive change** is defined as owner conduct that is not a formal change order but that has the effect of requiring the contractor to perform work different from that required by the original contract. Owners must pay the contractor for constructive changes that increase the project cost.

Constructive Change

Rule: Owners must pay the contractor for constructive changes that increase the project cost. A constructive change is defined as owner conduct that is not a formal change order but that has the effect of requiring the contractor to perform work different from that required by the original contract.

The constructive change rule is most frequently applied in cases in which

- the plans and/or specifications are defective and as a result the contractor is required to do extra work, or
- the owner's representative misinterprets the contract and requires additional work or rejects work that is in fact in compliance with the plans and specifications.

Case A: Defective Plans and/or Specifications

If the plans and specifications are defective, and the contractor is required to do extra work to remedy the defect, the contractor is entitled to reimbursement. This concept is a natural outgrowth of the *Spearin* doctrine, which states that the owner impliedly warrants that the contractor is not liable for damages related to defective plans and specifications. In the real world, many of the claims associated with construction contracts are resolved long after the project is completed. Neither party can halt the performance of the contract when minor breaches or problems arise (see Chapter 14, Termination of the Contract and Contract Damages). The parties must continue toward completion of the project. This means that *should a problem arise, the contractor cannot merely stop working until the problem is resolved; the contractor must continue working and resolve disputes at a later time.*

EXAMPLE:

In the case of *Appeal of M. A. Mortenson Co.*, the Corps of Engineers awarded a contract to M. A. Mortenson Co. for construction of a medical facility at Elmendorf Air Force Base in Alaska.[4] In order to provide protection from earthquakes, the contract called for the mechanical and electrical equipment to be in metal channels supported by strut posts hanging plumb from the supporting structure. A drawing detail indicated a strut mounting plate connection using a flat, rigid mounting plate.

---

[4]*Appeal of M. A. Mortenson Co.*, ASBCA No. 51241 (March 3, 1999), *Construction Claims Monthly*, April 1999.

None of the drawings indicated compound roof slopes, in which both east–west and north–south slopes occur on a single roof, but Mortenson's subcontractor encountered such a slope on one roof. This necessitated extensive reconfiguration and shimming of the strut mounting plates. Mortenson filed a claim for a constructive change, and the government denied the claim.

The government argued that the compound roof slope could and should have been detected from the drawings prior to bid submittal. The government also claimed that there was nothing defective in the original strut mounting design. Only "minor adjustments" had been required, and the amount claimed by Mortenson was excessive.

The Board of Contract Appeals (Board) ruled that "only [by] carefully analyzing and synthesizing the architectural and structural drawings taken together" could the contractor have detected the compound roof slope. The slope would then have to be compared with the strut connection detail. The Board ruled that contractors bidding on federal projects are not expected or required to conduct this level of design analysis. The Board determined that the contract had been constructively changed, and Mortenson was entitled to the additional sum.

Case B: Government's Representative Misinterprets the Contract

On a particular project the designer and the contractor may disagree on what is required by the plans and specifications. This is an issue of scope. Again, in the real world the contractor cannot stop performance until the issue is determined but must proceed with the work and resolve issues at a later time. The owner may order the contractor to complete the work as required by the designer, but later it may be determined, by a judge or arbitrator, that the owner or designer's interpretation of the scope was wrong. In effect, the owner has ordered the contractor do additional work not covered by the scope of the contract, and the owner must pay the contractor.

In a dispute involving this issue the judge or arbitrator will *first apply the scope rules to determine what the contract said. Second, if the contractor has been required to perform any work other than what the contract says, the owner will be required to compensate the contractor for the additional work done.* Additional work is discussed in more detail later.

For example, a bridge construction contract permitted a half-inch tolerance for the *bridge deck*. The owner's inspectors, however, insisted on exact compliance with the specified dimensions for the *bridge deck reinforcing steel*, insisting the half-inch tolerance was not for the bridge deck reinforcing steel, but only for the *final deck covering*. The contractor's costs to install the deck reinforcing steel without the tolerance was much greater. The contractor is entitled to additional payment because the owner's inspectors misinterpreted the contract, and the half-inch tolerance was also for the bridge deck reinforcing steel within the bridge deck.

Destruction of the Contract

It is possible, although extremely rare, for *the court to simply destroy the original contract between the parties when a large number of changes have been made.* The party performing the work is then paid a reasonable compensation for the work completed, usually under the legal principles of promissory estoppel.

Destruction of the Contract

Rule: When the owner makes a large number of changes to the contract,
the original contract is destroyed and contractor is paid a reasonable amount
for the work completed.

Although this concept appears in several forms in case law, no court actually uses the term *destruction of the contract.* This term is used in this text to aid in understanding the concepts of *abandonment* (state law term) and *cardinal change* (federal law term.) Under the concepts of abandonment and cardinal change, the contract is destroyed.

Every change to a contract has a cost associated with it. This cost may be small or large, depending on the change. In a very few cases a very large number of changes may cause such a decrease in efficiency that the contractor (or subcontractor) cannot realize any profit on the job or may in fact suffer a loss. In that case it will be to the contractor or subcontractor's advantage to claim that the original contract has been destroyed and seek payment for reasonable costs and profit in performing the work.

The advantage to the party who can convince the court that the contract has been destroyed is that the party to be paid is no longer paid pursuant to the original contract. That party is paid a "reasonable" amount, including profit and overhead.

The concepts of **abandonment** and **cardinal change** are not easily applied. These terms can be defined as a single large change or many small changes that are so great as to breach the original contract or destroy it.

> There is no exact formula for determining the point at which a single change or series of changes must be considered to be beyond the scope of the contract and necessarily in breach of it. Each case must be analyzed on its own facts and in light of its own circumstances, giving just consideration to the magnitude and quality of the changes ordered and their cumulative effect upon the project as a whole. The contractor cannot claim a breach of the contract if the project it ultimately constructed is essentially the same as the one it agreed in the contract to erect.[5]

For example, Havens, the general contractor subcontracted the installation of ductwork on a large project to the subcontractor, Randolph. Havens was to manufacture and

---

[5]*Wunderlich Constr. Co. v. U.S.*, 351 F.2d 956 (Ct.Cl. 1965).

provide the ductwork, and Randolph was to install it. The contract contained the schedule for the installation and the price to be paid to Randolph. Havens was not able to manufacture the ductwork per the schedule, and Havens provided it to Randolph on a totally different schedule from that in the original contract. Partway through the performance of the contract, Havens sent Randolph a change order, changing the schedule of installation and including a "No damage except time extension for delay" clause into the contract. This "no damage" clause stated that Havens did not have to pay Randolph any money for the delays Havens had caused but only had to grant Randolph additional time to complete the work. (No damages for delay clauses are discussed in Chapter 14, Termination of the Contract and Contract Damages.) Randolph promptly objected to both items in the change order but continued work on the project.

Randolph completed the installation of the ductwork, all at an increased cost, all due to late delivery of the ductwork by Havens. These increased costs were incurred because the buildings were in a greater stage of completion than originally scheduled for the ductwork installation. Thus, Randolph had to cut through walls, ceilings, and the like to install the ducts and had to repair the cuts. This installation cost Randolph a great deal of additional money, which Havens did not want to pay.

The court destroyed the original contract between Havens and Randolph, and it ruled that Randolph was entitled to all its reasonable costs in installing the ductwork and to a profit.[6]

Additional Work and Additional Payment

It is not uncommon for the parties on a project to promise to do additional work or to agree to pay an additional sum to another. **Additional or extra work** is work outside the scope of the original contract and in addition to it.

Promises to perform additional or extra work may or may not be enforceable contracts. For example, the contractor may agree to paint the existing hallway when the original contract originally called only for painting the addition. If the contractor later fails or refuses to do this, the owner may keep part of the retainage or sue the contractor for damages. The owner may agree to pay the contractor an increased sum when unexpected difficulties arise, and later renege on the promise. A supplier may refuse to deliver needed supplies unless the contractor agrees to an increase in the agreed-on contract.

Requirement of a Writing

In order to fully understand the law in this area, it is necessary to understand first what *the law is not*. Many people have the mistaken belief that contracts must be in writing in order for an arbitrator or judge to enforce them. This is incorrect. Although it is certainly easier to obtain enforcement of a written contract, oral contracts (except those listed in the box below) are enforceable once any factual issues relating to the contract are decided. For example, assume the contractor and the owners have a contract for the contractor to put a

---

[6]Facts and ruling slightly modified from case of *Havens vs. Randolph*, 613 F.Supp. 514 (DC Mo. 1985).

room addition onto a house. The contractor later claims that the owners asked him to paint some rooms in the existing structure to match the addition, and the parties agreed to a payment of $500 for this work. The owners dispute this and claim they never asked the contractor to paint the existing rooms. The owners refuse to pay for the additional painting, claiming they will not pay for work they did not order. The contractor sues the owners for $500. The existence of this contract is an issue of fact to be decided by a jury, judge, or arbitrator. If the trier of fact decides after listening to the conflicting testimony that the contractor is telling the truth, the contractor is entitled to $500 and any other costs. (See Chapter 14, Termination of the Contract and Contract Damages for a discussion of damages available to parties who win arbitrations and lawsuits.)

The law does not require any contract to be in writing. Many centuries ago the common law developed what was, and still is, called the **statute of frauds.** It was not a statute; it was common law, and it was developed to prevent fraud in contracts. Most states have codified the requirements of the statute of frauds. For example, the Uniform Commercial Code § 2-201 states the following writing requirement for sales of goods over $500:

> Contracts for the sale of goods totaling $500 or more are enforceable only if "there is some writing sufficient to indicate that a contract for sale has been made between the parties and signed by the party against whom enforcement is sought or by his authorized agent or broker. A writing is not insufficient because it omits or incorrectly states a term. . . .

Requirement of a Writing

Rule (known as the *Statute of Frauds*): The law does not require any contract to be in writing. The following contracts must be *evidenced* by a writing *signed* by the party to be charged:

1. Sales of goods valued over $500
2. An agreement that cannot be performed within a year from the making of the agreement
3. An agreement to purchase, mortgage, or lease (for more than 1 year) real property
4. A promise to answer for the debt, default, or miscarriage of another
5. Agency contracts
6. An agreement that cannot be performed during the life of the entity making the promise
7. Agreements based on consideration of marriage

Many students change the meaning of the phrase *evidenced by a writing* into the phrase *agreement must be in writing;* however, the written evidence need *not* be an agreement. The following example from the case of *Gillespie v. Pulsifer* shows how the *signed* letter of the seller, which stated, *"I do not wish to sell the farm to you . . ."* was the writing that satisfied the statue of frauds, and the *seller was forced to sell the farm:*[7]

---

[7]*Gillespie v. Pulsifer,* 655 S.W.2d 123 (1983).

Seller advertised her farm for sale, including the location and the amount of acreage (which later turned out to be slightly too high). Buyers called and negotiated for the purchase at a specific price. The seller agreed. Later, a dispute arose over the amount of acreage, and the seller attempted to back out of the contract and sent the following letter to the buyer:

"Dear Mr. and Mrs. [Buyer]:

This letter is in regard to your bid to purchase my farm described as follows (description of property omitted):

I am returning herewith the down payment. . . . I do not wish to sell the farm to you and I do not believe I am under any legal obligation to do so. . . .

1. There is no written contract, and a written contract is required by the Statute of Frauds . . ."

The preceding letter, signed by the seller, satisfied the requirement of the statute of frauds. The court said no written contract was required.

Contractor's Entitlement to Payment for Additional Work

In general, the contractor or subcontractor is entitled to be paid for *additional* or *extra* work (not *changed* work) only when a new contract has been formed between the owner and the contractor for this additional or extra work; however, three exceptions to this rule exist. The first exception is a relatively new one: the contractor is entitled to additional payment if the owner has agreed to the payment. In addition to this exception, the doctrines of promissory estoppel and waiver may be avenues available to the contractor or subcontractor seeking payment for additional work. All are discussed more fully below.

New Contract

If a new contract is formed between the owner and the contractor for the additional work, the contractor is entitled to payment. This contract need not be in writing, and it is separate and apart from any other contracts between the parties. For example, if the owner changes the color of the paint, the owner has changed the scope of the contract but has not asked the contractor to perform additional or extra work. If the scope of the contract is to paint the interior of the building, and the owner asks the contractor to paint the outside of the building also, the owner has requested additional or extra work. The owner is entitled to this additional work only if a new contract is formed to support it.

Contractor Entitled to Payment for Additional Work

Rule: The contractor is entitled to payment for additional or extra work when a contract has been formed between the contractor and the owner for additional or extra work.

A contract for additional or extra work is formed whenever all of the following elements exist:

- Offer; and
- Acceptance; and
- Consideration; and
- Parties have legal capacity to enter into a contract; and
- Contract must be for a legal purpose, and
- No fraud or force is involved

All these elements exist when the owner orders the contractor to perform additional or extra work and the contractor agrees to do it for a certain price.

In an attempt to prevent the formation of a new contract for additional or extra work, many contracts contain provisions attempting to *prevent* the formation of new contracts for extra work. These are relatively new, and it is unlikely these provisions will be enforced. The more common practice is to insert provisions into the contract detailing how extra work is to be handled and the price to be paid to the contractor, at least for some items such as overhead and profit. This type of provision is likely to be upheld as long as the contractor is paid some amount for the additional work.

Payment When Unexpected Difficulties Arise

As a general statement of the law the contractor is not entitled to additional payment when unexpected or unusual events occur that make the contract more costly to perform than originally anticipated. The contractor may refuse to complete an unprofitable project unless the owner agrees to pay it additional compensation. This is an example of the *holdup game*. The **holdup game** is a negotiating tactic whereby the party who is obligated attempts to get more value from the other party by refusing to perform when the time for performance arrives. The classic example is *Alaska Packers' Ass'n v. Domenico*.[8] In that case twenty-one seamen entered into a contract with Domenico to work as fishermen during the season for $50/day plus a commission on the amount of fish caught; however on arriving at the harbor they demanded an additional $50/day and Domenico agreed, since it was impossible for him to find additional fishermen in time to complete the fishing for that season. After returning from fishing Domenico refused to pay the additional $50/day, and the fishermen sued him. The court refused to uphold Domenico's promise because it was unsupported by consideration, and therefore no contract had been formed.

Consideration is what each party gives up and receives in an exchange. The law requires that both parties give up something and both receive something in order for consideration to exist. Figures 10–2 through 10–4 illustrate this concept.

---

[8]*Alaska Packers' Ass'n v. Domenico*, 117 F 99 (9th Cir. 1902).

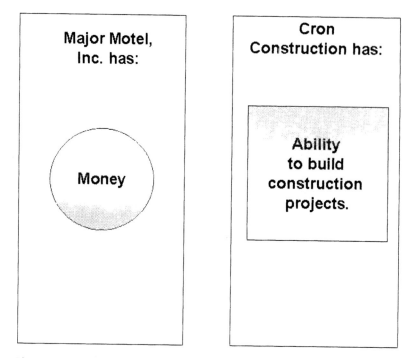

Figure 10–2 Both parties have something of value

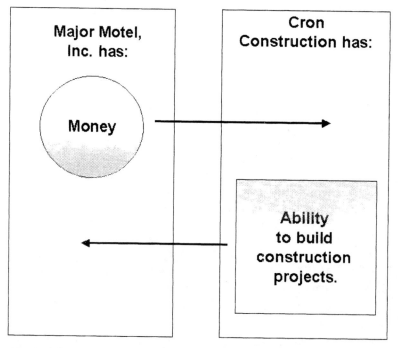

Figure 10–3 Each party gives up something of value to the other party

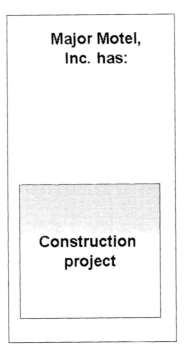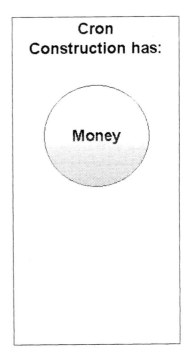

Figure 10-4 Both parties have something different of value

The contractor's promise to perform what it is already legally obligated to perform is not consideration. This is an example of a preexisting duty. A **preexisting duty** is a duty already legally owed to another and cannot be consideration for formation of a new contract.

Preexisting Duty Rule

Rule: A legal duty already owed to another cannot be consideration for a new contract.

A recent trend in the law, however, is to enforce any *voluntary* agreement between the parties. For example, in the case of *Angel v. Murray,* the contractor, Murray, had a five-year contract with the city to remove garbage at a set price.[9] After three years a large, new, unanticipated development in the city raised Murray's costs more than 25%. At a city council meeting the city agreed to an increase in the amount to be paid to Murray by $10,000 but later reneged on the promise. The court upheld the city's promise to pay the $10,000 despite the preexisting duty rule and made the following exception to that rule:

Agreements modifying contracts when unexpected or unanticipated difficulties arise during the course of the performance of a contract

---

[9] *Angel v. Murray,* 113 R.I. 482, 322 A.2d 630 (1974).

[are enforceable], even though there is no consideration for the modification,
as long as the parties agree voluntarily.

**Contractor Entitled to Payment for Additional Work When Unexpected
Difficulties Arise**

Rule: A contractor is entitled to payment of an additional sum *only* when
unexpected difficulties arise
if the owner voluntarily agrees to payment of the sum.

Owner's Entitlement to Performance of Additional Work

The owner is entitled to additional or extra work only when a new contract has been formed
covering the additional work. This contract, like all contracts, must be supported by consideration. The owner may believe the original consideration paid to the contractor covers additions; however, the owner will run into the preexisting duty rule. For example, assume the
owner asks the contractor to perform some additional work, and the contractor agrees.
Later, the contractor refuses to perform the additional work unless it is paid more money, but
the owner thought that the additional work was going to be covered by the original contract.

Owner Entitled to Performance of Additional Work

Rule: The owner is entitled to additional or extra work only if a contract has
been formed between the contractor and the owner for the work.

The owner faces the same problem as the contractor in the preceding section—the
owner has failed to give any consideration for the contractor's promise to do the additional
work, and therefore no contract is formed.

For example, in the case of *Steinbrecher v. Jones* the homeowners requested many,
many modifications to the original plans and specifications for their new home.[10] The contractor complied with many of these despite the fact it was not paid for any of them. After
the homeowners occupied the house, they continued to call the contractor and request
changes and modifications. The contractor refused to comply with any requests made by
the homeowners after they occupied the residence. The homeowners sued the contractor
for failing to comply with their requests and claimed the contractor had *waived* the provisions of the original contract. The court held that the contractor did not have to comply
with the requests. The court stated:

> *Not only must such modification or alterations be by [offer and acceptance]*
> *but must be based upon a valid consideration, and the original consideration*
> *of the construction of the house cannot be used as consideration for any*
> *agreement of modification or alteration in connection therewith.*

---

[10]*Steinbrecher v. Jones,* 153 S.E.2d 295 (W.Va. 1967).

Supplier's Entitlement to an Additional Payment

The *preexisting duty rule* also prevents the supplier from being entitled to additional payment. For example, assume a lumber supplier agreed to sell and deliver to the contractor a certain amount of lumber for $10,000. On the day the lumber is delivered, and framing is scheduled to begin, the lumber supplier refuses to unload the truck unless the contractor signs an invoice for $12,500. The lumber supplier claims decreases in the supply of lumber and increases in demand have raised the price of the lumber. The contractor signs the invoice in order to get the lumber unloaded. Is the lumber supplier entitled to $10,000 or $12,500? The answer is $10,000. The existence of the signed invoice and promise of the contractor to pay $12,500 is unsupported by consideration, and therefore no contract has been formed.

Implied Terms in Additional Work Contracts

If a contract is oral, as it often is with additional work, it may not contain many specific terms. When contracts, either oral or written, do not contain provisions covering a particular event the court may imply or add a term into the contract to cover that event. In other words, the court may imply *any* terms it deems necessary to compensate a party to a contract who has been damaged by the other's failure to perform. The concept of *implied terms* is discussed in more detail in Chapter 9, Scope.

Promissory Estoppel

An alternative theory available to the contractor (or subcontractor) seeking payment for changed or additional work is the doctrine of *promissory estoppel* introduced in Chapter 7, Mistakes in Bidding. Under this doctrine a contractor (or subcontractor) seeking payment for work is allowed recovery *even though no contract has been formed,* or the contractor has *failed to follow the procedures* outlined in the contract for changed work. The entity seeking payment for additional work or changed work under the doctrine of promissory estoppel must prove the following elements in order to recover:

1. Entity A (the party who should pay) has, by its actions or words, given Entity B (the party seeking payment) reason to believe Entity B will be paid for some service or product requested by Entity A; and

2. It is reasonable that Entity B would rely upon the above actions or words of Entity A; and

3. Entity B does rely upon the above actions or words of Entity A; and

4. Entity B performs the service or supplies the product to Entity A.

If all the listed elements are met, the court or arbitrator will order Entity A to pay Entity B.

EXAMPLE:

The original written agreement between the owner and the contractor was for the building of a home with a basement and the contractor completed this work. There was no written change order or written agreement between the parties concerning basement finishing or the amount to be paid to the contractor for that work. The basement finishing was outside the scope of the original agreement and not covered by it. The extra work was requested by the owner and was not voluntarily added by the contractor. It is unlikely a judge, jury, or arbitrator is going to believe that the contractor voluntarily decided to finish out the basement. A court or arbitrator is likely to hold that since the owner permitted the finishing work "under his very eyes," the owner is required to pay under the doctrine of promissory estoppel even though no contract had been formed. The court or arbitrator will determine a reasonable amount to be paid to the contractor for the additional work.   ■ ■ ■

Waiver

Another theory available to the contractor (or subcontractor) seeking payment for changed or additional work is the doctrine of *waiver.* **Waiver** is the knowing relinquishment of a known right. Waiver was discussed in detail Chapter 8, Specifications and Plans, but is useful in any number of situations in which the facts support its use.

In an effort to prevent claims arising from changes and/or additions to the contract, many contracts contain clauses requiring changes and/or additions to be in writing and signed by the owner or his representative before the changed or additional work commences. These clauses are an excellent idea as long as the parties follow the procedures outlined in the clauses; however, it is not uncommon for these clauses to be ignored. For example, assume that the contract on a certain project requires all changes and extras to be in writing and approved by the owner prior to completion of the work; however, on this job the owner has routinely paid for, without objection, changed work and additional work appearing on the contractor's monthly statements. The owner has *waived* the contractual requirement of an approved written change/extra order prior to the completion of the work. The exact point at which a waiver occurs depends on the specific facts of the case.

Waiver

Rule: Any provision of a contract can be waived, including provisions requiring approved written change orders or approved written orders for extras.

EXAMPLE:

In the case of *Doral Country Club, Inc. v. Curcie Brothers, Inc.*, Doral, the owner, contracted with Curcie, general contractor, for the construction of a nine-hole golf course.[11] The contract required all extras to be in writing, and it required that Curcie submit a "written request for additional compensation" in order to be paid for extras. Included in the original contract was a schedule specifying hourly rates for types of equipment and costs of materials. During construction Doral decided to add nine holes to the course and accordingly told Curcie. This necessitated an increase in the hours of construction equipment rental. Doral continued to pay the contractor based on the hours of equipment rental and the costs of materials listed in the contract. Computations were made on that basis and verified daily. Several payments were made for work done on the additional nine holes.

Later, Doral refused to pay for some of the rental charges, claiming that Curcie had not followed the procedure outlined in the contract for changes. The court said the continued payment by Doral, even in the absence of the written requests for additional compensation, and Doral's knowledge of the extra work, and the set procedure for calculating compensation that had been followed by Doral, amounted to proof that Doral had waived the provision requiring a written request for additional compensation. ■ ■ ■

10–2. THINK

What specific facts did Curcie prove that supported the court's decision that Doral had waived the provisions of the original contract?

Most jurisdictions allow waivers to be revoked. Using the preceding example, assume that the owner no longer wants to pay for changed work that appears for the first time on the contractor's monthly statements. The owner informs the contractor that *in the future it will require the contractor to comply with the terms of the contract.* The court will uphold the terms of the contract for all future changes, but not for past changes.

Revocation of Waiver

Rule: A provision that has been waived in the past can be reinstated for the future, as long as notice is given to the affected parties.

---

[11]*Doral Country Club, Inc. v. Curcie Brothers, Inc.*, 174 S. 2d 749 (Fla. App. 1965).

Vocabulary Checklist

Unilateral change
Change in scope of the
    contract
Change order
Construction change directive
Promissory estoppel
Waiver
Constructive change

Destruction of the contract
Abandonment
Cardinal change
Additional work
Extra work
Statute of frauds
Uniform Commercial Code
Holdup game

Preexisting duty
Contract formation
Offer
Acceptance
Consideration
Implied terms
Waiver
Revocation of waiver

Review Questions

1. What is a *unilateral change?*

2. Does the law normally enforce unilateral changes?

3. What is the difference in the law's attitude toward unilateral changes in construction contracts as compared with other types of contracts?

4. What is the law's attitude toward provisions in contracts requiring written change orders?

5. What should the contractor do when the owner orders changed work?

6. By whom should changes resulting in additional cost or a time extension be approved?

7. What is a *construction change directive?*

8. What five legal theories might a contractor who has *not* obtained a valid change order pursue in order to obtain payment?

9. What is the *additional work* doctrine?

10. What is the doctrine of *promissory estoppel?*

11. What is the *waiver* doctrine?

12. What is the *constructive change* doctrine?

13. What is the *destruction of the contract* doctrine?

14. Why must the contractor use the law of contract formation to support a claim for changed work under the *additional work* doctrine?

15. What is the *implied terms* doctrine?

16. Why is the implied terms doctrine useful when the additional work doctrine is employed to obtain payment for changed work without a valid change order?

17. What types of contracts, if any, *must* be in writing?

Problems

Answer the issue in each of the following problems by making a legal argument, including premises in support of your answer.

1. The construction contract allowed the contractor a time extension to complete a project in the event of "severe, heavy, unusual rain;" however, after a severe, heavy, unusual rain causing floods, the engineer refused to allow a reasonable time extension of two weeks, insisting that the project had to be completed on time because of a pending visit by the president of the United States. The engineer also stated that the provision did not allow for a time extension for floods, only for rain. The contractor informed the representative that it would have to put on an additional shift, and it gave the representative an accurate estimate of the additional costs it (the contractor) would incur to finish the project on time. The engineer refused to approve the additional sums to the contractor stating that its lawyer said the provision does not cover floods, and therefore the government need not grant a time extension. The contractor had complied with all contract provisions regarding notice of the additional charges. No other facts can be proved by a preponderance of the evidence.

   Issue: Is the contractor entitled to the extra costs it incurred in completing the project on time?

   Rule: (*Hint:* constructive change)

   Premises:

   Answer: Yes

   Question (can be answered only, if Chapter 3, Logic, has been studied): In problem 1 the engineer argued that the lawyer said the provision does not cover floods, and therefore the government did not need to grant a time extension. Which logical fallacy does this argument contain?

2. Owners, the Buxani family, awarded a contract to contractor Greg Nussbaum. The contract was for renovation and expansion of a jewelry store as outlined in the contract. The contract contained the following clause:

   > *Any alteration or deviation from the above specifications involving extra costs will be executed only upon written change orders and will become an extra charge.*

   During the course of the remodeling work, Buxani made oral requests for suspended ceilings, extra electrical work, one-way mirrors, additional painting and brickwork, and additional bathroom fixtures. None of these items were listed in the original contract; that is, they were not within the scope of the original contract. None of the changes were documented by a written change order; however, the contractor had documentation to support the costs associated with the work.[12]

   Issue: Is contractor entitled to payment for the suspended ceilings, extra electrical, and other additional work?

   Rule: (*Hint:* additional work, waiver)

   Premises:

   Answer: Yes

3. NASA awarded a contract to Valenzuela Engineering, Inc. for repairs to a building at a U.S. Air Force base. (This is a federal contract.) The work included installation of an infrared heating system. The total contract cost was $100,000.

---

[12]*Buxani v. Nussbaum*, 940 S.W.2d 350 (Tex. App. 1997).

The contract did not specify a particular brand or model of heating system, because federal law does not allow the government to do so. Federal law requires the government agency to use "or equal" specifications in this type of project; however, the specifications stated that the system must have a 2.5-hp pump in a certain location in the system. Only the Ray-Vac system contained such a pump in such a position. There was no indication the pump in that particular position was relevant to the operation of the system or to any part of the system. Valenzuela suspected that the government employee writing the specifications had some type of kickback deal with Ray-Vac; however, the contractor could not prove this at trial, so that fact never came before the administrative law judge at the Board of Contract Appeals.

Valenzuela submitted specifications for a Detroit system. The Detroit system was much cheaper than the Ray-Vac system, but the output and performance were identical with those of the Ray-Vac system. The government rejected the submittals and insisted on the Ray-Vac system. Valenzuela complied, but the increase in its costs for the Ray-Vac system was $10,000. No other facts can be proved by a preponderance of the evidence.[13]

Issue: Is Valenzuela entitled to the $10,000?

Rule: (*Hints:* Constructive change. Other law is given in the facts section of the problem. You can assume that law to be valid.)

Premises:

Answer: Yes

4. For twenty-five years preceding this dispute, Campbell Tower Maintenance had performed services for Major Telephone Company (MTC) on a number of different contracts. These contracts were Campbell's largest source of revenue. From 1988 to 1991, payments from MTC constituted 90% of Campbell's total income.

In December 1990 Campbell and MTC signed a contract for Campbell 's services for a project called the Lightguide Project. The Lightguide Project involved the burying of a 46-mile-long fiber-optic cable. The contract set Campbell's compensation at 23.5% of the "total project cost." The contract did not define "total project cost" but did place responsibility for calculating the total cost with MTC. The contracts contained a clause requiring all changes to be in writing.

After completion of the project MTC informed Campbell at a meeting in Santa Ana, California, that the total project cost was $6,514,891, and it paid Campbell based on that figure. Later, Campbell discovered an internal MTC accounting record, known as the "FD-10," which indicated that the total cost of the Lightguide Project was actually $7,229,874.

MTC accounted for the difference between the figure it gave at the Santa Ana meeting and the higher one in the FD-10 by noting that the FD-10 included many of MTC's internal expenses that the parties did not intend to include in the contract's "total project costs." Campbell filed suit against MTC based on a variety of contract, fraud, and tort claims.

In addition, at a pre-award meeting Campbell indicated that it intended to use Grade 2 inspectors on the project, and it bid according to the pay scale of Grade 2 inspectors. The contract indicated that Grade 1 inspectors were to be used. Grade 1 inspectors are more expensive to use than Grade 2 inspectors; however, partway through the project MTC demanded that Campbell use the Grade 1 inspectors. The additional cost to Campbell for these Grade 1 inspectors was $125,000 over the cost of the Grade 2 inspectors.

---

[13]Facts taken from CCM 4/98, p. 4, *Appeal of Valenzuela Engineering, Inc.*, ASBCA No. 50019 (1/16/98).

At trial Campbell claimed it agreed to use the Grade 1 inspectors because of its financial dependence on MTC. Campbell claimed the change from Grade 2 to Grade 1 inspectors was a change in the contract, and MTC must pay it. Campbell stated that it had no reasonable economic choice, and it made concessions because of the preponderance of the work—over 90% of its total—it was doing and had done for MTC for such a long time period.

Campbell sued MTC for the $125,000 paid to the inspectors and for $168,021, the difference it claimed it should be paid because the total cost of the Lightside project was $7,229,874, not $6,514,891.[14]

Issue 1: Who is required to pay for the Grade 1 inspectors?

Rule: Courts enforce written requirements for change orders.

Premises:

Answer: Campbell

Issue 2: Does MTC have to pay based on a total project cost of $6,514,891 or per the FD-10, which indicated that the total cost of the Lightguide Project was actually $7,229,874?

Rule: (*Hint:* Latent Ambiguity, Chapter 9, Scope)

Premises:

Answer: MTC must pay based on the FD-10.

5. Ahrens Development Co. planned to develop a residential subdivision and prepared a subdivision plat and construction plans for streets, sewers, water, sidewalks, and drainage. The plat indicated 35 lots. Ahrens awarded a fixed-price construction contract in the amount of $1,025,000 to Bailey Construction Co., Inc. for the site improvements. The contract stated it was "subject to the County not making any substantial changes to the storm drainage system." The County subsequently approved a subdivision plan with 55 lots.

Bailey sent Ahrens a letter outlining the additional construction work necessitated by the revised plan. Bailey submitted a number of progress payment requisitions containing items clearly labeled as "extra work." Ahrens paid those invoices over an 18-month period, but at the conclusion of the work, Ahrens said it was not obligated to pay more than the original fixed price of $1,025,000. Bailey said it was owed an additional $151,905.

Ahrens claimed the court cannot consider evidence outside an unambiguous fixed-price written contract, claiming that this case was governed by the parol evidence rule. Ahrens also claimed there had been no substantial changes to the storm drainage system, so that aspect of the contract had not been triggered.[15]

Issue: Is Bailey entitled to the additional payment?

Rule: (*Hint:* promissory estoppel)

Premises:

Answer: Yes

---

[14]Facts modified from *Strickland Tower Maintenance, Inc. v. AT&T Communications, Inc.,* 128 F.3d 1422 (10th Cir. 1997).

[15]Facts from *Cardinal Development Co. v. Stanley Construction Co., Inc.* 497 S.E.2d 847 (Va. 1998).

Question (can be answered only if Chapter 3, Logic, has been studied): Which logical fallacy does Ahrens's argument contain?

6. The U.S. government hired general contractor Pickens, Inc. to make improvements to a post office in Seattle, Washington. The contractor was to construct a new sloping roof over an existing flat roof. The contractor was to protect the interior of the building from the weather at all times. While anchoring the trusses to the roof the contractor penetrated the waterproofing of the existing flat roof. It rained the next day, and the interior of the building suffered water damage. The government directed the contractor to waterproof the existing roof and to repair the water damage, which the contractor did. The cost to waterproof the existing roof was $25,000. The cost to repair the damage to the building was $10,000. The contractor filed a claim for additional work or constructive change claiming that the waterproofing of the existing roof had not been called for in the contract and was unnecessary in light of the protection provided by the new roof. The contractor demanded additional compensation.[16]

Issue: Has there been a change in the contract?

Rule:

Premises:

Answer: No

7. The contract between the owner and the contractor, Glazetherm, was for the installation of windows in a motel and restaurant complex. Neither the contract nor the plans and specifications specified the color of the windows to be installed. A dispute arose over compensation to the contractor for the removal and replacement of white windows with bronze windows. At trial, Glazetherm testified that when the owner paid the first installment due under the contract, the owner verbally specified that white windows should be installed. Subsequently, Glazetherm began installing the white windows over a two-week period and installed 195 windows. After the 195 windows had been installed, Glazetherm testified that the owner's wife wanted to change the window color to bronze. Glazetherm immediately sent the owner a change order, and it included in it an estimate of $50,000 as the cost to install and remove the existing 195 white windows, and a time extension request of three weeks. The owner objected to the $50,000 and contended it had ordered bronze windows in the first instance. The owner did not object to the time extension, as the delay did not delay the completion of the entire project.

Glazetherm stopped work until the matter could be resolved because of the potential loss to it. A few days later a written agreement was entered into between the parties. Glazetherm signed a document agreeing it would "remove existing white windows and install bronze windows and bronze exterior trim at no additional cost."

At trial the owner testified the consideration paid to Glazetherm for the agreement to remove the existing windows and to install the bronze windows at no cost was the owner's agreement to make up the substantial loss to Glazetherm by awarding Glazetherm future lucrative contracts on other properties controlled by the owner. Glazetherm agrees with this, but the owner never awarded Glazetherm any future contracts. The owner agreed that it did not award Glazetherm any future contracts.[17] (The court's reasoning in the case was not based on the hints below.)

---

[16]Facts from *Appeal of C.E.F.A.P.* ASBCA No. 49704 (January 28, 1998).

[17]Facts modified from *Thermoglaze Inc. v. Morningside Gardens,* 23 Conn. App. 741, 583 A.2d. 1331, *appeal denied,* 217 Conn. 811 (1991).

Question: What issue of fact has been raised in this problem?

Assume the jury or arbitrator decides the issue of fact in favor of Glazetherm.

Issue 1: Has the owner made a change to the contract?

Rule:

Premises:

Answer: Yes

Issue 2: Is Glazetherm obligated to "remove existing white windows and install bronze windows and bronze exterior trim at no additional cost"?

Rule: (*Hint:* past consideration, contract formation)

Premises:

Answer: No

Issue 3: Is Glazetherm entitled to payment for removing the white windows?

Rule: (*Hint:* promissory estoppel)

Premises:

Answer: Yes

Answer to Selected Problem

1. The construction contract allowed the contractor a time extension to complete a project in the event of "severe, heavy, unusual rain;" however, . . .

   Issue: Is the contractor entitled to the extra costs it incurred in completing the project on time?

   Rule: Constructive change. A constructive change is defined as owner conduct that is not a formal change order but that has the effect of requiring the contractor to perform work different from that required by the original contract. In this situation the contractor may request additional time or money for changed work.

   Premises: The construction contract allowed the contractor a time extension to complete a project in the event of "severe, heavy, unusual rain"; however, after a severe, heavy, unusual rain causing floods, the engineer refused to allow a reasonable time extension of two weeks, insisting that the project had to be completed on time because of a pending visit by the president of the United States. Therefore, the engineer accelerated the project because the contractor was entitled, by the contract, to an additional two weeks.

   Answer: Yes

11

Delays and Acceleration

Delay to a project is an event or occurrence that prevents the project from being completed on the date specified in the contract. Any number of events can occur to delay the completion of a construction project. Bad weather, unavailability of the site, unavailability of materials, additional work requested by the owner, or changes in government regulations might cause delays in a project.

Every delay costs someone, if not everyone, on the project. No delay is "free." The cost may be small or large. For example, if the project is delayed one month, the design professional, general contractor, and subcontractors must pay employees (or lay them off) and home office overhead for an additional month; employees may lose income; and the owner loses the rentals or income the property would have generated in that month.

Good planning and effective management prevent most delays. Some delays, such as fire, can be insured against. Some delays are difficult to avoid, such as those caused by unexpected natural disasters, death, or government action. Since delay is so common, smart owners and contractors include provisions in their contracts specifying who is accepting the risks of delay. If the contract has not so specified, laws determine who is responsible.

In order to answer the question of who pays the costs associated with a delay, it is necessary to classify the delay as inexcusable, excusable, or compensatory. In industry, delays are classified from the *general contractor's perspective*. An **inexcusable delay** is one for which the contractor has no excuse and must pay the owner's costs or damages associated with the delay. An **excusable delay** is one for which the contractor has a valid excuse, and both parties absorb their own costs associated with the delay. A **compensable delay** is a delay for which the owner must pay the contractor's costs associated with the delay.

> Types of Delay
>
> **Inexcusable**—Contractor pays owner's damages.
> **Excusable**—Each party absorbs own damages.
> **Compensatory**—Owner pays contractor's damages.

Inexcusable Delay

As a general statement of the law, and absent any specific provision in the contract or the applicability of the legal theories discussed next, *the contractor pays the owner for the owner's costs associated with delay.* This assumes that the contract contains a completion date, which is generally the case in industry.

For example, most construction contracts can be simplified to the following:

> *"I, General Contractor, agree to build you, Owner, this project,
> by date X at cost Y."*

Pursuant to this simple construction contract, the contractor is agreeing to build a project according to the plans and specifications by a specific date for a specific price.

The preceding simple contract puts the risk of delay upon the contractor. The contractor must do *almost* everything it takes to get the job done by date X, or it breaches the contract. Events such as difficulty in obtaining materials or problems with subcontractors are no excuse.

> *It is well-established . . . that supervening circumstances making the
> performance of a promise more difficult and expensive than originally
> anticipated is not enough to excuse the promisor.*[1]

The *almost* is discussed in the sections "Objective Impossibility" and "Practical Impossibility."

Excusable Delay

An **excusable delay** is a delay for which the general contractor is excused or does not have to pay any damages to the owner relating to that delay. Of course, the contractor is not excused from paying its own costs associated with the delay. Two kinds of excusable delay exist: *delay excused by the contract* and *delay excused by the law.* It is not uncommon for the contract to contain many of the items that are also included in the list of items that excuse a delay by law.

---

[1]*Barnard-Curtis Co. v. U.S.,* 301 F.2d 909, 912 (Ct. Cl. 1962).

Delay Excused by the Contract

Whenever a contractor experiences a delay and there is a dispute with the owner about whether the delay is excusable or compensatory, the contractor should review its contract with the owner. For example, AIA A201 (1997) allows the contractor an excusable delay

> *if the Contractor is delayed at any time in the commencement or progress of the Work by . . . labor disputes, fire, unusual delay in deliveries, unavoidable casualties, or other causes beyond the Contractor's control, or by delay authorized by the Owner pending mediation and arbitration, or by other causes which the Architect determines may justify delay, then the Contractor Time shall be extended by Change order for such reasonable time as the Architect may determine.*

Because of the complexity of construction documents, no one can remember every term in them. When an issue arises it is a good idea to check the contract and see what it says about the problem. Although not every provision in a contract will be enforced by the law, the vast majority of them will be.

11-1. THINK

A problem arises and instead of reviewing the contract, you just "solve it." Later it is determined that your solution is contrary to the terms of the contract. What have you done to the original contract?

11-2. THINK

The following clause exists in a contract between an owner and a general contractor on a project to construct a retail store:

> *The contractor may be granted an extension of time because of changes ordered in the contract, or because of strikes, lockouts, fire, unusual delay in transportation, unavoidable casualties, unusual inclement weather, or any cause beyond the contractor's control, which constitutes a justifiable delay.*

A fire occurs and delays the project one month. Because of the fire the contractor has to pay an additional month of rental on scaffolding. Assume it is cheaper to pay the additional rental than to take down the rented scaffolding and return it. The owner loses one month of income from the store because of the delay. No other facts can be proved by a preponderance of the evidence.

(continued)

> *(continued)*
>
> Read the preceding clause carefully and answer the following questions:
>
> a. Is the contractor liable to the owner for delay damages?
> b. Who pays for the additional month of scaffolding rental?
> c. Is the owner agreeing to pay the contractor's costs associated with the delay?
> d. What is the owner agreeing to do?
> e. Who pays for the owner's lost rental income?

Delay Excused by the Law

The law in many jurisdictions excuses the contractor from some or all of the following delays, *whether or not* the contract so specifies:

Acts of God

Labor disputes, if unforeseeable

Acts of government

Criminal activity, if unforeseeable

The definition of acts of God generally varies from state to state but includes events such as fires, earthquakes, floods, and disease. Most contractors and owners have insurance that will pay for costs associated with acts of God.

Notice that some of the items are also included in many contracts. It is not uncommon for the contract to contain a provision "giving" the contractor something the law requires the owner to give the contractor.

It is important to realize that the preceding list is not complete. If an argument can be made that the delay is excusable, the law will allow an excusable delay. For example, in the case of *Carter Steel and Fabricating Co. v. Ohio Dept. of Transportation*, the contract documents required the subcontractor to obtain steel from a domestic supplier.[2] There was only one domestic supplier who could comply with the owner's specifications.

When the subcontractor had to reject noncomplying steel, the project was delayed. The owner assessed liquidated damages against the general contractor, who withheld the subcontractor's payment. The court held that because *the subcontractor was required to use the specified supplier, and the delays were beyond the control of the subcontractor, the delay was excusable.* The owner should have granted a time extension. The liquidated damages were improper and reimbursed to the contractor. The subcontractor recovered the amount due it under the subcontract.

---

[2]*Carter Steel and Fabricating Co. v. Ohio Dept. of Transportation*, 721 N.E.2d 1115 (Ohio Ct. Cl. 1999).

Compensable Delay

A **compensable delay** is a delay for which the owner pays the contractor its costs associated with the delay. Two kinds of compensable delay exist: *delay compensated per the contract* and *delay compensated by the law.*

Delay Compensated per the Contract

Although it is rarely done, contractors could negotiate for the right to compensable delay by contract provisions. For example, a contractor could negotiate a provision allowing for delay should the owner change design professionals during the course of the contract. In general, owners usually insert into the contract only the provisions that fall under the delay compensated by the law.

Delay Compensated by the Law

Whether or not the contract specifically requires the owner to pay for the contractor's costs associated with the following delays, the law in most states requires the owner to do so.

■ Hindrance, interference, or delay of the contractor by the owner or its agents, whether or not intentional

■ Delayed or restricted site access

■ Owner's failure to coordinate several prime contractors

■ Defective plans and/or specifications

■ Changes

■ Design professional delay of approvals

■ Failure to make timely progress payments

Acceleration

Acceleration is merely a specialized form of compensable delay. An **acceleration** is defined as a decrease by the owner in the amount of time given to the contractor to complete the job. It is possible for a contractor to accelerate a subcontract also. A decrease in the amount of time allowed for the completion of the project is a change, and the owner must pay the contractor for an acceleration. Changes are discussed more fully in Chapter 10, Changes.

An owner may accelerate the completion date of the contract in three ways, namely, by

1. decreasing the amount of time,

2. changing or increasing the amount of work, or

3. refusing to grant a time extension when the contract requires one.

An acceleration due to decreasing the amount of time is the most easily understood and recognized type of project acceleration. For example, if the contract has a completion date of May 1, and the owner changes the completion date to April 1, the owner has accelerated the project. This type of project acceleration seldom leads to legal claims and problems.

Changes and additions to the work also may increase the amount of time needed to complete the project. For example, assume the contractor and the subcontractor have a contract to put in the wiring for a new home, with the wiring to be completed by February. During the construction the owner decides to add a pool and gazebo, both with lighting, to the project. Assume it would take the average subcontractor two days to complete the additional wiring. If the owner fails to increase the amount of time for the project by two days, the owner has accelerated the project due to a work increase without a corresponding increase in time to complete the work.

Accelerations due to work increase can lead to claims disputing the actual amount of time required to complete the additional work. For example, the contractor may claim it should take the subcontractor only one day to complete the extra wiring, versus the two days requested by the subcontractor. It is not uncommon for contractors and subcontractors to overestimate the time it takes to perform the increased work in order to make up time for inexcusable delays.

The form of acceleration leading to the greatest numbers of delay-related claims occurs when an owner refuses to grant a contractor (or a contractor refuses to grant a subcontractor) an extension of time when the contractor (or subcontractor) is due an extension under the terms of the contract. For example, assume a contract between the owner and the contractor has a completion date of May 1 but also contains a clause that allows the contractor an extension of time should a labor strike occur. A labor strike does occur, but the owner demands that the contractor complete the project by May 1 anyway because opening ceremonies have been planned for the project, and it will cost the owner a great deal of money to reschedule. The owner has accelerated the project even though the contract completion date has not changed, nor has there been a change in the scope of the work. This concept can also be called a *constructive change,* which is discussed in Chapter 10, Changes and Additions to the Contract.

As another example, assume that Pike is the prime contractor on a certain project, and Bat Masonry is the masonry subcontractor. Bat has filed a claim against Pike for $53,000 for acceleration of the project. Bat claims that Pike instructed Bat to accelerate its performance of the masonry work. Bat Masonry's claim is based on the following letter from Pike and clause in the contract:

> *Letter:* This letter will serve as notice that our present schedule requires that the exterior masonry walls be expedited. The exterior walls in Areas E, D, and C need to be worked simultaneously. . . . You are directed to increase your manpower and equipment to facilitate working in the above-mentioned areas. All cost for the above will be discussed and negotiated for final settlement at a later date.

> *Contract clause:* Contractor may direct subcontractor to work overtime. . . . Contractor shall compensate subcontractor for the actual costs incurred by the subcontractor for such overtime.

The date for completing the entire project never changed. Pike claimed that because the date to complete the project had not changed, Bat was owed no additional sums. The court held that Bat was entitled to damages for the extra costs associated with the acceleration.[3]

Turning a Compensable Delay into an Excusable Delay

Owners generally want delay claims to be either excusable or inexcusable. This section discusses some common legal theories available to owners (or contractors) that may be used to change a compensable delay into an excusable delay. In the law this type of theory is often called a **defense to a claim.** It is less common for contractors to use these techniques in their contracts with subcontractors; however, their use is on the rise.

Figure 11–1 shows how delays can be transformed from one type into another. Note that this chart does not contain *all* the ways delays can be transformed, only the most common.

Refer to Figure 11–1. An inexcusable delay can be transformed into an excusable delay through the doctrines of Objective or Practical Impossibility (discussed in Chapter 8). Another route from inexcusable delay to excusable delay is through the waiver doctrine (discussed in Chapter 8). Compensable delays can be transformed into excusable delays if the contractor fails to give notice or if the contract has a limited damages for delay clause (discussed below).

---

[3]Facts and issue simplified from *Bat Masonry v. Pike-Paschen Joint Venture III*, 842 F. Supp. 174, 180–181 (E. Md. 1993).

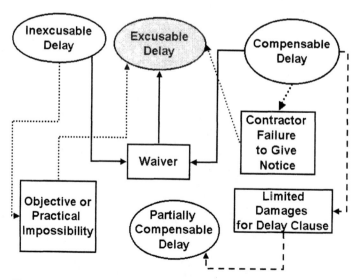

Figure 11-1 Transforming delays.

No Damages for Delay Clause

A **no damages for delay clause** in essence says that the owner is not required to pay the contractor damages for a compensable delay. In other words, it says, "I don't care what the law says, I don't have to pay you damages." For example, the contract may contain a provision that states the following:

> *Contractor agrees that should the owner or its agent delay the project for any reason, the contractor is not entitled to damages of any type.*

It is unlikely that a court or arbitrator will enforce such a clause. The judge or arbitrator will label it an exculpatory clause, onerous, or against public policy.

Limited Damages for Delay Clause

A variant of the no damage for delay clause is the **limited damages for delay clause.** It is common for this clause to be referred to as a "no damage for delay clause" in the industry. The limited damages for delay clause *limits, but does not eliminate,* the amount of money or damages to which the contractor is entitled. Many states uphold these clauses unless the owner's actions are unconscionable. The same is true for clauses by which general contractors attempt to limit damages of subcontractors.

The most common limited damages for delay clause in the construction industry is the **no damages other than a time extension clause.** This clause states that should the owner cause a delay, the only damages the contractor can get are an increase in the time to perform. Should the contractor incur *other* costs, such as additional equipment lease costs or increased overhead costs, the contractor is *not* entitled to those damages.

For example, assume that the contractor claims damages of $15,000 on a $1.5 million contract. No clause relating to delay damages exists in the contract. The damages resulted from delays caused by minor design errors, actions of other multiple prime contractors, and the state's failure to coordinate the several prime contracts. The $15,000 comes from additional rental on job site equipment, additional utility costs for the delay period, additional wages and salaries paid to personnel, and other types of costs. Assume that all these can be proved by a preponderance of the evidence. The contractor is entitled to $15,000 of damages from the owner.

Now, assume the exact same facts except with a contract that contains a "no damages other than a time extension" clause. In this case, in many jurisdictions the contractor would be entitled to nothing except additional time to perform the project. The contractor is *not* entitled to the $15,000.

These clauses are fairly new, and the law is still developing on their legality and the extent to which they can limit damages and not be held to be exculpatory or violations of public policy. Many state courts will enforce these clauses. See *City of Houston v. R. F. Ball Constr Co.* for a Texas opinion upholding the validity of this type of clause.[4]

---

[4]*City of Houston v. R. F. Ball Constr Co.*, 570 S.W.2d 75 (Tex. App. 1978).

Some states have laws limiting the effect of these clauses. For example, the state of Washington has enacted the following statute:[5]

> *Any contract, public or private, which contains a clause purporting to waive, release, or extinguish the rights of a contractor to damages for unreasonable delays is void and unenforceable as against public policy.*

11-3. THINK

Under the Washington statute, what types of damages *can* a contractor waive, release, or extinguish?

Numerous cases exist in which courts have refused to enforce no damages other than time extension clauses when the owner's actions have been unconscionable or intentional. For example, assume that a contract contains a "no damages other than a time extension" clause, and the architect routinely takes two weeks to approve change orders. The contractor routinely objects to this practice and sends an estimate of its costs associated with the delay to the owner. The owner does nothing about it because the owner believes the clause will protect it from having to pay anything for delays to the contractor. The project is delayed two months as a result. The contractor loses a lot of money in overhead costs associated with keeping the project open two additional months. It is unlikely that a court or arbitrator will enforce the clause but instead will award the contractor damages; however, because this issue is presently being litigated in various jurisdictions, specific legal research related to any particular jurisdiction is necessary to predict the outcome of any specific case.

Contractor Failure to Give Notice

Many contracts contain detailed requirements for notices to be sent to the owner when a delay occurs, but many contractors do not follow these requirements. Such failure by the contractor to follow the notice requirements demanded by the contract can defeat a contractor's claim for compensable delay. Judges and arbitrators will enforce these clauses.

Even though most contracts specify time frames and types of notices, *courts are not very picky on how notice was given, as long as it was given within the time frame.* For example in the case of *Seaboard Lumber Co. v. United States* the court said:[6]

> *Whether notice is constructive or written, therefore, is not critical. Instead, the question is whether the lack of notice caused any real prejudice to the [owner's] ability either to defend against the contractor's claim, or to limit damages.*

---

[5]*Wash. Rev. Code Sec.* 4.24.360.

[6]*Seaboard Lumber Co. v. United States*, 45 Fed. Cl. 404 (U.S. Claims 1999).

For example, assume that the contract requires the contractor to give the owner three days' written notice of the events giving rise to a delay. A major fire occurs, and the project is delayed two months. The contractor failed to give the required notice, but the architect was on site shortly after the fire, and correspondence between the owner and the architect concerning the fire and the delays was in the owner's file. The court is likely to uphold the contractor's delay claims despite the fact that proper notice was not given.

Waiver

A compensable delay can be turned into an excusable delay through the doctrine of waiver. If the contractor fails to make a claim for a delay, the contractor will be considered to have waived it. Waiver has been discussed previously in this text.

Float

The **float** is the extra time between the date the owner wants the project completed and the date the contractor sets for completion. For example, assume the contract calls for a project to be completed on June 1, and the contract contains a clause allowing the owner to make changes to the project. The contractor prepares a critical path method (CPM) schedule calling for completion on April 1. A contractor would do this to save overhead expenses and be able to move onto a new project. The contractor's profit on the project can be increased tremendously in this fashion. Owners generally have no objection to receiving a project early, and so they approve schedules with earlier completion dates than required by the contract.

An issue arises when the owner causes a delay in the project. For example, assume the architect is one day late (according to the contractor's CPM schedule) in approving a submittal. Does this mean the owner owes the contractor damages for one day of delay? The contractor is of the opinion that *any* owner-caused delay that causes the contract to extend past April 1 (using the preceding example) means the owner has to pay the contractor damages; however, unless the owner agrees to be bound by the shortened schedule *and* the contractor agrees to be bound, there is no consideration for the formation of a new contract and therefore the original contract stands. Remember, both parties must give up and get something in order for a contract to be formed or changed. This issue has not been decided by the courts yet, however.

Vocabulary Checklist

Delay	Compensatory delay	Waiver
Acceleration	No damage for delay clause	Limited damages for delay clause
Inexcusable delay	Objective impossibility	Float
Excusable delay	Practical impossibility	

Review Questions

1. What are the three types of delays?

2. What is the difference between a delay allowed by law and a delay allowed by contract?

3. How can a compensable delay be turned into a partially compensable delay?

4. How can a compensable delay be turned into an excusable delay?

5. How can an inexcusable delay be turned into excusable delay?

6. What is the difference between a no damages for delay clause and a limited damages for delay clause?

7. To what do owners most frequently limit the contractor's damages with a limited damages for delay clause?

8. Compare the following two clauses. Find five differences between them.

   Clause A: If the Contractor is delayed at any time in progress of the Work by an act or neglect of the Owner, or Architect, or of an employee of either, or of a separate contractor employed by the Owner, or by changes ordered in the Work, or by labor disputes, fire, unusual delay in deliveries, unavoidable casualties, or other causes beyond the Contractor's control, or by delay authorized by the Owner pending arbitration, or by other cause which the Architect determines may justify delay, then the Contract Time shall be extended by Change order for such reasonable time as the Architect may determine. Contractor must give written notice to the Architect of the cause of the delay within ten days of the event giving rise to the delay.

   Clause B: The contractor may be granted an extension of time because of changes ordered in the Contract, or because of strikes, lockouts, fire, unusual delay in transportation, unavoidable casualties, unusual inclement weather, or any cause beyond the Contractor's control, which constitutes a justifiable delay.

Problems

Answer the issue in each of the following problems by making a legal argument, including premises in support of your answer.

1. The contractor's project supervisor is killed in an automobile accident while returning home from a baseball game on the weekend. It takes the contractor one week to get a new project manager on the project and up to speed. The project is delayed one week. No other facts can be proved by a preponderance of the evidence.

   Note: The sentence "No other facts can be proved by a preponderance of the evidence" will not be repeated with every question; however, you should assume that only the facts given in any problem can be proved by a preponderance of the evidence.

   Issue: Is the contractor liable to the owner for delay damages?

   Rule: (*Hint:* Categorize the delay. Also, assume that auto accidents are not acts of God under state law.)

Premises:

Answer: Yes

2. Same facts as in problem 1, except that the contract contains the following clause:

> *The contractor may be granted an extension of time because of changes ordered in the Contract, or because of strikes, lockouts, fire, unusual delay in transportation, unavoidable casualties, unusual inclement weather, or any cause beyond the Contractor's control, which constitutes a justifiable delay.*

Issue: Is the contractor liable to the owner for delay damages?

Rule: (*Hint:* Categorize the delay.)

Premises:

Answer: No

3. The architect's project supervisor is killed in an automobile accident while returning home from a baseball game on the weekend. It takes the architect one week to get a new project manager on the project and get the project moving along again. The project is delayed one week due to the lack of approvals on an important aspect of the critical path. Assume that only very minor work could be done during this time.

Issue: Is the contractor entitled to a week's extension of the project or other damages for delay?

Rule: (*Hint:* Categorize the delay. Also, assume that auto accidents are not acts of God under state law.)

Premises:

Answer: Yes

4. The government contract allowed the contractor a time extension to complete a project in the event of "severe, heavy, unusual rain." However, after a severe, heavy, unusual rain *causing floods* that damaged the project site, the government representative refused to allow a reasonable time extension of two weeks, insisting that the project had to be completed on time because of a pending visit by the president of the United States. The representative also stated that the provision did not allow for a time extension for floods, only for rain. The contractor informed the representative that it would have to put on an additional shift, and it gave the representative an accurate estimate of the additional costs it (the contractor) would incur in order to finish the project on time. The government representative refused to approve the additional sums to the contractor. The contractor had complied with all contract provisions regarding notice of the additional charges.

Issue: Is the contractor entitled to the extra costs it incurred in completing the project on time?

Rule: (*Hint:* Categorize the delay, and accelerate the project.)

Premises:

Answer: Yes

5. Kold Developers, Inc., a closely held corporation owed by Mr. and Mrs. Kold, contracted with Little Bear City to build additional housing to accommodate workers on the Trans-Alaska pipeline, with the work to be completed by November 1. At the time the developer contracted

with the city, commencement of construction on the pipeline was imminent and the need for housing was great; however, shortly after the parties entered into the contract, a federal court issued an injunction that ordered a halt to all construction of the pipeline for six months. Kold refused to build the houses until the six months was over because it could not obtain financing at a cost to allow it to make any profit on the project until then. The city terminated the contract and threatened to sue the developer for liquidated damages pursuant to the damages clause that stated that Kold would pay $200/day in liquidated damages to the owner for each day after November 1 that the project was not completed. In addition, the owner threated to sue on the performance bond.

The city argued that the contractor should not win because the contractor's actions are the same as stealing from the taxpayers.

Question (can be answered only if Chapter 3, Logic, has been studied): Which fallacy of logic was committed by the city in its argument "that the contractor should not win because the contractor's actions are the same as stealing from the taxpayers"?

Note: See appendix to Chapter 18, Dispute Resolution, "Answer to Selected Problems" for a one-act play involving the preceding scenario. This exercise shows how this dispute might be negotiated using the following legal argument in the face of a fallacious and illogical argument.

Issue: Is the developer liable to the city?

Rule: A party must honor its contract (basic premise of contract law).

What other, more specialized, rule is available to the developer here? (*Hint:* Categorize the delay.)

Premises:

Answer: No

6. (Note the slight change in facts.) Kold Developers, a sole proprietorship owned by Mr. and Mrs. Kold, contracted with Little Bear City to build additional housing to accommodate workers on the Trans-Alaska pipeline, with the work to be completed by November 1. At the time the developer contracted with the city, commencement of construction on the pipeline was imminent and the need for housing was great; however, shortly after the parties entered into the contract, Kold's credit rating was revised, and it could not afford to get the financing. The city terminated the contract and hired another company to complete it, which it did; however, the project was delayed sixty days, and the city sued Kold Developers and Mr. and Mrs. Kold for liquidated damages pursuant to the damages clause that stated the Kold would pay $200/day in liquidated damages.

Issue: Is Kold Developer liable to the city?

Rule: (*Hint:* Categorize the delay.)

Premises:

Answer: Yes

Issue: Are Mr. and Mrs. Kold personally liable to the City?

Rule: (*Hint:* See Chapter 6, Relationships among the Parties on the Project.)

Premises:

Answer: Yes

7. A contractor claimed damages of $2000 on a $1.5 million contract. The damages resulted from delays caused by two minor design errors and the state's failure to coordinate the several prime contracts on one occasion during the course of the project. Assume that all damages are provable and not at issue. The damages resulted from decreased efficiency, home office overhead, and similar items. The contract contains a "limited damages except time extension for delay" clause.

   Issue: Is the contractor entitled to damages?

   Rule:

   Premises:

   Answer: No

8. The contractor claims damages of $215,000 on a $1.5 million contract. The damages resulted from delays caused by 324 minor design errors, fourteen incidents related to actions of other multiple prime contractors, and the state's failure to coordinate the several prime contracts on seventeen different occasions during the course of the project. Assume all damages are provable and not at issue. The damages resulted from decreased efficiency, home office overhead, and similar items. The contract contains a "limited damages except time extension for delay" clause.

   Issue: Is the contractor entitled to damages?

   Rule: (*Hint:* unconscionable)

   Premises:

   Answer: Yes

9. Piskun Electrical, a subcontractor, sued Johnston Construction, the prime contractor, because progress was retarded by the gross incompetence of one of the prime contractor's job superintendents, by the prime contractor's frequent replacement of its supervisors, by the prime contractor's failure to properly coordinate the work of the various subcontractors and failure to eliminate work redundancies and overlaps within its subcontractors. The contract between the prime contractor and the subcontractor contained a "no damages except time extension for delay" clause. The subcontractor's damages amounted to $25,000 on the $100,000 subcontract.

   Issue: Is the subcontractor entitled to damages?

   Rule:

   Premises: (*Hint:* unconscionable)

   Answer: Yes

10. A contract contains the following clause:

   > *2.1.1. If the Contractor is delayed at any time in progress of the Work by an act or neglect of the Owner or Architect, or of an employee of either, or of a separate contractor employed by the Owner, or by changes ordered in the Work, or by labor disputes, fire, unusual delay in deliveries, unavoidable casualties, or other causes beyond the Contractor's control, or by delay authorized by the Owner pending arbitration, or by other cause which the Architect determines may justify delay, then the Contract Time shall be extended by Change order for such reasonable time as the Architect may determine.*

2.1.2 Contractor must give written notice to the Architect of the cause of the delay within ten days of the event giving rise to the delay, or all damages shall be deemed waived.

The project was scheduled to be completed on June 1.

The contractor had trouble getting a certain type of tile because of an earthquake, which caused major damage to the plant in California where the tile was to be manufactured. The contractor was able to obtain replacement tile, but the architect insisted the project be completed by June 1, claiming that delay in delivery of materials is the contractor's responsibility. The contractor did, in fact, complete the project by June 1 by putting on an additional shift. The cost to the contractor to do this was $153,000 (assume this cost to be reasonable).

Issue: Is the contractor entitled to damages of $153,000?

Rule: (*Hint:* read the contract carefully.)

Premises:

Answer: Yes

11. The contract between the owner and the contractor contains the following clauses:

> *7.1: The contractor may be granted an extension of time because of changes ordered in the Contract, or because of strikes, lockouts, fire, unusual delay in transportation, unavoidable casualties, unusual inclement weather, or any cause beyond the Contractor's control, which constitutes a justifiable delay.*
>
> *7.2: Upon the occurrence of any event giving rise to a delay for which the contractor seeks an extension of time, the contractor must give written notice to the owner within three days of the events giving rise to the delay and a good faith estimate of the additional time needed by the contractor to complete the project. Failure to include a good faith estimate of the additional time needed is a* waiver *of any additional time needed (emphasis added).*
>
> *10.1 Liquidated damages: Contractor agrees to pay Owner the sum of $500/day liquidated damages for each day after February 1 up to and including the date the project is substantially completed.*

The project is delayed by one week due to unusual inclement weather, and the general contractor gives the following notice to the owner within three days as required by the contract:

> Dear Owner,
> Please accept this letter as notice pursuant to paragraph 7.1 of the contract that the project has been delayed by unusual inclement weather.
> (signed and dated)

The contractor incurs costs of $600 for rental of a crane during the three days the project is delayed. *The project is delivered three days late.*

Issue: Who owes damages to whom, if any?

Rule: (*Hint:* Three rules must be used simultaneously to come to the correct conclusion. Two are basic premises of contract law.)

Premises: (*Hint:* Compare what the contract *requires* the contractor to do when an event entitling it to delay damages occurs with what the contractor actually *did.*)

Answer: Contractor owes owner $1500 of liquidated damages. (*Note:* This case is a borderline case. More liberal jurisdictions might find that the letter was sufficient to put the owner on notice that a reasonable time extension was needed.)

12. A fire breaks out on the site causing damage to the existing framing. Perez Construction gives proper notice to Hillside Estates, Inc., the owner, and asks for three days of additional time to complete the project because of the damage. The architect refuses and says it should take only one day to redo the framing. Both parties agree that fire entitled the contractor to an extension of time under the contract; that is not an issue. *What is the issue?*

    The contractor calls its fire insurance company and makes a claim for $5000 for the materials and labor needed to replace the framing in one day. The insurance company pays $4000, saying it is responsible only for normal replacement costs, not the costs associated with redoing the framing in one day. In the opinion of the insurance company expert it should take three days to redo the damaged framing, and attempting to redo it in one day will cost overtime, which it is not obligated to pay.

    The contract between the owner and the general has a liquidated damages clause of $500/day for each day the project is late. Assume that this clause is reasonable.

    The contractor completes the project on time plus one day. The contractor had to pay employees $1000 in overtime to complete the project on time plus one day.

    Issue: Is the contractor entitled to the $1000? From whom and under what legal theory?

    Rule: (*Hint:* What has the owner done to the completion date?)

    Premises:

    Answer: Owner is liable to Perez for $1000 in damages.

13. The following clause exists in the contract between the owner and the contractor:

    > *The contractor may be granted an extension of time because of changes ordered in the contract, or because of labor strikes, lockouts, fire, unusual delay in transportation, unavoidable casualties, unusual inclement weather, or any cause beyond the contractor's control, which constitutes a justifiable delay.*

    A labor strike occurs, and the project is delayed one week while the matter is settled. The general contractor incurs the following costs during that week:

    Rental of scaffolding, cranes: $2000

    Extra security for the site: $1000

    Travel expenses for corporate executive to come to site to negotiate with the union: $1750

    Issue: Which of the costs listed is the owner responsible for?

    Rule: (*Hint:* Read the clause carefully.)

    Premises: (*Hint:* Read the clause carefully.)

    Answer: None

Answer to Selected Problems

1. The contractor's project supervisor is killed in an automobile accident while returning. . . .

Issue: Is the contractor liable to the owner for delay damages?

Rule: The law allows the contractor an excusable delay in the following circumstances: acts of God; labor disputes, if unforeseeable; acts of government, criminal activity, if unforeseeable.

Premises: There is no contract clause giving the contractor any rights to delay, so the only avenue available to the contractor is to see if law covers this delay. The death of the project manager is not in the list of delays allowed by law. Of course, in a real case the contractor's attorney might check the law of the state in which the project is located to see if it covers this type of unavoidable situation; however, if it does not, then the risk of such events is on the contractor. There are no facts to support the objective impossibility, practical impossibility, or waiver doctrines.

Answer: Yes

Appendix

CASE: UNITED STATES STEEL CORP. V. MISSOURI PACIFIC RAILROAD CO.

668 F.2d 435 (8th Cir. 1982)

The opinion of the court was delivered by Judge Hanson

> Mopac contracted with United States Steel's American Bridge Division (ABD) for alteration of the superstructure of two Mopac railroad bridges which spanned the Arkansas River at Little Rock, Arkansas. The initiation of ABD's field work was contingent upon the completion of certain work by the substructure contractor, Al Johnson Construction Co.

[Who are the parties and what is their function?]

> Johnson encountered unforeseen obstacles

[Note: Unforeseen obstacles are discussed in Chapter 12, Differing and Unforeseen Site Conditions.]

> which caused repeated revisions in its scheduled completion date. While ABD was contractually bound to apprise itself of Johnson's work progress and adjust its schedule accordingly, it was also bound to heed Mopac's notice to proceed and commence work when such notice was given. ABD commenced its work, suffering additional and unnecessary costs when its access to the construction site was delayed. United States

Steel, on behalf of ABD, brought this action to recover these increased costs from Mopac.

Following a bench trial, the district court found that Mopac, by giving notice to proceed to ABD when it knew that delay of Johnson's work was inevitable, actively interfered

[The court uses the term "actively interfered." You may substitute the term "unconscionable" or "breach of contract" here.]

with ABD's ability to maintain a flexible work schedule in the face of Johnson's difficulties; the result being that Mopac was liable for damages suffered by ABD while it waited for 175 days past its original start-up date to gain access to the job site. Mopac concedes liability for 25 days of this delay, but argues on appeal that the contract's no damage for delay clause precludes recovery by ABD for the remaining 150 days, that the evidence is insufficient to support the district court's conclusion of active interference and that certain aspects of the damage award were either not supported by the evidence or were improperly awarded. We affirm the lower court in all aspects.

[The preceding paragraph is a summary of the trial court's decision and this appeal court's decision. It is the conclusion of the argument. The remainder of the opinion contains the premises in support of this conclusion.]

I.

Mopac awarded ABD a contract to alter the superstructure of the Junction and Baring Cross Bridges on October 24, 1968. ABD could not begin its work until the substructure contractor, Johnson, completed work on the south pier of the Junction Bridge and constructed a "shoofly," which is a temporary bridge used to reroute rail traffic during construction. Johnson was under contract to complete this phase of its work within one year of receipt of notice to proceed, which was given by Mopac on August 6, 1968.

On November 22, 1968, Mopac issued a notice to proceed to ABD, which triggered the following provision in their contract:

> The contractor will be required to commence work under the contract within 10 calendar days after the date of receipt of Notice to Proceed, to prosecute and work with faithfulness and diligence so as to complete the entire work not later than the number of calendar days stipulated in Section 3 and the Proposal after date of receipt by the Contractor of written Notice to Proceed. Extension to the time allowed for completion may be granted pursuant only to the provisions set forth elsewhere in these Specifications.

Failure of ABD to respond to the notice to proceed would constitute breach. Consequently, when ABD received its notice, it began immediately to prepare shop drawings, place mill orders, begin steel fabrication, set dates for shipping equipment and materials, and prepare work schedules. ABD's first work schedule sent to Mopac indicated that it expected its start-up date for field work to be September 1, 1969. This date was based on the assumption that Johnson would complete its work as scheduled on August 6, 1969.

ABD's first indication that Johnson was encountering problems came when it made an on-site inspection on March 5, 1969, and discovered that Johnson was over three months behind schedule. ABD had no choice but to revise its schedule accordingly, setting a new start-up date at sometime in early November 1969.

On July 2, 1969, Mopac informed ABD that Johnson had again pushed back its completion date. ABD again revised its schedule, anticipating access to the job site in the first week of January 1970. In July Mopac notified ABD that Johnson did not expect the shoofly to be completed until January 11, 1970. ABD twice reset its start-up date to conform with these revisions.

ABD received no further word during the fall of 1969 about Johnson's work progress, but during an on-site visit on December 15, 1969, ABD learned that the shoofly would probably not be completed until February 1, 1970. ABD promptly informed Mopac that it was too late for it to stop shipments of fabricated steel to the job site, and that it would suffer extra expenses for the attendant demurrage, equipment rental, and overhead.

ABD's first steel shipment arrived at the job site on December 29, 1969, it moved onto the job site on January 5, 1970, and three days later Mopac disclosed that ABD could not start its work until the second week in February. ABD in fact was unable to commence work until February 23, 1970. The total delay from the originally scheduled start-up date of September 1, 1969, to February 23, 1970, was 175 days. Mopac informed ABD that the completion date for ABD's work would be adjusted 175 days thus relieving ABD from any claim for liquidated damages for failure to complete its work on schedule.

The delay in the project was caused by the failure of the plans and specifications (supplied by Mopac) which did not reveal, among other matters, that a rock ledge obstructed an area of the riverbed where the south pier was to be constructed. Johnson also found steel in the riverbed (the remains of an old, collapsed bridge) at other places where piles were to be driven. Recovery in a related suit by Johnson was permitted for the increased costs caused by these changed circumstances.

The trial court found that Mopac *knew* about the rock ledge and the steel in the riverbed before it issued the notice to proceed to ABD.

It also found that Mopac should have known delay by Johnson was inevitable because of these unforeseen circumstances.

The district court also found that once notice was given by Mopac to ABD, a series of events of great momentum were set in motion by ABD in order to be prepared to start construction on September 1, 1969. The lower court observed that ABD did its best to adjust its work schedules according to updates it received on Johnson's progress (or lack of it), but additional expenses to some degree were unavoidable.

The court concluded that Mopac, by issuing the notice to proceed with knowledge of Johnson's delay-causing problems, actively interfered with ABD's ability to plan and execute its work in a timely and economically efficient fashion. Following a separate hearing on damages, the court awarded ABD $364,232 which included compensation for increased costs incurred both by Mopac's active interference and by other delays during construction directly attributable to Mopac.

[The trial court upheld the validity of the "no damages for delay" clause, yet still charged Mopac for the delay damages. How did this result come about?]

II.

Mopac first argues that the following "no damage" clause in the contract precludes the award of damages to ABD for any delay caused by Johnson's untimely completion of its work: "Failure of the substructure contractor to complete his work on a specified date or dates shall not form a basis for claim for extra compensation by this superstructure contractor." Such no damage clauses, when clear and unambiguous, are regarded as valid, and will be enforced according to their terms. See *Peter Kiewit Sons' Co. v. Iowa Southern Utilities Co.*, 355 F. Supp. 376, 396–97 (S.D.Iowa 1973) and cases cited therein. Indeed, the district court in this case upheld the validity of the no damage clause, concluding that Johnson's nonperformance "cannot serve as the predicate for damages from the railroad, it having expressly and unambiguously shifted the risk of such nonperformance to (ABD.)" Mem. op. at 5.

[Are "no damages for delay clauses" valid?]

What Mopac actually challenges is the lower court's application of the principle of active interference, a judicially recognized exception to the no damage clause which permitted recovery. Given the harsh effect of no damage clauses, courts will strictly construe such provisions but generally enforce them absent delay (1) not contemplated by the parties under the provision, (2) amounting to an abandonment of the contract, (3) caused by bad faith, or (4) amounting to active interference. *Peter Kiewit Sons', supra*, 355 F. Supp. at 397; see *also E. C. Ernst, Inc. v. Manhattan Const. Co. of Texas*, 551 F.2d 1026, 1029 (5th

Cir. 1977), mod. on other grounds, 559 F.2d 268 (5th Cir. 1977), *cert. denied,* 434 United States 1067, 98 S. Ct. 1246, 55 L. Ed. 2d 769 (1978).

As the name implies, active interference requires a finding that defendant (Mopac in this case) committed some affirmative, willful act in bad faith which unreasonably interfered with the contractor's compliance with the terms of the construction contract. *Id.*

Courts have found active interference where the contractee, despite knowledge of delay-causing conditions, has issued notice to proceed to the contractor resulting in increased costs because of the contractor's premature initiation of its work. *Gasparini Excavating Co. v. Pennsylvania Turnpike Comm'n.,* 409 Pa. 465, 187 A.2d 157 (1963); *Garofano Construction Co. v. State,* 183 Misc. 1080, 52 N.Y.S.2d 186 (1944); *American Bridge Co. v. State,* 245 App. Div. 535, 283 N.Y.S. 577 (1935). In such a case the affirmative willful act is the issuance of the notice to proceed; the requisite bad faith is demonstrated by proof of the contractee's knowledge that delay-causing circumstances exist which will likely prevent the contractor from timely proceeding with its work.

Until the notice to proceed was issued, ABD had free choice and complete flexibility to reschedule its orders and its work force. But it lost this freedom and flexibility when Mopac issued the notice to proceed on November 22, 1968, at a time when Johnson had already encountered the unexpected rock ledge, redesigned its cofferdam, and found steel in the river bed, all of which should have indicated to Mopac that adjustment in schedules would be necessary because of the inevitable delay these changes would bring in the completion of the substructure work. The notice to proceed had a coercive and restricting effect upon ABD by virtue of the provisions of the contract.

Accordingly, the judgment of the district court is affirmed.

McMillian, Circuit Judge, dissenting.

I respectfully dissent. I would reverse and remand to the district court with instructions to reduce the damages award to an allowance of damages for only twenty-five days. First, I am of the opinion that the agreed upon "no damage" clause precludes recovery, and secondly, I can find no affirmative, willful bad faith act to support the active interference theory advanced by ABD.

[What is going on in the preceding paragraph?] ■ ■ ■

12

Differing and Unforeseen Site Conditions

A **differing site condition** is defined as a condition at the site that differs from a representation made in the contract, plans, or specifications. Notice that this does *not* mean a condition at the site that differs from what the contractor expects. **Unforeseen conditions** are conditions of an unusual nature, and many contracts contain a specific definition of unforeseen conditions. By definition, then, a differing site condition *cannot* be an unforeseen site condition. If the condition is indicated in the plans or specifications, there is no way that it can be considered unforeseen.

Differing Site Condition

Rule: The owner absorbs the costs associated with a differing site condition. A differing site condition is a condition at the site that is different from the condition as outlined in the plans and specifications.

The legal implications of differing and unforeseen site conditions are very different. Basically, *the law awards the contractor damages for a differing site condition.* The law does not award the contractor damages for an unforeseen site condition.

Unforeseen Site Conditions

Simplified Rule: The contractor absorbs the costs associated with unforeseen site conditions unless the condition arises to the level of objective or practical impossibility *or* the owner has agreed in the contract to accept this risk.

Federal government contracts and other literature addressing these issues call a differing site condition a "Type I Differing Site Condition." An unforeseen site condition is called a "Type II Differing Site Condition." These terms can cause confusion because they imply that the two types of conditions are similar in many ways; however, they are not similar, and the terms *differing site condition* and *unforeseen site condition* will be used in the text rather than Type I or Type II differing site conditions.

Differing Site Conditions

The law relating to differing site conditions is merely a specialized name applied to the concepts outlined in the *Spearin* case discussed in Chapter 8, Specifications and Plans. The *Spearin* warranty states that the owner warrants the plans and specifications, and the contractor can depend on them. If a problem exists in the project, and it is the result of a faulty plan or specification, then the owner bears the cost of fixing (remedying) the problem. If a problem exists on the site, and it is the result of faulty information in the contract, plans, or specifications, then the owner bears the cost of fixing (remedying) the problem (see Figure 12–1).

For example, assume that the contract documents state: "*no underground springs exist on the property.*" That statement is part of the contract, and the owner warrants through *Spearin* that no underground springs exist on the site. If the contractor encounters underground springs, then a differing site condition exists because the conditions at the site (springs) are different from the conditions stated in the contract (no springs.) The owner is responsible for any increased construction costs related to building around or over the springs.

As another example, in the case of *W. H. Lyman Construction Co. v. The Village Of Gurnee,* the contract documents required the contractor to seal manhole bases in a certain way, but because of high subsurface hydrostatic pressures the designed seal would not

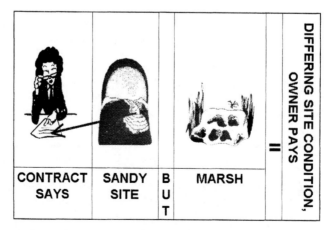

Figure 12-1   Differing site condition—owner pays.
© 2000–2001 *www.arttoday.com*

hold.[1] The contractor requested the use of a different sealing method, a method specifically prohibited by the contract documents. Approval was given for the revised design, and it proved to be adequate and necessary to complete the project. The contractor claimed that the higher-than-anticipated hydrostatic pressure was a differing site condition, and it claimed that the additional cost of completing the project (because of the higher-than-anticipated hydrostatic pressure) was owed to the contractor by the owner. The court disagreed and determined that no differing site condition existed *except* insofar as the design of the manhole bases. The contractor was entitled to increased construction costs associated with the sealing of the manhole bases but no other increased construction costs.

If the contract documents give no information about the site or about the specific condition(s), the contractor is complaining of, no differing site condition can exist. It is possible an unforeseen site condition might exist. That concept is discussed next.

Differing Site Condition

Rule: If the contract documents are silent about the condition found at the site, no differing site condition can exist; however, the condition may be an unforeseen site condition.

It is possible that the contract may be unclear or ambiguous as to the condition at the site. In that event the law must first decide what the contract says in order to determine if a differing site condition exists. To determine what a contract says refer to Chapter 9, Scope.

12–1. THINK

Outline the steps the law uses to determine what a contract says.

Unforeseen Site Conditions: Contractor Liability

An unforeseen site condition is a condition at the site that was not anticipated by the owner, the contractor, or both. Contracts frequently define unforeseen site conditions. The following is an example of a definition that might appear in a contract:

> *Unforeseen site condition: An unknown physical condition at the site of an unusual nature that differs materially from conditions ordinarily encountered in the type of work covered by this contract.*

---

[1] *W. H. Lyman Construction Co. v. The Village of Gurnee*, 84 Ill. App. 3d 28; 403 N.E.2d 1325 (1980).

The general rule is that the *contractor absorbs the costs associated with unforeseen site conditions, unless they rise to the level of objective or practical impossibility* (see Figure 12–2).

Unforeseen site conditions might include buried debris, unusual soil conditions, or a difference between the as-built drawings and the actual built system. *Nonphysical* conditions such as economic downturns, labor shortages, weather, and wars are not considered unforeseen site conditions.

If the unforeseen site condition is in the contractor's favor, then the contractor reaps the benefit. In other words, if the conditions at the site prove to be better than the contractor thought, the contractor does not refund any of the contract price to the owner. The opposite is also true; if the conditions at the site prove to be worse than the contractor thought, the contractor does not receive additional payment from the owner.

CONTRACTOR THINKS SANDY	BUT	MARSH =	UNFORESEEN SITE CONDITION, CONTRACTOR PAYS

Figure 12–2 Unforeseen site conditions: contractor pays.
© 2000–2001 www.arttoday.com

Unforeseen Site Conditions: Owner Liability

Under the following circumstances the owner is liable for unforeseen site conditions:

- Unforeseen site condition clause in the contract transfers liability to owner
- Objective or practical impossibility
- Nondisclosure/tort theories
- Differing site condition—an ambiguity in the contract makes the situation one of differing rather than unforeseen site condition

Figure 12–3 illustrates the theories that can transform liability for an unforeseen site condition from the contractor to the owner.

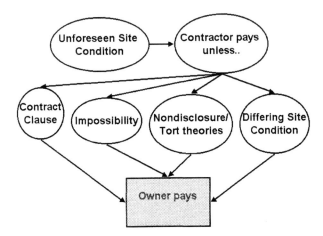

Figure 12–3 Transferring liability for an unforeseen site condition from contractor to owner.

Unforeseen Site Condition Clause in the Contract

Because of the impact of costs associated with unforeseen site conditions, few contractors will sign a contract without what is called an **unforeseen site condition clause.** The unforeseen site condition clause transfers the risk and costs of unforeseen site conditions to the owner and away from the contractor. The following is an example of an unforeseen site condition clause:

> If conditions are encountered at the site that are *unknown* physical conditions of an *unusual* nature and that *differ materially* from those ordinarily found to exist, and generally recognized as inherent in construction activities of the character provided for in the Contract Documents, then owner will make an equitable adjustment in the Contract Sum, or Contract Time, or both (emphasis added).

This clause does not pay the contractor for all unforeseen site conditions. In order to be entitled to payment for an unforeseen site condition the contractor must meet all the following criteria:

- The condition was unknown to the contractor; and
- the condition was unusual; and
- the condition was materially different.

If the condition is unknown but not unusual, the owner is not required to pay. If the condition is unknown and unusual but not materially different, the owner is not required to pay.

For example, assume that the entire contract between the owner and the contractor says:

> *Erect Olson prefabricated building Model #34RT on Owner's lot located on the northwest corner of Main Street and Hill Street, Madison, Tennessee, by June 1, 2001.*

The contractor must erect the building no matter what the conditions at the site are. This contract is extremely simple and is used only for the purposes of illustrating the ideas expressed in this section. According to this contract the contractor is accepting a great deal of risk on this project. Included in those risks are all risks associated with the conditions at the site, including unforeseen and unusual conditions. Should an unusual condition, such as a buried fertilizer storage tank be found, the contractor must bear the costs associated with removing the tank. (This example assumes that the buried fertilizer storage tank is unforeseen on this project and the contractor did not know it was located on the site.)

12-2. THINK

Why is the buried fertilizer tank *not* a differing site condition in the preceding scenario?

Objective and Practical Impossibility

If the costs associated with the unforeseen site condition rise to the level of objective or practical impossibility, the law will not require the contractor to perform the contract. Objective and practical impossibility are discussed in Chapter 8, Specifications and Plans.

Nondisclosure

Older common law held that there was no duty to volunteer information to the other party during contract negotiations. If the contractor did not specifically ask, "Did you perform a soil test, and what are the results?" the owner was not required to give this information to the contractor. If the contractor did ask, and the owner lied, the owner could be liable for fraud (discussed later). However, in recent decades the law has been changing, and most jurisdictions recognize a duty to report a known defect or problem that is not readily observable by the other party.

For example, in the case of *City of Salinas v. Souza & McCue Const. Co., Inc.*, the court held the city liable for damages to the contractor because its engineers knew of highly unstable conditions existing in the subsoils along the plotted line of a sewer and failed to inform the contractor.[2] The court said:

> *It is the general rule that by failing to impart its knowledge of difficulties to be encountered in a project, the owner will be liable for misrepresentation if the contractor is unable to perform according to the contract provisions.*

---

[2]*City of Salinas v. Souza & McCue Const. Co., Inc.*, 66 Cal. 2d 217, 424 P.2d 921 (1967).

Tort Theories

As a general rule of law, tort theories are not allowed to be raised in contract actions. As with all rules, this one is changing, and some jurisdictions allow parties who have a contract with each other (in other words, the parties are in *privity of contract*) to sue for torts in addition to any contract claims. The contractor might be able to support a claim of fraud, negligence, or negligent misrepresentation if an unforeseen condition exists. These concepts are discussed in Chapter 15, Torts and Tort Damages.

Ambiguity Resolved to Reveal Differing Site Condition

If the contract terms are ambiguous with regard to the offending condition at the site, the contractor might be able to first use the law outlined in Chapter 9, Scope, to obtain an interpretation of the contract that differs from the condition at the site. Once this occurs, the condition at the site becomes a differing rather than an unforeseen, site condition, and the contractor is entitled to damages.

For example, in the case of *Michels Pipe Line Construction, Inc., v. City Of Elgin*, the appeal court returned a case to the trial court to determine whether an ambiguity in the contract made the encountered condition a differing site condition or not.[3] Soil boring logs, technical specifications, and drawings had been given to the contractor. These documents described subsurface conditions, including the presence of boulders and water. Michels encountered more groundwater and boulders than expected; however, the contract contained conflicting provisions concerning the reliability of the supplied information. The appeal court said it was necessary to determine the ambiguity in the contract first in order to determine if a differing site condition existed.

As a further example, in the case of *S. J. Groves & Sons and Company v. North Carolina* the appeal court upheld the trial court's decision to award a contractor damages for a differing site condition (called "changed condition" in the opinion) on a highway construction project for excessive soil wetness.[4]

The specifications contained the following two items (and others):

> *(a) Soils should pose no great problems on this project except perhaps requiring some stabilization in the elastic A-5 soils.*

> *(b) Subsurface Investigation Report indicated that some cuts would contain "moist" to "damp" to "wet" materials, and further indicated that subsurface ground water would be encountered in the soils contained in the cut material.*

The contractor claimed that item (a) meant the contractor would face no great problems, when in fact it did because of excessive soil wetness. The excessive wetness was a differing site condition. The state claimed that the documents informed the contractor that

---

[3]*Michels Pipe Line Construction, Inc., v. City of Elgin*, 1998 U.S. Dist. LEXIS 7174.

[4]*S. J. Groves & Sons and Company v. State of North Carolina*, 50 N.C. App. 1; 273 S.E.2d 465 (1980 N.C. App.).

it would encounter wet materials and therefore no differing site condition existed. The contract was therefore ambiguous because it was capable of two different reasonable interpretations. The court was then faced with deciding which of the two competing interpretations would win. Using the whole-agreement rule (see Chapter 9, Slope) the court said:

> *When the report and other contract documents were and are considered together and in their entirety, there were and are affirmative indications that the ground water could be drained from the cuts in a practical manner and that the materials which were "wet" or "damp" could be dried in a practicable manner and used in the fills in a balanced grading operation and within a reasonable time. However, the soil could not be so used.*

The court determined that the contract had misled the contractor, and therefore a differing site condition existed.

Prebid Site Inspection

As a general rule contractors are *not* required to make a site inspection but are allowed to rely on the contract documents in preparing a bid; however, most written construction contracts require a site inspection. When a site inspection is required by the contract, the contractor is responsible for all damages—for example, increased construction costs—associated with any condition that is *visible*. The contractor cannot later make a claim for damages relating to a condition that is obvious and apparent on a visual inspection of the site. The law does not require the contractor to dig or analyze samples from the site, however—only to make a visual inspection.

Vocabulary Checklist

Differing site condition	*Spearin* doctrine	Practical impossibility
Unforeseen site condition	Objective impossibility	Prebid site inspection

Review Questions

1. Who pays for a differing site condition?
2. Who pays for an unforeseen site condition?
3. When does the owner pay for an unforeseen site condition?
4. What is the *Spearin* doctrine?
5. How is the *Spearin* doctrine related to unforeseen site conditions?
6. Fill in Figure 12–4 to indicate the theories that can be used by the contractor to place the costs associated with an unforeseen site condition on the owner:

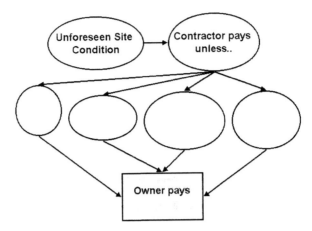

Figure 12–4 Student fill-in: Owner pays for unforeseen site condition.

Problems

Answer the issue in each of the following problems by making a legal argument, including premises in support of your answer.

1. The contract indicated that only silty and blue clays and a small amount of shale would be encountered on the site. A large quantity of shale was actually encountered instead of the silty and clayey material. The contractor had intended to use the excavated material of silt and clay for fill at another location on the job; however, the excavated material would not compact well, and the contractor had to purchase fill from another source.

   Issue: Is the owner responsible for the costs of the purchased fill?

   Rule: (*Hint:* Determine if this is a differing or unforeseen site condition.)

   Premises:

   Answer: Yes

2. The owner, Thornton University, solicited bids for the renovation of a wing of a university building. The contract included replacement of all windows and installations of a new drainage system around the foundation. The bid documents required bidders to conduct a pre-bid site inspection in order to familiarize themselves with the conditions in the field.

   Takao Contractor had performed renovations on a separate wing of the same building several years earlier and considered itself familiar with the conditions at the site. Nonetheless, Takao conducted a brief walk-through of the site and the wing to be renovated. Takao submitted the low bid and was awarded the contract.

   During performance of the work, Takao encountered two unanticipated problems. Whereas the other wing of the building had contained wooden framing around the windows, this wing had concealed metal framing, which impeded installation of the new windows. Additionally, Takao encountered subsurface sewer lines that interfered with excavation for the drainage system. Neither of these conditions had been indicated in the as-built drawings furnished by Thornton University, the owner. The location of the sewer line was shown in records available at the municipal wastewater authority.

Takao contractor submitted a claim alleging that both situations constituted a differing site condition. Takao claimed the as-built drawings should have indicated that the windows contained concealed metal framing and also should have indicated the sewer problem.

Takao Construction's expert testified that as-built drawings *normally contain* indications of sewer lines. As-built drawings do not normally contain indications of specific materials used in the construction, however.

The owner's expert testified that as-built drawings normally do *not* contain indications of sewer lines or indications of specific materials used in the construction.

Issue: Do as-built drawings normally contain indications of sewer lines?

Question: What type of issue is this?

Assume that the jury decides that the contractor's expert witness is better qualified and is telling the truth. Determine the legal issues presented next.

Issue 1: Is the contractor entitled to compensation for the window problem?

Rule: (*Hint:* no differing site condition)

Premises:

Answer: No

Issue 2: Is the contractor entitled to compensation for the sewer problem?

Rule: (*Hint:* differing site)

Premises:

Answer: Yes

Question (can be answered only if Chapter 3, Logic, has been studied): The owner argued that information about the sewer lines was available to the contractor at the municipal wastewater authority. Which logical fallacy does this argument contain?

3. (Note that the facts same as in problem 2.) Assume the contract contains the following clause:

> *If conditions are encountered at the site which are (1) subsurface or otherwise concealed physical conditions which differ materially from those indicated in the Contract Documents, or (2) unknown physical conditions of an unusual nature, which differ materially from those ordinarily found to exist and generally recognized as inherent in construction activities of the character provided for in the Contract Documents . . . the contractor shall be entitled to a reasonable addition to the contract sum and/or the contract time to complete the work.*

Question: Does the inclusion of this clause change the answers determined in problem 2?

4. The owner, Ivan, Inc. awarded a contract for construction of a small bridge over a river to Cornelius Construction, Inc. The design called for the bridge to be supported by concrete pilings resting on bedrock. The contract documents included boring logs from test borings taken along both banks. These logs indicated 6 to 10 feet of silt and gravel overlaying the bedrock. No test borings had been performed on the riverbed itself.

The contract documents also required bidders to conduct prebid site inspections prior to bid submittal.

The contract contained the following clause:

> *Claims for Concealed or Unknown Conditions. If conditions are encountered at the site which are (1) subsurface or otherwise concealed physical conditions which differ materially from those indicated in the Contract Documents, or (2) unknown physical conditions of an unusual nature, which differ materially from those ordinarily found to exist, and generally recognized as inherent in construction activities of the character proved for in the Contract Documents, then notice by the observing party shall be given to the other party promptly. . . . The Architect will promptly investigate such conditions, and if they differ materially, and cause an increase or decrease in the Contractor's cost of or time required for performance of, any part of the Work, will recommend an equitable adjustment in the Contract Sum, or Contract Time, or both.*

The contractor's prebid site inspection consisted of a visual examination of the site. The contractor's project manager, Ms. Kermit, was concerned about the lack of boring logs for the riverbed, and she wrote a memo to her superior expressing that concern. Ms. Kermit had previously supervised the building of another bridge 15 miles downstream on the same river, and she had found the depth of silt and gravel to be relatively uniform from bank to bank. Cornelius Construction's estimating team decided to price its bid on the assumption that the boring logs from the banks indicated the approximate depth to bedrock in the riverbed itself and on Ms. Kermit's previous experience along the same river. After contract award, the contractor, Cornelius Construction, Inc., discovered trenches and pockets of gravel and silt, some as deep as 18 feet.

These conditions would require an additional 10 working days to complete the project and an additional cost of $50,000 on the $1.5 million project. Cornelius Construction submitted a delay claim, claiming that the trenches in the riverbed were a differing and/or unforeseen site condition, and it was entitled to a delay pursuant to the contract and the law.

Ivan, Inc., responded that it had made no representations regarding conditions beneath the riverbed, and that soils maps available at a county office should have alerted the contractor to the possibility of these conditions. Ivan also informed the contractor that no time extension was to be granted, and Ivan expected the project to be completed per the contract schedule.

The contractor completed the project per the schedule with increased costs to place the bridge in the silt amounting to $20,000. Also, the contractor had to hire extra people and pay overtime to complete the project by the same date. The costs for this amounted to $10,000.

Issue 1: Is this an unforeseen site condition?

Rule:

Premises: (*Hint:* A fact exists that shows this is *not* an unforeseen site condition.)

Answer: No

Issue 2: Is this a differing site condition?

Rule:

Premises: (*Hint:* Look carefully at what the contract says. Is the description different from what was found?)

Answer: No

Question (can be answered only if Chapter 3, Logic, has been studied): The owner is correct in that it does not have to pay the contractor for either a differing or an unforeseen site condition. However, the owner raises the red herring logical fallacy in its argument. What is that argument and why is it a red herring?

5. Add the following fact to problem 4: The contractor's expert testifies that pockets of silt and gravel are not unusual on the river but that pockets as deep as 18 feet are very unusual. Several pockets of this depth located in close proximity are even more unusual.

Question: How and why does this additional fact allow the contractor to recover its costs?

Answer to Selected Problem

1. The contract indicated only silty and blue clays and a small amount of shale would be. . . .

Issue: Is the owner responsible for the costs of the purchased fill? It is either a differing or unforeseen site condition.

Rule: A differing site condition is a condition at the site that is different from what the contract says. The law awards the contractor damages for a differing site condition.

Premises: The contract stated that only silty and blue clays and a small amount of shale would be encountered on the site. Instead, the soil contained a large amount of shale. Thus the conditions stated in the contract differ from those actually in existence. The rule states the contractor is entitled to damages for a differing site condition. In this case the damages are the need to purchase suitable fill.

Answer: Yes

Appendix

CASE: RANDA/MADISON JOINT VENTURE III V. DAHLBERG

239 F.3d 1264 (Fed. Cir. 2001) (abridged)

Opinion: Linn, Circuit Judge

Randa/Madison Joint Venture III ("Randa") seeks review of a final decision of the Armed Services Board of Contract Appeals denying Randa's appeal from a deemed denial of its claim by the United States Army Corps of Engineers (the "Corps"). Randa's claim is that it encountered excessive groundwater in the performance of its contract with the government, constituting both a Type 1 and a Type 2 differing site condition, as defined by the contract. In re Randa/Madison Joint Venture III, No. 49452 (A.S.B.C.A. Aug. 27, 1999). Because the board's determination that Randa did not prove either a Type 1 or Type 2 differing site condition is supported by substantial evidence and does not otherwise contain any reversible error, we affirm the board's denial of Randa's appeal.

Background

The government, through the Corps, issued a solicitation on March 1, 1994, for work that included the construction of a sewage pumping station, also called a pump house. . . . The government retained a separate firm, CME Engineering, Inc. ("CME"), to prepare the design documents, which were to be "sufficiently detailed to permit construction contractors to submit responsive bids without the necessity to visit the project during bidding". . . . The Corps had agreed to perform the necessary geotechnical investigation, including drilling and testing to determine various characteristics of the subsurface, at CME's direction. *Id.*

The pump house foundation was to extend forty feet below the surface and it was necessary to determine the extent, if any, of subsurface water at the pump house location. Any subsurface water would have to be removed during construction to a depth of five feet below the foundation or forty-five feet below the surface. This process is called dewatering. . . .

The Corps drilled at least twelve holes, called soil borings, and performed specific tests on the soil that was removed. One of these soil borings, referred to as DH-11, was close to the pump house excavation and is, therefore, of particular relevance. . . .

After realizing that its initial approach to dewatering the site was not working, Randa's subcontractor drilled another soil boring, referred to as DW-3 . . . H-C subsequently performed a sieve analysis on the DW-3 soil samples and developed a gradation curve. . . . Randa asserts that the DW-3 data accurately depicts the conditions actually encountered at the site and that these conditions qualify as a differing site condition under the contract.

After finishing the dewatering operation, Randa filed a claim with the government for an increase in the contract price, alleging that it encountered a differing site condition. . . .

Discussion

B. Analysis

2. Type 1 Differing Site Condition

Randa's overriding theme is that this case involves impermissible burden shifting. In its first brief to this court, Randa asserts that the Differing Site Conditions clause "is intended to shift the risks associated with unanticipated adverse subsurface conditions from contractors to the Government." Randa argues that the board's decision contravenes this risk-shifting function, placing the burden for such conditions back on the contractor. If this risk is to be shifted by virtue of the Site Investigations Clause and the Explorations clause, then, Randa argues, there must be a warning in the contract documents that the boring logs alone are not reliable.

The government responds that substantial evidence supports the board's conclusion that each of the DH-11 boring log and the DH-11 gradation curves were individually adequate to predict the water encountered. . . .

We uphold the board's finding that there is no Type 1 differing site condition. . . .

This court has previously explained that "in order to establish entitlement to an equitable adjustment by reason of a Type 1 differing site condition[,] . . . the contractor must prove, by a preponderance of the evidence, that the conditions indicated in the contract differ materially from those it encounters during performance." *H. B. Mac, Inc. v. United States,* 153 F.3d 1338, 1345 (Fed. Cir. 1998) (quoting in part *Stuyvesant Dredging Co. v. United States,* 834 F.2d 1576, 1581 (Fed. Cir. 1987)) (quotations omitted). . . .

The board further found that it was "unable to conclude that boring log DW-3 [contractor's boring log] reflected conditions materially different from [those] indicated by boring log DH-11 [supplied by government]." . . . Thus, the board found that there was no material difference between the conditions indicated in the contract and those actually encountered. . . .

3. Type 2 Differing Site Condition

As mentioned earlier, FAR 52.236-2 was incorporated into the contract and defines Type 2 differing site conditions as "unknown physical conditions at the site, of an unusual nature, which differ materially from those ordinarily encountered and generally recognized as inhering in work of the character provided for in the contract." 48 C.F.R. § 52.236-2 (2000). The board found that no Type 2 differing site condition existed because there was no unknown condition.

We perform a de novo review of the question of whether the board applied the correct legal standards to determine if a Type 2 condition existed. Our precedent provides that in order to qualify as a Type 2 differing site condition, "the unknown physical condition must be one that could not be reasonably anticipated by the contractor from his study of the contract documents, his inspection of the site, and his general experience[,] if any, as a contractor in the area." *Perini Corp. v. United States,* 180 Ct. Cl. 768, 381 F.2d 403, 410 (Ct. Cl. 1967).

Again, because Randa has conceded that the DW-3 data [its own data] reflects the actual conditions encountered, the proper inquiry focuses on whether the DW-3 data shows an unknown condition. It does not. As detailed earlier, the DH-11 data virtually predicted the DW-3 data. Further, although the contract was intended to enable bids to be prepared without a site visit, a representative of Randa did make at least one site visit. . . . On that visit, he observed a creek bed, admittedly dry, but nonetheless a possible harbinger of underground water. *Id.* Accordingly, we hold that the board's decision that Randa did not establish that it was subjected to a Type 2 differing site condition is supported by substantial evidence and is not fraudulent, arbitrary, capricious or grossly erroneous.

Conclusion

We hold that the Board's determination of the absence of either a Type 1 or a Type 2 differing site condition is supported by substantial evidence and does not otherwise contain any reversible error. Affirmed.

■ ■ ■

13

Warranties

A **warranty** is merely a special type of contract. For example, an apartment lease is a special type of contract. A warranty guarantees that something will happen, or that a product or service will perform in a certain way in the future. For example, a one-year express written warranty on a compact disc player guarantees that the player will work for one year. The implied warranty of good and workmanlike construction guarantees that the contractor will build in a good and workmanlike manner. The basic principles of contract law apply to warranty contracts.

13-1. THINK

Name three different contracts.

Warranties can be divided into two categories—*express warranties* and *implied warranties.* An **express warranty** is a warranty given or *expressed* by the terms of a contract. It can be written or oral, but express warranties are generally written. You can see the warranty when you read the contract—the words *warrant* or *guarantee* are contained someplace in the contract. An **implied warranty** is a warranty added into the contract by the law. You may not see the implied warranty in the contract when you read it. You may know of the warranty's existence only if you know the law.

Some drafters of contracts are aware that the law implies warranties into contracts and will include them in the written contract. It makes no difference to the law whether the implied warranty is or is not in the written contract; the warranty exists either way.

Express Warranties

To determine the extent of an express warranty it is necessary to review the contract. Like all contracts, there is no requirement that the warranty contract be in writing; it is possible to have an oral warranty contract. Of course, it is always more difficult to prove an oral contract. Also, the statute of frauds might prevent a warranty contract of one year or more from being enforced because contracts that cannot be carried out in a year must be evidenced by a writing of some sort. The statute of frauds is a law that requires certain types of contracts to be evidenced by a writing and is discussed in Chapter 10, Changes and Additions to the Contract.

Express Warranty

A contract guaranteeing the performance of a product or service.
Usually written but may be oral in some circumstances.

A very simple example of a warranty in a contract is

"Parts and labor guaranteed for one year."

AIA A201—1997 §3.5 has a more complicated warranty:

The Contractor warrants to the Owner and Architect that materials and equipment furnished under the Contract will be of good quality and new unless otherwise required or permitted by the Contract Documents, that the Work will be free from defects not inherent in the quality required or permitted, and that the Work will conform to the requirements of the Contract Documents.

EXAMPLE 1:

STO Corporation warrants artificial stucco known as External Insulation Finish System (EIFS) manufactured by STO. STO warrants that EIFS, "if properly applied, will be free from defects in material for a period of seven years. STO's sole responsibility and liability under this warranty shall be to supply replacement materials and labor for any STO product warranted shown to be defective within seven years from the date of STO's original invoice to STO's supplier, distributor, contractor, applicator or owner, as the case may be." ■ ■ ■

EXAMPLE 2:

Contractor builds a new store. Six months later the roof leaks. The contract contains no warranty or language guaranteeing the construction. The contractor is not required under the contract terms to return and fix the roof. (However, see the discussion under "Implied Warranties.")

■ ■ ■

EXAMPLE 3:

Pearce Construction installs an air conditioner manufactured by Knight Corp. in a new home purchased by Mr. and Mrs. Compton, the owners. Knight Corp. warrants the air conditioner for five years. Pearce Construction has given the owners a two-year warranty on the construction of the home. After three years the air conditioner breaks down. Mr. Compton calls Knight and asks them to repair the air conditioner under the warranty. Knight refuses to repair or replace the air conditioner because they have no warranty contract with the Comptons. Knight is correct. Pearce Construction refuses to become involved because its two-year warranty period has elapsed. The Comptons have no recourse against Knight because there is no contract (no privity) between them and Knight. The warranty contract is between Knight and Pearce Construction, who purchased the product with the warranty. (*Note:* This is an example only. In most construction projects the manufacturers' warranties are transferred from the contractor to the owner.)

■ ■ ■

13-2. THINK

What is the difference between a contract to purchase an automobile and a warranty on that same automobile?

One problem a contractor can encounter in this area is the problem of being held liable under the *distributor's* express warranty. If the distributor supplies a brochure or other printed material containing the warranty, and the contractor prints or adds its name to the material, it could be concluded that the contractor is also giving a warranty. Statements or comments by the contractor may be sufficient to establish an oral express warranty. For example, in the case of *Weeks v. Slavick Builders, Inc.* the plaintiffs had purchased a new home construction by Slavick Builders.[1] One of the features of the home was a cement tile

---

[1]*Weeks v. Slavick Builders, Inc.* 24 Mich. App. 621; 180 N.W.2d 503 (Mich. App. 1970) *aff'd.* 384 Mich. 257.

roof supplied by Anza Industries of America, Inc. and it carried a warranty against leaks due to failure of the tile or its installation for the life of the building. The brochures used by appellant in promoting the sales of its homes contained a description of the lifetime roof. It was obvious that the manufacturer of the tile roof, Anza, had given a warranty. What was not so clear was whether statements made by the *contractor's* employees (and other factors not relevant here) might have given rise to an express warranty. The issue was ordered to be tried by a jury.

If the contract does not contain any verbiage guaranteeing or warranting the product or service, the product or service does not contain an *express* warranty; however the product or service may have *implied* warranties.

Implied Warranties

An **implied warranty** is a warranty established or required by law to be given to the purchaser. The four most common implied warranties in the construction industry are as follows:

- Owner's implied warranty of the plans and specifications (*Spearin* warranty)
- Contractor's implied warranty to build in a good and workmanlike manner
- Warranty of merchantability of goods
- Warranty of fitness of goods

Implied Warranty

A warranty established or required by law even if it is not expressed in the contract.

It is not uncommon when speaking of implied warranties to leave off the *implied* part of the name. This causes confusion among people who may not be familiar with the law. For example, it is common to read or to speak about the "owner's warranty of the plans and specifications." It is less common to read or talk about the "owner's *implied* warranty of the plans and specifications" even though this is the more accurate way of referring to the warranty. Each of the implied warranties is more fully discussed next.

The Four Most Common Implied Warranties in the Construction Industry

1. Owner's implied warranty of the plans and specifications
2. Contractor's warranty to build in a good and workmanlike manner
3. Warranty of merchantability
4. Warranty of fitness for a particular purpose

Implied warranties are a relatively recent innovation in the law. Until the 1960s the doctrine of **caveat emptor,** that is, "let the buyer beware" was the law applied to the sale of real property. In the 1960s most states began moving away from this doctrine and began to adopt implied warranties into the sale and construction of real property improvements. Because the law is relatively new (from a legal standpoint) many questions still remain on its application.

Spearin Warranty

The *Spearin* warranty or *Spearin* doctrine is discussed in detail in Chapter 8, Specifications and Plans. In summary, the courts have held that the owner gives the contractor an implied warranty that the plans and specifications are adequate to perform the project.

Contractor's Implied Warranty to Build in a Good and Workmanlike Manner

Most jurisdictions have decided that a construction contract contains an implied warranty that the contractor will build in a good and workmanlike manner. Good and workmanlike is defined more specifically in the case law of each jurisdiction. See the case *Mullis vs. Brennan* at the end of this chapter for an example.

The Contractor's Implied Warranty to Build in a
Good and Workmanlike Manner

Rule: The contractor warrants that it will build the project in a good and
workmanlike manner. Failure to do so is a breach of the contract.

The extent to which this theory has been developed varies widely among the jurisdictions. Some jurisdictions may refer to this warranty as the *implied warranty of habitability.* The warranty protects an owner's expectation that the home will be suitable for living in. Thus, if latent defects in the construction interfere with the inhabitant's reasonable expectation that the unit will be suitable for habitation, the contractor has breached the implied warranty of habitability.

If the contractor breaches this warranty, the contractor is liable to the owner for damages. In the preceding Example 2, in which the contractor builds a store, and the roof leaks six months later, the owner may be entitled to damages if it can prove that the contractor has *not* built in a good and workmanlike manner.

For example, in the case of *VonHoldt v. Barba & Barba Construction, Inc.,* the contractor constructed a multilevel addition to a single family residence.[2] Several years later

---

[2]*VonHoldt v. Barba & Barba Construction, Inc.,* 175 Ill. 2d 426, 677 N.E.2d 836 (1997).

the plaintiff, VanHoldt, purchased the home from the people who had originally bought it from Barba & Barba Construction. Shortly thereafter, VonHoldt noticed a depression in the floor plane that went unnoticed for a time because of the thickness of the carpet. Upon investigation it was determined that the addition had not been built according to the original approved plans. The variance caused excessive stress on the floor joists and inadequate support for a portion of the roof and ceiling, which created a greater-than-expected floor deflection. The contractor could be held liable for a breach of the implied warranty of habitability several years after the construction was completed and also by subsequent purchasers of the dwelling.

Implied Warranty of Merchantability

The implied warranty of merchantability is a warranty established by the Uniform Commercial Code (UCC), adopted in varying forms in every state. The UCC applies only to the sales of goods, such as toasters, nails, and lumber. It also applies only to manufacturers and commercial sellers. The UCC does not apply to service contracts, such as construction contracts. This warranty is important in the construction industry because the contracts for materials, appliances, and other goods installed in the construction project are governed by the UCC.

The Implied Warranty of Merchantability

Rule: The seller warrants the goods will be fit for the purpose
for which ordinarily sold.

Under the UCC the manufacturer or seller warrants to the buyer that the goods are of "like quality and performance of similar goods and fit for the purpose for which such goods are ordinarily sold." For example, the purchaser of a light bulb is given an implied warranty of merchantability that the light bulb is of like quality and performance to similar light bulbs and fit for the purpose for which light bulbs are normally sold. In this specific example that purpose is to provide light.

Implied Warranty of Fitness for a Particular Purpose

The implied warranty of fitness for a particular purpose is another warranty established by the UCC. This warranty arises only if the seller of the goods has recommended to the purchaser that the goods will be fit for some particular purpose.

The Implied Warranty of Fitness for a Particular Purpose

Rule: A seller who recommends goods warrants they will perform as recommended.

I want non-skid tile for my floor!	I got the right stuff right here!!	OOPS! Contractor liable.

Figure 13–1   Implied warranty of fitness for a particular purpose. *2000–2001 www.arttoday.com*

For example, a customer or purchaser goes to a paint store, asks for metal paint, and the clerk recommends XYZ paint. After the customer paints the metal door the paint begins to crack and peel because XYZ paint is suitable only for wood, not for metal. The seller has breached the implied warranty of fitness for a particular purpose. It is not uncommon for this warranty to be called *implied warranty of fitness* or *warranty of fitness* (see Figure 13–1).

Vocabulary Checklist

Express warranty
Implied warranty
Spearin warranty
Contractor's implied warranty to build in a

good and workmanlike manner
Implied warranty of habitability

Uniform Commercial Code
Warranty of merchantability
Warranty of fitness for a particular purpose

Review Questions

1. What is the difference between an express and an implied warranty?
2. Must a warranty be in writing?
3. What are the four types of implied warranties that are most likely to arise in the construction industry?
4. What is the difference between an implied warranty of merchantability and an implied warranty of fitness?
5. What types of contracts do the implied warranty of merchantability and the implied warranty of fitness cover?

Problems

Answer the issue in each of the following problems by making a legal argument, including premises in support of your answer.

1. Molkentine Department Store buys an air conditioner replacement part from Zayas Air Conditioning. Zayas also installs the part. No warranty is given on the part. The part is defective, stops working after one month, and cannot be repaired

   Issue: Does Molkentine have any legal recourse against Zayas?

   Rule: (*Hint:* warranty of merchantability)

   Premises:

   Answer: Yes

2. Spalten Contracting constructs a small storage shed behind Millner Brothers Rod and Reel, a retail business. It does not give the owners any warranty. The shed falls apart after six months due to defects in the workmanship. A normal shed of that type would have been expected to last about 20 years before needing fairly major repairs.

   Issue: Does Millner Brothers Rod and Reel have any legal recourse against Spalten?

   Rule: (*Hint:* warranty to build in a good and workmanlike manner)

   Premises:

   Answer: Yes

3. Woodley Farms contracts with Quintana Air Conditioning Company to provide an air conditioning unit that will cool its office building (6000 sq. ft.) to 75° given outdoor conditions of 110° and 80% humidity. The unit provided works but does not cool the area to the desired temperature. Quintana Air Conditioning Company gave no express warranties to Woodley Farms.

   Issue 1: Is the unit merchantable?

   Rule:

   Premises:

   Answer: Yes

   Issue 2: Does Woodley Farms have any legal recourse against Quintana Air Conditioning Company?

   Rule: (*Hint:* warranty of fitness)

   Premises:

   Answer: Yes

4. Hunt Arcade Games, Inc. sells and installs arcade games to the Tres Rios Miniature Golf and Recreation Center. Some of the games prove defective. Tres Rios wants to sue the contractor.

Issue: Is this case governed by the UCC?

Rule: (*Hint:* Read the section very carefully.)

Premises:

Answer: Yes

6. Yur state department of transportation awarded a contract to Border States Paving, Inc. to resurface 12 miles of road. The contract required Border States to mill off a portion of the existing asphalt surface, place a leveling course of asphalt, and place a wearing course of asphalt. The contract required the work to be completed by October 15, 1993.

Heavy rain prevented access to materials and caused delay. Border States requested an extension of the completion deadline to December 31 so it could finish the work that season and avoid remobilizing its forces in the spring.

The department reluctantly agreed to the extension, but the contract modification imposed strict limitations on temperatures and windchills in which asphalt could be batched and applied. The change order also stated: "In the spring of 1994, an inspection of the top of the road will made to determine if there is any raveling or any surface defect due to cold weather asphalt concrete work. If raveling or other surface defects are present, Border States will be required to repair or redo the work."

In the spring, defects were apparent in the work, and the state held Border States responsible for the repairs. The contractor responded that its interpretation of the contract and change order was that if it complied with the specifications for mixing and placing the asphalt, it would be in compliance with the contract. Border States said it had honored the temperature restrictions and should not be responsible for conditions beyond its control.

Issue: Is contractor responsible for the costs of repair?

Rule: (*Hint:* warranty of fitness)

Premises:

Answer:

Answer to Selected Problem

1. Molkentine Department Store buys an air conditioner replacement part from Zayas . . .

Issue: Does Molkentine have any legal recourse against Zayas?

Rule: Warranty of merchantability. Under the UCC the manufacturer or seller (if the seller's business is selling goods of the type indicated) warrants to the buyer that the goods are of "like quality and performance of similar goods and fit for the purpose for which such goods are sold."

Premises: Although no expert testimony is given in the problem, it is likely that a part such as this is expected to work longer than one month. It would be necessary to look at how long other air conditioner parts are normally expected to last.

Answer: Yes

Appendix

CASE: *MULLIS V. BRENNAN*

716 N.E.2d 58 (Ind. App. 1999)

Statement of the Case (*Note:* Part of the opinion has been deleted.)

Plaintiff-Appellant Richard Mullis ("Mullis"), Individually and d/b/a Mullis Building Corporation ("MBC") appeals the trial court's judgment in favor of Defendants-Appellees Shawn A. Brennan and Karen S. Brennan ("the Brennans.")

We affirm.

Issues

Mullis raises six issues for our review, which we consolidate and restate as:

III. Whether the trial court erred in finding that Mullis breached the contract with the Brennans by not performing in a workmanlike manner.

Facts

In April of 1996, the Brennans contacted Mullis to obtain estimates from Mullis on the cost of building an addition onto the Brennans' house. After negotiations, Mullis, individually, tendered a contract to the Brennans. The contract provided that Mullis, individually, would build the 24′ by 30′ room addition for the Brennans, and that the Brennans would pay Mullis, individually, the total sum of $43,500.00. MBC was not a party to the contract.

Problems between the Brennans and Mullis regarding his workmanship and performance of the contract began to develop immediately after he began the construction.

After Mullis left the project, the Brennans, through their own labor and that of various subcontractors hired by them, worked on the room addition to correct the problems left by Mullis and to complete the work contemplated by the contract. The room addition was completed in July, 1998.

Discussion and Decision

III. Breach of Contract

Mullis contends that the trial court erred in determining that he was liable for damages on the basis that he breached the home improvement contract with the Brennans. He argues, without citation to authority, that the Brennans breached first and that "arguably, this was an anticipatory breach of the contract by the Brennans." Appellant's Brief at 24.

The trial court found that the Brennans presented "overwhelming evidence" to show that Mullis was not performing his contract in a workmanlike manner, and that the room addition was not structurally sound and free of substantial defects at the time Mullis walked off the project. The trial court also found that Mullis's poor workmanship and lack of supervision of subcontractors created structural problems for the room addition. The trial court further found that the Brennans continually and clearly expressed their concerns about problems with the foundation, the frame, the roof, and the generally poor workmanship. Finally, the trial court found that:

In August or September, 1996, after several months of observing the poor quality work that was being done on their room addition, and after paying Mullis $10,500.00 of the contract price, and after asking Mullis numerous times to correct the many serious problems with his workmanship on the project, the Brennans demanded that Mullis correct the problems before any further payments or "draws" would be made to Mullis. Mullis refused to do any further work until he was paid his "draws" under the contract. Mullis walked off the project in September, 1996, and never returned. (Finding of Fact # 11.) The trial court then concluded that Mullis committed the first material breach of the contract by, inter alia, failing to perform the terms of the contract in a workmanlike manner, providing substandard and defective work, and walking off the project and failing to correct defective work and complete the work promised.

The law implies a duty in every contract for work or services that the work or services will be performed skillfully, carefully, diligently, and in a workmanlike manner. *Data Processing Services, Inc. v. L. H. Smith Oil Corp.,* 492 N.E.2d 314, 319 (Ind. Ct. App. 1986), *reh'g denied.* The term "workmanlike manner" has a fixed meaning in the building trade: "To do the work in the building of a house in a good workmanlike manner is to do the work as a skilled workman would do it." *Morris v. Fox,* 79 Ind. App. 389, 135 N.E. 663, 664 (1922). Failure to perform in a workmanlike manner may constitute a breach of contract. *Wilson v. Palmer,* 452 N.E.2d 426, 429 (Ind. Ct. App. 1983).

What duty or warranty is implied in the preceding paragraph? Notice that the language differs slightly from the language in this chapter.

Here, the record supports the trial court's finding that Mullis failed to perform in a workmanlike manner. The record also supports the trial court's finding that the Brennans requested that the defective work be cured and that Mullis refused to do so. This evidence is sufficient to support both the trial court's findings and its conclusion that Mullis breached the contract.　■　■　■

14

Termination of the Contract and Contract Damages

Material Breach versus Partial Breach

Terminating a construction contract is a very rare event. The law (common sense and economic principles support this approach also) is structured in such a way that it encourages the parties to work out the many problems that arise in a typical construction contract rather than terminate the contract. Basically, the law does *not* allow a party to terminate the construction contract, even if the other party breaches the contract. *A construction contract can be terminated only for a* **material** *or* **major breach** of the contract. If the party, usually the owner, terminates for a nonmaterial breach, that party is also in breach and must pay the damages. Since it may be difficult to predict what a major breach is, owners, or at least their attorneys, are very, very hesitant to terminate a construction contract.

An example of a partial/nonmaterial/nonsubstantial breach follows:

> *Contract calls for contractor's on-site project manager to have two telephone lines at the construction site. The project manager has only one telephone line. The owner's representative keeps telling project manager to get another phone line, but project manager does not obtain one.*

Material Breach

Rule: The owner may terminate a contract only for a material breach. Termination for a nonmaterial breach is itself a breach of the contract and subjects the terminating party to liability for damages.

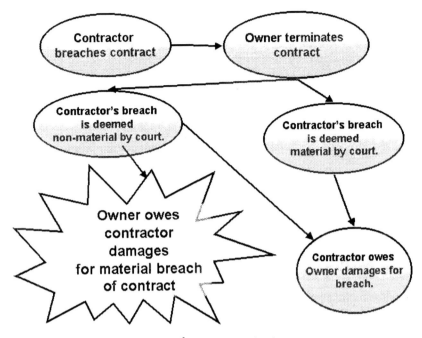

Figure 14-1 Consequences of contract termination.

In the case of *Collins v. Baldwin* the contractor on a motel project had breached the contract because a portion of the roof sagged, some leaks existed in some rooms, and there were other problems; however, the breaches did not rise to the level of a material breach of the contract.[1]

In the preceding two examples, the contractor *is in breach of the contract;* however, the owner cannot terminate the contract. If it does, it is liable to the contractor for damages, including contractor's lost profit. The owner must then finish the job with a new contractor *and* pay the former contractor. The cost to finish the job is greatly increased.

It is often difficult to draw the line between a material and a nonmaterial breach. The following examples illustrate some criteria for deciding that a material breach has occurred.

For example, in the case of *Prime Contractors, Inc., v. City Of Girard* a city advertised for bids for a road construction project.[2] It received three bids, and plaintiff Prime Contractors was the lowest at $96,816.75. The next two bids were approximately $125,000 and $130,000. The bidding proposal contained a provision requiring the contactor to attach a copy of a valid Certificate of Compliance issued by the State Equal Employment Opportunity Coordinator. This provision also indicated that the failure to meet these

---

[1]*Collins v. Baldwin* et al., 1965 OK 55; 405 P.2d 74 (Okla. 1965).

[2]*Prime Contractors, Inc., v. City Of Girard,* 101 Ohio App. 3d 249, 655 N.E.2d 411 (Ohio App. 1995).

requirements could cause the bid to be rejected. Prime Contractors attached a copy of an expired (by two weeks) *conditional* Certificate of Compliance to its bid. The city rejected Prime's bid based on the lack of the certificate and also on an investigation that led it to believe that the amount of Prime's bid was not sufficient to complete the project in the proper manner. The city awarded the contract to the contractor bidding $125,000. Prime sought injunctive relief to prevent the city from awarding the contract to any company other than Prime. The appeal court, however, upheld the trial court's determination that the attachment of an *expired* and *conditional* Certificate of Compliance was a material breach of the bid documents and the city was not required to award the contract to Prime even though it was the lowest bidder.

As another example, in the case of *Duall Building Restoration, Inc., v. 1143 East Jersey Avenue Associates, Inc.* Duall entered into a contract with 1143 East Jersey Avenue Associates to restore, clean, caulk and waterproof the masonry on three sides of a 10-story building.[3] The contract contained a five-year warranty against peeling or flaking. The waterproofing began peeling. A witness testified that "The entire building is peeling. It's . . . going wild. I mean . . . the surface is a whole bunch of spaghetti. Maybe noodles, I should say. It's curlicues of surface coming off all over the place." The court stated that Duall had materially breached the contract.

The owner must always be careful in terminating a contract for a material breach. For example, in the case of *Sinco, Inc. v. Metro-North Commuter R.R.* Metro-North awarded a contract to Sinco for a fall-protection system called "Sayfglida" to be installed at Grand Central Station, N.Y.[4] This system involved a harness worn by the worker, a network of cables, and metal clips or sleeves called "Sayflinks" that connected the worker's harness to the cables. The contract provided that Sinco deliver a reliable fall-protection system. The reliability of such a system was crucial; any failure of the fall-protection equipment easily could result in injury or loss of life.

On June 29, 1999, Sinco began a training session for Metro-North employees. During the session, a Metro-North employee was examining a Sayflink sleeve when the sleeve fell apart in his hands. The three other sample Sayflinks delivered by Sinco were found to have identical defects, and the training was immediately suspended. The court discussed in the opinion that termination of the contract at this point would *not* have been a valid termination for a material breach. Although Sinco had breached the contract, it had not yet *materially* breached the contract.

Within two days, Sinco manufactured and delivered two types of replacement clips: four replacement clips were staked by machine, and four had additional metal welded across the end of the stake as reinforcement. Sinco also included a videotape of a stress test performed on a welded Sayflink rather than a standard Sayflink; however, Metro-North rejected the replacement clips and terminated the contract. The court held that termination of the contract at this point *was* a valid termination for a material breach. The test in the video involved the application of stress in a different direction than the direction in which the failure occurred and did not show reliability over time and frequent use. Also, the videotape

---

[3]*Duall Building Restoration, Inc., v. 1143 East Jersey Avenue Associates, Inc.*, 279 N.J. Super. 346, 652 A.2d 1225 (N.J. App. 1995).

[4]*Sinco, Inc. v. Metro-North Commuter R.R.*, 133 F. Supp. 22 308 (S. Dist. N.Y. 2001).

was produced by Sinco itself, not by a disinterested and objective third party. Sinco could not prove it could provide a safe and reliable system.

Damages

Damages are one of the primary types of relief that courts can give or grant to parties that bring lawsuits. **Relief** is the term commonly used in the law to mean what the court will give to the winner of a legal claim. **Damages** are a sum of money to compensate for injuries or losses incurred. For example, $20,000 for lost profit is a form of damages.

Types of Relief Granted by Courts

Damages—Monetary compensation
Injunctive relief—An order to do or not to do a certain act
Specific performance—An order to comply with a contract

Other types of relief exist. For example, courts can grant **injunctive relief.** An **injunction** is an order telling a party to do or not to do something. An example of an injunctive order would be an order to remove a fence that is on someone else's property. **Specific performance** is similar to an injunction in that it is an order to comply with a contract. For example, if an owner of real estate enters into a contract to sell the real estate, then later changes his mind, the court might order him to sell it anyway under an order of specific performance.

So far this text has concentrated on the law relating to liability issues. All the following are examples of liability issues:

- Can the contractor rescind the contract?
- Is there a differing site condition?
- Has the owner breached the contract by refusing to grant a time extension?

This chapter discusses the damages a court is likely to award once such issues have been decided in favor of one or the other of the parties. This chapter discusses only contract damages. Tort damages are discussed in Chapter 15, Torts and Tort Damages.

Many types or categories of damages exist. The following is a list of potential types of contract damages recoverable in a breach of contract action:

- Cost of material to fix a mistake
- Cost of labor to fix a mistake
- Cost of rental of equipment
- Attorney fees
- Lost profit

The following list contains items that are generally *not* recoverable as contract damages:

- Medical expenses
- Pain and suffering
- Punitive damages

These items of damage are recoverable in tort actions, but not breach of contract actions.

Damages do not have to be proved exactly, but they must be proved by a preponderance of the evidence, like most other issues in civil matters. In the case of *Wunderlich Contracting Co. v. United States* the court said[5]

> *A claimant need not prove his damages with absolute certainty or mathematical exactitude. It is sufficient if he furnished the court with a reasonable basis for computation, even though the result is only approximate.*

It is common for expert witnesses to testify as to the amount of damages a party suffers.

Proof of Damages

Damages do not have to be proved exactly, but they must be proved by a preponderance of the evidence.

Proving damages is frequently the most difficult and time-consuming aspect of a construction claim, because proving damages entails the amassing and organizing of a large quantity of documents. If the project documentation has been sloppy, it may be impossible to prove an element of damages, and without proof the injured party cannot recover that item.

Actual versus Contract Damages

The law relating to damages is one of the most complex areas of law. Some of the terms used have different meanings in different jurisdictions. For the purposes of this text the following definitions will be used:

- **Actual damages** are all the damages suffered by anyone that are related to the breach of the contract duty. No court will award actual damages.

---

[5]*Wunderlich Contracting Co. v. United States*, 351 F.2d 956 (Ct. Cl. 1965).

- **Contract** or **foreseeable damages** are the portion of the actual damages that a court will award the nonbreaching party.
- **Unforeseeable damages** are the portion of the damages that the nonbreaching party must absorb. These may be covered by insurance.

Damages for Breach of Contract

Rule: Parties are entitled to contract or foreseeable damages for breach of a contract. Parties are not entitled to their actual damages.

Some courts call contract or foreseeable damages "actual" damages, because these are the "actual" damages that the law allows to be recovered. Because this terminology can cause confusion, in this text the term *actual* damages will be *all* damages, from any source, suffered by any person and related to the breach of duty.

Actual Damages

Actual damages include foreseeable and unforeseeable damages of all kinds. Some courts call actual damages **but-for damages,** that is, all damages that would *not* have occurred "but for" the act of the breaching party. For example:

> *Bendele Construction breaches the contract by failing to show up on the job on June 1, the first day. As a result the owner's representative, Felix Cuellar, must spend the day on the phone solving the problem. Felix cannot take his daughter to the doctor on June 1 and get a shot. The child gets sick and must be hospitalized for three days starting June 6. The doctors all agree that had the child been given the injection on June 1 she would not have been hospitalized. The hospital bills would not have been incurred but for the breach of the contract by Bendele Construction. These hospital bills are a part of the actual damages that resulted from Bendele's breach of the contract.*

No jurisdiction in the United States awards actual damages for breach of a contract.

Contract or Foreseeable Damages

Parties entitled to damages for breach of contract are entitled to foreseeable damages only. **Foreseeable damages** are those damages that a reasonable third party could envision as of the date the contract was entered into. For example, assume the contractor and the owner have just entered into a contract to build a project. Should the contractor be late in delivering the project, the foreseeable damages to the owner would include items such as lost profit or rental income generated by the project.

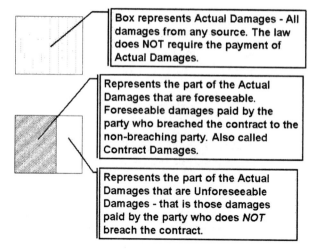

Figure 14-2 Actual versus contract damages.

The following is an example of foreseeable damages in a breach of contract action:[6]

EXAMPLE:

Owner contracted with Havens to fabricate, erect, and install uninsulated ductwork on a certain project. Havens *subcontracted* the erection and insulation (but not the fabrication) of the ductwork to Randolph. Havens had many problems with the fabrication of the ductwork and delayed supply of it to Randolph for over four months.

Because of Havens's delay in supplying the ductwork to Randolph, the buildings in which the ductwork was to be installed were in a far more advanced stage of construction than would otherwise have been the case had the ductwork been delivered on time. Randolph was required to perform extra work, such as cutting holes in walls, in order to get the ductwork installed per the plans and specifications. The following are a list of foreseeable damages suffered by Randolph:

- Total wages paid by Randolph to workers for extra work to install and insulate the ductwork, including overtime = $121,000
- Field office support: $30,000
- Prejudgment interest: At the legal rate
- Costs of suit: $5,000

■ ■ ■

---

[6]Facts slightly modified from *Havens Steel v. Randolph,* 613 F. Supp. 514 (W. D. Mo. 1985), aff'd 813 f. 22 186 (8th cir. 1986).

Damages for Breach of Contract

Rule: Parties are entitled to contract or foreseeable on damages for breach of a contract. Foreseeable damages are those damages that a reasonable third party could envision as of the date the contract was entered into.

The following is an outline of a simple argument determining the amount of damages owed in a simple case:

> *Owner causes delay to the contractor by turning over the site to the contractor late. (Notice that you have been told the owner delayed the project. You do not need to analyze this issue.) The contractor is damaged $2000 for equipment it had leased and had delivered to the site but could not use.*

Issue: What damages does the owner owe the contractor?

Rule: The party who breaches a contract must pay to the nonbreaching party reasonably foreseeable damages.

Premises: It is reasonably foreseeable that should the owner fail to turn over the site on the date indicated in the contract that the contractor would suffer damages for equipment it had leased and had delivered to the site but could not use.

Answer: $2000

The following is an example of *unforeseeable* damages that the contractor *cannot* collect from the owner. The owner, the U.S. government, delayed the contractor, Banks Construction, and the construction became more costly as a result of a flooded jobsite. The contractor had to put materials up on scaffolding and had to cover work with plastic, incurring increased labor charges amounting to $20,000. The drainage ditches that carried water away from the jobsite, which were under the owner's control, were inadequate to accommodate the *extraordinary* rainfall that had occurred. In addition, the entire project was delayed two weeks.[7]

A timeline is helpful for understanding this case:

January 2: Job is scheduled to start.

February 1: Job is scheduled to be completed.

February 2: Job is actually started because the owner was delayed in turning over the site to the contractor.

February 10: Extraordinary rainfall occurs.

March 15: Job is completed.

---

[7]Facts slightly modified from *Banks Construction Co v. U.S.*, 364 F.2d 357 (Ct. Cl. 1966).

Note that had the contractor started on January 1 the job would have been done by February 1, *before* the extraordinary rainfall. However, since the owner was late in turning over the site to the contractor, the contractor ran into the *extraordinary* rainfall of February 10. Extraordinary rainfall is, by definition, unforeseeable; therefore, the owner owes no damages to the contractor. In an actual case these damages would likely be covered by insurance.

A FIRPA outline of this example would look like this:

Issue: What damages does the owner owe the contractor?

Rule: The party who breaches a contract must pay to the nonbreaching party the foreseeable damages it incurs. Foreseeability is calculated from the date the contract is entered into.

Premises: An extraordinary rain is by definition unforeseeable, particularly as of the date the contract was entered into. Since the owner must pay the contractor only the foreseeable damages, the owner owes the contractor nothing. The contractor should check with its insurance company to determine if the costs are covered.

Answer: None

As a further example, in the case of *Vacuum Industrial Pollution, Inc., v. Union Oil Company of California,*[8] Vacuum Industrial entered into a contract with Union Oil to clean a tank containing chemical catalyst at Union Oil's refinery. Union Oil represented that no catalyst remained in the tank and agreed to provide two exits from the tank and to provide adequate lighting. All these agreements were breached, and two of Vacuum Industrial's workers were killed, and a third was injured.

Because of its connection with the fatal accident Vacuum Industrial suffered severe financial losses *even though it was not responsible for the accident.* It could no longer obtain similar work in that area and eventually had to close its office. In addition, it could obtain insurance only at a high cost—$750,000 for $1,000,000 of insurance. It eventually obtained insurance at three times its previous cost with an unrated company. Vacuum Industrial filed suit against Union Oil seeking damages for financial losses, the collapse of its business, the loss of future business, and the loss of favorable insurance policies. The court dismissed Vacuum Industrial's action and stated:

> *Rather, they [Vacuum Industrial's damages] are precisely the kind of remote damages not recoverable under the century-old doctrine enunciated in* Hadley v. Baxendale, 9 Ct. of Exch. 341 (1854) . . . *damages for breach of contract are limited to those that "may reasonably be supposed to have been in the contemplation of the parties, at the time they made the contract, as the probable result of the breach of it." The linchpin of this rule is foreseeability: only foreseeable damages are recoverable in a contract."*

[8]*Vacuum Industrial Pollution, Inc., v. Union Oil Company of California,* 764 F. Supp. 507 (N.D. Ill. 1991).

14-1. THINK

Is the owner responsible for any of the actual damages in the following problem?

The owner delayed the contractor, and the construction did not begin until February 2. Construction was supposed to have begun on January 2 and to have ended on February 2. This was the first out-of-state job for Lestor Construction, so Mr. Lestor went to supervise the job. His wife was pregnant and gave birth to their child on February 15. Unfortunately, since Lestor was not home, the wife's brother drove her to the hospital. The brother was only seventeen at the time and was nervous that the baby would be born before he got to the hospital. He collided with another car driven by Maria Rosario. The Lestors' baby was born on the roadway. Unfortunately, complications resulted, and the baby had to be rushed to the neonatal intensive care unit.

Actual damages are as follows:

- The baby's medical costs associated with the complications during delivery are $15,000.
- The damages to Maria Rosario's car are $1500.
- Maria Rosario's medical bills for whiplash are $2000.
- Maria Rosario's lost wages are $750.
- The damages to the brother's car are $1000.

A timeline if helpful for understanding this case:

January 2: Job is scheduled to start.

February 1: Job scheduled to be completed.

February 2: Job is actually started because the owner was delayed in turning over the site to the contractor.

February 15: Accident and birth of Baby Lestor.

March 15: Job completed

14-2. THINK

If the party who breaches the contract pays only for foreseeable contract damages, who pays for unforeseeable contract damages?

Eichleay Formula for Home-Office Overhead Home-office overhead is a foreseeable damage, and it is recoverable by the contractor when the owner has caused a delay.

Home-office overhead is the cost of running the home office during the time the project was delayed. Note that in some contracts the contractor specifically *waives* this item of damage. The law generally allows the parties to waive their rights to some, but not all, damages. The concept of limiting damages in the contract is discussed in the section "Limiting Contract Damages."

The **Eichleay formula** is a formula for calculating and allocating home-office overhead to a project. It was developed in the case of *Eichleay Corp.*[9] Since that time it has become the principal method for calculating recoverable home-office overhead (see *Capital Electric Co. v. United States*).[10]

The easiest way to see how recoverable home-office overhead is calculated is to look at an example of a small construction firm. Assume that the construction company has only one ongoing project. The construction company maintains a small home office with costs of $1000 per/month for office help, utilities, insurance, and other associated costs. Those costs are paid for by the one project. Now, assume that the owner delays the project one month. The contractor's home-office expenses continue—the contractor cannot call the landlord and ask for the rent to stop because the project has been delayed. Those costs are recoverable by the contractor as an element of foreseeable contract damages.

Because most construction companies have more than one ongoing project, the home-office overhead is absorbed by several projects, not just the delayed project. The *Eichleay* formula is used in allocating the home-office overhead among two or more projects, including the delayed project.

1. $\dfrac{\text{Billings planned for delayed project in period}}{\text{Total billings for all of contractor's projects}}$	$\times$	Total overhead for period	$=$	Allocable overhead	
2. Allocable overhead	$\div$	Days of performance	$=$	Daily overhead allocable to delayed project	
3. Daily overhead allocable to delayed project	$\times$	Number of days of delay	$=$	Overhead delay damages	

Impact Damages/Ripple Effect   **Impact damages** or **ripple effect damages** are another type of foreseeable damage recoverable by the damaged party. These are items that are indirect but still foreseeable. Thus, if the contractor fails to turn over the project on time, and the owner has to reprint flyers or advertising to accommodate a new opening date, the cost to reprint those items is a recoverable item of damage (see Figure 14–3).

For example, in the case of *Clarke Baridon, Inc. v. U.S.* the court ordered the owner to pay the contractor increased costs because excessive change orders increased the

---

[9]*Eichleay Corp.*, ASBCA 5183, 60-2 BCA ¶2688 (1960).

[10]*Capital Electric Co v. United States*, 729 F.2d 743 (Fed. Cir. 1984).

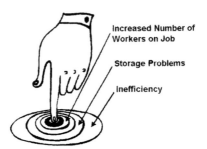

Figure 14-3 Ripple effect
damages caused delay.
©2000–2001 www.arttoday.com

demand for labor; however, only less efficient workers could be found in the remote area where the project was located.[11]

In the case of *Shinteck v. Group Constructors,* the court held that the contractor was entitled to damages for *loss in efficiency* caused by the owner.[12] The owner had

- failed to timely and continuously furnish material to the contractor as required in the contract;
- furnished erroneously prefabricated materials;
- made excessive design errors;
- made excessive changes and extra work orders; and
- refused to extend the work schedule despite the above.

The extent of the damages was proved by expert witness testimony.

Attorney Fees   Attorney fees are treated differently by different jurisdictions. A summary of the leading rules follows:

- **British rule:** Attorney fees are an element of damages and awarded to the winning party.
- **Federal rule:** Federal judges have some discretion in awarding attorney fees in any type of case.
- **American rule** (applicable in most state courts): Attorney fees are not damages and therefore not recoverable. *Caveat:* Attorney fees recoverable in contract actions *if* a provision in the contract allows for them.
- **Texas rule:** By statute, attorney fees are an element of damages and recoverable in *any* contract action, even oral contracts. No provision is required in the contract.

---

[11]*Clarke Baridon, Inc. v. U.S.,* 773 F.Supp. 335 (M.D. Fla. 1991).

[12]*Shinteck v. Group Constructors,* 688 S.W.2d 144 (Tex.App. Houston 1985)

Costs   The term *costs* can be confusing when used in a conversation between attorneys and nonattorneys. To an attorney the term *costs* has a specialized meaning. **Costs** are a set of damage items recoverable by the party winning a lawsuit. Costs include items such as the following:

- Court filing fees
- Fees for service of the complaint on the defendants
- Fees for service of subpoenas
- Jury fees
- Witness fees
- Costs of depositions

Most jurisdictions specifically list the types of costs recoverable by a party winning a lawsuit.

Interest   The winning party in a lawsuit is usually entitled to interest on the contract damages. The interest accrues from the date the specific item of damage occurred. For example, assume the contractor delayed the project one month, from February 1, 2001 until March 2, 2001. The owner's damages are determined to be $10,000. The parties file a lawsuit, and a court signs a judgment exactly one year later, on March 3, 2002, which states that the owner is entitled to the $10,000 in damages from the contractor. The owner is entitled to one year of **prejudgment interest,** which is the interest that accrued between March 3, 2001 and March 2, 2002. If the prejudgment interest rate in the jurisdiction is 10%, the contractor would owe the owner $10,000 plus prejudgment interest of $1000 on the date the judgment is signed.

If the contractor should fail to pay the $11,000 on March 2, 2002, the judgment would accrue interest, called **postjudgment interest.** Assume the contractor does not pay the owner for another full year and that the postjudgment interest in the jurisdiction is the prime rate plus 5%, or 14% for that year. The contractor would then owe the owner $10,000 in contract damages, $1000 in prejudgment interest, and $1400 in postjudgment interest on March 2, 2003. In most jurisdictions postjudgment interest does not accrue on prejudgment interest, nor is interest compounded.

Mitigation of Damages

A basic maxim of damage law is that damaged parties must *mitigate their damages*. **Mitigation of damages** means the damaged party must take all reasonable steps to limit his or her damages. A damaged party cannot take advantage of the injury to maximize the amount of recovery. If the court or arbitrator finds that the damaged party has not mitigated its damages, then the court or arbitrator can reduce the damage award. For this reason damages awards have a requirement that they be reasonable.

Mitigation of Damages

Rule: A damaged party must take all reasonable steps to limit or
mitigate their damages.

For example, in the case of *Center Court Associates Limited Partnership v.
Maitland/Strauss & Behr,* the court found that the architects had failed in their duty to reveal the extent of the bricked-in or toothed-in condition of windows on a historic building,
and the owner was damaged.[13] However, the owner could not recover the total cost of removing the brick in the toothed-in windows because the

> *credible evidence discloses that the means of the demolition of affected
> window openings, i.e., by sledge hammer or air hammer from the interior
> of the building, was unreasonably expensive and impractical. Moreover, this
> means of demolition in these circumstances was, largely due to the cost
> factor, not only impractical but rarely heard of in the business, especially
> considering the object to be accomplished. To persist in this method, . . .
> unreasonably aggravated the damages caused by the defendants'
> negligence.*

In the case of *Atlantic Contracting, Inc. v. International Fidelity Insurance Co.* the
court held that the defendant had not proved failure of mitigation.[14] In that case Dadonna,
Inc. subcontracted with Atlantic Contracting, Inc. for labor for excavating and site utility
work. Atlantic knew that Dadonna was experiencing financial difficulties, but Dadonna
assured Atlantic that the company was in the process of renegotiating its line of credit and
would be back on its feet shortly. Atlantis continued to supply labor to Dadonna for three
months even though Dadonna never paid any of Atlantic's invoices. Dadonna claimed that
Atlantic should have stopped providing it with labor after Dadonna failed to pay the first
invoice when due. Had Atlantic done this, the amount owed by Dadonna to Atlantic
would have been only approximately $20,000, rather than the eventual amount of over
$127,000. Atlantic offered testimony that it was a usual and customary practice in the
construction industry to wait for upward of 120 days for payment, despite the fact invoices required payment in thirty days. The court said that Dadonna had to prove that
Atlantic had not mitigated its damages, but that Dadonna had failed to do so. Atlantic was
awarded the entire $127,000.

---

[13]*Center Court Associates Limited Partnership v. Maitland/Strauss & Behr,* (1994 Conn.
Super. Unreported case).

[14]*Atlantic Contracting, Inc., v. International Fidelity Insurance Co.,* 86 F. Supp. 2d 479
(E. Dist. Pa. 2000).

Cost Rule versus Value Rule

The **cost rule** states that an injured party—for example, the owner,—is entitled to the amount of money required to repair the damage or breach. For example, if the contractor fails to paint the ceilings, the owner is entitled to the cost of hiring someone else to paint the ceilings.

The **value rule** states that an injured party,—for example, the owner,—is entitled to only the diminution in value of the project, not the cost of repair. This rule is used when the cost to repair (cost rule) is extremely large when compared with the value of the project.

Cost Rule and Value Rule

Cost Rule: The damaged party is entitled to the amount of money required to repair the damage.
Value Rule: The damaged party is entitled to the diminution of value of the project, not the cost to repair. This rule is used when the cost of repair is larger than the diminution in value (simplified rule).

For example, assume that the owner contracts to have a house built, and the value of that house should be $200,000 when completed; however, the contractor makes some errors in the construction and leaves out some items contracted for, so the value of the house as constructed is only $180,000. The cost to fix the items left out by the contractor is $40,000. The owner is entitled to only $20,000 to *make up the difference between what it got and what it should have gotten.* Naturally, should the cost to repair be less than $20,000, the contractor will be ordered to pay that sum.

In another example, the contractor departs from the specifications and pours defective slabs, which would cost $1 million to correct. The error is not detected until after substantial completion of the project. The value of the entire project is, at this point, $6.5 million. If the slabs were *not* defective, the value of the project would be $6.8 million. Assume that all the preceding is proved by a preponderance of the evidence, and no other facts can be proved by a preponderance of the evidence. The owner is entitled to only $300,000 in damages, not the $1 million it would cost to repair the slabs.

The cost and value rules produce interesting results when combined with the law regarding termination of the contract and mitigation of damages, as the following example reveals.

EXAMPLE:

The contractor, Hobson Construction, departs from the specifications and pours defective slabs, which would cost $1 million to correct. The entire value of the project is about $1.5 million. The error is noticed early on in the project. All experts, including the architect, estimate that the value of the project will be reduced by only $25,000 because of the defective slabs. The architect orders Hobson to fix the defective slabs anyway. Hobson refuses.

The owner terminates the contract and hires Pruitt Construction to complete the project. The owner does not fix the slabs because it does not want to pay Pruitt to do this at this time. Hobson's lost profit on the job is $100,000. All the preceding is proved by a preponderance of the evidence, and no other facts can be proved by a preponderance of the evidence. In this example the owner is entitled to $25,000 damages from Hobson because *Hobson did breach the contract,* but Hobson need pay damages only according to the value rule. Hobson is entitled to its lost profit because *the owner wrongfully terminated the contract for a nonmaterial breach.* Notice that Hobson did not materially breach the contract—the value of the project has been reduced by only $25,000 which is not a material breach on a project costing $1.5 million. The owner therefore owes Hobson $75,000 in contract damages. ■ ■ ■

The value rule can be used only as a shield and not as a sword. The value rule cannot be used to reward a contractor for bad faith and deliberate breach of contract. For example, if a contractor deliberately breaches a contract with the idea that the value rule will save it, the court is not likely to allow this to happen. In the case of *Groves v. Wunder Co.* the contractor deliberately breached a contract by failing to regrade land from which it had extracted gravel.[15] The cost of the regrading was approximately $60,000, but the value of the land would have been increased by only about $12,000. The court did not use the value rule but the cost rule and awarded the owner the $60,000.

Total Cost Claim or Rule

The value rule and the cost rule are often difficult to use. Parties, particularly contractors, like to depend on a calculation of damages known as the **total cost claim.** Under this rule the contractor merely takes the final cost of the project, subtracts the price to be paid according to the contract and claims the difference as the amount owed to it for delays or changes by the owner. The formula looks like this:

Cost to complete project − original contract price
= amount to be paid contractor for damages.

Numerous courts have rejected this formula.[16] The contractor must prove its damages in more detail.

---

[15]*Groves v. Wunder Co.,* 286 N.W. 235 (Minn. 1939).

[16]*Peter Scalamandre & Sons, Inc. Village Dock, Inc.,* 589 N.Y.S.2d 192, 193 (N.Y. App. 1986), *Boyajian v. U.S.,* 423 F.2d 1231 Cl. Ct. 1970. But see *Moorehead Constr. Co. v. City of Grand Forks,* 508 F.2d 1008, 1016 (8th Cir. 1975), where court allowed its use in limited circumstances.

Limiting and Controlling Contract Damages

Because the issue of damages is so important, and the legal standard "reasonably foresee-able" is vague, parties may attempt to stipulate the damages to be paid *in the contract* prior to any breaches of contract. The two most frequently used methods of adding certainty to damage issues are through the use of a "limited damage" clause and/or "liquidated dam-age" clause. A specific type of "limited damage" clause called a "no damages for delay" clause was discussed in Chapter 11, Delays and Acceleration.

Limiting or Controlling Contract Damages

Parties may attempt to limit or control the amount of damages they are required
to pay by contract through limited damage and liquidated damage clauses.

Limited or No Damage Clauses

Many jurisdictions allow the parties to enter into contracts with **limiting** or **no damage clauses** that limit or outline the amount of damages due upon breach of the contract. Al-though no jurisdiction would enforce a clause *totally* eliminating damages for breach, many will enforce clauses limiting or outlining the damages.

For example, Tates Roofing was hired to reroof a home for a family at a cost of $5000. The roofing was done incorrectly. (Assume this was proved by a preponderance of the evidence.) The contract between the roofer and the homeowner contained a one-year warranty *and* a contract provision that read,

> **HOMEOWNER AGREES THAT DAMAGES ARE LIMITED TO REPAIR OR REPLACEMENT OF THE ROOF.**

Assume this provision is in large, bold print. Three months after the roof was in-stalled it leaked, and the leaks were due to the incorrect installation of the roof. (Again, as-sume this was proved by a preponderance of the evidence.) The owner hired Bates Roofing to repair the roof at a cost of $2000. Assume this figure to be reasonable. In addition to the roof damage, the owners' furniture and carpets were destroyed. The value of the furniture and carpets on the date of the damage was proved to be $10,000.

The owners are entitled only to $2000 to have the roof repaired. The owner is *not* en-titled to compensation for the damage to the furniture or the carpets. Notice that the owner is not required to have the original contractor repair the roof either—the owner can hire someone else.

Liquidated Damages Clauses

A **liquidated damages clause** is a clause that sets a certain amount, usually per day, charged the contractor for each day beyond the scheduled termination date of the contract. For example the liquidated damages clause may state that the contractor must pay $500 per day damages to the owner for each day the project is late.

Liquidated damages are collected *in lieu of contract (foreseeable) damages*, not in addition to them. The advantage to this provision is that the parties need not prove each individual item of actual damages but can collect the specific sum.

Liquidated Damages Clause

Rule: Liquidated damages clauses are enforceable as long as the amount due is reasonably related to the contract damages and is not a penalty.

Courts will *not* enforce a liquidated damage provision that is a penalty. A liquidated damage provision is considered a penalty if it has no relation to the actual damages. *Liquidated damages must therefore be reasonably related to actual contract damages.*

Limited Damage Clauses and Liquidated Damage Clauses Compared

Notice the slight difference in the law regarding *limited* damages clauses and *liquidated* damages clauses. Limited damages clauses are generally upheld, no matter the amount of the limited damages. Liquidated damages clauses are upheld as long as they are reasonably related to the contract damages and are not a penalty.

The reason for this difference is that liquidated damage clauses are put into contracts by owners, and there is a tendency for owners to put in a large amount to be paid in order to give the contractor an incentive to complete the project on time. In other words, the liquidated damage clauses can be used as swords and abused by owners. For example, the owner may put in a clause requiring the contractor to pay $1 million per day for delay in completing the building of a minimall. The court will not uphold such a provision.

Limited damage clauses, on the other hand, are designed to allow the parties to limit their damages and take appropriate steps in light of the clause. Limited damages clauses are designed to be shields. American law has a tendency to be more accepting of shields other than swords. For example, assume that an alarm company sells you a home alarm system for $500, and that alarm system contains a $50 limitation of liability. If there is a burglary, and the alarm is somehow turned off by the burglar, and you lose $25,000 worth of personal property, the alarm company is liable for only $50. The alarm company is not agreeing to be an insurance company, so you must still purchase insurance if you want to recover the value of your stolen property.

Vocabulary Checklist

Termination of the contract
Material breach
Relief
Damages
Injunctive relief

Specific performance
Actual damages
Contract damages
Foreseeable damages
But-for damages

Home-office overhead
Eichleay formula
Impact damages
Ripple effect damages
Attorney fees

Costs	Cost rule	Limited damage clause
Interest	Value rule	No damage for delay clause
Mitigation of damages	Total cost claim	Liquidated damage clause

Review Questions

1. Can construction contracts be terminated if one party breaches the contract?

2. What is the difference between damages and injunctive relief?

3. Give an example of a *specific* type of allowable contract damage and a *specific* type of non-allowable contract damage. For example, a specific type of allowable contract damage is lost profit.

4. It is difficult, if not impossible, to calculate damages exactly. How can damages be proved?

5. What is the difference between actual and contract damages?

6. What is another name for contract damages?

7. What is the *Eichleay* formula?

8. What is the American rule regarding attorney fees?

9. What is meant by the term *costs*?

10. What are impact or ripple effect damages? Give an example.

11. What are the two types of interest recoverable by the winning party to a lawsuit? What is the difference between the two?

12. What is meant by the term *mitigation of damages*?

13. What is the cost rule?

14. What is the value rule?

15. What is the total cost rule?

16. What are the two ways parties can limit or add certainty to damage claims?

17. If the parties do not have a liquidated damages or a limited damages for delay clause in their contract, what are the damages that a breaching party must pay to the nonbreaching party?

Problems

Answer the issue in each of the following problems by making a legal argument, including premises in support of your answer.

1. The contract between Quintana Development, owner, and Najvar Construction, contractor, calls for Najvar's project manager to have a fireproof safe at the construction site. The project manager has a fireproof file cabinet instead.

   Issue: Can Quintana Development, owner, legally terminate the prime contract?

   Rule: A party must honor its contract (basic premise of contract law).

   What other rule is applicable here?

   Premises:

   Answer: No

2. Kotz Construction was retained to build a swimming pool for the County of Brazos. A major problem, well known to both the county and the contractor, was that much of the soil at the location is very hazardous to build on. The soil consists of 40 feet (deep) of sandy and clayey silt with occasional thin lenses of silty sand and gravel. The silt is dry, porous, and firm in its natural state but when wetted it becomes soft and compressible. Kotz Construction, with knowledge of the soil problem, represented to the county that a gunite pool, as he would construct it, would withstand the particular soil conditions. Kotz Construction designed and built a pool for the county.

One year after the pool was put to use it was noticed that there were extensive leaks. Kotz Construction agreed to repair the pool. The county retained an engineer to determine why the pool was leaking and had soil tests made. The engineer's recommendation was that the pool be removed and replaced by a different type of pool, placed on caissons. The engineer determined that it would be impossible to repair the existing pool. The pool was replaced per the engineer's recommendations. Assume that no other facts can be proved.[17]

Item of Damage	Amount
Cost of new pool	$50,000
Cost to remove old pool	$3,500
Costs of engineering study to be made to determine what caused the pool to lose water	$2,500
Prejudgement interest from the date the county paid for new pool.	$1,500

Issue 1: Did Kotz Construction breach its contract?

Rule: A party must honor its contract (basic premise of contract law).

Premises:

Answer: Yes

Issue 2: What damages, if any, is the county entitled to collect?

Rule: (*Hint:* foreseeable)

Premises:

Answer: (*Hint:* The court decided the engineering study was not foreseeable.)

3. After prolonged negotiations between Zanowiak Designers and Builders, and Warzak Hospital, the owner, a price of $3.60 million was agreed on concerning the cost of designing and constructing a new hospital building project. Subsequent to the date the contract was signed, the hospital requested changes and additions to the project. No written change orders were signed by the hospital or its construction manager agreeing to the exact cost of the changes and additions. The parties did have correspondence, approved plans and specifications, and other documentation concerning the changes and additions, including estimates of increased costs by Zanowiak. During the ensuing negotiations for the final cost of the project, Zanowiak demanded $4.2 million total payment for the original contract and the changes and additions. This figure was the amount it cost Zanowiak (including an amount for profit) to complete the project. The owners refused to pay this and agreed to pay only $4.0 million for the project.

---

[17]Facts modified from *Hendrie v. The Board of County Commissioners of Rio Blanco County,* 153 Colo. 432, 387 P.2d 266 (Co. 1963).

At trial the hospital's expert witness testified that $400,000 was the reasonable amount for the requested changes and additions made by the hospital. The design builder's expert witness testified that $600,000 was the reasonable amount for the requested changes and additions.

Question: What issue of fact has been raised?

(a) Assume the issue of fact is decided in favor of the design builder.

Issue: How much money is Zanowiak entitled to for the changes?
Rule: (*Hint:* Reasonable)
Premises:
Answer:

(b) Assume the issue of fact is decided in favor of the owner.

Issue: How much money is Zanowiak entitled to for the changes?
Rule: (*Hint:* Reasonable)
Premises:
Answer:

4. Wallace Construction has been awarded a contract to refurbish several buildings, all of which are in close proximity to one another. The work to be done on each building is about the same type and will take about two weeks to complete. Wallace Construction has prepared a critical path method (CPM) schedule, which the owner, the Harris Corporation, has agreed to. The owner causes a delay in turning over building 2 to Wallace Construction; however, building 3 is empty, and work can begin on it, even though the CPM calls for the work to begin on it in two weeks, and the work on building 2 is to begin now. The owner, refuses to issue a change order increasing the contract time by two weeks. The contractor waits, completes building 3 as per the schedule, and then at the end of the contract, finishes building 2. The contract completion date is therefore delayed by two weeks. Assume that no other problems were encountered in the CPM schedule or with anything else on this job.

Wallace Construction sues the Harris Corporation for two weeks of delay damages, including additional home-office and project site overhead, all of which can be adequately proved. The Harris Corporation lost two weeks of rental income because building 2 could not be rented out.

Issue 1: Can the contractor collect damages for delay?
Rule: (*Hint:* mitigation)
Premises:
Answer: No

Issue 2: Can the owner collect damages for delay?
Rule:
Premises:
Answer: Yes

5. (This problem was first presented in the problems in Chapter 8, Specifications and Plans.)

   A masonry subcontract required Milton Masonry, the subcontractor, to parge the inner face of a brick wall and to use Z brand galvanized ties. The subcontractor did not use the specified ties and did not parge the walls. The prime contractor's project manager, Ms. Pallanca, never objected, though she saw the work being done in this manner over a one-month period. The owner's representative, Mr. Rosen, never objected, even though he was on-site and saw the work being done in this manner on at least one occasion. The prime contractor withheld Milton's payment of $25,000 because the owner refused to pay for the work.

   The parties have filed an arbitration to decide who owes whom what in this scenario. Assume that all the expert testimony reveals that the value of the project without the parging of the inner face of the brick wall is $2000 less than the value of the project with the parging. The brand of galvanized ties makes no difference in the value of the building.

   Issue 1: What is the measure of damages that the owner owes the contractor? (*Hint:* The liability issues presented in this problem were FIRPAd at the end of Chapter 8, Specifications and Plans. You will need to know what the liability of the parties is in order to solve the damage issues presented here.)

   Rule:

   Premises:

   Answer:

   Issue 2: What is the measure of damages that the contractor owes the subcontractor?

   Rule:

   Premises:

   Answer: $25,000

6. Shima Construction and the Summerville Unified School District have entered into a contract for the installation of a sterile water system for $50,000. A contract specification states:

   > *Sterilize the water system with solution containing no less than 50 parts per million available chlorine. Allow chlorinating solution to remain in system for period of 8 hours, for 5 consecutive days. Have valves and faucets opened and closed several times during the period. After sterilization, flush the solution from the system with clean water until residual chlorine content is less than 0.2 parts per million.*

   The owner's construction manager was on-site and noticed that the contractor's employees flushed the system for only one day.

   Issue: Can the owner terminate the contract without incurring liability to the contractor?

   Rule: (*Hint:* material)

   Premises:

   Answer: Yes

7. (Note the difference in facts between this problem and the preceding problem.) Schmidt Construction entered into a contract with the state of Yur for the construction of a multimillion-

dollar Special Event Center on a major university campus located in Yur state. One component of the system was the installation of a sterile water system for $50,000. A contract specification states:

> *Sterilize the water system with solution containing no less than 50 parts per million available chlorine. Allow chlorinating solution to remain in system for period of 8 hours, for 5 consecutive days. Have valves and faucets opened and closed several times during the period. After sterilization, flush the solution from the system with clean water until residual chlorine content is less than 0.2 parts per million.* (This provision is the same as in the previous problem).

Schmidt Construction subcontracted the installation of the system to McGarvie Water Systems. The owner's construction manager was on-site and noticed that the subcontractor's employees flushed the system for only one day.

Issue 1: Can the state of Yur, the owner terminate its contract with Scmidt Construction contract without incurring liability to the contractor?

Rule: (*Hint:* material)

Premises:

Answer: No

Issue 2: Can Schmidt Construction terminate the subcontract with McGarvie Water Systems without incurring liability to the subcontractor?

Rule: (*Hint:* material)

Premises:

Answer: Yes

Questions:

(a) What is the difference between Issues 1 and 2?

(b) What does this tell you about breach of subcontracts as compared with prime contracts?

8. Bennett Construction and Humphrey Oil Company entered into a multimillion-dollar building contract to construct an industrial oil treatment facility. On a certain section of the project, the contract required galvanized iron pipe, lap welded, "of Reading Corp. manufacture." *During construction,* Humphrey's engineer discovered that some galvanized iron pipe was procured from Jerral Corporation, a competitor of Reading Corp's. The engineer ordered Bennett Construction to repipe, which would have required demolition of areas of work that had already been completed. There was no evidence that the Jerral pipe was inferior to the Reading pipe, though it was less costly. The quality and appearance of the two brands of pipe were virtually identical. Bennett Construction refused to repipe, and Humphrey Oil Company, the owner, terminated the contractor from the job at the suggestion of the engineer. Bennett's lost profit on the job was $150,000.

Humphrey Oil Company hired Hayes Construction to finish the project and repipe using the Reading Corp. pipe. The cost to Humphrey to have the piping redone was $50,000.

Issue 1: Who has breached the contract?

Rule: (*Hint:* This is *not* a damage issue.)

Premises:

Answer: Bennett

Issue 2: What is Humphrey Oil Company's measure of damages? In other words, how much does Bennett owe the owner because it breached the contract?

Rule:

Premises:

Answer: Nothing

Issue 3: Can the owner terminate the contract *without* incurring liability to the contractor?

Rule:

Premises:

Answer: No

Issue 4: What is Bennett Construction's measure of damages? In other words, how much does Humphrey Oil Company owe the contractor because it breached the contract?

Rule:

Premises:

Answer: $150,000

9. Lanik Construction and Ainsworth Oil Company entered into a multimillion-dollar building contract to construct an industrial oil treatment facility. On a certain section of the project, the contract required galvanized iron pipe, lap welded, "of Reading Corp. manufacture." *During construction,* Ainsworth's engineer discovered that some galvanized iron pipe was procured from Jerral Corporation, a competitor of Reading Corp's. The engineer ordered Lanik Construction to repipe, which would have required demolition of areas of work that had already been completed. There was no evidence that the Jerral pipe was inferior to the Reading pipe, though it was less costly. The quality and appearance of the two brands of pipe were virtually identical. Lanik Construction refused to repipe. (*Note:* These facts are the same as in the preceding problem.)

    Ainsworth Oil Company did *not* terminate the contract but held back a sum equal to the cost of the repiping ($50,000) from the retainage. (Assume that the rest of the retainage was paid to the contractor.) Lanik Construction filed an arbitration suit against Ainsworth Oil Company for the retainage.

Issue: Is the contractor entitled to the retainage?

Rule: (*Hint:* What damages must the contractor pay to the owner?)

Premises:

Answer: Yes

(*Note:* This is the more likely scenario a contractor will run into.)

10. Eval Sand and Gravel Company deliberately breached the contract by failing to regrade land after removing gravel, despite repeated requests by the owner, Mrs. Coots. The cost of

regrading was $50,000, and the value of the land would have been increased by only $10,000 had the contractor regraded it. Eval offered to pay Mrs. Coots $10,000. Eval remembered taking a law class in which he learned about the value rule and figured he could save $40,000.

Issue: What is the owner's measure of damages?

Rule: (*Hint:* shield, not sword)

Premises:

Answer: $50,000

11. Emmit Construction was delayed, and it incurred extra costs associated with defects in the designs of a hotel/restaurant project for the Marcus Corporation. The total cost of the project was $1.25 million. Emmit estimated that it cost $1.35 million to complete the project, including a figure for profit. Emmit calculated that the owner owes it $100,000 for delay damages. The Marcus Corporation employed an expert engineer and expert in construction delay claims to testify that the costs incurred by Emmit Construction related to the delay were $25,000.

Damages Issue: What is the measure of damages owed to the contractor?

Rule: Expert witnesses can estimate damages.[18]

Premises:

Answer: $25,000

12. Todd Construction is inexcusably delayed 177 days on a hotel/casino project owned by the Swenson Company. Swenson Company, the owner, terminates Todd Construction, and Todd Construction does not dispute the termination. (Notice that the liability issue has already been solved for you.) The contract contains the following two clauses:

> *35A: The contractor agrees to pay the owner $500 per day liquidated damages for lost income should the contractor delay in turning over the project to the owner on the date stipulated for completion of the project in the contract.*

> *35B: The contractor agrees to pay to the owner actual damages for all other damages incurred by the owner.*

The owner hires Patranella Construction to complete the project. Patranella is able to complete the project for $2.3 million, which is the amount remaining on the contract between Swenson and Todd Construction. The owner estimates that it lost $2.0 million in lost revenue from the casino because the project was turned over to it 177 days late.

Issue: What damages can Swenson collect from Todd?

Rule: (*Hint:* what type of clause is this?)

Premises:

Answer: $88,500

---

[18]*Iacobelli Constr. Inc. v. County of Monroe*, 32 F.3d 19 (1994), *Luria Bros, Co. v. United States*, 368 F.2d 701 (Ct. Cl. 1966).

13. Beck Construction is inexcusably delayed 150 days on a road-building project, the total cost of which is $5.0 million. The state department of transportation terminates Beck Construction, and Beck does not dispute the termination. (Notice that the liability issue has already been solved for you.) The contract calls for $50,000 per day liquidated damages for a total of $7.5 million in liquidated damages due from the contractor, to the state. The state hires another heavy highway contractor who is able to complete the project. Assume that no other facts can be proved.

    Issue: What damages can the owner collect?

    Rule:

    Premises:

    Answer: (*Hint:* not $7.5 million)

14. Richardson Construction, the prime contractor on a project to build a dam, caused delay through the failure of its subcontractors and materialmen to perform on time. The owner, the state of Yur, caused delay by constantly changing the design and by permitting its engineer to be late in furnishing drawings. (Notice that the liability issues have already been solved for you; both parties have delayed the project.) The owner claims damages of $50,000, and the contractor claims damages of $25,000. The evidence is, however, muddled, and it is hard for the court to tell how the various delays affected one another and the nondelayed work.

    Issue: Can either or both of the parties collect its damages?

    Rule: (*Hint: Wunderlich Contracting Co. v. United States* case.)

    Premises:

    Answer: No

15. Flores Construction prepared a bid of $1 million for the construction of an addition to the privately owned Doctors' Hospital. The profit margin was typical for that of the industry, approximately 3%.

    At the bid opening the following five bids came in:

    Nottingham Construction: $1.15 million

    Cullison Construction: $1.2 million

    Lehenbauer Construction: $1.09 million

    Goza Construction: $1.1 million

    Flores Construction: $1.0 million

    Flores was awarded the contract and gave the owner a bond that assured the owner that Flores would complete the project.

    On February 15, Flores was informed of a privately owned retirement home construction project with an owner who wanted to enter into a negotiated project (contract) with Flores. The owner, Singleton, Inc., was willing to pay a profit margin of 7%, but only if construction could begin on August 1. Flores estimated its profit on this job to exceed $500,000, plus there existed the possibility of additional negotiated work with the retirement home owners.

    Flores was unable to handle both the hospital project and the retirement home project due to a limitation of project management employees. Flores called the hospital and rescinded the contract, explaining it would not perform because it would rather do the retirement home project.

Issue 1: If Flores refuses to complete the hospital project, will it be in breach of the contract?

Rule:

Premises:

Answer: Yes

However, Flores does offer to pay Doctors' Hospital $90,000 if the hospital will not make a demand on the bonding company. This $90,000 is the difference between Flores's bid and Lehenbauer's bid. The hospital accepts and awards the project to Lehenbauer. Lehenbauer accepts. The bonding company is never informed that Flores did not perform the hospital project.

Issue 2: Does the hospital company have any further recourse against Flores?

Rule:

Premises:

Answer: No

Ethical issue: Has Flores been unethical? *Hint:* In economics the preceding is called an "economic breach of contract" and is encouraged as being efficient.

Answers to Selected Problems

1. Contract between Quinta Development, owner and Najvar Construction. . . .

   Issue: Can Quintana Development, owner, legally terminate the prime contract?

   Rule: A party must honor its contract (basic premise of contract law). What other rule is applicable here? A construction contract can be terminated only for a material or major breach of the contract.

   Premises: Although failing to have a fireproof safe at the site is a breach of the contract, it is not a major or material breach. Since the law allows for termination of the contract only when the breach is material, the owner cannot terminate the contract.

   Answer: No

9. Lanik Construction and Ainsworth Oil Company entered into a multimillion-dollar. . . .

   Issue: Is the contractor entitled to the retainage?

   Rule: What damages must the contractor pay to the owner? The owner is entitled to either the cost of repair or the difference in the value of what it got over what it should have gotten (value rule) whichever is less.

   Premises: Since the pipe is virtually identical and there is no decrease in quality, the value of the project is unchanged. No damages exist.

   Answer: Yes

15

Torts and Tort Damages

In a very broad sense the law is concerned with fundamental rights and duties of people and other entities, such as corporations and governments, to one another. So far this text has concentrated on voluntary duties parties assume toward one another, also called *contracts*. This chapter reviews *duties established by law independent of any contractual relationship between the parties.* These duties are called **tort duties.**

The person or entity that breaches, or is alleged to have breached, a tort duty is called a **tortfeasor.** The person or entity that has been damaged or alleges damage is called the **victim** or **injured party.**

The following are some torts with which you may be familiar:

- **Negligence**—acting unreasonably
- **Fraud**—cheating someone out of something of value
- **Libel**—writing something untrue about a person
- **Slander**—saying something untrue about a person
- **Battery**—touching another person without their consent
- **Assault**—threatening to touch someone without their consent

Many other legal or tort duties exist, and the names may be different depending on the jurisdiction.

Many torts resemble crimes; however, it is important to remember that a tort and a crime are different. Crimes are discussed in Chapter 1, Introduction to the Legal System and the Maxims of Law.

Although tort law certainly discourages people and entities from engaging in unacceptable behaviors, the concept of punishment is generally absent from tort law with the exception of intentional torts, discussed later in this chapter. *Tort laws are designed to make people pay damages for injuries resulting from certain acts they commit.* The payment of money to the injured party is the primary result of a tort action (see Figure 15–1).

In this text tort law is divided into the following four categories:

- **Negligence.** Negligence is the failure to be reasonable and is the most common tort.

- **Intentional torts.** An intentional tort is the intentional harming of another.

- **Strict liability.** Strict liability is liability for damages to another regardless of fault or negligence. The most common form of strict liability is the liability of manufacturers for dangerous products they make.

- **Deceptive trade practices.** Most states have passed deceptive trade practices acts in recent years. These acts outline certain practices that are considered deceptive and have historically been covered by common law. A major difference between these statutes and the common law is that intent to deceive need not be proved, as it must under the common-law theory. Another difference is that the financial damages imposed for committing the acts are much greater than those normally awarded under common law.

Common Divisions of Tort Law

Negligence
Intentional torts
Strict liability
Deceptive trade practices

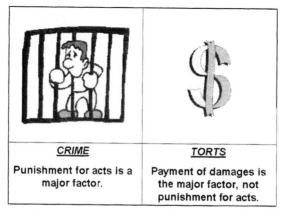

CRIME	TORTS
Punishment for acts is a major factor.	Payment of damages is the major factor, not punishment for acts.

Figure 15-1 *Crime and Tort Compared.*
© *2000–2001 www.arttoday.com*

Every tort can be described in terms of **elements.** These elements are similar to a "recipe" of the facts needed to prove the tort. Evidence of facts to prove all the elements *must* exist in order for an injured party to win a tort case. For example, the elements of negligence are duty, breach of duty, causation, and damages. In order for a person to win a negligence lawsuit the injured party must prove *each* of these elements.

It is important to remember, however, that torts are not mutually exclusive. In any given case it is possible that the same facts may support two, three, or more torts such as the tort of negligence and fraud. It is typical in a tort lawsuit for the suit to contain claims (also called **causes of action**) that the tortfeasor has committed several different torts. For example, if a previous owner fails to inform the buyer of a property of hazardous materials on the site, the lawsuit may consist of both negligence and fraud causes of action.

Negligence

Basically, the tort of *negligence is the failure to act reasonably and consequently to cause injury or damage (simplified rule).* This simplified rule can be used to determine whether negligence has occurred in the examples given in this text.

Simplified Rule of Negligence

A person is negligent if they act unreasonably and cause injury.

The more complete legal definition or elements of a cause of action for negligence are:

1. Existence of a duty to be reasonable toward another, *and*
2. Breach of the above duty, *and*
3. Damages, *and*
4. Causation.

Many, many cases exist that have explored each of these elements in great detail. This text merely introduces you to these concepts. The following problem is used to clarify these concepts:

> *Achim Driver is driving down a residential street shortly after a spring rain. Achim is driving fifty-five miles per hour. The speed limit in the residential area is twenty-five miles per hour. Achim loses control of the vehicle and runs into a group of pedestrians walking on the sidewalk. The pedestrians are Maria, age seventy-four; her son, Mike, age thirty; and her grandaughter, Kia, age four months. Kia is in a stroller. Maria and Mike see the automobile,*

and they run out of the way. Mike is actually grazed by the bumper and receives a bruise on the leg. Maria is able to run out of the path of the car and pushes the stroller out of the path. Maria falls and receives cuts and bruises on her face, knees, and hands. She requires three stitches to her forehead.

Duty

The first issue or question that arises in a negligence claim is whether the alleged tortfeasor has any *duty* toward the injured party. In the Achim example many cases have established that the driver of an automobile has a duty to pedestrians and other drivers. The duty is to drive in a safe manner given the conditions of the road.

The basic duty is to act reasonably

In general, the duty owed to others is the *duty to act reasonably* given the situation. This element of duty is usually the easiest to establish. Many cases outline in much more detail exactly what "acting reasonably" means in specific situations. For example, there are cases establishing the *reasonable* duties of doctors, lawyers, contractors, architects, engineers, bus drivers, gas station attendants, store owners, circus owners, ice cream manufacturers, and others.

In the following case the general contractor was *not negligent* because the mode of transportation on the site was reasonable. (The court's decision was based on other legal theory, however):

> Aerojet was a general contractor that had undertaken a construction project for Union Carbide Corporation. Hamrick was an employee of Dougherty Company, Inc., one of Aerojet's subcontractors. Hamrick arrived on the site, and found it was necessary to ascend to the third floor of the project. Hamrick chose to utilize the "man-lift" instead of a staircase that was equally accessible. The man-lift is a conveyor belt that stands perpendicular to the ground, has footholds and handles that allow persons to secure themselves, and serves as a crude mode of elevator. Having mounted the lift, Hamrick failed to realize that he had gone beyond the floor level of the top floor and was approaching the point at which the belt would make a 180° turn and begin its descent. As a consequence, he was forced to jump off the lift. On impact with the floor, he sustained serious damage to his ankle. *The general contractor was not negligent because the jury determined the man-lift was a reasonable form of transportation at a construction site.*[1]

---

[1]Facts from *Grady Hamrick v. Aerojet-General*, 528 F.2d 65 (4th Cir. 1975).

15–1. THINK

> In looking at the issue of duty it is very important to specify the parties, their relationship, and the duty you believe exists between them. In the Aerojet example name the parties and the duty the victim claims is owed to him.

Not everyone has a duty to every other person. In the following case Baker & Taylor Company were found not negligent because they had *no duty* to George Gray: (The court's decision was based on other legal issues, however.)

> Gray was employed by J. D. Hodges Trucking Co., Inc., as a truck driver. Baker & Taylor Company hired J. D. Hodges Trucking Co., Inc., to haul some casing pipe from Baker & Taylor's yard in Canadian, Texas, to a drilling rig in that vicinity. The temperature was below 32°, and the ground, the roads, and the pipe were icy. Gray used Baker & Taylor's forklift to load the pipe onto his truck. During the process of loading the truck, several joints of pipe fell from the truck and injured Gray. *He alleged that Baker & Taylor committed actionable negligence by requesting J. D. Hodges Trucking Co., Inc. to haul the pipe during the icy weather conditions, and by furnishing the forklift to load the pipe onto Hodges's truck during such weather.*[2]

Note that the *specific act* the plaintiff, Gray, claims to be negligent or unreasonable is very clearly identified. This is a must in a case of negligence. The court disagreed with Gray and stated that Gray was an employee of an independent contractor, and Baker & Taylor had no duty to him.

In the construction industry many jurisdictions have refused to recognize a duty between two of the major players: the designer and the contractor. Many states have held that *architects/engineers have no duty to prime or subcontractors.* This concept is discussed more fully in the section entitled "Liability of Designers to Contractors and Subcontractors." The result of this law is that *contractors/subcontractors cannot sue or recover from an architect/engineer for negligence.* The contractor can, however, recover from the owner, because the architect/engineer is the agent of the owner. See Chapter 6, Relationships among the Parties on the Project, for discussion of this concept.

Breach of Duty

The second element a person claiming negligence must prove is *breach of duty.* The victim must prove that the person possessing the duty has failed to uphold that duty. In the Achim example, the driver's duty was to drive in a reasonable manner. Breach of that duty is proved by his *driving on a residential street at the excessive speed of fifty-five miles per hour shortly after a spring rain.* Notice that specific facts are needed to prove the breach of duty.

---

[2]*Gray v. Baker & Taylor Drilling,* 602 S.W.2d (Tex. App. 1980).

15-2. THINK

In the Aerojet example what is the claimed breach of duty?

Damages

The third element to be proved is *damages.* In order to recover for a tort the injured person must prove damages or injury. In other words, if the injured party is not actually injured, he or she cannot recover, even if the tortfeasor acted unreasonably. In the Achim example Kia was not injured. Therefore, even though Achim had a duty to drive safely, which he breached by driving fifty-five miles per hour after a rain, he owes her nothing because she was not damaged.

As another example assume that Dr. Sleepy misdiagnoses Patty Patient and tells her she has the flu. Patty Patient does not recover and goes to another doctor, Dr. Careful, several weeks later. Dr. Careful correctly diagnoses Patty Patient with a rare form of incurable blood disease. Assume that it is proved that even if Dr. Sleepy had correctly diagnosed Patty, she could not have been cured. Patty Patient is not entitled to any damages from Dr. Sleepy because she did not suffer any damages.

Causation

The fourth and final element to be proved is *causation.* That is, the injured party must prove that the *damage was caused by the breach of duty.* In other words, the damage cannot be from some other unrelated source. In the Achim example assume Maria has a history of heart disease and arthritis. Maria is not entitled to recover medical costs associated with the heart disease or arthritis from Achim because causation does not exist. That is, the breach by Achim, driving too fast in a residential area and losing control of the car, did not *cause* her heart disease and arthritis.

A tortfeasor *is liable for aggravation of an existing condition* of the injured party, however. This is often called the "eggshell skull" theory. In the Achim example, assume that Mike has a rare blood disease that causes his blood to coagulate very slowly. He must be very careful of bruises and other slight injuries to prevent large internal blood losses. Even though the automobile driven by Achim only grazed Mike, he must be rushed to the hospital and given special medication, and treatment to prevent internal bleeding. Achim is responsible for the medical bills incurred by Mike, even though a bruise on the average person would not require such treatment.

In the following example all the elements of negligence exist. The owner, Palm Bay Corporation, was found negligent toward John Stinson:

> *John Stinson was a supervisor for a landscape contractor and he*
> *sustained an injury to his shoulder when he tripped over an electrical*
> *conduit protruding from a concrete parking deck at a construction site.*
> *Stinson sued Palm Bay Corporation, the owner/developer of the site,*
> *and GCA General Contractors, Inc. Palm Bay had failed to discover the*

conduit and remove it, despite their daily inspections of the job site for hazards. GCA had a contractual duty to remove the concrete island including the conduit approximately three weeks before the accident, but failed to do so.[3]

The owner in the preceding example was negligent because

- It had a *duty* to be reasonable and, specifically, to make the area safe. A reasonable inspector would have noticed the conduit and had it removed.
- It *breached the duty* because even though it made daily inspections of the site for safety, it did not notice the hazard of the protruding conduit.
- Stinson suffered an injury to his shoulder.
- The shoulder injury was *caused* by tripping on the conduit, not by some other unrelated incident.

An argument could be made that the contractor, CGA Construction, and John Stinson are also negligent; however, even if the contractor and John Stinson are also negligent, the owner is still negligent. One party is not relieved of its liability for negligence merely because another party may also be negligent. This concept is discussed in Chapter 16, Joint Liability and Indemnity.

15-3. THINK

> Make the argument that the contractor is negligent. All the elements of negligence—duty, breach, causation, and damages—are present. Can you find them?

In the following example the steel subcontractor, Steele Construction, was negligent and liable to Csaranko's family for damages.

Steele Construction was the steel erection subcontractor on a certain job. Csaranko was an employee of the roofing subcontractor. The roofing subcontractor is not a party to the lawsuit. Csaranko fell through a hole in the roof and died as a result of injuries he sustained on the job. At the time of the accident Steele's employees were performing certain steelwork on the roof. Their work necessitated that a hole be left open from the roof to the floor below. Steele's employees failed to cover the opening nor did they erect any barriers around it when they were not working on it.

---

[3]Facts modified from *General Contractors of America, Inc., v. Stinson*, 524 So. 2d 1148 (Fla. 1988).

> *Csaranko fell through the hole when carrying a load of materials across the roof.*[4]

The jury determined that Steele was negligent because

- It had a *duty* to the employees of other subcontractors who might be working on the roof.
- It *breached the duty* because it failed to erected a barrier or otherwise protect the area.
- Csaranko was *injured,* that is *damaged,* and in fact died.
- Falling through the hole, not some other unrelated incident, *caused* Csaranko's death.

In essence, the jury determined that Steele Construction employees were not acting reasonably. The jury believed that a *reasonable subcontractor* would have erected a barrier or otherwise protected the area so that others working on the site would not be injured.

Mistakes and Negligence

It is not uncommon for people to think that whenever a mistake is made the person who made the mistake is negligent. *Making a mistake does not automatically mean that a person has breached a duty or been unreasonable or negligent.* For example, if an architect makes a mistake in her calculations for a staircase, and the stairwell collapses, and you are injured, you are not necessarily entitled to recover for your injuries. *You are entitled to recover only if a reasonable architect would not have made the same mistake.* Of course, different people have different definitions of reasonable and unreasonable behavior, particularly for professionals. Expert witnesses must testify as to the reasonableness of the architect's error. The law does not expect perfection. This is ultimately an issue of fact and will be decided by a jury or arbitrator.

Who are all these "reasonable" architects, engineers, contractors, and subcontractors? They do not show up in court and testify. The jury or arbitrator decides what a reasonable person would do in the given situation. The arbitrator or jury can use the testimony of expert witnesses in coming to a decision. An arbitrator will likely depend on his or her own experience to some extent.

Negligent Misrepresentation

A specialized form of negligence is negligent misrepresentation. **Negligent misrepresentation** is the making of a statement without reasonable grounds for believing it to be true. The law requires persons in certain situations to be careful and reasonable in the statements

---

[4]Facts modified from *Csaranko v. Robilt,* 226 A.2d 43, 93 N.J. Super. 428 (1967).

they make. For example, assume that the designer makes a statement about the type of soil at the site. Also assume that the designer has no familiarity with the site and has not ordered any testing of the soil. The designer is liable for damages should the contractor rely on the designer's statements in making its bid.

Negligent Misrepresentation

Rule: A party making a statement without reasonable grounds for believing it to be true is liable for damages (simplified rule).

The five elements of negligent misrepresentation are as follows:

1. A statement of fact (not opinion) is made; *and*
2. The statement is false; *and*
3. The statement is made with no reasonable grounds for believing it to be true; *and*
4. The injured party is justified in relying on the statement; *and*
5. Actual damage results.

The following is an example of negligent misrepresentation on the part of Mr. Reyes:

EXAMPLE:

Industrias Trele, a Mexico-based maker of commercial and home cabinetry, entered into an agreement on May 14, 1992, with Intertex, Inc., a San Antonio–based company, to provide all the cabinetry for a project in San Antonio, Texas. Mr. Reyes signed the agreement on behalf of Intertex. Trele's employees testified that Reyes's reputation and involvement in Intertex was a major reason for entering into the deal; it was undisputed that Reyes met with Trele's representatives at the time the contract was signed.

Trele shipped trailerloads of product in October, November, and December 1992 to Intertex and was paid a small fraction of the invoice price. In July 1993, after making several demands for payment, Trele representatives visited the warehouse property supposedly leased by Intertex and found it abandoned. Trele sued Reyes individually for negligent misrepresentation and won. Intertex, Inc. had gone out of business and was not part of the suit.

Trele claimed that Reyes negligently misrepresented his involvement in Intertex to Trele. In fact, Reyes was not an officer or

employee of Intertex, Inc., although he was in the process of
negotiating an employment contract. The jury believed the testimony
and found Reyes liable for negligent misrepresentation.[5]   ■ ■ ■

Negligence per se

Negligence per se is negligence based on the violation of a statute. Under this doctrine a
party who violates a statute and causes injury is liable for damages. The injured party does
not have to prove duty or breach. *Proof of violation of the statute is sufficient to prove
negligence.* Note this is a simplified rule; the five elements necessary to prove a claim of
negligence per se are as follows:

> Negligence per se
>
> *Rule:* A person who violates a statute and thereby causes injury
> is liable for damages (simplified rule).

1. A valid ordinance was violated; *and*
2. The injured party is a member of the class that the statute was enacted to protect; *and*
3. The harm or injury suffered by the plaintiff was of the type that statute was designed
   to prevent; *and*
4. The violation of the statute caused the damages; *and*
5. Damages or injury resulted.

For example, if the law required stairs to have rails, and the designer did not design
a rail along the stairs, the designer could be liable to a person who fell off the stairs under
the negligence per se rule. The injured party would have to prove only the existence of the
statute, the designer's failure to follow the statute, causation, and damages.

The existence of thousands of OSHA regulations has made this doctrine very important in the construction industry. Under this doctrine the violation of an OSHA regulation
coupled with the remaining elements could lead to contractor liability for negligence per
se. *At present the courts are not in agreement on this issue.* Some courts have imposed
negligence per se liability on a contractor who violated an OSHA regulation, and others
have not. For a more detailed analysis of this issue see the case of *Cowan v. Laughridge
Constr.*[6]

---

[5]Modified from *Industrias Trele v. Reyes*, 1997 Tex. App. LEXIS 4855 (unpublished opinion).

[6]See *Cowan v. Laughridge Constr. Co*, 291 S.E. 287 (N.C. Ct. App. 1982).

Liability of Designers to Subsequent Users of the Designed Product

Designers are liable to subsequent users of the projects they design under the law of negligence. For example, in the case of *Fox v. Stanley J. How & Assoc.* a patient in a hospital sued a designer for negligent design of a window through which the patient walked.[7] Designers have a duty to subsequent users of the designed area to design it in a reasonable manner so as to prevent injury.

Liability of Designers to Contractors and Subcontractors

The following four rules have been developed in the various U.S. jurisdictions to deal with the liability of designers to contractors and subcontractors. Legal citations in support of these rules appear in Appendix B at the end of the chapter.

Liability of Designers to Contractors and Subcontractors

Majority Rule: Contractors and subcontractors cannot collect economic damages from the designer.

California Rule: A balancing test is used to determine if the designer is liable to the contractor or subcontractor.

Designers are liable to contractors and subcontractors under a theory of negligence.

Designers have no duty to contractors and subcontractors and therefore cannot be liable to them under a theory of negligence.

---

1. Majority rule: A contractor or subcontractor who is damaged as the result of the designer's negligence in preparing plans and/or specifications is *precluded* from collecting "economic" losses related to the negligence. The term *economic* does not have the standard dictionary meaning. **Economic losses** are damages for inadequate value, costs of repair, replacement of a defect, and loss of profits and are *not recoverable by the contractor* from the designer. These damages may be recoverable by the contractor from the owner. See Chapter 6, Relationships among the Parties on the Project, and Chapter 14, Termination of the Contract and Contract Damages, which discusses various methods owners use to limit their liability for such damages.

    The injured party is *not* precluded from collecting damages related to *other* property or for *personal injury*. For example, if the architect negligently designs an

---

[7]*Fox v. Stanley J. How & Assocs.*, 309 N.W.2d 520 (Iowa 1981).

arch, and the arch falls on the contractor's truck while the contractor is in it, the contractor can recover for damage to the truck and his medical bills from the architect. The contractor cannot, however, recover the cost to rebuild the arch from the architect because that is an economic loss. The contractor can recover the cost to rebuild the arch from the owner.

2. A third party, including a subcontractor or contractor, who is damaged as the result of the designer's negligence in preparing plans and/or specifications has a valid negligence claim against the design professional. No privity of contract is required.

3. California rule: The following balancing test is used to determine the liability of the designer to third parties:

   a. The foreseeability of harm to the plaintiff;

   b. The degree of certainty that the plaintiff suffered injury;

   c. The closeness of the defendant's connection between the conduct and the injury suffered;

   d. The policy of preventing future harm; and

   e. Moral blame for a design professional's actions and preventing future harm. Balancing tests are difficult to implement, and this law is still undergoing modification in the court system.

4. Designers have no duty to contractors and subcontractors and therefore cannot be sued for negligence.

Intentional Torts and Fraud

Recall that negligence is basically the failure to act reasonably. **Intentional torts** contain an element of actual intent to cause injury to another person or entity. For example, the intentional tort of battery is the intentional touching of another without consent. Hitting someone in the nose during a fight is a battery, as is kissing them while they are asleep.

Intent is difficult to prove, as few parties will admit they intended to cause harm; intent can be inferred from the evidence by the arbitrator or jury, however.

Intentional Torts

An intentional tort involves an action that is actually intended to cause harm.

The most common intentional tort alleged in the construction industry is **fraud,** sometimes called **deceit** or **misrepresentation.** The elements of fraud are as follows:

1. A false representation or nondisclosure of material fact(s); and

2. The intent to deceive; and

3. The statement has been relied on by the complaining party; and

4. Actual damage results.

Fraud

Rule:

1. A false representation is made, or there is nondisclosure of material fact(s); *and*
2. There was intent to deceive; *and*
3. The statement was relied on by the complaining party; *and*
4. Actual damage results.

For example, if the owner *deliberately* misrepresents the existing topography, zoning, or cost of project, it can be a fraud. A state inspector's failure to provide full disclosure to a plumbing contractor who was taking over a partially completed project might be fraud. A contractor who conceals major defects is liable for fraud. It is unlikely a party will admit to intent to deceive, but the jury or arbitrator can infer intent to deceive from the evidence.

Deceptive Trade Practices

Most states have adopted a deceptive or false trade practices act to discourage businesses from cheating consumers.[8] Appendix C to this chapter contains selected sections of the Uniform Deceptive Trade Practices Act (1966).

Deceptive trade practices acts generally differ from traditional fraud causes of action in that *it is not always necessary to prove the element of intent.* The concept of deception is inherent in the forbidden act. In addition, most of these acts contain provisions for increased damages and even attorney fees. (See Appendix C to this chapter, Section 3, Remedies.)

The following are two examples of cases of actual deceptive trade practices acts:

> After construction of a home, the buyers sued the builder claiming the builder failed to construct the house in a good and workmanlike manner. Buyers contended that the builder failed to supervise workers, and there were many defects and variances, which were not corrected. The appeals court did not decide that the builder *had* committed a deceptive trade practices act violation, only that the matter must go to a jury.[9]

---

[8]For example, Texas Bus. & Comm. C Sec. 17.41 et seq., Colorado: §§ 6-1-101 to 6-1-115, Delaware: §§ 2531–2536, Georgia: §§ 10-1-370 to 10-1-375, Hawaii: §§481A-1 to 481A-5, Minnesota: §§ 325D.43 to 325D.48, Nebraska: §§ 87-301 to 87-306, Oklahoma: 78 §§ 51 to 55, Oregon: §§ 646.605 to 646.656.

[9]*Kennemore v. Bennett*, 755 S.W.3d 89 (Tex. 1988).

A purchaser bought a lot from the owner, an oil company, and built a home on it. Later it was learned that several abandoned oil wells were located under the lot. Because of the abandoned wells, the house was not habitable.[10]

Contorts

Historically, one of the basic principles of civil law has been that *it is not possible to turn a breach of contract into a tort*. Since the amount and types of damages are different and often (not always) greater in tort actions than in contract actions, there is a tendency to attempt to sue in tort rather than contract. Litigants (and others) tend to pursue avenues that offer the greatest advantages to them.

Torts and Contracts

Rule: It is not possible to turn a breach of contract into a tort.

Tort damages include some unforeseeable damages and also damages for emotional distress. Tort damages are discussed more fully later in the chapter. Contract damages are discussed in Chapter 14, Termination of the Contract and Contract Damages. (See the case of *Erlich v. Menezes,* in the appendix to Chapter 4, Preparing Legal Arguments, for a discussion of why damages for emotional distress are *not* recoverable for the negligent breach of a contract to construct a house.[11])

Notice that this principle, that one cannot turn a breach of a contract into a tort, is limited only to that specific situation—attempting to turn a breach of contract into a tort. Having a contract with someone does not preclude him or her from being liable for tortious activity engaged in.

In recent years, however, a number of cases permitting recovery of tort damages in breach of contract cases have arisen. These cases are often referred to as **contorts** because they are a combination of contract and tort principles; however, contorts typically involve some type of *personal* contract such as an infant injured during childbirth,[12] or misdiagnosis of venereal disease and subsequent failure of marriage.[13]

The only area in which persons involved in the construction industry may run into contorts is in the relationship between the owner and the designer. Since this is an agency relationship, the law tends to protect and safeguard that relationship to a high degree. One way of doing that is by allowing tort damages for breach of the agency relationship.

---

[10]*Guest v. Phillips Petroleum Co.,* 981 F.2d 218 (5th Cir.1993).

[11]*Erlich v. Menezes,* 21 Cal. 4th 543, 981 P.2d 978, 87 Cal. Rptr. 2d 886; (Calif. 1999).

[12]*Burgess v. Superior Court,* 2 Cal. 4th 1064, 1072, 831 P.2d 1197 (1992).

[13]*Molien v. Kaiser Foundation Hospitals,* 27 Cal. 3d 916, 167 Cal. Rptr. 831, 616 P.2d 813 (1980).

Some jurisdictions have causes of action entitled "negligent building" or some similar term. This terminology can cause confusion between tort and contract principles; however, review of the law of those states generally reveals that these apparently tortious causes of action are actually breaches of contract and are treated as such.

Strict Liability

Strict liability is liability for damages without fault. Strict liability is applied in only very limited types of cases. For example the law of strict liability does cover blasting—a fairly common occurrence in the construction industry. A company that engages in blasting is strictly liable for any damage caused.

Strict Liability

Rule: Manufacturers of defective products are liable for injuries caused by those products.

Most jurisdictions have law holding manufacturers of *defective products* strictly liable for injuries caused by those products.

Because of the large numbers of manufactured products that become part of the construction project, strict liability can be an issue. The manufacturers of those products are liable for injuries caused by defective products attached to the realty. Contractors are not normally considered manufacturers, though specialty subcontractors may be. For example, the general contractor on a building project is not considered a manufacturer of the cabinets that go into the project, but the cabinet subcontractor would be.

A product is defective if it is marketed with any of the following characteristics:

1. A flaw is present at the time the product is sold, and the flaw causes injury; *or*
2. The manufacturer fails to adequately warn of a risk or hazard associated with the product's use; *or*
3. The product was defectively designed.

An example of the first type of defective product is an automobile sold with a cracked gasoline tank. Gas leaks from the crack and causes the automobile to catch fire, and the occupants are injured. The manufacturer of the automobile is liable for the injuries. Of course, *the injured party must prove that the flaw existed at the time the product was sold.* This is often impossible to do, and so recovery under this theory is rare.

An example of the second type of defective product is a lawn mower with rotors that throw out rocks and other debris from under the mower. The manufacturer does not warn the user of the mower that the rotors may throw out rocks and other debris and cause injury. The manufacturers of lawn mowers typically warn the users that rocks and debris can cause injury, and advise the user to use the mower only with foot and leg protection in place.

The third type of defective product is one that is defectively designed. For example, the Ford Pinto was designed with the gas tank in a spot that caused it to explode even in a minor collision. Heavy machinery without guards has been found to be defectively designed. It is necessary to bring in expert witnesses to prove that the design was defective. The law in this area is extremely complex and beyond the scope of this text.

Assumption of the Risk

Assumption of the risk is a common defense to a tort action related to the construction industry. A defense is like a shield and prevents liability from attaching.

Assumption of the Risk

Rule: Injured parties are responsible for their own injuries if they voluntarily assumed the risks inherent in the activity they engaged in.

Assumption of the risk holds that the injured party is responsible for his or her own injuries if he or she voluntarily assumed the risks inherent in the activity engaged in. For example, if a person roller skates, the law generally recognizes that the person has assumed the risk that another skater may bump him or her, causing a fall. If this occurs, the skating rink is not liable for the injuries to the person who fell. However, if the proprietor of the skating rink does not tighten and lubricate the wheels on the skates periodically, and they fall off, and the skater is injured, the proprietor can be liable for negligence. The skater has not assumed the risk that the proprietor will not take reasonable care.

Tort Damages or Proximate Cause Damages

Tort damages are generally (not always) greater than contract damages because they are designed to put the party back into the position it would have been in had the injury not occurred. *Recoverable tort damages include foreseeable and some (not all) unforeseeable damages* (see Figure 15–2). The term given to recoverable tort damages is **proximate cause damages.** Contract damages are limited to foreseeable damages and are discussed in Chapter 14, Termination of the Contract and Contract Damages.

Maxims of Damage Law

Contract breaches of duty: The nonbreaching party is entitled to the benefit of its bargain, but no more.
Tort breaches: The victim is entitled to be put back into the same position it would have been in had the tort not occurred.

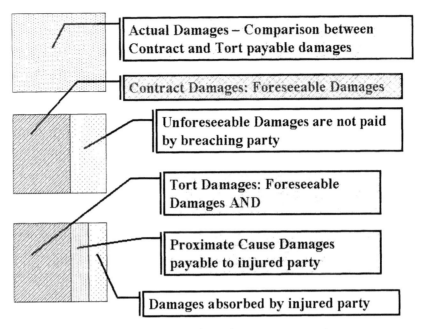

Figure 15-2 Actual, contract, and tort damages compared.

The following example illustrates tort or proximate cause damages:

EXAMPLE:

Jo operated a backhoe for a small construction company, Impact Construction. Donald's Diner hired Impact to expand their existing facility. The opening date of the new expanded diner was to be October 1. Impact's supervisor, Mr. Impact, knew that the backhoe was in need of repairs; however, he was short of cash and wanted to delay repairs until after this job. Because the needed repairs were not completed, the shovel was blasted away from the backhoe, flew several feet into the air, and crashed into Donald's Diner's construction manager's truck, which happened to be on-site at the time. Other parts of the backhoe damaged the existing structure's walls and windows. Jo was injured by flying debris and sustained several cuts needing stitches. In addition, his clothing was damaged and his eyeglasses were broken. He was upset at all the damage and with his injury.

The impact of the backhoe shovel pieces pushed Donald's Diner's construction manager's truck into the street, causing Donna, a passing driver, to swerve onto the lot adjoining Donald's Diner. Donna hit and felled an oak tree on that lot. The oak tree was very old and weakened by termites. The lot (and the tree) were owned by Shaleh Corporation, which operated a small retail outlet of fine china and antiques in a building on the lot. The oak tree crashed into Shaleh Corporation's building, causing a wall to collapse and destroy several thousand dollars' worth of merchandise in the store.

In addition, Donna sustained a whiplash injury and was out of work two days. She went to a chiropractor. After Donna returned to work, her boss, Mr. Bhig, began to give her a hard time because he believes that chiropractors are quacks and do not do anyone good. After two months he dreamed up some excuse to fire Donna. Donna was out of work for six months until she could find another similar job.

Donna had three children. While she was out of work for those six months they missed a lot of school because Donna kept the thermostat at 55° all the time, and the children got colds. Donna and the children became depressed and worried because they were not sure if they would have a roof over their heads and enough food to eat. In addition, a passing motorist hit the dog during this time. Donna did not have enough money for the necessary surgery but had the dog euthanized instead. The children were devastated by the death of their family pet, particularly at this time in their lives.

Donna's boss hired Tim to replace Donna; however, Tim stole $7000 from the company in the first month, and the boss fired him. After he was fired, Tim robbed a store and shot the clerk, Mabel, in the arm.

Completion of the diner was delayed two weeks while Impact obtained insurance money to pay for a new backhoe; however, Mr. Donald became upset with Impact and terminated the construction contract with Impact. Donald's Diner obtained another contractor, Smart Construction, to finish the job. Smart was able to finish the job and open the diner on October 1; however, the cost to Donald's Diner was an additional $50,000 over the Impact contract. ■ ■ ■

Everyone sued everyone else. Assume that the following damages can be proved by a preponderance of the evidence. All are considered actual damages or but-for damages. No court will order all these damages to be paid, however. Pain and suffering is one item of proximate cause or tort damages. It is discussed more fully later in the chapter.

Impact's Damages

Cost to repair backhoe: $2000

Lost profit on the Donald's Diner job: $25,000 (Contract damage only—not recoverable in tort. May be due Impact because Diner terminated project for a nonmaterial breach. See Chapter 14).

Jo's Damages

Medical bills: $500 (Note that workers' compensation statutes would affect this recovery.)

Pain and suffering: $5000

New glasses: $200

Donald's Diner's Construction Manager's Damages

Damage to truck: $4000

Donald's Diner's Damages

Damage to Donald's Diner's walls and windows: $5000

Payment to Smart to complete the project: $50,000 (Contract damage only—not recoverable in tort. May not be due from Impact because Diner terminated Impact for a nonmaterial breach. See Chapter 14.)

Donna's Damages

Donna's car: $2,500

Loss of work for two days: $200

Chiropractic bills: $3,500

Loss of work for six months: $12,600

Pain and suffering: $150,000 ($3000)

Donna's Children's Damages (each)

Pain and suffering: $150,000

Shaleh's Damages

Loss of tree: $750

Damage to building: $4575

Loss of antiques in store: $17,500

Mr. Bigh's Damages:

Theft by Tim: $7000

Mabel's Damages

Medical bills: $15,000

Lost wages: $5000

Who, if anyone, is responsible for what damages and why? The basic maxim of tort law is that the injured parties are to be put into the same position they would have be in had the injury not occurred; however, the court limits the damages to those that are *proximately caused* by the tortfeasor's actions. Exactly what damages are and are not proximately caused is the subject of much negotiation and litigation, and an in-depth review of the law in this area is beyond the scope of this course.

Assume that the jury finds Impact negligent because a reasonable contractor would not have used defective equipment. This is a tort cause of action. Impact is responsible for all damages "proximately caused" by its actions. *Which damages are proximately caused will be decided by the jury.* The items in italics represent proximately caused or tort damages. Shaleh's antiques (underlined) are borderline between proximately caused damages and remotely caused damages. Some juries might award them, and some might not. Donna would probably be awarded some compensation for her pain and suffering, but not in the amount requested. The amount in parenthesis, $3000, is an estimate of what a jury might award her. It is unlikely a jury would find or the judge would hold the other damages, for example, Mr. Bigh's damages—to be proximately caused by Impact's negligence.

15-4. THINK

What is the law or rule that Impact might use to recover its lost profit from Donald's Diner? *Hint:* See Chapter 14, Termination of the Contract and Contract Damages.

Pain and Suffering

Tort law allows injured parties to recover a sum to compensate them for the pain and suffering they have experienced. This sum is always difficult to estimate and is decided by a jury, usually on a per diem basis. For example the jury might award the injured party $100 per day to compensate him or her for pain and suffering. The amount may vary over time, compensating an injured party more at the beginning of the injury, when pain is greatest, and less as the injury heals.

The pain associated with a burn injury is generally considered to be among the worst. A burned victim might recover hundreds of thousands or even millions of dollars from the tortfeasor for pain and suffering. In contrast, the pain from a whiplash is less severe, and a jury will award a much smaller amount.

Punitive Damages

As a general rule, tort law does not punish a tortfeasor. Tort law is designed to compensate injured parties for their damages. Criminal law is designed to punish people who engage in socially unacceptable behavior; however, in extreme cases of *intentional tortious conduct* the law will punish a tortfeasor by awarding the plaintiff **punitive damages** to punish the tortfeasor. Punitive damages are in addition to proximate cause damages. Another name for punitive damages is **exemplary damages.** Punitive damage awards are extremely rare, and when they do occur the court frequently reduces the amount of the award.

Many students have heard about the McDonald's coffee case and the $2.7 million in punitive damages awarded to the plaintiff. Here is a letter from the attorney representing the plaintiff in that case. It explains the purpose and effect of punitive damages as only a real case can:

EXAMPLE:

I am the lawyer who tried Stella Liebeck's case in Albuquerque. There has been a great uproar from people displeased at the size of the verdict, who see it as an example of . . . a runaway jury and a plaintiff who will not accept responsibility for her actions.

Stella Liebeck, 79, purchased a cup of McDonald's coffee while a passenger in her grandson's automobile. Ms. Liebeck attempted to hold the cup securely between her knees while she removed the plastic lid. It tipped over causing third-degree burns that necessitated hospitalization for eight days, whirlpool treatment for debridement [which is the surgical removal of foreign matter and dead tissue] of her wounds, and skin grafting, and led to permanent scarring, and disability for more than two years. The jury awarded her $200,000 in compensatory damages, reduced by 20% for her own negligence, and $2.7 million in punitive damages.

The following information was presented to an impartial jury which found that the product is unreasonably dangerous and is sold in breach of the implied warranty of fitness imposed by the Uniform Commercial Code:

McDonald's Corporation sold its coffee at 180–190 degrees Fahrenheit by corporate specification. McDonald's coffee if spilled could cause full-thickness burns (third degree to the muscle/fatty tissue layer) in two to seven seconds.

McDonald's knew about this unacceptable risk for more than 10 years; it was brought to the company's attention by other lawsuits (more than 700 reported claims from 1982 to 1992.) The company's witnesses testified that it did not intend to turn down the heat. McDonald's generates revenues in excess of $1.3 million daily from the sale of coffee.

Ms. Liebeck's treating physician testified that this was one of the worst scald burns he had ever seen. Other expert witnesses termed the risk of harm from McDonald's coffee to be unacceptable.

Most consumers don't know that coffee this hot causes such injuries. Nor do they know McDonald's made a practice of serving its coffee this hot.

The jury applied the law of punitive damages to deter McDonald's and other similarly situated corporations from exposing consumers to this risk. It imposed a penalty of two days' revenue from coffee sales, or $2.7 million, for willfully ignoring the safety of customers who feed the McDonald's money tree. The system has numerous methods of overturning a verdict that is excessive. [Author's note: In this very case the award was reduced to $450,000.]

Why should we tolerate corporate irresponsibility? What's wrong with penalizing irresponsible behavior that injures consumers?

The news media, the day after the verdict, established that coffee at the McDonald's in Albuquerque is now sold at 158 degrees. At that temperature, it would take about 60 seconds to cause third-degree burns. Mission accomplished.

S. Reed Morgan
Morgan & Associates, Houston,
Letters, National Law Journal, p. A20 (October 24, 1994) ■ ■ ■

Vocabulary Checklist

Tort duties
Victim or injured party
Tortfeasor
Negligence
Fraud
Libel
Slander
Battery

Assault
Negligence
Intentional torts
Strict liability
Deceptive trade
  practices
Elements
Causes of action

Negligent
  misrepresentation
Negligence per se
Contorts
Assumption of the risk
Proximate cause damages
Pain and suffering
Punitive damages

Review Questions

1. In a broad sense, with what is the law concerned?

2. What are the two ways in which duties can arise between two people?

3. What is the difference between a tort and a crime?

4. What is a tort "recipe"?

5. What is the simplified rule of negligence?

6. What is the actual rule of negligence?

7. In the following situations what are some things a reasonable person would do?

   a. Steele Co. is the subcontractor on the steelwork on a certain job. The work necessitates that a hole be left open from the roof to the foundation below. The roofing subcontractor is beginning to roof the building.

   b. The architect is preparing the plans and specifications for a certain project. Part of the project will necessitate the demolition of a certain concrete slab. Embedded in the slab are high-voltage wires.

8. What duties, do you think, does person A have to person B?

   a. *Person A:* George Kurved, a father who collects guns

      Person B: Jamie, the 4-year-old best friend of George's son, Davey.

   b. *Person A:* Dr. Toni Hynds, a college professor

      Person B: Jun-Young, a student in the front row sitting near the overhead projector cart.

   c. *Person A:* Mr. David Hudson, the OSHA inspector on a particular job.

      Person B: Carol Jenks, an employee of the masonry subcontractor on the particular job.

   d. *Person A:* Dr. Diane Paquin, a veterinarian.

      Person B: Dr. Steve Platts, who brings his dog, Quincy, in for a checkup.

9. Give an example of how Person A might breach the duty he or she owes to Person B in each part of question 8. Give an example of how Person B might be damaged by the breach of Person A.

10. What is the "eggshell skull" theory?

11. What would a *reasonable person* (not the person named in the example) do in each of the following scenarios?

    a. Mr. Newsom is driving his friends to work and gets in an accident. One of his passengers is bleeding from a cut on the forehead and has been knocked unconscious.

    b. Murphey's grocery store has an aisle where fruits and vegetables are located for sale to the public. It is common for fruits and vegetables to fall on the floor.

    c. Bluebell Power has people painting the inside of one of its high-voltage power substations. It is not possible to turn off all the electricity throughout the substation, only to certain sections at a time.

12. Give an example of something an *unreasonable person* (not the person named in the example) might do in each of the scenarios in question 11.

13. What is the simplified rule of negligent misrepresentation?

14. What is the actual rule of negligent misrepresentation?

15. What is the simplified rule of negligence per se?

16. What is the actual rule of negligence per se?

17. Why is the answer to the following question *not* yes or no? *Question:* Are designers liable in negligence to contractors and subcontractors?

18. What are the four rules regarding designer liability for negligence to contractors and subcontractors?

19. What are economic losses?

20. What is the difference between fraud and negligent misrepresentation?

21. What is the difference between a deceptive trade practices act and tort law?

22. Name two specific deceptive trade practices.

23. In what circumstance is a contort most likely to arise in the construction industry?

24. Why are the concepts of strict liability important in the construction industry?

25. When is a product defective?

26. What is the only defense to a tort action that was discussed in this chapter?

27. What is another name for *tort damages?*

28. What is the primary difference between tort damages and contract damages?

29. What is meant by the term *pain and suffering?*

30. When are punitive damages recoverable?

31. What is another name for *punitive damages?*

32. In the McDonald's coffee case, why was the plaintiff awarded punitive damages? In other words, what are the specific facts that supported an award of punitive damages?

Problems

Answer the issue in each of the following problems by making a legal argument, including premises in support of your answer.

    1. B&B Petroleum Corporation, the owner, hired Jacobs Inc., an independent contractor, to co-ordinate and supervise the expansion of B&B's Lake Tia refinery. On-site was Mr. McNab, B&B's construction manager. B&B hired other independent contractors to perform other

specific segments of the project. One such contractor was Dufus Construction, who employed Mr. Royer. On the day of Royer's fall Dufus was responsible for connecting two completed sections of work. Royer attached himself to the wheel of a valve and lowered himself to do some work. *Dufus had assembled the valve* and welded it to B&B's existing pipe work. The valve wheel came off and Royer fell. The *improper assembly of the valve,* rather than any defect of its individual components, caused the valve unit to be defective. Assume this to be an admission of fact.[14]

Issue: Are B&B and Jacobs liable to Royer for negligence?

Rule: (*Hint:* duty)

Premises:

Answer: No

2. The Missouri Highway and Transportation Commission (MHTC) awarded a contract to FW, Inc. for improvements to a state highway. The projects included clearing, excavating, and grading in an area adjacent to Shady Valley Park & Pool, Inc., a fish-breeding and fishing-for-fee establishment. The contract documents required FW to "take every precaution to insure mud and siltation are kept to a minimum during grading operations."

FW cleared and grubbed the area in accordance with MHTC's specifications. Siltation immediately began to affect Shady Valley's manmade lakes. FW put up a line of sandbags around the construction site to prevent water and silt from entering the lakes, but the problem continued even after the highway project had been completed and accepted. Shady Valley went out of business. Shady Valley sued FW and MHTC.[15]

Issue: Is Fred Weber, Inc., negligent?

Rule:

Premises: (*Hint:* A duty can be established by a contract.)

Answer:

3. Eli Torres, an employee of a subcontractor, was using the upper or "fly," section of an extension ladder belonging to the general contractor to tie a sheet-metal duct to an overhead roof fan on a jobsite. He fell and sustained serious injury. The fly section had been removed from the lower section of the ladder. No one knows by whom or when. The manufacturer's instructions printed on the ladder specifically warned users not to remove the two sections and use the fly section independently of the lower section. At the time of the accident Torres was the job foreman and had several years of experience in the industry.[16]

Issue: Is the general contractor liable to Torres for damages?

Rule: (*Hint:* assumption)

Premises:

Answer: No, the contractor is not liable to Torres for damages.

---

[14] Facts modified from *Royer v. Citgo Petroleum Corp.,* 53 F.3d 116 (1995).

[15] *Shady Valley Park & Pool, Inc. v. Fred Weber, Inc.* 913 S.W.2d 28 (Mo. App. 1995).

[16] *Colantuoni v. Alfred Calcagni & Sons, Inc.,* 44 F.3d 1 (1st Cir. 1994).

4. On March 13, 1998, Smith, an employee of Paisano Inc., was driving a tractor-trailer rig for his employer on the shoulder of State Highway 37, 4.5 miles east of Pleasanton. At that point his rig climbed the guardrail, fell off an overpass, and struck a train, causing damage to the train. Smith died in the accident. No one knows why he was on the shoulder. No witnesses to the accident exist. The railroad sued Paisano, Inc. for damages to its train.[17]

A state statute says the following:

> *Sec. 54A. A driver may operate a vehicle on an improved shoulder to the right of the main traveled portion of the roadway as long as necessary, and when the operation may be done in safety, only under the following circumstances:*
>
> > *a. to stop, stand, or park;*
> > *b. to accelerate prior to entering the main traveled lane of traffic;*
> > *c. to decelerate prior to making a right turn;*
> > *d. to overtake and pass another vehicle that is slowing or stopped on the main traveled portion of the highway, disabled, or preparing to make a left turn;*
> > *e. to allow other vehicles to pass that are traveling at a greater speed;*
> > *f. when permitted or required by an official traffic control device; or*
> > *g. at any time to avoid a collision.*

Issue 1: Was Smith negligent per se?

Rule:

Premises: (*Hint:* lack of evidence)

Answer: No

Issue 2: Was Smith negligent?

Rule:

Premises:

Answer: No

5. Owen Owner sold a piece of property to D.R. Development and Construction Company. The land was located on an old landfill. Owen Owner did not tell D.R. that the land was located over a landfill, though documents in the escrow file obtained through discovery reveal that this information was supplied to Owen Owner. Owen Owner had no documents that revealed this information, and he denied knowing that the property had been an old landfill. D.R. built a house on the land, and he tried to sell it but could not because of harmful gases that had built up over time from the old landfill. D.R. knew nothing of the landfill at the time it purchased the land. D.R. lost $40,000 on the project.

Question: What issue of fact must be determined before liability can be decided in this case?

Assume that the jury finds that Owen Owner knew that the land was located over a landfill.

Issue: Has Owen Owner committed any tort?

Rule: (*Hint:* intentional tort)

Premises:

Answer: Yes

---

[17]Facts from *Cudworth v. South Texas Paisano Constr. Co.*, 705 S.W.2d 315 (Tex. App. 1986).

Assume that the jury finds that Owen Owner did not know the land was located over a landfill.

Issue: Has Owen Owner been negligent?

Rule:

Premises:

Answer: Yes

6. You are about ready to graduate from college with an undergraduate degree in multicultural studies. You and some of your fellow students get wind of a good deal on some property and form a small joint venture, called Trippin' Along, to develop the property into a strip mall.

  You hire Dewey and Howe, Inc., licensed architects, to design the plans for the strip mall. Your main dealings with the firm are through Mr. Slick, who you thought was a licensed architect. You find out later he is, in fact, not a licensed architect but a draftsperson. He does have many years of experience with the firm in projects similar to yours.

  Mr. Slick recommends you use C-tile™ for the outside paving. He tells you it will be suitable for this purpose and will bear traffic, weather, and loads well.

  Shortly after completion of the project the C-tile™ begins to break and deteriorate, and it is proved by a preponderance of the evidence to be totally unsuitable for the use to which it has been put. (You can assume all facts given to you can be proved by a preponderance of the evidence, unless you are specifically told of a conflict.) It will cost approximately $135,000 to remove the existing tile and replace it with X-tile™, a suitable tile for the job.

  In addition to the preceding, a patron of the center, Dana Formosa, falls on a piece of deteriorated C-tile™ and sustains $10,000 in medical bills for damage to her knee and ankle, and $500 in lost wages damages. All damages are related to the fall only.

  It is determined that C-tile™ is, in fact a brand new product that has not had much, if any, application similar to yours. It is, however, much cheaper than other types of tiles. It cost only $35,000 to install, whereas a tile more appropriate to the job, such as X-tile™ would have cost $70,000.[18]

  FIRPA each of the following scenarios:

  Hint: Check the *facts* and *law* to see if facts and law exist to support each cause of action.

  Hint: Some of the following causes of action are not supportable, either because of a lack of facts *or* a lack of legal support. It is just as important to recognize what facts and law you *do not have* in support of a cause of action as it is to recognize what facts and law support a cause of action.

Formosa vs. Mr. Slick for *negligent misrepresentation*

Formosa vs. Trippin' Along for *negligence.*

Trippin' Along vs. Mr. Slick for *fraud.*

Trippin' Along vs. Dewey and Howe, Inc., for *negligent misrepresentation.*

Questions:

a. The preceding list is not a complete list of the possible causes of action the various parties might want to explore. What other causes of action could be added to the list?

---

[18]Facts modified from *The White Budd Van Ness Partnership v. Major-Gladys Drive Joint Venture,* 798 S.W.2d 805 (Tex. App.—Beaumont 1990).

b. What is your personal liability for the damages to Formosa should a jury find Trippin' Along negligent? (*Hint:* See Chapter 6, Relationships among the Parties on the Project.)

7. Ifte Choudhury, then an employee of Segner & Granddaughter Industrial Painting Company, Inc., sustained severe injuries when he came into contact with high-voltage electricity while painting an electric substation owned and operated by the Bluebell Power and Light. Bluebell had hired Segner & Granddaughter, an independent contractor, to perform the painting work at several of Bluebell's electric substations. The substation involved in the lawsuit was a "transmission" substation through which high-voltage electricity flowed. The evidence indicated that it was not feasible to shut off the entire flow of electricity through the substation during the painting work. Specifically, the evidence indicated that to shut down the entire flow of electricity through the substation would have resulted in a loss of power to thousands of Bluebell's customers; however, it was possible to stop the flow of electricity through selected conductors in selected areas of the substation without interrupting service to its customers.

Bob Segner, the president of Segner & Granddaughter, was the supervisor of the painting crew. Each day, prior to the commencement of the painting work, Bluebell's employees would confer with Segner, in the presence of the painters, to inform them which conductors were "hot" (energized) and which had been deactivated. Segner would then convey or repeat that information to the painters. After informing Segner of the energized and deenergized areas, a representative of Bluebell would remain at the substation to answer questions and to ensure that the painting work was properly completed. Bluebell's agents would also occasionally speak directly to the painters, but these conversations were generally limited to the topic of which electrical lines or circuits were active and which had been deenergized.

At all times, Bluebell retained exclusive control over the determination of which electrical circuits or lines would be deenergized at the substation. Bluebell also retained exclusive control over the process of activating and deactivating the lines.

Choudhury, the injured party, testified that he had asked Bluebell's representative prior to the accident whether there were any warning flags that could be hung from the electrical lines to help the painters distinguish between the hot (energized) and cold (deenergized) areas, Bluebell's representative stated there were no flags at that substation. Choudhury was severely injured while descending from painting a certain portion of the work. He came into contact with a part of area that was energized.[19]

Issue: Was Bluebell negligent?

Rule:

Premises: (*Hint:* What facts can be used to show that the owner was unreasonable?)

Answer:

8. Donald Kind brought an action to recover for injuries he received while working on a shopping center in April 1999. He "was removing a cement plaster soffit from the canopy of the shopping center when the suspension system for the soffit suddenly and catastrophically failed." He claimed that the suspension system's failure was caused by the negligence of the shopping center's architects, Schroeder & Holt Architects, Ltd.

The architects were alleged to be negligent for failing to adequately design the suspension system and supervise its construction in 1984. The specifications for the 1984 construction omitted details regarding how the soffit should be suspended.

---

[19]Facts from *Sopkovich v. Ohio Edison Co.*, 81 Ohio St. 3d 628, 693 N.E.2d 233 (1998).

The testimony of the architects was as follows: "It is customary and ordinary to omit certain details because it is within the common knowledge of the contractor to know how to suspend a soffit ceiling" of the type used in the shopping center. "It is ordinary and customary in the architectural profession to omit certain details from specifications, designs and drawings, when it is understood that the omitted information is within the common knowledge of the general and/or subcontractors. If detail is omitted from an architect's specifications, designs or drawings for which the contractor needs further explanation, the contractor knows that it may question the architect when he periodically visits the job site."

The architect also testified in his deposition that the canopy could be dangerous if it were not adequately suspended.

The architects periodically visited the construction site in 1984 and "were available" to answer any questions that the contractor might have had concerning the suspension of the canopy ceiling. The architects were "generally aware of how the canopy ceiling was being suspended and did not note a problem with it."

The general contractor's project supervisor on the shopping center job testified at a deposition that he agreed with the general proposition that architects' drawings were not always as clear as he would like. If a detail on the drawing was omitted, or he was uncertain as to how something should be accomplished he "would feel that he should ask the architect." He also testified that instructions for suspending the canopy were not shown in the architect's drawings for the shopping center job and that he never asked the architect how the soffit should be hung.[20]

Kind is claiming the architects committed *two* separate acts of negligence. Put the first in Issue 1 and the second in Issue 2, then answer the issues.

Issue 1: Was the architect negligent for failing to_____?

Rule:

Premises: In the interest of brevity, the example has been simplified, and much of the testimony in the actual case has been eliminated; however, an argument can be made using only the facts given. What additional type of testimony might be presented to the jury to help them come to a conclusion in this matter?

Answer:

Issue 2: Was the architect negligent for failing to_____?

Rule:

Premises: What additional type of testimony might be presented to the jury to help them come to a conclusion in this matter?

Answer:

9. Paul Ed Mallow, a workman on a construction site, was killed while employed on the job by R. E. Hazard, Jr., Inc. (Contractor) as it remodeled a motel on the premises of Camino del Rio Properties, Inc. (Owner). Defendant Tucker, Sadler & Bennett, Architects and Engineers, Inc. (Architect) independently contracted with Owner to act as the architect for this construction project. The workman, Paul Mallow, was electrocuted and killed while jackhammering

---

[20] Facts from *Transportation Insurance Co., Inc. v. Hunzinger Construction Co.,* 507 N.W.2d 136, 179 Wis. 2d 281 (1993).

footings in the ground at the place called for by Architect's plans; the jackhammer broke into an underground high-voltage transmission line.

The complaint alleged (1) negligence of Owner in failing to make the premises safe for decedent's use, and a failure to warn of known danger, and (2) negligence of Architect in failing to warn of the existence and location of the high-voltage line, specifically, by not showing it on the plans it prepared for the construction.[21]

Issue 1: Was the owner negligent?

Rule:

Premises:

Answer: Yes

Issue 2: Was the Architect negligent?

Rule:

Premises:

Answer: Yes

10. Billy Ray Clark was an employee of Halliburton Industrial Services Division, which was hired by CCA to clean the interior of industrial pipes known as "liquor lines" at CCA's Brewton, Alabama, paper mill. Halliburton cleaned the lines by *hydrojetting,* a process in which water is pumped at extremely high pressures through a hose and nozzle fitted into the lines. Clark was one of the Halliburton employees responsible for inserting and removing the hose, and he was seriously injured during the course of his work at the CCA facility. Clark had removed the hose from a line so the line could be inspected, and he was returning to pick up the hose when the water came on unexpectedly. The hose began spraying wildly, and Clark was struck repeatedly by the jet of water.

Halliburton supplied the equipment and personnel for the hydrojetting operation. At CCA, CCA employees were routinely assigned by CCA supervisors to assist Halliburton personnel with the hydrojetting operation. At the time of Clark's accident, CCA employee Tommy Still was operating the foot pedal that served as a safety switch for activating and deactivating the pump. It is undisputed that at the time of the accident, instead of operating the pedal with his foot and leaving the switch box on the ground as it was designed to be operated, Still held the box in one hand and operated the switch with the other hand. Still testified that he had done so because the ground where he needed to stand was covered by water and other liquids, and he had not felt that it was safe to operate an electrical switch on the ground in those conditions.

Clark testified that before the accident occurred he had become displeased with Still's operation of the switch. Still was not paying sufficient attention to his hand signals, Clark felt, and as a result the hose had twice lost pressure unexpectedly, falling out of the line and to the ground some distance below the catwalk where Clark worked among the lines. Approximately twenty minutes before the accident, Clark confronted Still about his alleged lack of attention, and Still, Clark testified, had replied to the effect that he worked for CCA and did not have to take orders from Clark. At trial, Still admitted to having released the switch at least once when he thought he heard someone (other than Clark) shout "shut it off!" He also admitted that the confrontation between him and Clark occurred, although he denied having made the remarks

---

[21]Facts from *Mallow v. Tucker, Sadler & Bennet,* 245 Cal.App 700, 54 Cal.Rptr. 174 (1966).

attributed to him by Clark. He emphatically denied pressing the switch and activating the pump while the hose was not secured into a line; in other words, he denied causing Clark's injuries.[22]

Question: What is the factual issue raised in this scenario?

Factual issue:

Assume that the jury believes Clark's testimony but not Still's testimony. Analyze the following issue:

Issue: Has CCA been negligent? (Why can you assume that if Still is negligent, then CCA is responsible. *Hint:* See Chapter 6, Relationships among the Parties on the Project.)

Rule:

Premises:

Answer: Yes

11. Sam was the new salesperson at a local hardware store. He had never worked in that type of work before, and he had little knowledge of paint and other types of hardware. Mrs. Bixby, a 58-year-old widow entered the store looking to buy exterior pain for an outdoor storage shed in which she stored her gardening equipment. She told Sam that she needed paint that could be used on metal siding. Sam indicated that a type of wood paint would be useful. Mrs. Bixby mentioned that the paint said on the side of the can that it was good for wood. Sam told her it was not just for wood, but for any surface. In fact, the paint would not adhere to the metal of the shed. Mrs. Bixby had never painted any metal surface before, though she had occasionally painted wood trim on her home. The paint purchased from Sam peeled off within two weeks.

Issue: Is Sam negligent?

Rule: (*Hint:* What specific type of negligence is this?)

Premises:

Answer:

Question: You saw a similar problem in Chapter 13, Warranties. Why might Mrs. Bixby sue for negligence rather than breach of warranty?

12. You supervise a road repair crew and are employed by We 'R Pavement, Inc. Riverside County contracted road construction and renovation of a certain section of county road to We 'R Pavement. One day your crew was filling potholes on Highway 21 in Riverside County. One of the employees, Bubba, improperly mixed the asphalt, and it would not harden adequately. This bad asphalt was used to fill the potholes. Debbie Ann, who lives off Highway 21 drove over a patched pothole a few days later. The asphalt collapsed, and the front right tire of her automobile wedged into the hole, bending the front axle. Debbie Ann found out about the asphalt and all the preceding details because her husband is Bubba's next-door neighbor's fishing buddy; however, no records were kept of the exact type of mix used or the problem with the asphalt. (How convenient!)

---

[22]From *Clark v. Container Corporation of America, Inc.,* 936 F.2d 1220 (11th Cir. 1991).

Expert testimony states that asphalt of this particular age and at locations similar to the conditions on Highway 21 does not normally collapse under vehicular weight unless it is improperly prepared.

Issue: Can Debbie Ann collect damages to her car? (*Note:* It is common for government entities to require that certain notices and other requirements be followed before they can be sued. Assume that all such details are not an issue.)

Rule:

Premises:

Answer: Yes

13. In August 1990, Lynn Codec flew from his home in New York to Houston where he entered into negotiations with Grand Contractors, Inc. to employ him. Lynn Codec met with Lasko in Houston to discuss the details of his employment contract. Rick Tinat, representing Grand, negotiated some of the final terms of the employment contract and then flew to New York to obtain Lynn Codec's signature. Lynn Codec signed the employment contract on August 28, 1990.

In October 1990, Lynn Codec moved from New York to Houston and began working for Grand. The relationship between the parties soon disintegrated. Grand was unhappy with Lynn Codec's performance as an employee. The jury heard evidence that Lynn Codec kept irregular hours and was not carrying his share of the work. He had difficulty working in the office, and several female employees had complained about his behavior. He belittled and embarrassed sales representatives in front of customers and sent sexually suggestive memos to sales representatives in an attempt to be humorous. One sales representative testified that he made a pass at her. There was also some evidence that he negotiated agreements without any provision for profit to the company.

At trial, Lynn Codec claimed that Rick Tinat, a representative of Grand, made several negligent misrepresentations during the employment negotiations that induced Lynn Codec to move to Houston and accept employment with Grand. Specifically, Lynn Codec claimed that Tinat misrepresented that Lynn Codec would have an ownership interest in Grand, and that he would receive certain benefits upon his transfer to Houston. The jury awarded Lynn Codec $50,000 for damages arising from Tinat's negligent misrepresentations.[23]

Question: The appeal court overturned the award of $50,000 damages for *negligent misrepresentation*. Why?

Answers to Selected Problems

1. B&B Petroleum Corporation, the owner, hired Jacobs Inc. an independent. . . .

Issue: Are B&B and Jacobs liable to Royer for negligence?

Rule: Duty. Persons generally have a duty to act reasonably.

Premises: Even though the facts state that the damage was caused because of the improper assembly, Dufus did not have a duty to assemble the valve in such a way as to support a person's weight. Valves are not usually used in such a manner.

Answer: No

---

[23]Modified from *Innovo Group, Inc., v. Tedesco*, 1996. TX.26550, (unpublished opinion).

4. On March 13, 1998, Smith, an employee of Paisano Inc., was driving a tractor. . . .

Issue 1: Was Smith negligent per se?

Rule: The following are the elements of a cause of action for negligence per se:

a. Violation of a valid ordinance; and

b. Injured party is a member of the class that the statute was enacted to protect; and

c. The harm or injury suffered by the plaintiff was of the type that statute was contemplated to prevent; and

d. Causation; and

e. Damages

Premises: No proof exists that Smith violated any ordinance. Sec. 54A allows driving on the shoulder under some circumstances. Also parts (b) and (d) of the above rule are not satisfied. The statute to prevent driving on shoulders was not enacted to prevent trains from being hit by trucks falling off of shoulders. In addition, the harm suffered by plaintiff (damage to train) was not the type of harm section 54A was designed to prevent.

Answer: No

Appendix A Case: *McCaughtry v. Barwood Homes Association*

981 S.W.2d 325 (Tex. App. 1998)
Affirmed in Part; Reversed and Remanded in Part, and Opinion filed July 30, 1998. [Original opinion has been modified for student use.]

I. Background

Barwood owns and operates a clubhouse and recreational facilities, including a swimming pool and a tennis court, in Cypress, Texas. A chain link fence surrounds the tennis court, which has six light standards located outside the fence. The light standards are approximately twenty-five feet in height. A high voltage power line, with the lower line approximately [25 feet above the ground], or the same height as the light standards, carrying approximately 19,900 volts of power, runs diagonally through the Barwood property. At one point the power line is approximately nine to nine and one-half feet from one of the tennis court light standards. HL&P owns the power line.

[Summarize the facts of the case here:
Hint: This was done for you in Chapter 4, in the section "Briefing Cases."]

In August 1993, Barwood entered into a contract with C.L. Sports, owned by Craig Littlefield (Littlefield), for the refurbishment of its tennis court and the painting of the light standards surrounding the court. Littlefield hired McCaughtry and Dennis Espinoza (Espinoza) for the Barwood job.

[Draw a relationship chart including all the parties.]

When it came time to paint the light standards, Littlefield, McCaughtry and Espinoza assembled a scaffold so McCaughtry and Espinoza could reach the top of the light standards with roller brushes. For the painting of the first five standards, the scaffold was placed on the tennis court, inside the fence. For the painting of the final light standard, the scaffold was placed outside the fence. Although the scaffold had been placed inside the fence when the primer coat was applied to the sixth light standard, it was decided the scaffold should be placed outside the fence because it would be easier to reach the top of the light standard.

On August 17, 1993, McCaughtry ascended the top of the scaffold and proceeded to paint the top of the sixth light standard with an aluminum extended-handle paint roller. While painting the light standard, the handle of McCaughtry's paint roller came into contact with the high voltage power line. Espinoza, who was on the ground, heard a loud noise and looked up to see the paint roller flying in the air, and McCaughtry fall over the rail of the scaffold to the ground. McCaughtry sustained personal injuries, including a fractured right ankle, third degree burns over sixty percent of his body, internal injuries, a closed head injury, and the amputation of his left leg below the knee.

On September 16, 1993, McCaughtry brought suit against HL&P and Barwood for negligence. . . .

In four points of error, McCaughtry claims the trial court erred in granting summary judgment because Barwood failed to establish that it: (1) complied with its duty to warn McCaughtry of a hazardous condition, or that there was no duty to warn McCaughtry of a known hazard; (2) maintained the premises in a safe manner at the time of the accident; and (3) was in compliance with the applicable safety standards for high voltage power lines. . . .

III. Premises Liability

[Note: This is a negligence cause of action claiming that the owner of the premises did not act reasonably.]

A. Duty to Warn

In his second point of error, McCaughtry claims Barwood failed to establish that it had complied with its duty to warn him of a hazardous condition—that a high voltage power line was located at its nearest point, nine feet from one of the light standards—or that it had no duty to warn McCaughtry of a known hazard.

[Who made this error?]

An owner or occupier of land has a duty to use reasonable care to protect an employee of a contractor working on the premises from reasonably foreseeable injuries [all citations removed]. This duty is discharged by warning the employee of unreasonable risks of harm either known to the owner or which would be known to him by reasonable inspection or making the premises reasonably safe. . . .

[What is the duty of an owner or occupier of land?]

The duty of an owner or occupier of land to keep the premises in a safe condition may subject him to liability in two situations: (1) those arising from a defect in the premises and (2) those arising from an activity or instrumentality. First, are those cases in which the dangerous condition existed at the time the contractor's employee entered the property for business purposes, or was created by someone, or through some means unrelated to the injured employee. Under this situation, the owner of the premises is in a superior position to know of or discover the hidden dangerous conditions on his premises [all citations removed].

McCaughtry contends that although Barwood knew of the danger of a high voltage power line being adjacent to and within nine or nine and one-half feet of the light standard, it nonetheless failed to warn him of the potential danger of the situation. According to McCaughtry, maintaining a high voltage power line is a pre-existing dangerous condition about which Barwood had the duty to warn him. McCaughtry cites *Edwards* in support of this conclusion [citations removed].

[McCaughtry is claiming Barwood was negligent for failing to do what?]

In the *Edwards* case, the plaintiff was an employee of an independent contractor employed by Shell to construct a pipeline on premises which Shell controlled. The plaintiff was operating a ditching machine when he dug up the guy anchor line causing a loose guy line, which was not adequately insulated, to come to come into contact with a high voltage power line. The plaintiff then came into contact with the energized guy line. Shell argued the accident arose out of the plaintiff's activity, not a pre-existing dangerous activity.

[What are the facts of the Edwards *case?]*

The court, considering expert testimony that guy lines should be properly insulated because they can come loose, rejected Shell's argument and found the maintenance of an improperly insulated guy line was a pre-existing dangerous condition. The guy line in question went into the ground at an angle and continued underground at an angle. The plaintiff was not aware that it continued underground at such an angle. There also was evidence Shell had assured the contractor that the ditch line was not going to run into the guy line.

McCaughtry argues that just as the uninsulated guy line located in close proximity to the work site was a pre-existing dangerous condition in *Edwards*, so too was the location of the light standard—nine and one-half feet from the power line—particularly when Barwood had contracted to have the light standard painted.

We find, however, *Edwards* is distinguishable from the facts of this case. In *Edwards*, the court specifically found the condition was dangerous because the guy line was not properly insulated, and the line continued underground at an angle of which the plaintiff was not aware. Also, Shell had assured the plaintiff's employer that the ditch would not run into the guy line. Here, there is no evidence showing either (1) the power line was in poor condition, or it was any way not visible, or (2) that Barwood made any representations regarding the location of the power line with respect to the light standard.

[The judge writing this opinion says that Edwards *does not apply to McCaughtry's case. Why not?]*

McCaughtry further argues the mere observation of the location of a power line is not sufficient to charge the contractor's employee with knowledge of a dangerous condition. See *Sun Oil Co. v. Massey.* In *Sun Oil Co.,* the plaintiff, while working on a workover crew servicing an oil well owned by Sun Oil, which was powered by electricity from a visible high voltage power line, received severe injuries when he was electrocuted. In order to anchor the rig so that it would not topple over, the crew ran guy wires from the top of the derrick to the ground. While the crew was in the process of running the fourth guy line, the cable the crew was using came into contact with a power line. There was testimony the crew had been misled by Sun Oil into believing that power in the lines had been shut off. Sun Oil argued the well-site was safe because the power line was visible.

[What are the facts of the Sun Oil *case?]*

The court observed that "the hazard posed by the live power lines was not obvious despite their visibility since the location of the lines was only one component of the danger, the other being that they were charged with electricity." The court concluded the accident would not have happened either if the lines had been located farther away from the well or if the current had been turned off. The court further found the evidence showed Sun Oil was at least partially responsible for the initial placing of the power lines unusually close to the well. Thus, the evidence supported the jury's finding that (1) Sun Oil had created or maintained a dangerous condition, (2) it failed to make the premises safe, and (3) its failure was a proximate cause of the accident.

[The preceding paragraph mentions "the court." What court is being referred to?]

Sun Oil Co. is also distinguishable from this case. First, a Sun Oil employee had represented that the power line had been de-energized. Second, Sun Oil was at least initially responsible for placing the power line so close to the well. Here, there is no evidence Barwood was responsible for the location of the power line. Indeed, Forney testified he did not know if the power line had been installed prior to the installation of the light standards on the Barwood property. Moreover, McCaughtry has not even alleged that Barwood made any representation that it had made arrangements to deenergize the power line. . . .

[Why does the McCaughtry court say that Sun Oil *does not apply to McCaughtry's case?]*

Barwood asserts McCaughtry's injuries did not arise from a defect in the premises, but rather, from McCaughtry's work itself, for which Barwood had no control. Therefore, no duty to warn arose. Barwood argues it was not possible for a person to come into contact with the power line because it was suspended twenty-five feet over the ground. McCaughtry's standing on the scaffold combined with the use of a paint roller with an extended handle enabled him to come into contact with the power line. Barwood cites two courts of appeals summary judgment cases addressing *facts analogous* to those of this case, each finding there was no premise defect and, therefore, no duty to warn.

[What does "facts analogous" mean?]

First, in *Corpus v. K-J Oil Co.,* the plaintiff, an employee of an independent contractor hired to "pull" a well, which included removing pipe and other underground equipment from the well, suffered severe injuries when the workover rig boom touched an overhead electric power line [cite removed]. The court concluded the power line, as constructed, was not dangerous to those working below until the foreman caused the boom to come into contact with or in close proximity to the power line. The power line was not a hidden danger on the premises. The court stated the fact that the foremen and other crewmen "were not paying attention did not change the presence of the high line from a reasonably apparent condition into a dangerous condition about which the occupier of the premises had a duty to warn." Because the danger arose from the performance of the independent contractor's work, the occupier of the premises owed no duty to warn.

[What are the facts in the Corpus *case?]*

Second, in *Bryant v. Gulf Oil Corp.,* an employee of an independent contractor hired by the defendant was electrocuted when the gin pole on a workover unit touched an electrical wire during a well-repair job [cite removed]. The workover unit had a "gin pole" which could telescope out to sixty feet in height. The court, noting Gulf Oil did not have control over the installation or maintenance of the high line, held the power line did not become dangerous to those working below until the independent contractor's employee caused the gin pole to contact it.

[What are the facts in the Bryant *case?]*

Under the reasoning set forth in *Corpus* and *Bryant,* we conclude the proximity of the power line to the light standard does not constitute a premise defect. McCaughtry's injuries, therefore, were caused by the performance of his duties in painting the light standard. Generally, the owner or occupier of the premises is not responsible for injuries arising from an activity being performed by an independent contractor.

[What rule does the court state in the preceding paragraph?]

This point of error is overruled.

In order to hold Barwood liable for his injuries arising from his work on the Barwood property, McCaughtry must show that his case falls within an exception to this general rule of liability.

[The general rule of liability mentioned above is the following:
The owner or occupier of the premises is not responsible for injuries arising from an activity being performed by an independent contractor.]

[The court says that despite the above rule, Barwood could be held responsible for McCaughtry's injuries.]

C. Control over Work Details

Generally, the owner or occupier of the premises does not have a duty to see that an independent contractor performs the work in a safe manner [all citations removed]. Under these circumstances, the independent contractor is in a superior position to prevent, inspect for, eliminate or protect against the dangerous condition [all citations removed].

The Texas Supreme Court, however, in adopting the Restatement (Second) of Torts § 414 (1977), set forth an exception to this general rule of premises liability with respect to the owner of the premises and the independent contractor. The Restatement provides:

> *One who entrusts work to an independent contractor, but who retains the*
> *control of any part of the work, is subject to liability for physical harm to*
> *others for whose safety the employer owes a duty to exercise reasonable care,*
> *which is caused by his failure to exercise his control with reasonable care.*

This rule applies to circumstances where the [owner] retains some control over the manner in which the independent contractor's work is performed, but does not retain the degree of control which would subject him to liability as a master. The court further defined the "degree of control" required to impose liability. Specifically, the owner's role must be more than a general right to order the work to start or stop, to inspect progress, or receive reports.

The owner may retain only the power to direct the order in which the work shall be done, or to forbid its being done in a manner likely to be dangerous to himself or others.

Next, McCaughtry contends Barwood is liable because it exercised control over the details and manner of his and Espinoza's work refurbishing the tennis court. In support of this assertion, McCaughtry relies on Espinoza's deposition testimony wherein he states the chairwoman of Barwood instructed them on what needed to be painted or the way in which the painting should be done:

[McCaughtry is claiming that Barwood is responsible because its action come under one of the exceptions to the general rule of liability. What exception is that? What evidence is McCaughtry offering to prove the existence of this exception?]

Q. Now, before the accident, did you personally talk to anyone from Barwood Homes about this job?

A. There was a lady, a chairman of the Barwood Association. She would just come and, you know, look around and see, what we were doing, you know.

Q. What did you hear her say about this job prior to the accident?

A. No. She would just say, "This needs to be painted," or, "Do it this way," or something like that. Anyway, she is representing Barwood, so I will have to listen to her.

Q. Was she pointing out maybe a missed spot in the paint?

A. Probably. I mean it's not like I saw her several times. If I saw her, it was probably—if I talked to her, it was probably once or twice at the most.

The above testimony reflects that Barwood merely checked the progress of McCaughtry's and Espinoza's work. In *Bryant,* the court found where a supervisor employed by the owner of the premises who visited the crew at the work site to "see how they doing with the job, if they working or goofing off, see if they've got any problem," was not sufficient to establish that the defendant had control over the details of the work to establish liability [citation removed]. Moreover, Littlefield testified that no one other than he and McCaughtry directed any of the details of work or how the work was to be done. Also, Barwood did not provide any of the tools or equipment used in that job. McCaughtry has failed to establish the requisite control over the details of his and Espinoza's work to establish Barwood's liability for his injuries.

McCaughtry has failed to raise any fact issues that Barwood maintained control over the manner in which the refurbishment of the tennis courts was to be done.

This point of error is overruled.

[remainder of opinion omitted]

Appendix B Citations for Four Rules of Liability of Designers to Contractors and Subcontractors

1. *Majority Rule:* A contractor or subcontractor who is damaged as the proximate result of the designer's negligence in preparing plans and/or specifications is *precluded* from collecting "economic" losses related to the negligence. The term *economic* does not have the standard dictionary meaning. Economic losses are damages for inadequate value, costs of repair, replacement of a defect, and loss of profits. These are all typical types of damages for breach of contract. In other words, the injured party must sue for breach of contract or warranty, not negligence. However, the injured party is not precluded from collecting damages for other tort actions related to damage to other property or for personal injury.

   Moorman Mfg. Co. v. National Tank Co., 91 Ill. 2d 69, 435 N.E.2d 443 (1982), *Bryant v. Murray-Jones,* 653 F. Supp. 1015 (ED Mo. 1985); *Thomson v. Espey Huston & Asso., Inc.,* 899 S.W.2d 415 (Tex. App—Austin 1995); *Bryant Elec. Co. v. City of Fredericksburg,* 762 F.2d 1192 (4th Cir. 1985); *Florida Power & Light Co. v. Westinghouse Elec. Corp,* 510 So. 2d 899 (Fla. 1987); *Hennepin Drainage & Levee Dist. v . Klinger,* 187 Ill. App. 3d 710, 543 N.E.2d 967 (1989), *app. den.; Floor Craft Floor Covering, Inc. v. Parma Community Gen. Hosp.,* 54 Ohio St. 3d 1, 560 N.E.2d 206 (1990); *Blake Constr. Co. v. Alley,* 233 Va. 31, 353 S.E.2d 724 (1987).

2. A third party, including a subcontractor or contractor, who is damaged as the proximate result of the engineer/engineer's negligence in preparing plans and/or specifications *has a valid negligence claim* against the design professional. No privity is required. *A. R. Moyer, Inc. v. Graham,* 285 So.2d 397 (1973); *Colbert v. B.F. Carvin Constr. Co.,* 600 S0.2d 719 (La. Ct. App.), *cert. denied,* 604 So.2d 1311 (La. 1992); *United States v. Rogers & Rogers,* 161 F. Supp. 132 (SD Cal. 1958); *Waldor Pump & Equip. Co. v. Orr-Schelen-Mayeron & Asso.,* 386 N.W.2d 375 (Minn. Ct. App. 1986); *E. C. Ernst, Inc. v. Manhattan Constr. Co.,* 551 F.2d 1026 (5th Cir.

1977) *reh'g denied in part, granted in part,* 559 F.2d 268 (5th Cir. 1977), *cert. denied,* 434 United States 1067 (1968); *US v. Rogers & Rogers,* 161 F. Supp. 132 (SDCal 1958); *Mayor of Columbus v. Clark-Dietz,* 550 F. Supp. 624 (ED Miss. 1982); *Bryant v. Murray Jones Murray, Inc.* 653 F. Supp. 1015 (ED Mo. 1985); *Merchants Natl Bank and Trust,* 876 F.2d 1202 (5th Cir. 1989).

3. The following *balancing test* is used to determine the liability of the engineer to third parties:

   a. The foreseeability of harm to the plaintiff;

   b. The degree of certainty that the plaintiff suffered injury;

   c. The closeness of the defendant's connection between the conduct and the injury suffered;

   d. The policy of preventing future harm; and

   e. Moral blame for a design professional's actions and preventing future harm.

   Dale v. Cooper, 56 Cal. App. 3d 860, 128 Cal. Rptr. 724, 729 (1976).

4. Engineers and architects have no duty to contractors and subcontractors and therefore cannot be sued for negligence.

   Amazon v. British Am. Dev. Corp., 216 A.D.2d 702, 628 N.Y.S.2d 204 (1995); *Widett v. US Fidelity,* 815 F.2d 885(2d Cir. 1987); *Edward B. Fitzpatrick, Jr. Constr. Corp. v. County of Suffolk,* 138 A.D.2d 446, 525 N.Y.S.2d 863 (1988) *reconsideration, denied,* 73 N.Y.2d 918, 539 N.Y.S.2d 302, 536 N.E.2d 631 (1989); *Williams & Sons Erectors, Inc. v. South Carolina Steel Corp.,* 983 F.2d 1176 (2nd Cir. 1993); *Reber v. Chandler High School Dist.,* 13 Ariz. App. 133, 474 P.2d 852 (1970); *Barnes v. Rakow,* 78 Ill. App. 3d 404, 396 N.E.2d 1168 (1979); *McDonough v. Whalen,* 364 Mass. 837, 313 N.E.2d 435 (1974); *Cutlip v. Lucky Stores, Inc.,* 22 Md. Ap. 673, 325 A.2d 432 (1974).

Appendix C Selected Sections of the Uniform Deceptive Trade Practices Act

Revised Uniform Deceptive Trade Practices Act (1966) Section 2, 3

Copies of all Uniform and Model Acts and other printed matter issued by the Conference may be obtained from National Conference of Commissioners on Uniform State Laws, 1155 East Sixtieth Street, Chicago, Illinois 60637

SECTION 2. Deceptive Trade Practices

a. A person engages in a deceptive trade practice when, in the course of his business, vocation or occupation, he:

   1. passes off goods or services as those of another;

   2. causes likelihood of confusion or of misunderstanding as to the source, sponsorship, approval, or certification of goods, or services;

   3. causes likelihood of confusion or of misunderstanding as to affiliation, connection, or association with, or certification by, another;

4. uses deceptive representations or designations of geographic origin in connection with goods or services;

5. represents that goods or services have sponsorship, approval, characteristics, ingredients, uses, benefits, or quantities that they do not have, or that a person has a sponsorship, approval, status, affiliation or connection that he does not have;

6. represents that goods are original or new if they are deteriorated, altered, reconditioned, reclaimed, used, or second-hand;

7. represents that goods or services are of a particular standard, quality, or grade, or that goods are of a particular style, or model, if they are of another;

8. disparages the goods, services or business of another by false or misleading representation of fact;

9. advertises goods or services with intent not to sell them as advertised;

10. advertises goods or services with intent not to supply reasonably expectable public demand, unless the advertisement discloses a limitation of quantity;

11. makes false or misleading statements of fact concerning the reasons for, existence of, or amounts of price reductions; or

12. engages in any other conduct which similarly creates a likelihood of confusion or of misunderstanding.

b. In order to prevail in an action under this Act, a complainant need not prove competition between the parties, or actual confusion, or misunderstanding.

c. This section does not affect unfair trade practices otherwise actionable at common law or under other statutes of this state.

SECTION 3. Remedies

a. A person likely to be damaged by a deceptive trade practice of another may be granted an injunction against it under the principles of equity and on terms that the court considers reasonable. Proof of monetary damage, loss of profits or intent to deceive is not required. Relief granted for the copying of an article shall be limited to the prevention of confusion or misunderstanding as to source.

b. Costs shall be allowed to the prevailing party unless the court otherwise directs. The court [in its discretion] may award attorneys' fees to the prevailing party if (1) the party complaining of a deceptive trade practice has brought an action which he knew to be groundless, or (2) the party charged with a deceptive trade practice has willfully engaged in the trade practice knowing it to be deceptive.

c. The relief provided in this section is in addition to remedies otherwise available against the same conduct under the common law or other statutes of this state.

16

Joint Liability and Indemnity

Joint Liability

The law recognizes that *several people* and/or entities may contribute to *one loss*. For example, a stairway may collapse. The collapse may be caused *in part* by an engineering design error, *in part* by improper construction techniques of the subcontractor, and *in part* because of improper supervision by the general contractor. In such a case *each party*—the engineer, the subcontractor, and the contractor—will have to pay for the loss *in proportion to the amount of their liability*. The engineer, the subcontractor, and the contractor are said to be **jointly liable** for the *one loss*. If the parties cannot agree on the percentage of liability each must pay, a jury or arbitrator will decide that issue.

People involved in construction claims often try to point the finger at others involved in the construction process and say that only the "others" have to pay because the "others" are "primarily responsible for the damage," or have caused "more of the damage" than they have. For example, the contractor may attempt to claim it is not responsible for the damages caused by the collapsing stairwell because the subcontractor or the engineer is "more responsible" or is "primarily responsible." *This is not a legally valid excuse, or defense.* The law is that all parties who have contributed to an injury pay in proportion to their liability. Note that the term used in the law for a legally valid excuse is **defense.** Figure 16–1 shows how several people have contributed to the injury of the person sitting in the center of the figure. In Figure 16–2 the damages suffered by the injured person are represented by the entire box. The amount of damages payable by each party is represented by a part of the whole box.

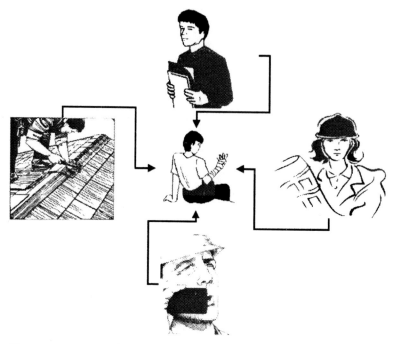

Figure 16–1 Joint liability: Several parties contribute to one injury.
© 2000–2001 www.arttoday.com

Indemnity and *contribution* are terms describing the specific situation in which one of the jointly liable parties has paid, or is likely to pay, damages to the injured party and wants to make sure that all the jointly liable parties pay their share. An **indemnity action** is one in which one party brings in another party it thinks is liable for at least some of the damages. For example, if the injured party in Figure 16–1 were to sue only the contractor, the contractor could bring in the owner and the designer into the lawsuit. **Contribution actions** arise when one party has already paid an injured party and is seeking reimbursement from other jointly liable parties. Both of these concepts are discussed in more detail later in this chapter.

The following problem will be used to discuss the concepts of joint liability and indemnification.

EXAMPLE:

Facts: Acme Supplier supplied defective switches, model #25B, to Sung Lee Electrical on a job to build a retail food and beverage business called Lorelei Tea and Coffee Room. Sung Lee is a local

TOTAL DAMAGES

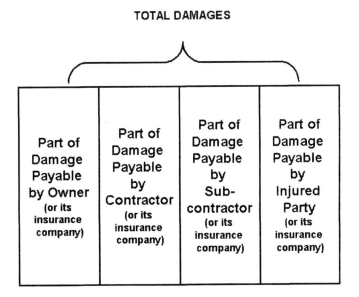

Figure 16–2 Damages split among jointly liable parties.

electrical subcontractor. Lorelei Tea and Coffee is owned and operated by George and Debbie Akima in Santa Fe, New Mexico, and is a franchise purchased by the Akimas from Lorelei Tea and Coffee, Inc. As part of the franchise agreement, the Akimas agreed to use a particular design and construction firm, Construct Construction Inc., to build out the space at the Sunset Mall according to the specifications supplied by Lorelei Tea and Coffee, Inc. The mall is owned by Sunset Mall Corporation, and space is leased to the Akimas.

Switch #25B was manufactured by Dante, Inc., a small company located on one of the Marshall Islands in the Pacific Ocean. This particular switch was required by the design supplied by Lorelei. The architect, Sondern and Blemith, Architects, required these switches because they were inexpensive, even though both Sondern, and Blemith had had problems with defective #25B switches on two other recent Lorelei projects. The contractor knew that these particular switches had a history of being defective and shorting out.

Dot Washington, a customer in the store on the day of the grand opening of the Lorelei Tea and Coffee Room, was electrocuted when turning on a #25B switch in the rest room. Dot Washington had a pacemaker in her heart, and the electrical shock caused a problem with the pacemaker. Dot was rushed to the hospital and treated, but she died. The defect in the switch was determined by scientific evidence through expert testimony.

Nathan Washington, Dot's husband, sues on his behalf and on behalf of his and Dot's minor child, Tanika. ■ ■ ■

16–1. THINK

What types of damages do you suppose have been suffered by Nathan and Tanika? Make a list. Check your list against the Jury Charge in Appendix A at the end of Chapter 1, Introduction to the Legal System and the Maxims of Law.

16–2. THINK

Dot's estate (through her husband) sues all the entities that might be jointly liable for her injuries. Who are those entities? Make a list. Check your list against the Jury Charge in Appendix A at the end of Chapter 1.

16–3. THINK

Why is it extremely unlikely, given only the preceding facts, that the following entities would be liable for any of Dot's damages under a theory of negligence?

Sunset Mall, Corporation, owner of the building

The Akimas

Dot Washington

Assume that this case was tried to a jury, and the jury found each of the following parties negligent as indicated in Table 16–1. Total damages for all plaintiffs were found to be $5,000,000. In addition to finding each of the parties negligent, the jury decided the percentage of liability for each of the parties to be as indicated.

Notice that none of the parties are insurance companies. Although it is extremely likely that insurance companies might have retained the lawyers to defend the various parties, *the insurance companies themselves are not parties to the lawsuit.* For example, the architect, Sondern and Blemith, might have errors and omissions insurance. When it received the lawsuit or a letter from Dot Washington's attorney, it would have contacted the company's insurance carrier, who would defend the lawsuit on its behalf.

Table 16–1 Tort Liability and Damages Payable by Jointly Liable Parties

Party	Liability	Damages (All Parties)
Owner (Sunset Mall Corporation)	0%	0
Franchisee/Lessor (the Akimas)	0%	0
Franchisor (Lorelei Tea, and Coffee, Inc.)	Liable for agent (architect) and employee (Construct) actions	Will have to pay architect and/or contractor's portions if architect or contractor cannot pay
Architect (Sondern and Blemith)	20%	$1,000,000
Prime contractor (Construct)	15%	$750,000
Subcontractor (Sung Lee)	0%	0
Supplier of switch (Acme)	5%	$250,000
Manufacturer of switch (Dante)	60%	$3,000,000
Customer (Dot Washington)	0%	0
TOTAL	100%	$5,000,000

Problems occur when one or more of the parties do not have the funds to pay their share of the damages. Who should pay the damages? Damages do not just disappear; someone always pays damages. If a tortfeasor cannot pay, then the injured party (or the injured party's insurance company) will have to absorb the damages.

16–4. THINK

When are the tortfeasor and the injured party the same?

Now, assume that the manufacturer of the switch, Dante, Inc., has no assets in the United States, or has gone out of business. Because damages do not disappear, the customer (or her estate in this case) would be required to absorb the damages related to the manufacturer's liability ($3,000,000 as shown in Table 16–2) if the law did not take this type of occurrence into account.

Should the innocent party, Dot, the customer, pay for the damages the manufacturer cannot pay? In this situation the law in most states requires the other tortfeasors, not the

Table 16–2 Damages Paid by Injured Party When One Jointly Liable Party Cannot Pay

Party	Liability as Determined by Jury	Damages
Architect (Sondern and Blemith)	20%	$1,000,000
Prime contractor (Construct)	15%	$750,000
Supplier of switch (Acme)	5%	$250,000
Manufacturer of switch (Dante)	60%	0
Customer (Dot Washington)	0%	$3,000,000

injured party, to pay. This is the concept of **joint and severable liability,** which says that each tortfeasor is *jointly* liable with the other tortfeasors for the total damages and is also *individually* liable for *all* the damages should none of the other tortfeasors be able to pay the damages.

Joint and Severable Liability

Rule: Each tortfeasor is jointly liable with the other tortfeasors for the total
damages suffered by the injured party, and
each tortfeasor is also individually liable (that is severably liable) for *all* the
damages suffered by the injured party
should none of the other tortfeasors be able to pay.

Dante's portion of the damages are calculated and paid by the other tortfeasors as follows: Each party's additional liability is determined by dividing its percentage of liability, as determined by the jury, by the sum of the percentages of the liability of the parties that are able to pay (in this case, 20% + 15% + 5% = 40%). This fraction is then multiplied by the amount of the damages owed by the party that cannot pay. Thus, the additional liability of the architect is (20%/40%) $\times$ $3,000,000 = $1,500,000. Table 16–3 shows the additional liability of each of the parties due to the inability of Dante to pay.

Because the architect, the contractor, and the supplier have paid for part of the liability of another tortfeasor, Dante, those parties have a claim for *contribution* against Dante.

Table 16-3   Damages Paid by Jointly and Severally Liable Parties When One Party Does Not Pay

Party	Liability as Determined by Jury	Liability if Manufacturer Does Not Pay	Additional Liability by Law	Total Liability of Party Including Portion of Manufacturer's Damages
Architect (Sondern (and Blemith)	20%	$1,000,000	$1,500,000	$2,500,000
Prime contractor (Construct)	15%	$750,000	$1,125,000	$1,875,000
Supplier of switch (Acme)	5%	$250,000	$375,000	$625,000
Manufacturer of switch (Dante)	60%	$0	$0	$0
Customer (Dot Washington)	0%	$3,000,000	$0	$0
TOTAL	100%	$5,000,000	$5,000,000	$5,000,000

Should Dante ever be financially able to pay, the architect, contractor, and supplier could attempt to collect from Dante. *The law puts the responsibility for obtaining these funds on the other tortfeasors, not on the injured party.* Of course, it is extremely unlikely the paying tortfeasors will be able to get any money from the manufacturer, Dante, Inc.

Settlement by a Jointly Liable Party

The concept of joint liability is further complicated when one or more parties settle prior to trial. *The law encourages settlement.* This is a basic legal maxim. Because of this legal maxim, it is possible for nonsettling parties to be required to pay a portion of the settling party's liability. This situation occurs when it is later determined that the settling party paid less than its percentage of liability—a very common occurrence in settlement. It is *not* uncommon for an injured party to accept less from a settling tortfeasor than will be awarded by the jury. This is one of the reasons settlement works—parties often pay less in settlement than they would by going to trial. Of course, they may pay more.

For example, referring again to the Dot Washington problem, assume that the manufacturer of the switch, Dante, Inc., agrees to settle for $1 million prior to trial; however, the other defendants refuse to settle. The jury comes back with the same verdict as outlined in Table 16–1. If the nonsettling defendants have to pay only their original liability, the law would thus not encourage the parties to this lawsuit, nor parties to future lawsuits, to settle. The following result, *not encouraging settlement,* would occur (see Table 16–4).

16–5. THINK

Why would the injured party settle for only $1 million from the manufacturer Dante, Inc., rather than for the $3 million that the jury would award?

Table 16-4 Damages Paid by Jointly and Severally Liable Parties When One Party Settles (Scenario 1)

Party	Liability as Determined by Jury	Damages Paid, Including Amount by Settling Party, Dante
Architect (Sondern and Blemith)	20%	$1,000,000
Prime Contractor (Construct)	15%	$750,000
Supplier of switch (Acme)	5%	$250,000
Manufacturer of switch (Dante)	60%	$1,000,000
Customer (Dot Washington)	0%	$2,000,000
TOTAL	100%	$5,000,000

However, in many jurisdictions the nonsettling parties would pay an increased amount, as indicated in Table 16–5. The law in this area varies widely by jurisdiction and is currently being tested and changed. Local law must be consulted on this issue.

Indemnification and Contribution

In the defective switch example assume that Nathan Washington sued *only* the franchisor, Lorelei Tea and Coffee, Inc. Perhaps Nathan did not know who the prime contractor was, who the architect was, or who manufactured the switch. The franchisor, Lorelei Tea and Coffee, Inc., would likely seek indemnification from the other parties for their share of the damage liability to Nathan and Tanika. The franchisor can do this by bringing the other parties it believes to be jointly liable into the lawsuit. The court or jury will ultimately determine which party is liable for what.

Contribution refers to situations in which one jointly liable party has paid for damages and seeks to be reimbursed by other jointly liable parties. Sometimes one party (or, more likely, that party's insurance company) settles with the injured party and pays the injured party's damages. The paying party (or insurance company) may later seek to be reimbursed for some or all of the damages it has paid to the injured party from *other* jointly liable parties. In the defective switch example, if the manufacturer, Dante, or the manufacturer's insurance company were to pay $1,000,000 to Nathan Washington in settlement of the claim, Dante could seek contribution from the architect, the prime contractor, the subcontractor, and the supplier.

A common example of this recovery of payment occurs in the area of automobile accident claims. Assume you cause injury to Peter Pedestrian by striking him with your car while running a stop sign. You were on an errand for your employer to pick up some tools

Table 16-5 Damages Paid by Jointly and Severally Liable Parties When One Party Settles (Scenario 2)

Party	Liability as Determined by Jury	Damages Paid, Including Amount by Settling Party, Dante, if Law Did Not Encourage Settlement	Additional Damages because Party Refused to Settle	Total Damages Paid by Each Defendant
Architect (Sondern and Blemith)	20%	$1,000,000	$1,000,000	$2,000,000
Prime contractor (Construct)	15%	$750,000	$750,000	$1,500,000
Supplier of switch (Acme)	5%	$250,000	$250,000	$500,000
Manufacturer of switch (Dante)	60%	$1,000,000	0	$1,000,000
Customer (Dot Washington)	0%	$2,000,000	0	0
TOTAL		$5,000,000	$2,000,000	$5,000,000

and supplies needed on a particular job. Peter Pedestrian's health insurance company pays for Peter's medical bills. The health insurance company can sue you and your employer for contribution—that is, reimbursement for the money it has paid.

Indemnity and Indemnity Clauses

Because of the complexity of the construction process, issues of joint liability are extremely common. In order to reduce attorney fees and other associated costs, it is common for the parties involved in a particular project to agree that one party will bear all the liability for certain events or risks. The specific name for this type of contract is an **indemnity clause.** Note that many clauses in the construction contract allocate risk among the parties for various events. Indemnity clauses are specialized clauses that have been developed to allocate risks associated with *joint liability for torts and accidents.*

For example, the general contractor may agree to be responsible for any damage caused by fire, no matter how the fire occurs. The contractor usually obtains insurance for this risk. If the employee of a subcontractor starts a fire, the contractor, or its insurance company will be responsible for the damages. This reduces the insurance costs on a project because the subcontractors and owners do not need to purchase fire insurance also.

Because of its power to transfer risk, it is not uncommon for the stronger or less hungry party in a negotiation to transfer or attempt to transfer all types of risk away from itself and onto the weaker, hungrier party. (This is not a new concept—this has been going on for centuries in all kinds of relationships, both business and personal.) The law may look carefully at these clauses and strike them or modify them if they are onerous. Onerous clauses are discussed in Chapter 8, Specifications and Plans.

Indemnity clauses also have the effect of lessening the amount of care exercised by the entity that has transferred the risk to another. For example, if the owner inserts a clause that states that the contractor is liable for all damages caused by fire, then the owner's employees and the subcontractors' employees are likely to be less careful of fire prevention. The law does not encourage people to be less careful, and if the amount of care is drastically reduced, the law may not uphold the clause.

It is impossible to transfer all risk, however. Even if risk has been transferred, there are costs associated in making sure that the risk acceptor will comply with the risk-transferring agreement. Also, there is no way to transfer the risk that a lawsuit may be filed, because anyone can sue anyone for anything at any time. There may be legal and financial repercussions or punishments for filing frivolous lawsuits, but there is no legal way to prevent anyone from *filing* a lawsuit.

Three types of indemnity clauses exist:

- Limited
- Intermediate
- Broad

Indemnity clauses are some of the most difficult clauses in a contract to understand; however, the effects of the different clauses are so great that it is always important to understand which clause your contract contains.

Limited Form Indemnity Clause

The **limited form indemnity clause** states that one party will pay *only* for damages it causes. This clause is merely a restatement of the law and does not change the relationships of the parties. The following is a very simple limited indemnity clause:

> *The contractor agrees to repay the owner for any damages or sums that the owner pays to an injured party on account of the acts of the contractor.*

It is extremely unlikely that such a simple clause would appear in a contract. It has been included here merely to help you understand the following more realistic example of a limited indemnity clause that might be found in a construction contract.

Limited Form Indemnity Clause

A party agrees to be responsible for damages caused by that party.

In this clause the subcontractor is agreeing to be responsible to the owner and prime contractor *only for damages the subcontractor causes* should the subcontractor and some other party be jointly liable for damages for some event:

> *Subcontractor shall at all times indemnify, defend, and hold harmless General Contractor and Owner from all loss, damage, lawsuits, arbitrations, mechanic's liens, legal actions of any kind, attorney's fees, and/or costs caused or contributed to by, or claimed to be caused or contributed to by, any act, omission, fault, and/or negligence, whether passive, or active, of Subcontractor or its agents or employees, in connection with the Work but only to the extent caused by the Subcontractor or its agents or employees.*

In the defective switch example, a limited indemnity clause such as the preceding might exist in the contracts between the various parties. In that event each party would pay the damages as outlined in Table 16–1. This clause does not change the law or the risk of any of the parties.

Intermediate Form Indemnity Clause

The **intermediate form clause** states that one party will pay for *all damages* even if it is only *partially* responsible for the damage. This type of clause changes the law and the amount of damages a party would otherwise have to pay. This clause shifts the legal liability off of one party and onto another if both are partially liable. Parties agree to this clause for several reasons, the primary one being that the party accepting the liability buys an insurance policy covering the risk, relieving the other parties of the need to purchase such insurance. The following is a very simple intermediate indemnity clause:

> *The contractor agrees to pay all damages to any injured party, as long as the contractor is at least partially at fault for the damage.*

It is extremely unlikely that such a simple clause would appear in a contract. It has been included here merely to help you understand the following more realistic example of an intermediate indemnity clause.

Intermediate Form Indemnity Clause

A party agrees to be responsible for *all* damages even if it was only partially responsible for the damages.

In this clause the contractor is agreeing to be responsible to the owner for *all* damages (not just the contractor's portion) should the contractor *and* the owner/designer be jointly liable for some event. This clause is very difficult to read, so striking out or highlighting certain language in the clause helps decipher it. This trick is often helpful in understanding difficult clauses. Just remember that the stricken language will have an effect in some situations, so you must be careful when employing this trick. Reading only the bold type in the following clause will simplify the language for you and help you understand what is being said.

> To the fullest extent permitted by law, **Contractor shall indemnify and hold harmless Owner,** its consultants and agents and employees of any of them **from** and against claims, **damages,** losses, and expenses, including but not limited to attorney's fees, arising out of or resulting from performance of the Work, provided that such claim, damage, loss, or expense is attributable to bodily injury, sickness, disease, or death, or to injury to or destruction of tangible property (other than the work itself) including loss of use resulting therefrom, **whether caused in whole or *in part* by negligent acts or omissions of the Contractor** or anyone directly or indirectly employed by them or anyone for whose acts they may be liable, regardless of whether or not such claim, damage, loss, or expense is caused in part by a party indemnified hereunder.

In the defective switch example, the damages paid by the parties as indicated in Table 16–1 would change as shown in Table 16–6 if the preceding clause existed in the construction contracts between the owner, architect, prime contractor, and subcontractor.

Table 16–6 Damages Paid with Intermediate Form Clause

Party	Liability	Damages Paid by Party
Owner (Sunset Mall)	0%	0
Franchisee/Lessor (the Akimas)	0%	0
Franchisor (Lorelei Tea and Coffee, Inc.)	Liable for agent (architect) and employee (Construct) actions	Will have to pay architect and/or contractor's portions if architect or contractor cannot pay
Architect (Sondern and Blemith)	20%—payable by contractor pursuant to indemnity clause	0
Prime Contractor (Construct)	15%	$5,000,000
Subcontractor (Sung Lee)	0%	0
Supplier of switch (Acme)	5%—payable by contractor pursuant to indemnity clause	0
Manufacturer of switch (Dante)	60%—payable by contractor pursuant to indemnity clause	0
Customer (Dot Washington)	0%	0

16–6. THINK

In the defective switch example, assume that the subcontract between the contractor, Construct, and the subcontractor, Sung Lee, contains the following clause:

> The subcontractor agrees to pay all damages to any injured party, as long as the subcontractor is at least partially at fault for the damage.

Sung Lee still does not owe any damages to anyone. Why not?

16–7. THINK

In the defective switch example, assume that the contract between the owner and the prime contractor contains an intermediate form indemnity clause. Assume the following additional information:

Architect's attorney fees and costs	$10,000
Subcontractor's attorney fees and costs	$10,000

a. For how much of the architect's attorney fees is the prime contractor liable?

b. For how much of the subcontractor's attorney fees is the prime contractor liable?

Intermediate clauses are unlawful in some jurisdictions, or are lawful only if the clause is in bold type or is otherwise brought to the risk-absorbing-party's attention. See Appendix A to this chapter for a list of state statutes that limit the enforceability of indemnity clauses to some extent.

Broad Form Indemnity Clause

A **broad form indemnity clause** states that one party will pay for *all damages* even if that one party has *not* caused *any* of the damage. This clause shifts the legal liability off one party and onto another for all events. For example, assume that the following simplified broad form clause exists in the contract between the prime contractor, Constructor, and the subcontractor, Sung Lee, in the Dot Washington case:

> *The subcontractor agrees to pay all damages to any party injured as a result of the work of this project.*

It is extremely unlikely such a simple clause would appear in a contract. It has been included here merely to help you understand the following more realistic broad form indemnity clause.

Broad Form Indemnity Clause

A party agrees to be responsible for all damages, whether that party has any legal liability or not.

Like the limited form indemnity clause this clause is difficult to read. Certain parts have been highlighted to aid you in understanding the clause. In this clause the subcontractor is agreeing to be responsible to the owner and architect for *all* damages relating to an event, even if the subcontractor has no liability.

> To the fullest extent permitted by law, **Subcontractor shall indemnify and hold harmless Contractor, Owner,** its consultants and agents and employees of any of them **from** and against claims, **damages,** losses, and expenses, including but not limited to attorney's fees, arising out of or resulting from performance of the Work, provided that such claim, damage, loss, or expense is attributable to bodily injury, sickness, disease, or death, or to injury to or destruction of tangible property (other than the work itself) including loss of use resulting therefrom, **for any negligent acts or omissions of the Subcontractor or the Contractor or the Designer** or anyone directly or indirectly employed by them or anyone for whose acts they may be liable, regardless of **whether or not** such claim, damage, loss, or expense is **caused in whole or in part by the Subcontractor.**

Table 16-7   Damages Payable with Broad Form Clause

Party	Liability	Damages
Owner (C-Mall Corporation)	0%	0
Franchisee/Lessor (the Akimas)	0%	0
Franchisor (Lorelei Tea and Coffee, Inc.)	Liable for agent (architect) and employee (Construct) actions	Will have to pay architect and/or contractor's portions if architect or contractor cannot pay
Architect (Sondern and Blemith)	20%	0
Prime contractor (Construct)	15%	0
Subcontractor (Sung Lee)	0%	$5,000,000
Supplier of switch (Acme)	5%	0
Manufacturer of switch (Dante)	60%	0
Customer (Dot Washington)	0%	0

Compare Table 16–7 with the preceding tables illustrating the defective switch example. In all previous tables the subcontractor has been found not negligent and therefore owes nothing either to Dot Washington or to any other party; however, the result of the preceding broad form indemnity clause is that the subcontractor is now liable for *all* the damages.

Broad form indemnity clauses have come under the most legal attack and are unlawful in many jurisdictions. See Appendix A to this chapter for a list of state statutes that limit indemnity clauses to some extent.

Insurance Coverage and Indemnity Clauses

The effect of intermediate and broad form indemnification clauses can be financially devastating. It is important to be aware of the types of indemnification clauses in your contracts. Parties agreeing to such clauses may believe their insurance company will automatically cover the increased risk, but this is not generally the case.

Insurance does *not* automatically cover the risks accepted by a party through an indemnity clause. Unless the party accepting the risk has informed its insurance company that it has accepted additional risk through a limited or broad form indemnification clause, the party may *not* be covered by insurance for that risk. If the party is not covered by insurance, then the party is personally liable for any damages that become due under the clause. The existence of insurance is irrelevant to the applicability of an indemnity clause!

Insurance Coverage and Indemnity Clauses

Insurance does not automatically protect a party who accepts liability or risk under an intermediate or broad form indemnity clause.

Be sure to confer with your insurance agent when you agree to indemnify anyone because your existing policy may or may not cover any losses incurred. For example, assume that you have a policy protecting *you* from damages caused by fire on the site. By contract you agree to indemnify the owner for damages related to fire, including fire damage to areas adjacent to the work site. A fire occurs on the construction site and spreads to an adjacent building (not part of your project) owned by the owner. Some of your tools are destroyed in the fire.

Your insurance company will pay you for your tools. *You* will pay for the damage to the owner's building. Your insurance policy will not pay for the damage to the owner's property because it protects only *you*. In order to obtain insurance for the risk you have accepted you need to obtain a policy that insures you *and* the *owner.*

Additional Insured

Many contracts require one party—for example, the contractor—to add another party—for example, the owner—onto an insurance policy. This clause shifts the legal liability off of one party and onto the insurance carrier for all covered events. For example, assume that the contract requires the contractor to add the owner onto the contractor's general liability insurance policy as an **additional insured** entity under the policy. In the event of a claim, the contractor's insurance will defend the owner and will pay damages due from the owner.

Additional Insured

A party agrees to add another party onto the first party's insurance.

The practical effect of requiring someone to be named an additional insured is the same as the broad form indemnity provision. For reasons beyond the scope of this text, requiring someone to be named as an additional insured is not as abhorrent to the law as the broad form indemnity clause. It is likely that the court or arbitrator will uphold the validity of an additional insured clause.

Vocabulary Checklist

Joint liability	Joint and severable liability	Intermediate form indemnity clause
Defense	Indemnity clauses	Broad form indemnity clause
Indemnity action	Limited form indemnity clause	Additional insured
Contribution action		

Review Questions

1. How is it possible for several people to cause or contribute to one loss?

2. What does the law say should happen when several parties have contributed to one loss?

3. How and why do problems occur when one (or more) of the parties causing an injury does not have the funds to pay its share of the damages?

4. Assume that several people and businesses contribute to one injury. Under what circumstances would *one* of these parties be forced to pay *all* the damages?

5. How does the law encourage the settlement of multiparty claims?

6. Is there some way that a tortfeasor paying more than its share of the damages can try to recoup some of the amounts paid from other parties?

7. Why do owners and contractors put indemnity clauses in their contracts?

8. Why is naming someone as an additional insured on your policy the same as a broad form indemnity clause?

Problems

Answer the issue in each of the following problems by making a legal argument, including premises in support of your answer.

1. Mr. Zanowiak, architect on a certain project, makes an error in the plans and specifications relating to the design of a stairwell. The contractor, Mr. Ovidio, builds *exactly* according to the plans and specs. The architect's error causes a stairwell to collapse and injure an employee of the contractor, Ms. Takao, who is working on the site. Workers' compensation insurance and law is not an issue.

   Issue: Are the architect and the contractor jointly liable for the injuries to the employee?
   Rule: (*Hint:* causation)
   Premises:
   Answer: No

2. The architect, Ms. Alphonse, makes an error in the plans and specs relating to the design of a stairwell. The contractor, Dwarshus Construction, builds exactly according to the plans and specifications; however, one of its employees allows too much water in the concrete mix, causing weak concrete. The architect's error and the contractor's error cause a stairwell to collapse and injure a customer, Mark Linen, using the stairway shortly after the project is terminated. (Assume no statute of limitations or repose issues in this problem.) Expert witnesses testify that neither error alone would have caused the collapse of the stairwell, but the two errors operating together did cause the accident. Experts also testify that reasonable architects and contractors would have procedures in place to find and correct this type of error.

   Issue: Are the architect and the contractor jointly liable for the injuries to Mark Linen?
   Rule: (*Hint:* negligence, you have to use information in Chapter 15, Torts and Tort Damages, to find the rule and prepare your argument.)

Premises:

Answer: Yes

3. Assume the same facts as in problem 2, except that the following clause exists in the contract between the prime contractor and the owner:

> 14.3: **Contractor** agrees to indemnify and hold harmless owner and its employees from any and all claims, causes of action, damage, or liability due to personal injury or property damage, or both, including loss of use, arising from or on account of the fault of contractor or **caused in part by any act** or omission, whether passive, or active, **of owner** and anyone directly or indirectly employed by owner [emphasis added].

Assume that the law in the jurisdiction will uphold all forms of indemnification clauses.

Issue: Is the contractor responsible for all or part of the damages to the employee?

Rule: (*Hint:* Just apply the provision.)

Premises:

Answer:

4. Assume the same facts as in problem 2, except that the following clause exists in the contract between the prime contractor and the owner:

> *31.3: Contractor agrees to indemnify and hold harmless Owner and the Architect from any and all claims, causes of action, damage, or liability due to personal injury or property damage, or both, including loss of use, arising from or on account of the fault of Contractor and anyone directly or indirectly employed by Contractor.*

Assume that the law in the jurisdiction will uphold all forms of indemnification clauses.

Issue: Is the contractor responsible for all or part of the damages to the employee?

Rule: (*Hint:* Just apply the provision.)

Premises:

Answer:

What is difference between the preceding clause and the clause in problem 3?

5. Borough Inc., the general contractor, contracted with Noble Design to prepare the initial plans for a subdivision. The contract between Borough and Noble contained the following clause:

> *Noble agrees to indemnify and hold harmless Borough from any and all claims, causes of action, damage, or liability due to personal injury or property damage, or both, including loss of use, arising from or on account of the fault of Noble and anyone directly or indirectly employed by Noble.*

A road-building contractor, Boram Heavy Construction, encountered extreme difficulties meeting the specifications prepared by Noble for the project and filed suit against Noble and Borough, alleging design deficiencies, negligence, and professional malpractice. Borough hired an attorney, Joe Basham, to represent it in the litigation. Mr. Basham filed a cross-claim for indemnity against Noble. Mr. Basham also sent his monthly bills to Noble for payment.

Assume that the law in the jurisdiction will uphold all forms of indemnification clauses.

Issue 1: Must Noble Design indemnify Borough?

Rule: (*Hint:* Just apply the provision.)

Premises:

Answer: Yes

Issue 2: Must Noble Design pay Mr. Basham's attorney fee bills?

Rule: (*Hint:* Just apply the provision.)

Premises:

Answer: No

6. Assume the same facts as in problem 5, except the clause in the contract between Noble and Borough is as follows:

> To the fullest extent permitted by law, Noble Design shall indemnify and hold harmless Borough, its consultants and agents and employees of any of them from and against claims, damages, losses, and expenses, including but not limited to attorney's fees, arising out of or resulting from performance of the Work, provided that such claim, damage, loss, or expense is attributable to bodily injury, sickness, disease, or death, or to injury to or destruction of tangible property (other than the work itself) including loss of use resulting therefrom, but only to the extent caused in whole or in part by negligent acts or omissions of Noble Design or anyone directly or indirectly employed by them or anyone for whose acts they may be liable, regardless of whether or not such claim, damage, loss, or expense is caused in part by a party indemnified hereunder.

Assume that the law in the jurisdiction will uphold all forms of indemnification clauses.

Issue 1: Must Noble Design indemnify Borough?

Rule: (*Hint:* Just apply the provision.)

Premises:

Answer: Yes

Issue 2: Must Noble Design pay Mr. Basham's attorney fee bills?

Rule: (*Hint:* Just apply the provision.)

Premises:

Answer: Yes

Question: What is the difference in meaning between the preceding clause and the clause in problem 5 above?

7. The following clause exists in the contract between Summerville Construction and Thomas McGarvie, Owner: (*Note:* This is the same clause as in the preceding problem—only the names are changed.)

> To the fullest extent permitted by law, the Contractor shall indemnify and hold harmless the Owner, Architect, Architect's consultants and agents and employees of any of them from and against claims, damages, losses, and expenses, including but not limited to attorney's fees, arising out of or resulting from performance of the Work, provided that such claim, damage, loss, or expense is attributable to bodily injury, sickness, disease, or death, or to injury to or destruction of tangible property (other than the work itself) including loss of use resulting therefrom, but only to the extent caused in whole or in part by negligent acts or omissions of the Contractor, a Subcontractor, anyone directly or indirectly employed by them, or anyone for whose acts they may be liable, regardless of whether or not such claim, damage, loss, or expense is caused in part by a party indemnified hereunder.

Contractor's subcontractor, Jerral, was placing a very large strut. While placing the strut, Jerral dropped it. Parts of the project collapsed, injuring several persons, including an employee of the subcontractor, an employee of the prime contractor, an employee of the designer, and a group of Girl Scouts who were visiting the site. The total medical bills and lost wages of these injured parties were $450,000. The designer's architect spent $250,000 defending the lawsuits. In addition, the work was damaged and had to be redone. The cost for doing this was $300,000. Workers' compensation insurance and law is not an issue.

All experts testify that the architect's design for placing the strut was defective. No experts testify that the contractor was in any way negligent.

Issue: Who is liable for the damages?

Rule: (*Hint:* Apply the provision.)

Premises:

Answer: (*Hint:* Contractor is liable for only part of the damages if negligent.)

Questions: What are the damages? Who is likely to pay for the damages for which the contractor is *not* liable?

8. Sylvester, the subcontractor on a new stadium project, was placing a very large and heavy strut. He complained to the prime (independent) contractor's supervisor, Ms. Kalahan, that the operation was very dangerous because the design of the support structures and the type of material required by the plans and specs did not appear to the subcontractor to be strong enough to hold the strut. Sylvester said the likelihood of collapse was great. Sylvester had over thirty years of experience but was not an engineer. In fact, he did not finish high school. Ms. Kalahan, the supervisor, said, "Don't worry about it. That's the engineer's problem, and we are just following the plans and specifications."

The support structures for the strut collapsed and injured employees of other subcontractors on the site. The jury or arbitrator decided the liability for the accident was 95% the fault of the engineer and 5% the fault of the prime contractor for failing to heed the advice of Sylvester and to do something that might have prevented the accident. Workers' compensation insurance and law is not an issue.

Issue: Who is liable for the damages to the injured employees?

Rule: (*Hint:* There is no contract provision.)

Premises:

Answer:

9. Assume the same facts as in problem 8, except that the following provision exists in the contract:

> *To the fullest extent permitted by law, the Contractor shall indemnify and hold harmless the Owner, Architect, Architect's consultants and agents and employees of any of them from and against claims, damages, losses, and expenses, including but not limited to attorney's fees, arising out of or resulting from performance of the Work, provided that such claim, damage, loss, or expense is attributable to bodily injury, sickness, disease, or death, or to injury to or destruction of tangible property (other than the work itself) including loss of use resulting therefrom, but only to the extent caused in whole or in part by negligent acts or omissions of the Contractor, a Subcontractor, anyone directly or indirectly employed by them, or anyone for whose acts they may be liable, regardless of whether or not such claim, damage, loss, or expense is caused in part by a party indemnified hereunder.*

Assume the jurisdiction is one that will enforce any type of indemnity clause.

Issue: Who is liable for the damages to the injured employees?

Rule: (*Hint:* There *is* a contract provision.)

Premises:

Answer:

10. Assume the same facts as in problem 8, except that the following provision exists in the contract:

> *Contractor shall at all times indemnify, defend and hold harmless Owner and its agents and employees from all loss and damage, lawsuits, arbitrations, mechanic's liens, legal actions of any kind, attorney's fees, and/or costs caused or contributed by, or claimed to be caused or contributed to by, any act, omission, fault, and/or negligence, whether passive or active, of Contractor or its agents or employees, in connection with the Work but only to the extent caused by the Contractor or its agents or employees.*

Issue: Who is liable for the damages to the injured employees?

Rule: (*Hint:* Apply the contract provision.)

Premises:

Answer:

Answers to Selected Problems

1. Mr. Zanowiak, architect on a certain project, makes an error in the plans and. . . .

   Issue: Are the architect and the contractor jointly liable for the injuries to the employee?

   Rule: Causation. Parties are responsible only for damages they cause.

   Premises: Only the architect is responsible, because only the architect's error caused the stairwell to collapse. Mr. Ovidio did nothing to cause the stairwell to collapse.

   Answer: No

5. Borough Inc., the general contractor, contracted with Noble Design to prepare. . . .

   Issue 1: Must Noble Design indemnify Borough?

   Rule: Basic maxim of contract law: A party must honor its contract.

   Premises: The contract states "Noble agrees to indemnify and hold harmless Borough from any and all claims. . . damages." Noble is responsible. This is an intermediate form indemnity clause.

   Answer: Yes

Appendix A State Statutes Limiting Indemnity Clauses

Alaska: § 45.45.900 (1999)

Arizona: A.R.S. § 32-1159 (1999)

California: Cal. Civ. Code § 1668 (1999)

Connecticut: Conn. Gen. Stat. § 52-572-k (1999)

Florida: Florida Stat. § 725.06 (1999)

Georgia: O.C.G.A. § 13-8-2 (1999)

Illinois: 740 ILCS 35/1 (1999)

Indiana: Burns Ind. Code § 26-2-5-1 (1999)

Maryland: Courts and Judicial Proceedings Code Ann. § 5-401 (1999)

Massachusetts: Mass. Ann. Laws ch. 106, § 2-316A (1999)

Michigan: MSA § 26.1146(1) (1999)

Mississippi: Miss. Code Ann. § 31-5-41 (1999)

Missouri: § 434.100 R.S.Mo. (1999)

Montana: Mont. Code Ann. § 2802-702 (1999)

New York: NY CLS Gen. Oblig. § 5-322.1 (1999)

North Dakota: N.D. Cent. Code § 31-11-05[34] (1999)

Ohio: Ohio Rev. Code Ann. 2305.31 (Anderson 1999)

Puerto Rico: 31 L.P.R.A. § 3372 (1999)

Rhode Island: R.I. Gen. Laws § 6-34-1 (1999)

South Carolina: S.C. Code Ann. § 32-2-10 (1998)

South Dakota: S.D. Codified Laws § 56-3-16 (1999)

Tennessee: Tenn. Code Ann. § 62-6-123 (1999)

Texas: Tex. Civ. Prac. & Rem. § 130.002 (1999)

Utah: Utah Code Ann. § 13-8-1 (1999)

Virginia: Va. Code Ann. § 11-4.1 (1999)

Washington: Rev. Code Wash. (ARCW) § 4.24.115 (1999)

17

Bankruptcy

Introduction

Federal bankruptcy law accomplishes many different goals for many different types of entities: businesses, people, railroads, and municipalities, to name a few. This chapter briefly reviews fundamental federal bankruptcy law relating to individuals and to business entities *only.* Many states have laws similar to federal bankruptcy law; however, state law is not as widely used and will not be reviewed here. Bankruptcy proceedings can be very complicated, and the advice of an attorney is recommended.

What happens when a bankruptcy is filed? In extremely simplified terms, the case is turned over to a **bankruptcy trustee,** who is an independent person charged by the law to handle the bankruptcy. The person filing the bankruptcy is called the **debtor,** and the entities to which the debtor owes money are called the **creditors.** In rehabilitation bankruptcies a creditor committee is often formed to make suggestions and review acts of the trustee and the debtor. The bankruptcy trustee does many things including helping to make sure that the debtor and the creditors follow the law. The trustee will attempt to marshal (collect), and liquidate (sell) the *nonexempt* assets of the debtor and use the money to pay off the creditors. Exempt assets are discussed more fully later.

Types of Bankruptcy

It is common to refer to a bankruptcy by the chapter of the Bankruptcy Code under which the bankruptcy has been filed, for example, Chapter 7 bankruptcy. The three most common forms of bankruptcy in the personal and business arenas and the ones reviewed in this chapter, are:

- Chapter 7, or debt liquidation
- Chapter 11, or business reorganization, and
- Chapter 13, or individual reorganization.

Other chapters of the Bankruptcy Code handle bankruptcies for government bodies, railroads, and other situations beyond the scope of this text.

Chapter 7: Liquidation

Under Chapter 7 of the Bankruptcy Code certain *unsecured debts of individuals are discharged.* **Discharged** means wiped out or done away with. An **unsecured debt** is a debt for which the creditor holds no security. For example, credit card debts are unsecured, but home loans are usually secured by a home and the real estate on which it sits.

The most common types of unsecured debt that are discharged are credit card debts and personal loans. Child support debts and student loans are examples of unsecured debts that cannot be discharged. Damages owed for the commission of an intentional tort are not dischargeable, but negligence damages are dischargeable. Very specific laws outline which debts are and are not dischargeable.

Businesses may file under this chapter, but *the debts of a business are never discharged.* In theory, the debts could be collected if the business should have sufficient assets at some point in the future; however, in actual practice, businesses that file for liquidation seldom if ever operate again, and so the debts are uncollectable.

Secured debts are never discharged in bankruptcy. Secured debts and the assets that secure them flow through the bankruptcy, for the most part unaffected by the bankruptcy. **Secured debts** are debts for which the creditor holds an interest in some asset as security for the debt. This interest is generally called *security* or a *secured interest.*

For example, when you buy a new car on credit you do not have free and clear title or the sole interest in the car. The title or interest in the car, is divided between you and the lender. In effect, the lender has a part of the title or interest in the car until you have paid it off. Because the lender has an interest in the car, the lender can come and take your car should you fail to make payments. In such a case the lender is taking back only what it already has an interest in—your car.

17-1. THINK

List any unsecured debts you have.

17-2. THINK

List any secured debts you have. List any secured debts you are likely to incur in the future.

17–3. THINK

A small electrical subcontractor, Jason Cheng, makes a mistake in the wiring of a building, causing it to burn to the ground and kill twelve people. The estimated damages to these people and the building are in the millions of dollars. Mr. Cheng files a Chapter 7 bankruptcy listing the estimated damages as one of his debts. Can this debt be discharged in the bankruptcy?

All persons filing a bankruptcy are allowed to keep some of their assets, and the remaining assets are sold to pay off the debts. The assets the debtor keeps are called **exempt assets** or **exemptions.** All the states and the federal government have a list of exempt assets. For example, the list usually allows the debtor to keep household items such as dishes and furniture. The debtor is generally free to choose which list will apply. Appendix A to this chapter contains a list of selected federal bankruptcy exemptions.

People are sometimes amazed that a person can file bankruptcy and still keep a fancy car and a nice house. There may be several reasons for this. The most common reason for a debtor's keeping the valuable property is that the property is security for a debt, and there is very little equity in the asset. Secured debts and the assets that secure the debts merely flow through the bankruptcy. Only if the debtor stops making the payments on the secured asset will the item be foreclosed on by the creditors. If the debtor is able to maintain the payments, the debtor can keep the property.

The debtor may be able to keep a very expensive home because some states, such as Florida and Texas, have very liberal exemption laws for homes. The debtor may be entitled to keep the property if it is leased. If the property is leased, it does not belong to the debtor. Some leasehold interests may become assets of the estate. This issue is beyond the scope of this text.

Chapter 11: Business Reorganization

A Chapter 11 bankruptcy is often referred to as **business reorganization** bankruptcy. It is designed to give a business some breathing room in order to allow it to get back on its feet.

Once the reorganization bankruptcy is filed the debtor continues to operate the business. At this point the debtor is often referred to as the **debtor-in-possession** because the debtor is in possession of the business. The debtor can operate the business, but it does so under the watchful eye of the bankruptcy trustee and the creditors. The debtor must pay all bills incurred after the filing of the bankruptcy. If the debtor fails to pay all new debts incurred after the date of filing the bankruptcy, it can be forced into a Chapter 7 bankruptcy. This will result in the liquidation of all assets and generally the closure of the business. Most people operating businesses do not want the business to be closed—if they did, they would have filed a liquidation or Chapter 7 bankruptcy in the first place.

Chapter 13: Individual Reorganization

A Chapter 13 bankruptcy is similar to a Chapter 11 except that it is designed to allow individuals time to pay off their debts. One significant difference between a Chapter 13 and a Chapter 11 bankruptcy is that the *individual may choose to pay only a portion of his or her unsecured debts.* Some of the unsecured debts can be discharged as if the bankruptcy were a Chapter 7 bankruptcy. The exact amount the individual must repay varies and is beyond the scope of this text.

A Chapter 13 bankruptcy is advantageous to the individual in that his or her assets are not liquidated, and some but not all of the unsecured debts can be discharged. This type of bankruptcy usually does not have as adverse an effect on the debtor's credit.

Automatic Stay

One of the most important things a businessperson needs to know about bankruptcy is that the *filing* of a bankruptcy invokes the *automatic stay.* The **automatic stay** is a court order preventing the creditors from attempting to collect any debts or harming the bankruptcy estate. The stay is effective nationwide and is operative without any formal notice. It comes into force as soon as the court clerk stamps the bankruptcy papers for filing; however, the court will send a notice of the stay to all creditors listed by the debtor in the papers filed with the court, so most creditors become aware of the stay within a few days of the filing of the bankruptcy.

Failure to abide by the stay is punishable by contempt proceedings, which can include fines and imprisonment. For example, the creditor cannot call the debtor and try to coerce the debtor into paying the debt once the bankruptcy is filed. Although most courts will not punish actions in violation of the stay if the creditor has no notice of the stay, the courts will require *return of any assets seized* even if the creditor had no notice of the bankruptcy.

For example, assume that the owner files for a bankruptcy. The automatic stay prevents the contractor from terminating a construction project without approval from the bankruptcy trustee and the court. At first glance this may sound like a problem to the contractor, but in reality it is usually a relief to the contractor. The owner need *not* pay other creditors but *must* pay the contractor or risk being forced into a liquidation bankruptcy.

Some examples of acts stayed by the automatic stay are:

- Commencement/continuation of creditors' lawsuits against the debtor (but not vice versa)
- Enforcement of a judgment
- Collection of debts or claims
- Setoffs of debt
- Termination of a contract

17–4. THINK

> AIA A201 gives the contractor the right to terminate the contract should the owner not pay the contractor. The owner files for bankruptcy prior to one of the scheduled payments. Can the contractor terminate the contract? Why or why not?

Mechanic's Liens and the Automatic Stay

The law is not entirely settled, but most jurisdictions allow the perfection of a mechanic's lien after a bankruptcy has been filed. **Perfection** is the term used to indicate that all the state laws and recording requirements necessary to have a valid and enforceable mechanic's lien, have been complied with. The automatic stay will prevent the *foreclosure* of the mechanic's lien, however. This means the contractor or subcontractor can file all the necessary papers as required by the state law to protect the lien but cannot foreclose on it.

Executory Contracts

The bankruptcy code gives the bankruptcy trustee or the debtor-in-possession the power, with court approval, to assume or reject executory contracts and unexpired leases.[1] An **executory contract** is one in which the parties continue to have duties and obligations to each other under the contract. Construction contracts are executory contracts until the last item on the punch list has been completed.

In other words, once the owner files a bankruptcy, the bankruptcy trustee or the owner has the power to continue with a construction project. Although it is likely the bankruptcy trustee and/or owner will want to continue with the project, he or she does not have to. The project is likely to be completed because a completed project is worth more than an uncompleted project. It is much more costly to bring in a new contractor to complete a project than it is to finish the project with the existing contractor.

Fraudulent Transfers and Preferences

When a bankruptcy is filed the bankruptcy trustee is given the power to void or nullify certain transfers of money or property made *up to one year prior* to the filing of the bankruptcy.[2] For example, assume that the debtor transfers assets to family members or other businesses to remove them from debtor's estate. The debtor then files bankruptcy. These transfers will be labeled **fraudulent transfers,** and the trustee can void them and force the recipient to return the money or property to the estate.

Another power of the trustee is the nullification of preferential payments.[3] A **preferential payment** is a payment made by the debtor for which the debtor has not received new value. For example, the debtor may owe his mother $50,000 for money borrowed a few years ago to start up the business. The debtor also owes $50,000 in credit card bills. The debtor pays his mother $50,000, then files bankruptcy attempting to have the credit card bills discharged. It is possible for the trustee to force the mother to deposit the $50,000 into

---

[1] 11 U.S.C. § 365.

[2] 11 U.S.C. § 548.

[3] 11 U.S.C. § 547(b).

the bankruptcy estate. The trustee can void preferential payments made ninety days prior to the filing of a bankruptcy.

If the payment is made by the debtor in exchange for an asset, then the payment is not considered preferential. This is because the asset is part of the estate. For example, if the debtor pays the supplier of parts for those parts, the debt is not preferential. If the debtor pays the supplier on an outstanding invoice, the payment is preferential.

Specific Effects of Bankruptcy on Construction Contracts

The following can occur in a construction-related bankruptcy:

- The trustee may force you to return payments made to you by the debtor. (See the discussion of fraudulent transfers and preferences.)
- Lien rights may be altered. (See the discussion of the automatic stay.)
- You may be dealing with a trustee, not the owner, or contractor on a project, or you may be dealing with a creditors' committee.
- If the debtor is an owner, the retainage becomes an asset of the bankruptcy estate and not an amount owed to the contractor. Most contracts allow the owner to keep or retain a percentage of the amount due the contractor until the project is completed. This amount is called the **retainage.**

Involuntary Bankruptcy

Although rare, it is possible to force a business or a person into a Chapter 7 or 11 bankruptcy. This helps preserve the debtor's assets, as the bankruptcy trustee will attempt to control the debtor to prevent assets from disappearing or being wasted. The rules for this type of proceeding are very detailed and beyond the scope of this text; however, if an entity owing you a large sum of money appears to be siphoning off assets of the company, it may be worthwhile to explore this avenue with your attorney.

Vocabulary Checklist

Bankruptcy estate	Unsecured debt	Perfection of mechanic's lien
Bankruptcy trustee	Secured debt	Executory contract
Debtor	Exempt assets	Fraudulent transfer
Creditor	Exemptions	Preferences or preferential
Chapter 7 bankruptcy	Secured debts	payment
Chapter 11 bankruptcy	Unsecured debts	Involuntary bankruptcy
Chapter 13 bankruptcy	Debtor-in-possession	
Discharged debt	Automatic stay	

Review Questions

1. What happens when a bankruptcy is filed?

2. What are secured debts, and how are they treated in a bankruptcy?

3. What are unsecured debts, and how are they treated in a bankruptcy?

4. Must a person who files for a bankruptcy give up all the possessions to be liquidated so that debts can be paid?

5. What is the automatic stay designed to do?

6. What are some examples of the types of acts stayed by the automatic stay?

7. How are mechanic's liens handled in a bankruptcy?

8. What is an executory contract, and how are executory contracts handled in a bankruptcy?

9. The trustee can void fraudulent transfers, and preferential payments. What is the difference in time for which these transactions can be voided?

10. What are some of the special effects a bankruptcy can have on a construction project?

11. Why would someone want to force another person or business into bankruptcy?

12. Using the appendix, list two exemptions from the federal law.

Problems

Answer the issue in each of the following problems by making a legal argument, including premises in support of your answer.

1. Benjamin Sewell, Inc. is the prime contractor on a major construction project. The owner, Ranella Corporation, has made only partial payments on the last three progress reports, citing numerous defects in the construction, which Sewell thinks are bogus. Sewell has filed several claims and has negotiated with the owner's representative to no avail. The contract contains a clause allowing the contractor to terminate the contract for failure of the owner to make timely progress payments. Sewell is getting ready to terminate the contract and put its crew on a new project that the company has just been awarded.

    Mr. Sewell's secretary gets a call from Ranella Corporation's secretary saying that Ranella Corporation filed a Chapter 11 bankruptcy two hours ago.

    Issue: Can Sewell terminate the contract, and put its crew onto the new project?

    Rule:

    Premises:

    Answer: No

2. Melvin Beck is the project manager for Lanik Construction, which is working on a large hotel project with Wayfarer Corporation, owner. Wayfarer Corporation has not paid and/or only partially paid the last three progress payments. Lanik Construction has approximately $500,000 in unpaid subcontractor/material/labor bills in connection with the project. Lanik is having difficulty paying these bills because of the nonpayment by the owner.

Mr. Beck advises his supervisors that the construction has reached a point that discontinuing performance will not damage the existing structure. Lanik decides to stop further work until something can be worked out with the owner. Mr. Beck tells all personnel on the project to clean up and report to work on Monday on the Frost project located across town.

That same afternoon Mr. Beck gets a call from Wayfarer's construction manager informing him that Wayfarer filed a bankruptcy petition yesterday.

Issue: Can Lanik terminate the contract and put his crew onto the Frost project?

Rule:

Premises:

Answer: No

3. Mohammed Akat is the project manager for Bowers Engineering, Inc., the design–build contractor on a large renovation project for an industrial facility owned by Nocal Oil. The owner's bank, American Commerce, has not paid and/or only partially paid the last three progress payments. Bowers Engineering has approximately $500,000 in unpaid subcontractor/material/labor bills in connection with the project, which Bowers is having difficulty paying because of the nonpayment by the owner.

The bank had been paying the progress payments, but for some reason the bank is not returning any of Akat's calls concerning the project. Akat calls the owner's construction manager, Emily Todd. Todd expresses some concern to Akat that other owners of major construction projects in the area are having similar problems with American Commerce Bank. She suspects problems with the bank's ownership and fears that assets are being depleted.

Question: What can Bowers and Nocal do?

4. Markston was a lumber supplier who dealt regularly with Spade Construction. On September 1 Spade gave Markston a check for $100,000 for lumber delivered to a project. Markston continued to deliver lumber to Spade's projects until the check was dishonored by the bank. On November 1 Spade delivered Markston a certified check for $100,000. Markston did not deliver any further lumber to Spade. On December 1 Spade filed a bankruptcy.

Issue: Can Markston be forced to turn over $100,000 to the bankruptcy trustee?

Rule:

Premises:

Answer: Yes

5. Dr. Wit is a physician practicing medicine in California. He was being sued for medical malpractice and filed a Chapter 7 bankruptcy. At the time of filing the bankruptcy his retirement plan was worth approximately $1.8 million.[4]

Issue: Can Dr. Wit be forced to turn over his retirement plan assets to the bankruptcy trustee?

Rule: The assets of a retirement plan are exempt assets (California exemption law).

Premises:

Answer: No

---

[4]*In re* Witwer, 148 B.R. 930 (1992).

6. Johns-Manville Corporation is a major corporation that manufactures a variety of products, including insulation used in buildings. This insulation contained asbestos, which was determined to cause illness in humans exposed to it. Approximately 120,000 asbestos-related lawsuits were filed against the corporation.[5]

Issue: Can Johns-Manville Corporation file for a Chapter 11 bankruptcy?

Rule:

Premises:

Answer:

7. In 1999 Ed and Ginny Tab paid off their home valued at $200,000. Two years later they began operating an ice cream store, but unfortunately they did not make any money at it and in fact incurred debts of approximately $100,000. On October 1 they deeded the home to their three daughters, ages 9, 19, and 20 for consideration of $1. They continued to reside at the house and to pay for upkeep and taxes. On the following August 1 they filed a Chapter 7 bankruptcy.

Issue: Can the trustee set aside the deed to the daughters?

Rule:

Premises:

Answer: Yes

Answer to Selected Problems

1. Benjamin Sewell, Inc. is the prime contractor on a major construction project.

Issue: Can Sewell terminate the contract and put his crew onto the new project?

Rule: As soon as a party files a bankruptcy the automatic stay comes into effect. This stay is a court order that prevents the creditors from attempting to collect any debts or harming the bankruptcy estate.

Premises: Terminating the contract will certainly harm the estate. A project that is being completed is worth more than one where the contractor has walked off the job and a new contractor and crew must be brought in to complete it. The existence of the contract provision is irrelevant. The law prevails over the contract provision.

Answer: No

Appendix A Selected Bankruptcy Exemptions

11 USCS § 522(d) (2000) Exemptions (selected sections)

The following property may be exempted under subsection (b)(1) of this section:

1. The debtor's aggregate interest, not to exceed $16,150 in value, in real property or personal property that the debtor or a dependent of the debtor uses as a residence, in

---

[5]*In re* Johns-Manville Corp., 36 B.R. 727 (1984).

a cooperative that owns property that the debtor or a dependent of the debtor uses as a residence, or in a burial plot for the debtor or a dependent of the debtor.

2. The debtor's interest, not to exceed $2,575 in value, in one motor vehicle.

3. The debtor's interest, not to exceed $425 in value in any particular item or $8,625 in aggregate value, in household furnishings, household goods, wearing apparel, appliances, books, animals, crops, or musical instruments, that are held primarily for the personal, family, or household use of the debtor or a dependent of the debtor.

4. The debtor's aggregate interest, not to exceed $1,075 in value, in jewelry held primarily for the personal, family, or household use of the debtor or a dependent of the debtor.

5. The debtor's aggregate interest in any property, not to exceed in value $850 plus up to $8,075 of any unused amount of the exemption provided under paragraph (1) of this subsection.

6. The debtor's aggregate interest, not to exceed $1,625 in value, in any implements, professional books, or tools, of the trade of the debtor or the trade of a dependent of the debtor.

7. Any unmatured life insurance contract owned by the debtor, other than a credit life insurance contract.

8. The debtor's aggregate interest, not to exceed in value $8,625 less any amount of property of the estate transferred in the manner specified in section 542(d) of this title, in any accrued dividend or interest under, or loan value of, any unmatured life insurance contract owned by the debtor under which the insured is the debtor or an individual of whom the debtor is a dependent.

9. Professionally prescribed health aids for the debtor or a dependent of the debtor.

18

Dispute Resolution

---

*"Avoid lawsuits beyond all things; they impair your health, &
dissipate your property."—J. de La Bruyère*

Disputes and conflicts between people are a fact of life. They can be minor or major. This
chapter discusses some of the most common methods for resolving disputes in the construction industry. The methods discussed are avoidance, intimidation, negotiation, mediation, arbitration, and litigation. It is possible for any one conflict to use all or any of these
techniques. The term **alternative dispute resolution** is generally used to refer to arbitration and mediation as methods of resolving disputes alternative to litigation.

Avoidance

Avoidance is probably the most common form of dispute resolution. Most people engage
in it unconsciously on many occasions. By **avoidance** is meant that one or both people to
the dispute make no attempt to interact with the other to resolve the dispute; the dispute or
conflict is ignored. This technique is inappropriate for important or major conflicts because
they can turn into bigger problems.

18-1. THINK

In the last week what conflicts have you avoided? What conflicts have you caused
that others avoided?

Intimidation

The use of threats or violence to obtain the agreement of one party to another party's particular viewpoint is **intimidation.** Any argument containing threats or violence is logically fallacious. Logical fallacies are discussed in Chapter 3, Logic.

Threatening to file a lawsuit is a common appeal to force in American business. It has replaced the threat of punching someone in the nose but is still a form of intimidation.

When faced with any type of intimidation the suggested response is to leave the intimidator's presence if possible. If you have been threatened with a lawsuit, you may want to seek the advice of an attorney if you believe the argument has some merit. If you are actually served with a lawsuit, you definitely should seek the advice of an attorney.

Negotiation (Attorneys Not Involved)

Negotiation is affirmative communication between parties to a dispute and designed to resolve a dispute. It can be verbal, written, or another type of interaction.

Principles and Forces that Make Prelawsuit Negotiation Different
from Postlawsuit Negotiation

■ The attorney makes money from the dispute and may not be interested in an early settlement.

■ The attorney must avoid admitting any weakness in the case.

■ The client's legal rights are not necessarily the same as the client's best interests.

■ The goal of winning.

By *negotiation* in this chapter is meant *nonlegal* or *prelawsuit* or *without the aid of attorneys* negotiation. Although it is true the majority of lawsuits are settled through negotiation and mediation, rather than by trial, *negotiation and mediation after the filing of a lawsuit,* or *postlawsuit negotiation, is usually very different from prelawsuit negotiation.* Once the parties have filed a lawsuit, different principles and forces come into play in the negotiation.

Negotiation usually involves looking at alternatives and compromise by both parties in order to terminate the conflict. The negotiated solution may not be completely agreeable to the parties involved but is accepted because alternatives are less acceptable. In the literature of negotiation the term *BATNA* is common. This acronym stands for **best alternative to a negotiated agreement.** If a disputant believes something other than negotiation, such as litigation, will likely produce a more advantageous solution, it is unlikely the disputant will negotiate. The alternative may not actually be better; however, the disputant may not know this.

Attorney-Assisted Negotiation

The term **attorney-assisted negotiation** is used in this text to mean negotiation with the aid of attorneys. It is not the same as negotiation, for many reasons. Attorneys are not, in general, paid to settle claims quickly and easily. Attorneys are generally paid to protect the rights of a party. These two factors are not usually compatible.

18-2. THINK

Why would a person choose to have an attorney assist with a negotiation?

Litigation attorneys generally want to litigate, and the longer the litigation, the more income they may make on the dispute. In addition, litigation attorneys are trained to see situations in black and white and to use the power of the legal system to win their client's case. Litigation attorneys are not always amenable to negotiation, which requires an ability to see and accept the gray in any situation. In fact, in many firms it is common to have one litigation attorney and one negotiating attorney working on a case. This practice avoids some of the appearance of weakness that willingness to negotiate gives to the other side. A willingness to negotiate is interpreted as a sign of weakness in American culture, but not in all cultures.

Litigation attorneys are trained to win. If winning is the most important goal, other goals including fairness, efficiency, legality, morality, or ethics may be compromised. In Western cultures winning is synonymous with strength, rightness, and goodness. Negotiation and settlement are synonymous with weakness and wrongness.

Mediation

Mediation is the use of a third party to help parties resolve a dispute. The mediator, unlike a judge or arbitrator, does not decide who is right or who is wrong. The mediator does not decide issues. The mediator may discuss strengths and weaknesses of issues but does not make any decision one way or the other. The mediator helps the parties come to a completely voluntary settlement.

Mediators meet with all the parties and their attorneys, if any. Each side tells the mediator its side. The mediator requires the parties to listen to the opposing side or argument without interrupting. The mediator does not need to know and generally has no actual interest in either party's side or argument; however, it is amazing that the mediation is often the *first time* parties actually listen to each other without interrupting.

The mediator cares about the *issues*, both legal and nonlegal. The mediator is not as interested in arguments or conclusions to arguments. It is common for mediators to use such phrases as

- Correct me if I am wrong but I perceive that. . . .
- It is my understanding that your concern is. . . .
- I understand your position, and unless there is anything else, I would like to look at the specific issues in this matter.

Notice that many of these statements are what is referred to as *I-statements*. An **I-statement** is a statement about what the speaker thinks, feels, understands, or believes. A **you-statement** is a statement about what the speaker thinks, feels, understands, or believes the other party thinks, feels, understands, or believes. *You-statements are to be avoided* whenever possible in negotiation and mediation. Try to use I-statements only.

The interest in issues, rather than conclusions, is one of the main differences between mediators and arbitrators and judges. Arbitrators and judges must reach conclusions and therefore are very interested in the arguments of the opposing sides as an aid in coming to a conclusion. In mediation the *parties* are going to come to a conclusion, so the mediator is not as interested in the arguments.

It is not uncommon for the mediators to separate the parties at some point and speak to them individually. This almost never happens in a trial or arbitration. It is generally considered unethical for an arbitrator or judge to confer with a party unless all the parties and their attorneys are present. The mediator encourages the parties to come to compromise and to generate new and different types of settlements. The mediator goes back and forth between the parties with offers and counteroffers.

The mediator keeps the parties on track with their negotiation, although it is common for nonlegal issues to be important. Personal or emotional issues may be preventing the parties from settling the dispute. Often, it is the recognition of an emotional issue by the mediator that helps one or more parties reach a settlement. Of course, violence is avoided at all times.

Recognizing and addressing, although not necessarily resolving, nonlegal issues is another area where mediation and litigation/arbitration differ. Judges and arbitrators deal only with *legal* issues.

Arbitration

Arbitration is very similar to litigation in that the parties present their cases to an arbitrator or arbitrators who then decide who wins and who loses. Arbitrators decide all legal and factual issues; no jury is involved. Arbitration produces a win–lose result. Mediation and negotiation can produce win–win results.

Arbitrators are employed by private associations that have facilities or arrange for facilities in which to hold the arbitration. For example, in the United States the American Arbitration Association is one of the major sources of arbitration services. In the construction industry it is common for the parties to stipulate in their agreements that should an arbitration be filed, it will be filed with this group.

Arbitration has several advantages over litigation: (1) Arbitration is usually much faster. Whereas parties may have to wait years for a trial, parties usually have to wait only a few months for an arbitration hearing. (2) Arbitration is usually cheaper, since the attorneys, if any, are not employed for as long a period of time. (3) In addition, the amount of discovery in arbitration is limited, and this saves money. Finally, (4) most parties stipulate to binding arbitration. This means the parties agree that they cannot appeal the arbitrator's decision. Although a court will overturn an arbitrator's decision in the event of fraud or other very limited reasons, it is very unusual for courts to do so.

Litigation

Litigation is the use of the government-provided dispute resolutions system. A negative aspect of this system is that it is complex and time-consuming. As such it usually requires the use of paid professionals—that is, lawyers—to help persons navigate the system. Another drawback to litigation from a business standpoint is that the court system in the United States is open to the public. Although it is possible to have judgments sealed from public view, most litigation proceedings are subject to public scrutiny. Public scrutiny is a *not* a drawback in many circumstances. For example, the public nature of criminal trials helps protect the rights of people who become involved in the criminal justice system. The government's actions are subject to public scrutiny, particularly by the media, and the citizens are kept informed. The legal system of the United States is more fully outlined in Chapter 1.

Approaching a Negotiation/Mediation

Most people engage in negotiation, at least occasionally, even if only with friends or family. Friends negotiate where they will go for the evening, and partners negotiate how they will spend income.

Most people negotiate without any formal training in specific negotiating techniques. Untrained negotiators may unconsciously use a variety of illogical techniques to settle a disagreement. One of the problems with negotiated and mediated settlements is that the parties will often make fallacious arguments in order to obtain agreement for their position. Be careful of fallacious arguments and do not be swayed by them. Fallacious arguments are discussed in Chapter 3, Logic.

Some of the illogical techniques used in negotiation or mediation include anger, bullying, and guilt. Although it is true many trained negotiators resort to such illogical or emotional techniques, they do so with a greater understanding of the advantages and disadvantages of using them. Trained negotiators also develop other skills—skills that help them settle disputes in a more professional manner.

Many different styles of negotiation exist. Some people are loud, some are quiet, some are friendly, and some are distant. No style is more effective than another. In fact, good negotiators use a variety of styles depending on the situation and the parties involved.

No matter what your style of negotiation, always start with a clear outline of the facts of the case. Know what the factual disputes are and what evidence exists to support a particular dispute. Each of the problems at the end of Chapters 6 through 17 are examples containing an outline of the facts of a particular case.

The problems at the end of the chapters have not concerned themselves with the source of any particular fact or piece of evidence, but in real life the source of the evidence is very important because it weighs heavily upon its reliability. For example, the factual dispute might be whether the light was red or green when Dot Driver went through the intersection and struck Stan Striver. Dot Driver has herself and three nuns returning home from spending a year in a mission in Africa to testify the light was green. Stan Striver has himself and three ten-year-olds, one of whom is his child, to testify the light was red. Although it is true the jury could choose to believe the Stan and the children, it is likely they will believe Dot and the nuns; therefore, Dot's argument is stronger, and Stan should negotiate rather than go to trial/arbitration.

In addition to the facts, the parties need a well-defined statement of the damages together with the proof for the items. Cases will not settle at early stages if the injured party has not adequately proved its damages. Often, in cases where it is obvious the defendant is liable, the injured party believes this obvious liability entitles it to whatever damages it can dream up. For example, although it may be obvious that one party has breached a contract, this is insufficient evidence to win a lawsuit. Damages must also be proved.

It is not uncommon for injured parties to inflate damages, particularly when liability is strong. Remember, there is no connection between liability and damages. A strong case of liability does not necessarily translate into dollars. Dollars must be proved separately.

Most negotiated or mediated settlements contain, at most, the preceding two items— namely, facts and damages. *Adding an informed discussion of the legal principles involved may strengthen a position.* Many negotiated or mediated settlements, and to some extent arbitrated settlements, are based on legally erroneous concepts because the parties do not understand or know the law. This is not necessarily bad, because settlement is more important than legality; however, one of the major purposes of a course such as this is to help you understand the legal implications of the events giving rise to the dispute and strengthen your negotiating or mediating posture. You must exercise caution, however. Introducing legal arguments into a negotiation or mediation prior to the filing of a lawsuit may turn the dispute into a legal one.

The Actual Negotiation/Mediation

Never approach a negotiation or mediation with a firm position such as, "We will not take anything less than $200,000 in settlement." This is called **positional negotiation,** that is, stating a firm position and refusing to budge from it. It is seldom effective. In fact, it is one of the best and most effective ways of *preventing* any type of settlement.

Other effective ways of ensuring, or almost ensuring, that a settlement will *not* be reached include:

- not allowing anyone with settlement authority to attend the negotiation or mediation;
- becoming verbally or physically abusive.

Approach the negotiation or mediation with the idea that settlement is *not* the primary purpose of the meeting but that the purpose is to come up with lists of viable options for a workable settlement. After a list of options is generated, it is often easier to find one that is agreeable to all parties or to craft one that is agreeable by combining several on the table.

The following technique works well in many negotiations or mediations:

a. Write on a board or flip chart all suggested settlements *without comment of any sort* by any person present. This technique often produces funny or ridiculous options such as the project manager and the architect need to take a trip to Jamaica. However, these types of humorous suggestions may be just what are needed to break the tension and get the parties working together.

b. When no more alternative suggestions are forthcoming, go through the options and outline *only* the strengths of each.

c. Next, list the weaknesses or negative points of each option.

d. Reduce the list to some viable alternatives.

Characteristics of a Good Negotiator

Listens
Does not dictate
Does not ridicule others
Does not insult others
Is considerate and polite

Approach negotiation or mediation with the idea of *listening* to the other side, not *telling* them. It is amazing how little listening actually goes on among the parties to a dispute and yet how often just listening and understanding the opposing views can lead to settlement. In the United States listening to and understanding the other party's viewpoint too often means agreeing to it or giving in. It is thought of as weak; however, just listening to someone does not mean you agree with him or her. Even if settlement does not occur, the parties will have exchanged information and will have a better understanding of the problems involved. Note that some parties approach negotiation and mediation for the sole purpose of obtaining information that can later be used against the opponent. Techniques for handling untrustworthy opponents are beyond the scope of this text.

Unfortunately, the parties to a dispute may have a history of ill will and dislike. If this is the case, it is generally a good idea *not* to have those particular people involved in the negotiations. They may have difficulty separating their emotions from the actual issues. Other representatives of the company should handle the negotiation.

Types of Negotiators to Watch Out For

The Mind-Changer

This person is so afraid he has not gotten the best possible deal or has not negotiated you down to your minimum acceptable solution that he will change his mind once it comes to actually signing on the dotted line. For example, if you agree to pay $500, he will say to himself, "If they agreed to pay $500, they would probably have agreed to pay $550, so I won't sign unless the amount is changed to $550."

This technique is often effective because the additional step is often so small in comparison with the total that the other party is willing to give in. Unfortunately, it can escalate. The mind-changer may say, "If they agreed to pay $550, they would probably have agreed to pay $600, so I won't sign unless the amount is changed to $600." The primary way of stopping this type of negotiation is to walk away.

The Bits-and-Pieces Negotiator

If a claim has several parts or items of damage, this person will attempt to get you to negotiate and settle each part independently of other parts. All complex claims have weak and strong points, important and less important points. You are more likely to give in or take less for weaker or less important points; however, when it comes to stronger and more important points you will have fewer bargaining chips to negotiate with if you have already settled your weaker or less important points. In addition, if you settle the other side's weak and important points, leaving her with only her strong and/or unimportant points to negotiate, she may refuse to negotiate and tell you to "file a lawsuit," since her claims are strong or unimportant to them.

This type of negotiation can be avoided by informing the party that you are negotiating an entire package and that any agreement on a particular point is contingent on agreement on all points. You may have to remind the other negotiator of this during the negotiation.

Starts Ridiculously Low or High Negotiator

Starting ridiculously low or high is a common ploy, and if possible you should ignore it and continue on with the negotiation or mediation. This technique is often effective when one side has not adequately prepared its claim and is not sure of the value of its claim. An unprepared negotiator when faced with a ridiculously low offer may think, "My claim must not be as strong as I thought if they are offering only 1% of what I have demanded." The unprepared negotiator may then settle for less than the claim is worth. A prepared negotiator will ignore this ploy.

Often, a ridiculously low or high demand so alienates the opposing side that settlement becomes impossible. Do not allow this technique to anger you. Recognize it for a common negotiating technique, let the other side know you recognize it, and continue negotiating.

Vocabulary Checklist

Alternative dispute resolution	Attorney-assisted negotiation	Litigation
Avoidance	Mediation	The mind-changer
Intimidation	I-statement	Bits-and-pieces negotiator
Negotiation	You-statement	Starts ridiculously low or high negotiator
BATNA	Arbitration	

Review Questions

1. What is usually meant by the term *alternative dispute resolution*?
2. In addition to alternative dispute resolution, what types of dispute resolution methods does this chapter discuss?
3. What is probably the most common form of dispute resolution?
4. When is avoidance a good method for resolving disputes? When is it a poor method?
5. What term is applied to the use of threats or violence to obtain agreement on a particular viewpoint?
6. The form of dispute resolution referred to in question 5 is logically defective. Why is that?
7. What is one of the most common appeals to force in dispute resolution in the United States?
8. When faced with any type of intimidation what should you do?
9. What is the definition of *negotiation* in the text?
10. What does negotiation usually involve?
11. What is a *BATNA*?
12. What happens if your opponent in a negotiation has a BATNA?
13. List four ways in which negotiation differs from attorney-assisted negotiation.
14. Why is it common in many firms to have one litigation attorney and one negotiating attorney working on a case?
15. In Western cultures winning is perceived to be synonymous with what?
16. In the United States negotiation and settlement are perceived to be synonymous with what?
17. In the United States compromise is perceived to be synonymous with what?
18. Why does an attorney not want to let the opposing side know of any weakness in the case?
19. What is *mediation*?
20. What does a mediator do in a dispute that an arbitrator or judge does not do?

21. Who settles a mediated dispute?

22. What is one of the first things mediators require the parties to do?

23. What is the mediator's attitude toward each party's side of the argument?

24. A mediator, as compared with an arbitrator or judge, is concerned with what?

25. A mediator is not concerned with what?

26. Arbitrators and judges, as compared with mediators, care about what aspect of the dispute?

27. Why do mediators and arbitrators or judges care about different aspects of the dispute?

28. What technique that almost never is used in a trial or arbitration do mediators employ?

29. Who generally presents the offers and counteroffers to the opposing parties during mediation?

30. What types of issues (that are not usually raised at trial) will the mediator allow the parties to discuss or bring up?

31. Why is it effective to allow the issues referred to in question 30 to be discussed?

32. What is *arbitration*?

33. What types of issues do arbitrators decide?

34. What are some of the advantages of arbitration over litigation?

35. Name an instance in which an arbitration decision can be overturned.

36. What is *litigation*?

37. What are some disadvantages of litigation?

38. What is *positional negotiation*?

39. Give an example of positional negotiation.

40. Why is positional negotiation a problem?

41. The text gives three effective ways that will help ensure that a settlement will *not* be reached. What are they?

42. With what idea should negotiation be approached?

43. Detail the one method outlined in the text for handling a negotiation.

44. What problem arises when a negotiation/mediation is approached with the idea of *telling* instead of listening?

45. What cultural belief or norm prevents Americans from listening to opposing views?

46. If the parties to a dispute have a history of ill will and dislike, what should be done at the negotiation?

47. What is a *mind-changer*?

48. What can be done to neutralize the technique referred to in question 47?

49. What is a *bits-and-pieces negotiator*?

50. What can be done to neutralize the technique referred to in question 49?

51. What is the danger with allowing a bits-and-pieces negotiator to control the negotiation?

52. What is a "starts ridiculously low or high negotiator"?

53. What can be done to neutralize the technique referred to in question 52?

54. In what types of situations is the technique referred to in question 52 effective?

55. What problem can result from using the "starts ridiculously low or high" technique?

Problems

1. Prepare a one-act play in which the parties in the following scenario *negotiate* the matter to a solution. Write dialogue for each party and include *all* the following facts and arguments, including the fallacious argument. Assume that all parties know *all* of the following facts. This problem is from Chapter 11, Delays and Accelerations.

    > Kold Developers, Inc., a closely held corporation owned by Mr. and Mrs. Kold, contracted with Little Bear City to build additional housing to accommodate workers on the Trans-Alaska pipeline, with the work to be completed by November 1. At the time the developer contracted with the city, commencement of construction on the pipeline was imminent and the need for housing was great; however, shortly after the parties entered into the contract, a federal court issued an injunction that ordered a halt to all construction of the pipeline for six months. Kold refused to build the houses until the six months was over because it could not obtain financing at a cost to allow it to make any profit on the project until then. The city terminated the contract and threatened to sue the developer for liquidated damages pursuant to the damages clause that stated that Kold would pay \$200/day in liquidated damages to the owner for each day after November 1 that the project was not completed. In addition, the owner threated to sue on the performance bond.

    > The city argued that the contractor should not win because the contractor's actions are the same as stealing from the taxpayers.

    Issue: Is the developer liable to the city?

    Rule: A party must honor its contract (basic premise of contract law).

    What other, more specialized, rule is available to the developer here?

    Premises: (*Hint:* Categorize the delay.)

    Answer: No

2. Prepare a one-act play in which the parties in the following scenario *negotiate* the matter to a solution. Write dialogue for each party and include *all* the following facts and arguments made below, including the fallacious argument. Assume that all parties know *all* of the following facts. This problem is from Chapter 7, Mistakes in Bidding.

    > Zayas and Spalten General Contracting submits a bid to an owner on a prime contract. Zayas has obtained several bids for the concrete, as follows:

    > | Fryas Concrete: | \$150,000 |
    > |---|---|
    > | Millner Concrete: | \$142,000 |
    > | Bradley Concrete: | \$145,000 |
    > | Williams Concrete: | \$ 90,000 |

    > After being awarded the contract, Zayas and Spalten General Contracting contacts Woodley Concrete and Quintana Concrete in an effort to get a bid for the concrete that is even lower than Williams Concrete's bid. Neither Woodley nor Quintana will do the job for less than \$90,000.

Williams Concrete realizes it made an error in its calculations and informs Zayas and Spalten General Contracting that it will not perform the subcontract, saying its business will probably fold if it is required to perform the contract for $90,000. No other facts can be proved by a preponderance of the evidence.

Issue: Can Williams Concrete rescind its bid without incurring any liability to Zayas and Spalten General Contracting?

Rule: Detrimental reliance by the prime on the sub's bid is the cornerstone on which the courts have based their decisions in holding subcontractors to their bids. It is important that after receipt of the contract the prime not cast doubt on the existence of that reliance. The courts have construed prime contractor bid shopping after contract award as reflecting that the prime did not rely on the original subbid but merely used the subbids to ascertain the approximate prices it should bid on each item.

3. Prepare a one-act play in which the parties in the following scenario *arbitrate* the matter to a solution. Write dialogue for each party, including the arbitrator. Assume that all parties know all of the following facts. This problem is from Chapter 8, Specifications and Plans. You will have to know the law in order to arbitrate to a solution.

The following specification exists in a certain construction contract between Kevin Construction and the owner:

"a. Install drainage course on horizontal and vertical surfaces in accordance with the manufacturer's recommendations."

After the project is completed, a storm hits the area. The drainage course proves inadequate to handle the runoff and causes leakage that causes some damage to ceiling and flooring tiles amounting to $10,000. The owner makes a claim against the contractor for those damages, claiming the contractor did not install the drainage course per the manufacturer's recommendations. The owner argues that any decent contractor would have installed the drainage course properly or would at least pay the damages. The drainage course extended for approximately 137 feet, and two screws were found to be lacking. No other facts can be proved by a preponderance of the evidence.

Issue: Is Kevin Construction liable to the owner for the damage to the ceiling and flooring?

Issue: (*Hint:* causation)

Rule: (*Hint:* causation)

Premises:

Answer: No

4. Prepare a one-act play in which the parties in the following scenario *litigate* the matter to a solution. Write dialogue for each party, including the judge and attorney for each party. Assume that all parties know all of the following facts. This problem is from Chapter 9, Scope. You will have to know the law in order to litigate to a solution. You will have to prepare conflicting arguments for both attorneys.

Sanchez Construction was awarded a fixed-price contract with the U.S. Army in connection with the construction of an artificial battlefield. A safety manual was provided by the army and was incorporated as one of the contract documents. The contract required the installation of several electrical systems including interior wiring and an underground electrical distribution system. The contractor intended to use a particular *trenching machine* to dig the trenches required by the contract.

Prior to the bid the contractor had a conversation with an authorized representative of the owner, during which he mentioned he intended to use a particular trenching machine to dig the trenches required by the contract, and he asked if a rollover protective structure (ROPS) would be required to be installed on that trenching machine. The representative said no. The contract was bid accordingly.

After contract performance had begun, the army required the contractor to install a ROPS on the trencher. Contractor complied and filed a claim for additional funds.

The safety manual provided by the army (on this and prior jobs) stated that ROPS

"shall be installed on crawler and rubber-tire tractors such as dozers, push-and-pull tractors, winch tractors, mowers, off-the-highway self-propelled pneumatic-tire earth movers such as trucks, pans, scrapers, bottom dumps, and end dumps, motor graders."

No other facts can be proved by a preponderance of the evidence.

Another authorized government representative said that the contract was not ambiguous and required the contractor to install a ROPS. The contractor did so and filed a claim for the additional cost of the equipment with a ROPS. No other facts can be proved by a preponderance of the evidence.

Issue: Is Sanchez entitled to payment for the ROPS?

Subissue 1: Is the contract ambiguous?

Rule:

Premises: Be sure to clearly state what each party wants the contract to say and where in the contract, if any where, they have support for this interpretation.

Answer: Yes

Subissue 2: Which rules can be applied?

Rule: (*Hint:* parol evidence rule)

Premises:

Answer: Sanchez prevails.

Answer: Yes, Sanchez is entitled to payment.

Answer to Selected Problem

1. *CHARACTERS:*

Kold: Project manager for Kold Developers

Owner's representative: Project manager for Little Bear City

The parties have not yet filed a lawsuit but have met informally to see if they can settle this matter. The six months has not yet passed, and the federal injunction is still in force, and the project cannot be built.

Kold: Good morning, _____(owner's rep.) I am glad that you agreed to meet with me today to see if we can settle this matter.

Owner's rep: I don't care if you are glad or not. Get to the point. You are going to owe the city a lot of money in liquidated damages because you agreed to complete the project by November 1 and that is not going to happen. and don't think we won't blink an eye about contacting your bonding company—you know what that means. You will never get another bond in this state and won't be able to do any more work. The city has agreed to settle this matter if you write us a check for $200,000 today. Otherwise the settlement is off and we will go to court and sue you.

Kold: I understand that the contract has stated that Kold will complete the project by November 1, but with the federal court injunction in place neither Kold nor any other developer can obtain the financing to complete the project.

Owner's rep: I don't care about your problems. You can get financing someplace—sure it might be a lot more money than you thought you would have to pay, but that is your problem. You have a contract to finish this project by November 1. Can you do that?

Kold: No, you know I cannot complete the project by November 1.

Owner's rep: Well then, you are clearly in breach of the contract. The only issue here is how much in damages are we willing to settle for. I told you, the city will settle this case with you if you write us a check for $200,000 today. Did you bring your checkbook? I understand you just bought a new house outside of town—well, you know that if you don't pay us, we can get your house and your car, and don't even think about sending your kids to college.

Kold: I think the real issue here is whether or not the law allows me a delay. If I am legally entitled to a delay, then I am not in breach of the contract.

Owner's rep: What are you talking about? The law allows you a delay? We have a contract—it says you will complete the project by November; you say you can't do it. That is a breach of contract. You are nothing more than a thief, trying to steal money from the taxpayers of this state. You should honor your obligations. All you developers are alike—just a bunch of lazy robbers, trying to get something for nothing.

Kold: I know that I have a contract with you and that failing to fulfill the terms of that contract can be a breach, but not in all circumstances. In some circumstances the law gives the parties to a contract a break—when things happen, like what is happening here with the federal court injunction. When unusual things like that happen, then the law gives the developer/contractor the right to delay the performance of the contract.

Owner's rep: Where does the law say that?

Kold: Right here in this reference book. It says: *Delay Excused by Law.*

The law in many jurisdictions excuses the contractor from some or all of these delays, whether or not the contract so specifies:

Acts of God

Labor disputes, if unforeseeable

Acts of government

Criminal activity, if unforeseeable

I think the federal court injunction is an act of government entitling me to a delay.

Especially in a case like this where the city does not even need the housing—the city needs the housing to house the workers who are going to be working on the pipeline, but the pipeline can't be started for at least another six months. What if the pipeline is delayed indefinitely? Then the city won't *ever* need the housing, and it will have spent a lot of money for nothing. This way, if we wait to see if the injunction is lifted to do the project, then the city won't have to spend money for housing it does not need.

Owner's rep: You mean you agree that if the injunction is never lifted, we can just trash this contract? You won't sue the city and the city won't sue you?

Kold: Sure—if the city does not need the housing, then I will agree that the contract will be terminated. In fact, it might be better just to keep the contract terminated—the city has already terminated the contract. I can accept that. If the injunction is lifted, the city can put the project out for bid, and I can bid on it, just like any other bidder.

Owner's rep: I don't know; I will have to take this back to the main office to see if we can do that.

Kold: Why don't I have my attorney draw up a document terminating the contract, and both parties will waive all claims relating to it. I will send it to you and you can have your office look at it and see if it is OK and if not, we can work on it.

Owner's rep: OK, but I am not promising anything.

Note: Another legal argument exists to support the developer's claim that it is entitled to a delay. What is it?

19

Frequently Asked Questions

What Are Some Current Topics of Importance in the Construction Industry?

What Is a Certified Professional Constructor?

As the construction industry continues to become more complex, the need for competent managers remains critical. Many of the students using this text will become construction professionals managing various aspects of the construction process. The profession is attempting to professionalize itself by testing people and issuing a credential to those who pass. Presently the American Institute of Constructors (AIC) has a testing procedure to certify **professional constructors.** The test consists of two parts. Normally, the first part is taken while the applicant is still in college or shortly thereafter. The second part of the exam is taken after the candidate has been working in the industry for several years. All students planning on entering the construction industry should think seriously about taking this exam.

What Is a Sick Building and What Is Indoor Air Quality?

The term **sick building** has been gaining recognition in the industry and law in recent years. This term refers to a building that causes occupants to suffer from illnesses such as headaches, itchy and watery eyes, stuffy noses, sinus drainage, sore throats, and fatigue. Asthma sufferers may be particularly prone. Just as outdoor air pollution is a major problem in many areas, indoor air pollution has recently been recognized as a major health hazard in some buildings. The quality of the air inside a building or working environment can affect the health of the occupants of the structure.

Several causes exist for sick buildings. In the 1970s the United States suffered an energy crisis, and owners began demanding more energy-efficient buildings. Designers complied by designing more tightly sealed buildings and reducing indoor air ventilation. Other causes of sick buildings are the emission of formaldehyde and volatile organic compounds (VOCs) from construction materials, furnishings, office equipment, and cleaning and maintenance supplies. For example, rugs may be composed of synthetic fibers that withstand a great deal of traffic but emit harmful chemicals into the air. Mold and mildew are biological contaminants that contribute to sick buildings.

What Is Design–Build?

In **traditional construction project delivery** the project drawings and specifications are completed by the designer and put out for bid to the general contractors; construction then commences. The relationships between the parties in traditional construction project delivery systems are diagrammed in Figure 6–1, Chapter 6, Relationships among the Parties on the Project.

Design–build is an alternative delivery system. In **design–build** the owner contracts for design and construction services from one company. This method usually speeds up the delivery time and prevents antagonism between the designer and the contractor, as both work for the same entity. The relationships between the parties in design–build project delivery are diagrammed in Figure 6–3, Chapter 6, Relationships among the Parties on the Project.

Any construction project delivery method that varies from the traditional construction project delivery method is called an **alternative delivery system.** Design–build is only one of several alternatives being tested in the market. Another alternative delivery system is a *public–private partnership*. A **public–private partnership** is a contractual relationship whereby the private company enters into a contract with a public entity to build some type of public project—for example, a road or a bridge. The private company agrees to build and maintain the project for some amount of time. The private company may be entitled to tolls or other revenues generated by the project.

What Is Expert Testimony?

Construction litigation is very likely to require the use of *expert witnesses* to explain processes and procedures to the judge, jury, or arbitrator. For example, if a case involves a claim that the foundation is defective, someone is going to have to explain how the foundation is defective and what effect the defect has on the structure to the judge, jury, or arbitrator. The person brought in to explain will be an *expert witness*—someone who has specialized knowledge of the area. The judge, jury, or arbitrator (the trier of fact) then has the power to decide if, in fact, the slab was defective. Most construction contracts contain binding arbitration clauses, so it is likely that arbitrators with construction experience will decide these issues.

Being an expert witness in a case can be very lucrative. The pay is in the hundreds of dollars per hour. In addition, juries tend to place a great deal of trust in expert testimony. The pressures in the system are to hire an expert to say whatever it is the party wants the expert to say. Lawsuits can often become a matter of dueling experts.

In the case of *Daubert v. Merrell Dow Pharmaceuticals*, the United States Supreme Court ruled for the first time on the admissibility of expert scientific evidence.[1] Of course this ruling applies only to federal cases, but similar law is being adopted by states. Admissibility of expert testimony is beyond the scope of this text; however, practitioners in the industry should realize that judges or arbitrators will decide whether the expert evidence will be admitted according to established rules. Not every expert or every theory can be presented.

What Is a Waiver of Claim?

Parties frequently try to draft clauses that *prevent* lawsuits and claims rather than merely establish alternative dispute resolution methods such as mediation or arbitration. Party O is certainly in a much stronger negotiating position if it can get party C to *waive* any claims or disputes *before they arise*. This is certainly convenient for party O, who need not worry about pesky things like laws, ethics, rights, being careful, or even abiding by the contract because party C has agreed to waive all its claims.

Be careful of clauses such as the following in your contract:

> By submitting a bid each bidder agrees to **waive** *any claim* it has or may have against the Owner, the Architect/Engineer, and their respective employees, arising out of or in connection with the administration, evaluation, or recommendation of any bid; waiver of any requirements under the Bid Documents; or the Contract Documents; acceptance or rejection of any bids; and award of the Contract (emphasis added).

Many courts will refuse to enforce these clauses because they are exculpatory or onerous in many circumstances, but many courts will uphold them in some circumstances. The preceding clause was held to prevent a bidder's suit against the architectural firm that recommended rejection of its low bid.[2]

What Are Some of the Most Common Areas of Problems/Claims in the Industry?

The most common areas of problems in the industry are problems relating to the following:

Changes

Notice provisions

Scope of the contract

Differing and unforeseen site conditions

Damages and limitation of damages

---

[1] *Daubert v. Merrell Dow Pharmaceuticals*, 509, U.S. 579, 595 (1993).
[2] See *Sedona Contracting v. Ford, Powell, & Carson*, 995 S.W.2d 192 (Tex. App.—1999).

What Are the Most Important Skills Needed in the Industry?

Many people might think that it is necessary to possess a great deal of technical knowledge to do well in the construction industry. Although that knowledge is certainly extremely important, the following are the most important skills needed by persons entering the construction industry:

1. Ability to get along with people.

   The construction industry is a prime example of how cooperation among individuals and specialization of labor can produce the most complex and astounding creations of the human race. It is possible to create these projects only when people cooperate. Not all people have this skill, however, and disputes and confrontations are probably more common at more levels in the construction industry than in other industries.

2. Ability to read.

   When students are asked how they prefer to learn, many students today respond, "visually; I do not like to read." Although drawings are certainly an important aspect of the construction industry, written contracts and specifications are extremely important. Reading and the ability to understand what you read are important skills for construction managers.

3. Ability to write.

   Whenever people from industry get together with professors they lament the inability of college graduates to write. If your job entails going to meetings or managing others, you will have to write. You will have to prepare agendas for meetings, you will have to take notes at meetings, and you will have to write memos detailing what needs to be done, how to do it, what has been done, and what has not been done.

You can write a comprehensible memo on any topic by following the FIRPA format. It may be that your memo will not involve each of these elements—it is not likely that you will be given the power to make conclusions until you have more experience; however, no matter what the problem, using this format will help you.

How Can I Avoid a Lawsuit?

1. Do not lie, cheat, or steal.
2. Give a dollar's worth of work and a thank you for every dollar *paid to you.* Smiles are nice, too.
3. Pay a dollar and say thank you for every dollar's worth of work done *for you.* Smiles are nice, too.
4. Do not sweat the small stuff, and remember, almost everything is small stuff.
5. Work together and try to fix mistakes.

6. Realize that you and others will make mistakes. Learn how to fix mistakes. It is necessary to establish blame only when the mistake is repetitive and something can be done to lessen the frequency of occurrence of the mistake in the future.

7. Seek to understand before seeking to be understood (Steve Covey).

8. Listen to others. Remember that *Listen = Listen; Listen ≠ Agreement.* Frequently, the speaker does not even want your agreement, the speaker wants you only to listen.

9. Treat *every* person you meet with respect. Every person includes any person who thinks or acts differently than you. Every person includes the most inexperienced laborer to the president of the company. Every person on the job deserves to be treated with respect because they are important contributors to the project. Without them someone else would have to do their job, or the job would go undone. Every person includes people who may want to sue you or file a claim against you. You may be surprised to learn that treating people with respect prevents a lot of claims and lawsuits.

10. Remember that *Different = Different; Different ≠ Bad.* In fact, *Different = Good* is true in many, many situations. Otherwise we would not have indoor plumbing or _____. (Fill in the blank with any change that has occurred since humans dug holes in the ground to plant seeds. Planting seeds was different from what came before it, and it was good.)

11. Do not let your ego prevent you from accomplishing your goals and others from accomplishing theirs. Many problems in the construction industry are related to overblown egos.

12. Never sue because "It is the principle of the thing" unless *you* are willing to spend a lot of money to enforce your principles. Attorneys are not likely to want to spend *their* money upholding *your* principles.

13. Ask your lawyer what it will cost—then double that amount. This will give you a conservative estimate of your attorney fees and costs. After getting an estimate of the attorney fees and costs, add in an estimate for *your* lost time and resources. This is likely to be greater than the attorney fees and costs, depending on the complexity of the matter. Add both together to get a conservative estimate of how much a lawsuit is going to cost you. Arbitrations are must less costly, but still expensive.

What Should I Do When I Make a Mistake?

Mistakes will occur in the construction process. As emphasized throughout this book, mistakes are to be fixed, not taken advantage of; however, one element not mentioned previously is people's emotional reaction to a mistake. Mistakes cost people time and money. Do not be surprised when someone becomes angry when you make a mistake.

For example, if you have ever been rear-ended while sitting at a stop sign you know the anger and frustration you feel when a stranger intrudes into your life and costs you time and effort to fix a problem someone else has caused. You, not the person who hit you, has to call your insurance company, take your car around town for a couple of estimates, take your car in to be fixed, and get someone to drive you to pick it up. *You will have to expend your time and effort rectifying someone else's mistake, and you will never be compensated for it.* This is likely to cause a certain amount of anger and frustration in you.

Be prepared for the eruption of emotions such as anger and frustration when a mistake occurs. Mature persons get angry and/or frustrated *with the mistake—not with the person* involved in the mistake. This is a very big difference, one that is achieved with experience and maturity.

When a mistake occurs, yours or another person's, say, "I am sorry this mistake/problem happened." This tends to diffuse the anger and frustration that are likely to arise in the face of a mistake. Even if you are not at fault, you can still be sorry that the mistake or problem happened. After all, an apology just means you are sorry a certain event has occurred. You might be sorry that 10 million Russians were killed in World War II, even though you did nothing to cause that event. *An apology, properly worded, is not an admission of guilt, fault, or liability.* Note that in Oriental cultures an apology is often an admission of guilt, fault, or liability but not in Western culture, depending on the wording of the apology. If you say, "I am sorry I caused this accident," then you are admitting fault.

From a legal standpoint it is recommended that you *not* admit fault or responsibility when apologizing. For some people it is part of their nature, for whatever reason, to say, "I am sorry, it's all my fault. I will take care of it." It may *not* be your fault or it may be only *partially* your fault (see Chapter 16, Joint Liability and Indemnity); however, if you admit that the mistake is your fault, that admission can be used against you should the matter come to trial or arbitration.

If the mistake is the result of something you did or did not do or you somehow contributed to the mistake, another very good way to diffuse the anger and frustration caused by the mistake is to offer to help fix the problem and to actually do something to help fix it. Again, *offering to fix a problem is not an admission of guilt, fault, or liability.* When people stop to help perfect strangers fix flat tires they are not taking any responsibility for the flat tire. Fix the problem now and sort out the liability later if necessary.

Several times this text has mentioned that social interaction and cooperation increase the standard of living and allow the building of complex projects and social institutions. Remember that *everything* has a cost. The anger and frustration that results when social interaction and cooperation fail is part of the cost of the benefits we reap from a cooperative society. Unless you move to a very tiny, very deserted island, you have no control or choice over this. Your life is constantly influenced and altered by people you do not even know and do not want to know. Of course, people you know influence your life also, and you, too, influence the lives of people you do not know.

In summary:

- Mistakes will occur.
- People will experience anger and frustration.
- Apologize for the situation without admitting fault.
- Fix the mistake or help fix it if possible.

When Should I Call an Attorney?

It is always good to discuss legal matters with an attorney before taking any action. The following are some of the *most* essential times you will need an attorney immediately:

1. When you get served with court papers.
2. If you want to terminate, quit, or walk off a construction job.
3. If someone files a bankruptcy or you need to file a bankruptcy.

What Are Some Killer Clauses?

Termination for Convenience Clause

A fairly recent development in the industry is the **termination for convenience** clause. This clause allows the owner to terminate the contract at the owner's convenience. Under this clause the owner can terminate the entire contract only—the owner cannot terminate bits and pieces of the contract.

For example, suppose the government issued an invitation for bids for a fixed-price contract for maintenance services at a certain air base. Bids ranged from $11.3 million to $29.1 million. By law the award should be given to the lowest responsive and responsible bidder; however, the officer can award the contract and then immediately terminate it for convenience if the contract contains such a clause.

This clause is *not* necessarily a bad thing because it allows the owner to terminate a project when a major error is found in the plans or specifications, or if an unforeseen site condition is encountered.

For example, the Army Corps of Engineers awarded a contract for demolition of two buildings to Krygoski. After contract award, the government discovered that the actual quantity of asbestos in the buildings far exceeded its estimate. The contractor submitted a change order proposal calling for a 33% increase in the contract price. The government considered this unreasonable and elected to terminate the entire contract for convenience. The termination for convenience was upheld. The court held that the government is free to terminate a contract for convenience for any reason, so long as it does not abuse its discretion or act in bad faith.[3]

Unforeseen Site Condition Clause

This clause states that the owner will pay the contractor costs associated with unforeseen site conditions. The law normally puts the risk of unforeseen site conditions on the contractor, but pursuant to this clause the owner accepts the risk. This concept is discussed in Chapter 12, Differing and Unforeseen Site Conditions.

---

[3]*Krygoski Construction Co. v. United States*, 94 F.3d 1537 (Fed. Cir. 1996).

Delay Clauses

Most contracts will list events that result in excusable and compensable delays. For example, it is common for contracts to grant the contractor a delay for "unusual delay in delivery of materials." Many contractors are not aware of when they are entitled to a delay and so waive rights given them under these clauses. Delay clauses are discussed in Chapter 11, Delays and Acceleration.

Notice Provisions

Notice provisions are discussed at several points in the text. Basically, the law will uphold notice provisions, and so parties should be aware of the notice provisions in the contract. Courts will uphold provisions requiring notice of damage or delay to be given within a certain period of time. Check the time limits required by your contract.

For example, the subcontract between Martin K. Eby Construction Co., Inc., (prime contractor) and Associated Mechanical Contractors, Inc. (AMC, the subcontractor) on a prison project contained the following provision:

> *Any claim for delay must be filed in writing with the Contractor within ten (10) days from the commencement of the alleged damage and a full accounting filed within ten (10) days after the extent of damage is known or the cause of damage ceases, whichever is sooner; otherwise, any such claims will be considered void.*

AMC subsequently complained that Eby had *repeatedly* resequenced the work, forcing the subcontractor to stop and start and filed a claim for additional compensation. Eby responded that the claim was barred because AMC had not provided timely written notice of the delay, as required by the provision of the subcontract. Eby's position was upheld by the trial court, and AMC could not collect damages.[4]

Damages Clauses

Most construction contracts contain clauses limiting or eliminating the amount or types of damages the owner must pay. Limited damages for delay clauses are discussed in Chapter 14, Termination of the Contract and Contract Damages. Basically this type of clause limits the damages a contractor or subcontractor is entitled to should a delay occur. The damages are usually limited to a time extension, and the owner need not pay a sum of money to the contractor should the owner delay the project.

The contract may contain clauses limiting the amount of overhead and profit the contractor can charge to change orders clauses may eliminate home-office overhead as an allowable element of damages clauses may allow winning parties to be entitled to attorney fees. These types of clauses are generally upheld.

---

[4]*Associated Mechanical Contractors, Inc. v. Martin K. Eby Construction Co., Inc.* 983 F. Supp. 1121 (M.D.Ga. 1997).

The 1997 AIA-A201 § 4.3.10 contains a waiver of *consequential damages*. Exactly what damages are consequential may depend on state law, but the clause itself includes the following items:

- Owner's damages for loss of use, income, profit, financing, business and reputation, and loss of management or employee productivity.
- Contractor's damages for principal office expense (home-office overhead), losses of financing, business and reputation, and for loss of profit except anticipated profit arising directly from the work.

Another common damage clause is the liquidated damages clause. This clause states that the owner is entitled to a certain specific sum from the contractor should the contractor delay the project. For example, the contractor may owe the owner $100 per day in damages.

Indemnification Provisions

Indemnification provisions are discussed in Chapter 16, Joint Liability and Indemnity. Intermediate and broad form indemnification clauses force the contractor to pay for the owner's liability in some circumstances. Such clauses can have devastating effects if insufficient insurance is not obtained.

Flow-down Clauses

A **flow-down** clause is a contract provision in the prime contract causing duties between the owner and the contractor (as expressed in the prime contract) to flow down to the subcontractor or material supplier. Common duties that flow down are warranties, service agreements, and dispute resolution procedures. Subcontractors need to be aware of any provisions in the prime contract that flow down to them. Figure 19–1 illustrates the duties possessed by the parties absent a flow-down clause. Figure 19–2 illustrates how these duties are altered by the flow-down clause.

For example, L & B Construction subcontracted the electrical work to Ragan Enterprises, Inc. on a certain project. The subcontract between L & B and Ragan incorporated the prime contract (between L & B and the owner) into the subcontract and was made a part thereof. The subcontract also stated:

> *The Subcontractor agrees to be bound to the Contractor by the terms of the contract documents and assume toward the Contractor all of the obligations and responsibilities that the Contractor by aforesaid document assumes toward the Owner.*

The project was delayed two years, and Ragan brought a delay claim against L & B. The prime contractor raised the no damage other than a time extension for delay clause in its

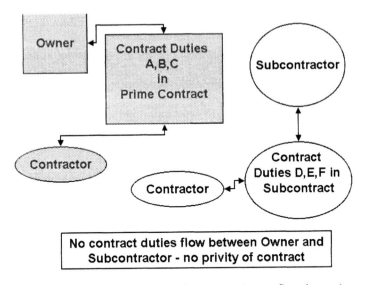

Figure 19–1 Responsibilities of parties without a flow-down clause.

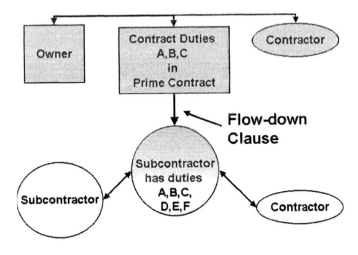

Figure 19–2 Responsibilities of parties with a flow-down clause.

---

[5]*L & B Contruction Co. v. Ragan Enterprises, Inc.* 482 S.E.2d (Ga. 1997).

contract with the owner as a defense. The Supreme court of Georgia said Georgia law has long recognized the validity of flow-down clauses in subcontracts. The court concluded that the flow-down clause incorporated the no damage other than a time extension for delay clause into the subcontract, and the clause barred Ragan's delay claim against L & B.[5] Not all state law agrees with this result.

Pay When Paid Clauses

The **pay when paid clause** states that the subcontractor will not be paid until the owner pays the contractor. Under normal contract law the subcontract is between the subcontractor and the prime contractor. It makes no difference to the subcontractor whether or not the prime contractor is paid—the subcontractor wants to be paid pursuant to its contract with the prime contractor; however, a pay when paid clause shifts the risk of owner failure to pay from the contractor to the subcontractor. In other words, this clause prevents the prime contractor from being forced to pay the subcontractor if the owner does not pay the prime.

The following is an example of a pay when paid clause:

> *Subcontractor is relying upon the financial responsibility of Owner in performing the work. It is understood by Subcontractor that payment for the work is to be made from funds received from Owner by Contractor in respect to the work.*

Relying on ancient precedent, a Colorado court enforced a pay when paid clause in a subcontract despite the absence of language expressly shifting the risk of owner nonpayment to the subcontractors. The Southern Group, Inc., awarded a contract to Printz Services Corp. to build a casino facility. The subcontracts between Printz and the subcontractors contained the following provision:

> *Contractor shall make final payment to Subcontractor after work is complete and accepted by Owner and Architect provided like payment shall have been made by Owner to Contractor.*

The Southern Group, Inc., did not pay Printz Services Corp., and Printz did not pay the subcontractors. Printz claimed the subcontractors were not entitled to payment because the preceding clause stated that the subcontractors would be paid only if Printz were paid. The court agreed.[6]

---

[6]*Printz Services Corp. v. Main Electric, Ltd.* 949 P.2d 77 (Colo. App. 1997).

Here is another example of a pay when paid clause:

> *PROGRESS PAYMENTS and FINAL PAYMENT. Notwithstanding anything to the contrary in the preceding paragraphs of this agreement, subcontractor agrees as a condition precedent to payment, of either progress or final payment, that the owner shall have first paid the payment applied for to the contractor and that payment for either progress payments or final payment is not due and owing to the subcontractor as provided for herein until the owner has made such payment to the contractor. The subcontractor recognizes that the source of funding for this subcontract agreement is the progress and final payments that are to be made by the owner to contractor.*

The preceding clause makes payment by the owner a **condition precedent** (something that must happen before) to the contractor's obligation to pay the subcontractor. Some courts require the magic words *condition precedent* in the clause before the clause is enforced.[7] Other courts will enforce a clause that does not contain the words.[8]

Dispute Resolution Clauses

Many prime contracts require the owner and the contractor to submit claims to binding arbitration. This means that disputes will be determined by arbitrators and not by a judge and/or jury. Matters can be complicated if the problem is with a subcontractor and the subcontractor is *not* required to arbitrate the claim. In this circumstance some claims will be arbitrated and some litigated.

For example, the City and County of Denver (Denver) awarded a contract to Harbert to construct a terminal building at Denver International Airport. The contract contained the following provision:

> *It is agreed and understood by the parties hereto that disputes regarding this contract shall be resolved by administrative hearing under procedures described in Revised Municipal Code section 56-106.*

The code section referenced in the contract was promulgated to resolve disputes involving *sewer rate charges*. Under that statute the Manager of Public Works conducts a hearing and renders a decision that is reviewable by a court on questions of law or fact. Harbert sued Denver on several claims for extras relating to the airport project and a return

---

[7]*L. Harvey Concrete, Inc. v. Agro Construction and Supply Co.*, 939 P.2d 811 (Ariz. App. 1997). *Christman Co. v. Anthony S. Brown Development Co., Inc.*, 533 N.W.2d 838 (Mich. App. 1995); *Gilbane Building Co. v. Brisk Waterproofing Co., Inc.* 565 A.2d 248 (Md. App. 1991).

[8]*Robert F. Wilson, Inc. v. Post-Tensioned Structures, Inc.*, 522 So. 2d 79 (Fla. App. 1988); *Printz Services Corp. v. Main Electric, Ltd.* 949 P.2d 77 (Colo. App. 1997); *St. Paul Fire and Marine Insurance Co. v. Georgia Interstate Electric Co.*, 370 S.E.2d 829 (Ga. App. 1988); *Gilbane Building Co. v. Brisk Waterproofing Co., Inc.*, 565 A.2d 248 (Md. App. 1991).

of the retainage. The city moved to dismiss the court and compel arbitration. The appeal court upheld the arbitration clause and ordered the matter to arbitration.[9]

Questions to Ask about the Prime Contract

1. Is the scope of work complete and adequate?

2. How are change orders and additional work to be handled?

3. What is the payment schedule?

4. Who is paying for what insurance?

5. What are the warranty provisions?

6. Is there an unforeseen site condition clause?

7. Are there any flow-down provisions? Contractors need to make sure their sub-contracts contain clauses to incorporate the duties that flow down.

8. What happens with delays? Are there excusable delays?

9. Can the owner suspend the work? If yes, what happens to the contract?

10. Can the owner terminate for convenience? When can the owner terminate?

11. Is there a provision allowing the contractor to stop work if payment is late or not made.

12. Is there a provision allowing the owner to complete the work and charge it to the contractor should the contractor fail to perform?

13. Are damages payable to either the owner or the contractor limited in any way? For example, is there a no damage for delay provision, or a provision that allows only a time extension for delay?

14. What is the retention and how is it handled?

15. Are there any indemnification clauses, and what do they say? Does insurance cover risks assumed here?

16. Are there any alternative dispute resolution clauses? Is the right to trial eliminated?

Questions to Ask about the Subcontract

In addition to the preceding 16 items:

17. Is there a pay when paid clause? If you are a subcontractor, this will drastically affect your cash flow.

---

[9]*City and County of Denver v. District Court*, 939 P.2d 1353 (Colo. 1997).

18. Are there any flow-down clauses? If there are, what duties flow down from the prime contract to the subcontractor?
19. Are provisions for terminating the subcontract clearly specified?
20. Can the contractor terminate the subcontractor and finish the subcontract at the subcontractor's expense?

Vocabulary Checklist

Certified professional
   constructor
Sick building
Indoor air quality
Traditional construction
   project delivery

Design–build
Alternative delivery systems
Public–private partnership
Expert testimony
Dueling experts

Waiver of claim
Termination for convenience clause
Flow-down clause
Pay when paid clause

Review Questions

1. What are some substances that can cause indoor air to be a health hazard?
2. Must the court allow any expert witness to testify?
3. What is the most ignored clause in the construction contract?
4. How can problems with the changes clause be avoided?
5. Is the law picky about notice requirements?
6. According to the text, what are the three most important skills needed by persons involved in the construction industry?
7. How can you write a comprehensible memo on any topic?
8. What is the first rule to follow to avoid lawsuits?
9. What is the second?
10. Why should you treat *every* person you meet with respect?
11. Why should you treat people who may want to sue you or file a claim against you with respect?
12. Why is *different* good in many situations?
13. How should you estimate what it will cost to bring a lawsuit?
14. What should you do when you make a mistake?
15. The text mentions one cost to individuals of social interaction and cooperation. What is it?
16. How do people you do not even know influence your life?
17. When should you call an attorney?
18. What is a termination for convenience clause?
19. What is a limited damages for delay clause?
20. Why are delay clauses important to the contractor?

21. Is the contractor's right to delay limited by what the contract says?

22. If a delay occurs, what should the contractor do?

23. Why should the contractor check the contract for damages clauses?

24. What are the three types of indemnification provisions and their effects?

25. What is a flow-down clause?

26. What is a pay when paid clause?

27. Why should the contractor or subcontractor check the dispute resolution clauses in the contract?

Index